A Language Older
Than Words

Also by Derrick Jensen

Railroads and Clearcuts

Listening to the Land

A Language Older Than Words

Derrick Jensen

CONTEXT BOOKS NEW YORK 2000

www.contextbooks.com

Designer: Julie Burke
Jacket Design: Julie Burke
Cover Photograph: Jerry N. Uelsmann
Illustrations: Jean McAlister
Production: Larry Flusser
Typeface: Garamond

Context Books
368 Broadway
Suite 314
New York, NY 10013

Library of Congress catalog card number: 00-131025

ISBN 1-893956-03-2

Parts of this book have appeared in somewhat different form in the
The Sun, The New York Times Magazine, Earth Island Journal, the Earth
First! Journal, The Anderson Valley Advertiser, Interspecies Communication,
The Spokesman-Review, The Pacific Northwest Inlander, Wild Forest Review,
Native Voice, Food and Water Journal, Free Spirit, Earth Ethics, Transitions,
and The Road-RIPorter. One part was included in the anthology Against
Civilization, and another in the anthology Prayers For A Thousand Years.

9   8   7   6   5   4   3

Manufactured in the United States of America

Contents

Preface

THE GENESIS OF THIS book was an event. I used to raise chickens and ducks for food. After a couple of years, a pack of coyotes discovered the easy meals, and I began to lose birds. I scared the coyotes away when I happened to be home, but I knew I could not forever stand guard. One day, when I saw a coyote stalking chickens I asked it to stop. I did this more out of frustration than conviction.

The odd thing was, the coyote *did* stop, and neither it nor other pack members returned. I was skeptical about the significance of this. Indeed, it took quite a long time and many more interactions with the coyotes before I began to suspect that interspecies communication might be real. This created a new concern. What I was experiencing went against everything I'd been taught—at school, on television, at church, in the newspaper—and especially went against my training in the sciences.

I began to question my sanity, which further piqued my curiosity.

Crazy or not, I soon discovered I wasn't alone. I began to ask people if they too experienced these conversations, and overwhelmingly they said *yes*. Pigs, dogs, coyotes, squirrels, even rivers, trees, and rocks: all these, according to the stories I was hearing, were speaking *and listening* if only we too would enter into conversation. Almost without exception, the people I asked said they'd never told these stories, for fear that others would think they were crazy.

The path for the book seemed clear: I would document these stories so that others could learn through the number, variety, and dailiness of these interactions to begin trusting that their own experiences of interspecies communication might be real. I hoped they would learn that just because they speak to their tabby, or because their cocker spaniel responds to their words and intents, that they may not be crazy after all. Or at least if they *are* crazy, far from being alone they outnumber the skeptical sane.

What promised to emerge from this exploration was a feel-good book. It seemed to have *New York Times* best-seller list written all over it.

I tried to write that book, and couldn't do it. Not if I wanted to be honest. One reason is that the conversation with the coyotes was not in truth my first interaction of this kind. It was simply the most obvious I'd experienced in a long time. I recollected that as a child, I had routinely participated in this sort of conversation, listening especially rapt to what the stars had told me almost nightly. I remembered in fact that the stars had saved my life.

Soon it became clear that an honest examination had to begin further back than my experience with the coyotes. At the very least it would need to start with the story of the stars. And in order to fully tell that story, I would also need to tell the story of my childhood; how I came to listen to the stars, and why their message was important to me.

At that point another storyline emerged, and it became clear that what I had to write, regardless of my relative youth, was a memoir: How did I later come to deny my experience in favor of what I had been taught? How and why does this happen to each of us as we grow up? Suddenly the book took on epic proportions. Question led to question, each one more difficult and disturbing than the one before. How and why do we numb ourselves to our own experiences? How and why do we deafen ourselves to the voices of others? Who benefits? Who suffers? Is there a connection between the silencing of women, to use one example, and the silencing of the natural world? I wanted to write a memoir that moved beyond the microcosm of my personal experience to the macrocosm of the world in which we live.

Thus a second reason I couldn't write the feel-good book. As a long-time environmental activist, I am intimately acquainted with the landscape of loss, and have grown accustomed to carrying the daily weight of despair. When it comes to our relationship with nature, there is little to feel good about. A happy reckoning of this relationship would not only be dishonest, it would be unworthy of the subject matter, of the great runs of salmon we're destroying, of the billions of chickens forced to live miserable lives, of the beautiful forests our children will never see.

If the salmon or the chickens or the forests could write a book, what would it be like? More to the point, if we were to take time to listen to what they might already be saying, do you think their stories would be cheery and bright?

Yet that is precisely what public discourse demands. I cannot count the number of times I've been commissioned to write environmental pieces, and the editors have said to me, "Make sure it's positive." Never once has an editor said, "Make sure the piece is honest." This unwillingness to face the truth about our time is another form of silencing. Before we can fix our troubled relationship with nature, we must be willing to look at it.

It became clear that this book had to be different. If I were to be honest, it could only be a cry of outrage, a lamentation, and at the same time a love story about that which is and that which was but is no longer. It would have to be about the potential for life and love and happiness we each carry inside but are too afraid to explore. The book would have to be raw and difficult, but it would also have to offer redemption.

As Franz Kafka put it, you may not destroy someone's world unless you are prepared to offer a better one. But no redemption can be found in the avoidance of difficult issues. Redemption comes only after we have moved through the horrors of our present situation to the better world that lies beyond it. By confronting the problem as courageously as we can and at the same time presenting alternatives, our barriers to clarity, including our false hopes, may crumble to reveal previously unseen possibilities.

A Language Older Than Words

Silencing

"Our behavior is a function of our experience. We act according to the way we see things. *If our experience is destroyed, our behavior will be destructive.* If our experience is destroyed, we have lost our own selves."
R.D. Laing

THERE IS A LANGUAGE older by far and deeper than words. It is the language of bodies, of body on body, wind on snow, rain on trees, wave on stone. It is the language of dream, gesture, symbol, memory. We have forgotten this language. We do not even remember that it exists.

In order for us to maintain our way of living, we must, in a broad sense, tell lies to each other, and especially to ourselves. It is not necessary that the lies be particularly believable. The lies act as barriers to truth. These barriers to truth are necessary because without them many deplorable acts would become impossibilities. Truth must at all costs be avoided. When we do allow self-evident truths to percolate past our defenses and into our consciousness, they are treated like so many hand grenades rolling across the dance floor of an improbably macabre party. We try to stay out of harm's way, afraid they will go off, shatter our delusions, and leave us exposed to what we have done to the world and to ourselves, exposed as the hollow people we have become. And so we avoid these truths, these self-evident truths, and continue the dance of world destruction.

As is true for most children, when I was young I heard the world speak. Stars sang. Stones had preferences. Trees had bad days. Toads held lively discussions, crowed over a good day's catch. Like static on a radio, schooling and other forms of socialization began to interfere with my perception of the animate world, and for a number of years I almost believed that only humans spoke. The gap between what I experienced and what I almost believed confused me deeply. It wasn't until later that I began to understand the personal, political, social, ecological, and economic implications of living in a silenced world.

This silencing is central to the workings of our culture. The staunch refusal to hear the voices of those we exploit is crucial to our domination of them. Religion, science, philosophy, politics, education, psychology, medicine, literature, linguistics, and art have all been pressed into service as tools to rationalize the silencing and degradation of women, children, other races, other cultures, the natural world and its members, our emotions, our consciences, our experiences, and our cultural and personal histories.

My own introduction to this silencing—and this is similarly true for a great percentage of children as well within many families—came at the hands (and genitals) of my father, who beat my mother, my brothers, and my sisters, and who raped my mother, my sister, and me.

I can only speculate that because I was the youngest, my father somehow thought it best that instead of beating me, he would force me to watch, and listen. I remember scenes—vaguely, as from a dream or a movie—of arms flailing, of my father chasing my brother Rob around and around the house. I remember my mother pulling my father into their bedroom to absorb blows that may have otherwise landed on her children. We sat stone-faced in the kitchen, captive audience to stifled groans that escaped through walls that were just too thin.

The vagueness with which I recollect these formative images is the point here, because the worst thing my father did went beyond the hitting and the raping to the denial *that any of it ever occurred.* Not only bodies were broken, but broken also was the bedrock connection between memory and experience, between psyche and reality. His denial made sense, not only because an admission of violence would have harmed his image as a socially respected, wealthy, and deeply religious attorney, but more simply because the man who would beat his children could not speak about it honestly and continue to do it.

We became a family of amnesiacs. There's no place in the mind to sufficiently contain these experiences, and as there was effectively no way out, it would have served no purpose for us to consciously remember the atrocities. So we learned, day after day, that we could not trust our perceptions, and that we were better off not listening to our emotions. Daily we forgot, and if a memory pushed its way to the surface we forgot again. There'd be a beating, followed by brief contrition and my father asking, "Why did you make me do it?" And then? Nothing, save the inconvenient evidence: a broken door, urine-soaked underwear, a wooden room divider my brother repeatedly tore from the wall trying to pick up speed around the corner. Once these were fixed, there was nothing left to remember. So we "forgot," and the pattern continued.

This willingness to forget is the essence of silencing. When I realized that, I began to pay more attention to the "how" and the "why" of forgetting—and thus began a journey back to remembering.

What else do we forget? Do we think about nuclear devastation, or the wisdom of producing tons of plutonium, which is lethal even in microscopic doses for well over 250,000 years? Does global warming invade our dreams? In our most serious moments do we consider that industrial civilization has initiated the greatest mass extinction in the history of the planet? How often do we consider that our culture commits genocide against every indigenous culture it encounters? As one consumes the products manufactured by our culture, is s/he concerned about the atrocities that make them possible?

We don't stop these atrocities, because we don't talk about them. We don't talk about them, because we don't think about them. We don't think about them, because they're too horrific to comprehend. As trauma expert Judith Herman writes, "The ordinary response to atrocities is to banish them from consciousness. Certain violations of the social compact are too terrible to utter aloud: this is the meaning of the word *unspeakable.*"

As the ecological fabric of the natural world unravels around us, perhaps it is time that we begin to speak of the unspeakable, and to listen to that which we have deemed unhearable.

A grenade rolls across the floor. Look. It won't go away.

Here's what I've heard about your typical slaughterhouse.

The room sounds for all the world like a factory. You hear the clang of steam in pipes and the hiss of its release, the clank of steel on steel as chains pull taut, the whirr of rolling wheels on metal runners, all punctuated every thirty seconds or so by the pop of the stunner.

The rooms are always humid, and smell of grease as much as blood. The walls are often pale, the floor usually concrete. I have a picture from a slaughterhouse that will forever be etched in my mind. No matter how I try to look elsewhere, my eyes return to the newly painted chute that leads in from outside, not only because of the chute's contents, but because the color—electric blue—contrasts almost painfully with the drabness of the rest of the room.

Inside the chute, facing a blank wall, stands a steer. Until the last moment he does not seem to notice when a worker places a steam-driven stunner at the ridge of his forehead. I do not know what the steer feels in those last moments, or what he thinks. The pressure of contact triggers the stunner, which shoots a re-tractable bolt into the brain of the steer. The steer falls, some-times stunned, sometimes dead, sometimes screaming, and another worker climbs down to attach a chain to the creature's hind leg. Task completed, he nods, and the first worker—the one who applied the stunner—pushes a black button. There's the whine of a hoist, and the steer dangles from a suspended rail, blood dripping red to join the coagulating river on the floor.

The steer sways as wheels roll along the rail, causing the fall-ing blood to describe a sinusoidal curve on the way to another worker, who slits his throat. There is barely time to follow his path before the chute door opens and another animal is pushed in. There goes the stunner again, the hoist, metal, steam, the grind of meshing gears. It happens again and again, like clock-work, every half-minute.

We live in a world of make-believe. Think of it as a little game—the only problem being that the repercussions are real. Bang! Bang! You're dead—only the other person doesn't get up. My father, in order to rationalize his behavior, had to live in a world of make-believe. He had to make *us* believe that the beatings and rapes made sense, that all was as it should, and must, be. Now, it will be obvious to everyone that my father's game of make-believe was far from fun—it was destructive. My father rewrote the script on a day-to-day basis, thereby making everything right—he *created* the reality that he *required* in order to continue his behavior.

In attempting to describe the world in make-believe terms, we have forgotten what is real and what isn't. We pretend the world is silent, whereas in reality it is filled with conversations. We pretend we are not animals, whereas in reality the laws of ecology apply as much to us as the rest of "God's Creation." We pretend we're at the top of a great chain of being, although evolution is nonhierarchical.

Here's what I think: it's a sham. It's a giant game of make-believe. We pretend that animals feel no pain, and that we have no ethical responsibility toward them. But how do we know? We pretend that other humans—the women who are raped, for example (a full twenty-five percent of all women in this culture have been raped, and an additional nineteen percent have had to fend off rape attempts), or the one hundred and fifty million children who are enslaved to make soccer balls, tennis shoes, Barbie dolls, and the like—are happy and unaffected by it all. We pretend all is well as we dissipate our lives in quiet desperation.

We pretend that death is an enemy, although it is an integral part of life. We pretend we don't have to die, that modern medicine can cure what ails us, no matter what it is. But can modern medicine cure a dying soul?

We pretend that violence is inevitable, and in some ways it is. But can it be mitigated through better science? Rather than answer that question, most often we pretend, sheepishly, that violence doesn't exist.

Science, politics, economics, and everyday life do not exist separately from ethics. But we act like they do.

The problem is not difficult to understand: we pretend that anything we do not understand—anything that cannot be measured, quantified, and controlled—does not exist. We pretend that animals are resources to be conserved or consumed, when, in reality, they have purposes entirely independent of us. It is wrong to make believe that people are nothing more than "Human Resources" to be efficiently utilized, when they too have independent existences and preferences. And it is wrong to make believe that animals are not sentient, that they do not form social communities in which members nurture, love, sustain, and grieve for each other, that they do not manifest ethical behavior.

We act like these pretenses are reasonable, but none of them are intuitive or instinctual; nor are they logically, empirically, or ethically defensible. Taken together, a way of life based on these pretenses is destroying life on this planet.

But a real world still awaits us, one that is ready to speak to us if only we would remember how to listen.

When I was a child, the stars saved my life. I did not die because they spoke to me.

Between the ages of seven and nine, I often crept outside at night to lie on the grass and talk to the stars. Each night I gave them memories to hold for me—memories of beatings witnessed, of rapes endured. I gave them emotions too large and sharp for me to feel. In return the stars gave me understanding. They said to me, "This is not how it is supposed to be. This is not your fault. You will survive. *We* love you. You are good."

I cannot overstress the importance of this message. Had I never known an alternative existed—had I believed that the cruelty I witnessed and suffered was natural or inevitable—I would have died.

My parents divorced during my early teens. It was a bitter divorce in which my father used judges, attorneys, psychologists, and most of all money, with the same fury and relentlessness with which he had once used fists, feet, and genitals. The stars continued to foster me, speaking softly whenever I chose to listen.

Time passed. I grew older. I went to college, received a degree in physics, and on my own read a fair amount of psychology. I came to a new understanding of my place in the world. It had not been the stars that saved me, but my own mind. My earlier thesis—that the stars cared for me, spoke to me, held me—made no physical sense. Stars are inanimate. They don't *say* anything. They can't, and they certainly couldn't care about me. And even if they had cared there remained the problem of distance. How could a star a thousand light-years away respond to my emotional needs in a timely fashion? It became clear that some part of my own psyche had known precisely the words I needed to hear in order to endure, and had projected those words onto the stars. It was a pretty neat trick on the part of my unconscious, and this projection business seemed a wonderful adaptive mechanism for surviving in a world that I had come to recognize as largely insensate, with the exception of its supreme tenant—humankind.

I've often wished that I could have been in the room when Descartes came up with his famous quip, "I think, therefore I am." I would have put my arm around his shoulder and gently tapped, or I would have punched him in the nose, or I might have taken his hands in mine, kissed him full on the lips, and said, "René, my friend, don't you *feel* anything?"

I used to believe that Descartes' most famous statement was arbitrary. Why hadn't he said, "I love, therefore I am," or "I breathe, therefore I have lungs," or "I defecate, therefore I must have eaten," or "I feel the weight of the quill on my fingers and rejoice in the fact that I am alive, therefore I must be"? Later I grew to see even these statements as superfluous; for anyone living in the real world, life *is:* existence itself is wondrously sufficient proof of its own existence.

I no longer see Descartes' statement as arbitrary. It is representative of our culture's narcissism. This narcissism leads to a disturbing disrespect for direct experience and a negation of the body.

Descartes had been attempting to find one point of certainty in the universe, to find some piece of information he could trust. He stated, "I suppose, then, that all the things that I see are false; I persuade myself that nothing has ever existed of all that my fallacious memory represents to me. I consider that I possess no senses; I imagine that body, figure, extension, movement and place are but the fictions of my mind. What then can be esteemed as true? I was persuaded that there was nothing in all the world." Estranged from all of life, Descartes thought that everything was a dream, and he the dreamer.

You may have played this game, too. During tenth grade I occasionally bedeviled a friend of mine by saying, "Jon, the entire world doesn't exist. You'll be glad to know that includes you.

You are nothing more than a figment of my imagination. Because you don't exist, everything you do is a result of my having willed it." Since Jon was a good friend, and because we were high school sophomores, his response was a fairly straightforward sock in the arm. I then countered by smiling and saying, "I willed you to do that." He'd throw a couple more jabs for good measure, and then we'd go to the gym and shoot baskets.

I guess Descartes didn't have a close friend with Jon's good sensibilities. So, instead of going to play basketball, he found himself pushing his philosophy of narcissism to its logical, albeit empty, conclusion. He realized that since he was thinking his thoughts—because he was doubting the existence of the universe—then he must exist to be doing the doubting. "I think, therefore I am." So far, so good. But as Descartes continued his line of reasoning, the world congealed for him into two groups, the thinker, in this case Descartes (or more precisely his disembodied thought processes), and that which he thought (i.e., everything and everyone else). He who matters, and that which doesn't.

Had Descartes stopped there, the response by other philosophers would probably have been similar to Jon's: a violent backlash at having been philosophized out of subjective existence. But he didn't. He and many other philosophers eventually agreed that subjective personhood should certainly be granted to all of them, as well as to others with political, economic, or military power, while they decided that just as certainly it should not be granted to those who could not speak, or at least those whose voices they chose not to hear.

The latter group of course included women: "Let the woman learn in silence with all subjection. But I suffer not a woman to teach, nor to usurp authority over the man, but to be in silence." It also included Africans, because they were "extremely ugly and loathsome, if one may give the name of Men to such Animals," and because "when they speak they fart with their tongues in their mouths." But the bottom line was that these thinkers thought it was "a greatt pittie that such creattures as they bee should injoy so sweett a country." The subjective persons—those who actually existed—set out immediately to rectify this situation by exterminating these "creattures" and appropriating their land. The same logic was used to deal with Native Americans, who also occupied land the Europeans wanted. It was ethical to steal their land because they were "animals who do not feel reason, but are ruled by their passions," and who "were born for [forced labor]." It included non-Christians, whose poor choice of religion meant they were not fully human, and so could be enslaved. It included children born to non-Christians, whose poor choice of parents meant they too were not fully human, and so too could be enslaved. The definition of those precluded from being fully subjective and rational beings included *anyone* whom those in power wished to exploit.

Regarding the world of nonhumans (i.e., "animals") we find a contemporary of Descartes who reported that "scientists administered beatings to dogs with perfect indifference and made fun of those who pitied the creatures as if they felt pain. They said the animals were clocks; that the cries they emitted when struck were only the noise of a little spring that had been touched, but that the whole body was without feeling. They nailed the poor animals up on boards by their four paws to vivisect them to see the circulation of the blood, which was a great subject of controversy."

Searching for certainty, René Descartes became the father of modern science and philosophy. Even if his philosophy were not such an easy justification for exploitation, his search was fatally flawed before it began. Because life is uncertain, and because we die, the only way Descartes could gain the certainty he sought was in the world of abstraction. By substituting the illusion of disembodied thought for experience (disembodied thought being, of course, not possible for anyone with a body), by substituting mathematical equations for living relations, and most importantly by substituting control, or the attempt to control, for the full participation in the wild and unpredictable process of living, Descartes became the prototypical modern man. He also established the single most important rule of Western philosophy: if it doesn't fit the model, it doesn't exist.

Welcome to industrial civilization.

. . .

I do not know what my father was thinking or feeling during those days and nights of violence when I was young. I do not know what was in his heart or mind as he cocked his fist to strike my sister, or as he lunged across the table at my brother, or as he stood beside my bed and unzipped his pants. Throughout my childhood an unarticulated question hung in the air, then settled deep in my bones, not to be defined or spoken until it had worked its way back to the surface many years later: If his violence isn't making him happy, why is he doing it?

I will never know what my father was feeling or thinking during those moments. For him, at least consciously, the moments don't exist. To this day and despite all of the evidence, he continues to deny his acts of violence. This is often the first response to the undeniable evidence of an awful truth; one simply denies it. This is true whether the evidence pertains to a father's rape of his children, the murder of millions of Jews or scores of millions of indigenous peoples, or the destruction of life on the planet.

I would imagine this denial of evidence is often unconscious. My father is not the only person in my family whose recollection for those years is unaccountable. As he leapt across the table, do you know what I did? I continued eating, because that is what you do at the table, and because I did not want to be noticed. I ate, but I do not know what I felt or thought as I brought the sandwich to my mouth, or the spoonful of stew, or the bean soup.

I do not know how I arrived at it, but I do know that I had a deal with my unconscious, a deal that, as I hope will be clear by the end of this book, has been made in one form or another by nearly everyone living in our culture. Because I was spared the beatings, I pretended—*pretended* is not the right word, perhaps it would be more accurate to say I *made believe* because the process became in time virtually transparent—that if I did not consciously acknowledge the abuse, it would not be visited directly on me. I believed that if I focused on my own moment-to-moment survival—on remaining motionless on the couch, or forcing beans down a too-tight throat—then my already untenable situation would get no worse.

My father's first visit to my bedroom did not abrogate the deal. It couldn't because without the deal I could not have survived the violence he did to me, just as I'm sure that without a similar deal, that removed *him* from *his* own experience, my father could not have perpetrated the violence. In order to maintain the illusion that if I ignored the abuse I would be spared the worst of it—in order to maintain the illusion of control in an uncontrollably painful situation, or simply to stay alive, even if I had to divorce myself from my emotions and bodily sensations— the events in my bedroom necessarily did not happen. His body behind mine, his penis between my legs, these sensations and images slipped in and out of my mind as easily and quickly as he slipped into and out of my room.

It's probably best if you don't believe a word I say.

What I wrote about my father beating and raping us simply isn't true. I was not only wrong, I was lying. My childhood was nothing like that, because if it had been, I couldn't have survived. No one could survive that. So the truth not only *is* but especially *must be* that my father never chased Rob around the house, and my mother and sisters never threw pans and glasses of water on him trying to make him stop. That would all have been just too implausible. Oh, he may have gotten a little out of control when he spanked one or the other of us, but he never beat anyone to the ground, then kicked her again and again. And rape? Out of the question. The constant insomnia, the incessant nightmares, the painful and itching anus, all these had their origin in some source other than my father. The same was true for my nightly ritual of searching my room, and later, barricading my door. Doesn't every child have a terror of someone catching him asleep?

I do not remember—I *specifically* do not remember—sitting at the table for dinner early one summer evening, and I do not remember my father asking my brother where he was the night before. I don't recollect if my brother said he went to an amusement park. But if my brother *had* said that, my father would never have asked him how much it cost to get in. And most certainly if my brother *had* said an amount, in response to this question that was never asked, my father would not have lunged at him across the table, not even if my brother's answer was incorrect, meaning my brother had not gone to the amusement park but instead perhaps to a bar. Food would not have scattered. My brother would not have made a break for the door, only to be cut off by the bottleneck at the refrigerator. My father would never have called him a cocksucking asshole stupid fuck, nor would he have begun to pummel him. My sisters would not have screamed, and my mother would not have clutched at my father's back. My brother would not have broken free only to stumble, fall, and get kicked in the kidneys. None of this happened. None of it could have happened. I swear to you. My brother could not have made it to his feet, and made it out the door and to his car, a pink Camaro, if you can believe *that*. My brother would not have locked the doors, and even if he had it would never have occurred to my father to kick in the side of the car. And even if by some strange chance all this did happen, I can tell you for certain that I do not remember continuing to sit at the table, a seven-year-old trying desperately not to be noticed, trying to disappear.

I can tell you for certain also that I was never, even as a young child, awakened and summoned to the living room to watch someone get beaten. This did not happen daily, weekly, or even monthly. And even had the beatings occurred—which I need to reassure both you and me that they did not—they could never have been made into such a spectacle. Who could endure such a thing? And who could perpetrate it? I have no recollection of sitting frozen on the couch, eyes directly forward, feeling more than seeing my siblings near to me, none of us touching, none of us moving, none of us making a sound, each of us simultaneously absent and preternaturally present, hyperaware of every one of my father's movements. I do not remember my father's leg frozen in mid-kick, nor can I see his face closed off with fury. I recollect nothing of this. Because it didn't happen. My brother doesn't have epilepsy, and if he does it could not have been caused by blows to the head. My sister never wakes up screaming that someone is in her room, in her bed. She never fears that someone will step out from behind a door to hit her, or to push her onto a bed. The smell of alcohol on a lover's breath does not terrify me, because my father did not drink. And even if he had, he would never have become drunk. And even if he would have become drunk, he would never have entered my room.

And the worst of it all is that even if he would have, I would never have remembered a thing.

Do not believe a word that I write in this book, about my father, about the culture, about anything. It's much better that way.

A study of Holocaust survivors by the psychologists Allport, Bruner, and Jandorf revealed a pattern of active resistance to unpleasant ideas and an acute unwillingness to face the seriousness of the situation. As late as 1936, many Jews who had been fortunate enough to leave Germany continued to return on business trips. Others simply stayed at home, escaping on weekends into the countryside so they would not have to think about their experiences. One survivor recollected that his orchestra did not miss a *beat* in the Mozart piece they were playing as they pretended not to notice the smoke from the synagogue being burned next door.

And what do we make of the good German citizens who stood by? By what means did they suppress their own experiences and their own consciences in order to participate or (similarly) not resist? How did they distract themselves from the grenade that slowly rolled across the floor?

Think for a moment about the figure I gave earlier: twenty-five percent of all women in this culture are raped during their lifetimes. One out of four. Next, think for a moment about the number of children beaten, or of the one hundred and fifty million children—*one hundred and fifty million*—enslaved, carrying bricks, chained to looms, chained to beds. If you were not one of the women raped, if you were not one of the children beaten, if you were not one of the children enslaved, these numbers probably don't mean very much to you. This is understandable. Consider your own life, and the ways you deny your own experience, the ways you have to deaden your own empathies to get through the day.

We live our lives, grateful that things aren't worse than they are. But there has to be a threshold beyond which we can no longer ignore the destructiveness of our way of living. What is that threshold? One in two women raped? Every woman raped? 500 million children enslaved? 750 million? A billion? All of them? The disappearance of flocks of passenger pigeons so large they darkened the sky for days at a time? The death of salmon runs so thick that it was impossible to dip an oar without "striking a silvery back"? The collapse of earthworm populations?

This deal by which we adapt ourselves to the receiving, witnessing, and committing of violence by refusing to perceive its effects on ourselves and on others is ubiquitous. And it is a bad deal. As R.D. Laing has written about our culture, "The condition of alienation, of being asleep, of being unconscious, of being out of one's mind, is the condition of the normal man. Society highly values its normal man. It educates children to lose themselves and to become absurd, and thus to be normal. Normal men have killed perhaps 100,000,000 of their fellow normal men in the last fifty years."

The question still hangs heavy in the air: If our behavior is not making us happy, why do we act this way?

The zoologist and philosopher Neil Evernden tells the familiar story of how we silence the world. During the nineteenth century, many vivisectionists routinely severed the vocal cords before operating on an animal. This meant that during the experiment the animals could not scream (referred to in the literature as emitting "high-pitched vocalization"). By cutting the vocal cords experimenters simultaneously denied reality—by pretending a silent animal feels no pain—and they affirmed it by implicitly acknowledging that the animal's cries would have told them what they already knew, that the creature was a sentient, feeling (and, during the vivisection, tortured) being.

As Evernden comments, "The rite of passage into the scientific," or, I would add, modern, "way of being centres on the ability to apply the knife to the vocal cords, not just of the dog on the table, but of life itself. Inwardly, he [the modern human being] must be able to sever the cords of his own consciousness. Outwardly, the effect must be the destruction of the larynx of the biosphere, an action essential to the transformation of the world into a material object." This is no less true for our relations with fellow humans.

If we are to survive, we must learn a new way to live, or relearn an old way. There have existed, and for the time being still exist, many cultures whose members refuse to cut the vocal cords of the planet, and refuse to enter into the deadening deal which we daily accept as part of living. It is perhaps significant that prior to contact with Western Civilization many of these cultures did not have rape, nor did they have child abuse (the Okanagans of what is now British Columbia, to provide just one example, had neither word nor concept in their language corresponding to the abuse of a child. They did have a word corresponding to the violation of a woman: literally translated it means "someone looked at me in a way I don't like"). It is perhaps significant as well that these cultures did not drive the passenger pigeon to extinction, nor the salmon, the wood bison, the sea mink, the Labrador heath hen, the Eskimo curlew, the Taipei tree frog. Would that we could say the same. It is perhaps significant that members of these cultures listen attentively (as though their lives depend on it, which of course they do) to what plants, animals, rocks, rivers, and stars have to say, and that these cultures have been able to do what we can only dream of, which is to live in dynamic equilibrium with the rest of the world.

The task ahead of us is awesome, to meet human needs without imperiling life on the planet.

Coyotes, Kittens, and Conversations

"We are the land. . . . That is the fundamental idea of Native American life: the land and the people are the same."
Paula Gunn Allen

"Since nature makes nothing purposeless or in vain, it is undeniably true that she has made all animals for the sake of man."
Aristotle

strongholds and castles." At no time did Bacon hide his agenda: "I am come in very truth leading you to Nature with all her children to bind her to your service and make her your slave . . . the mechanical inventions of recent years do not merely exert a gentle guidance over Nature's courses, they have the power to conquer and subdue her, to shake her to her foundations."

It would be as pointless as it would be easy to blame Descartes, Bacon, and other early scientists and philosophers for the sorry tradition of exploitation that has been handed down to us by our elders. These people merely articulated, brilliantly, urges that are woven together throughout our culture like rivulets in sand. These are the urge to deny the body and the urge to dominate the bodies of others, the urge to silence one's self and the urge to silence others. The urge to exploit. The urge to deny death and the urge to cause the deaths of others—or more accurately, as we shall see, to cause their annihilation. These urges are clear in the philosophy of Aristotle, and they are vivid—blood-red—in the Bible. They go as far back as Gilgamesh and the other formative myths of our culture, and they are as close as today's newspaper, where new mythmakers continue in the path of Descartes and Bacon, attempting to provide rational justification for that which cannot be justified.

The examples are everywhere. Yesterday, I saw a modern echo of Descartes' megalomania as rendered by the prominent theoretical physicist Gerard J. Milburn: "The aim of modern science is to reach an understanding of the world, not merely for purely aesthetic reasons, but that it may be ordered to our purpose."

The day before, I had seen an account of scientists at Tokyo University, who have created what they call Robo-roach, an insect which (or who) has "been surgically implanted with a microrobotic backpack that allows researchers to control its [or rather his or her] movements." The scientists remove the roaches' wings and antennae and place electrodes in the wounds. As if they were playing a video game, the scientists are then able to push one button on a remote control to force the roach to move left. Another button causes it to move right. There are buttons for forward and backward as well. Once the "bugs" are worked out, these half-creature/half-robots will be fitted with television cameras and used as miniature spies. Not surprisingly, the scientists like their artificial roaches better than the real thing: "They are not very nice insects. They are a little smelly, and there's something about the way they move their antennae. But they look nicer when you put a little circuit on their backs and remove their wings."

I wasn't convinced I was crazy when the coyotes failed to show up the day after I asked them not to. At first I didn't even notice; it had been the coyotes' pattern to show up only occasionally. When a week passed, and then two, I began to wonder at the coincidence, and after a month I began to consider that their absence might not be coincidental after all.

About the same time, my dogs commenced eating eggs. Since I don't pen the chickens, the hens lay wherever they want, which means I've often found eggs in an old barrel, atop stored stacks of bee boxes, on a folded tarp nestled on a shelf between cloth softball bases and an icebox, and especially in a corner outside the barn beneath and behind thick pfitzers. Only occasionally—and even then I think by accident—does a hen lay in one of the nesting boxes I've set up for them.

Sometimes the dogs found eggs before I did, and I'd see only an empty spot where I'd expected an egg, or rarely, if it had been raining or snowing, I would see large paw prints heading into the thick bushes. I suspected that the larger of the dogs was also taking eggs off the waist-high shelf—books or beekeeping equipment I'd placed in front of the tarp would be strangely disarranged—but I could never pin anything on him.

Still, I had the paw prints, which seemed enough to convict him, or at least convince me that he was doing it. At first I tried being authoritarian: whenever I picked up an egg and the dogs happened to be around, I'd hold it at arm's length, between thumb and forefinger, and say in a deep, stentorian voice, "No eggs! No!" This quickly taught the dogs to roll on their backs and wag their tales whenever I picked up an egg. As soon as I went inside they continued to do as they pleased.

Finally it occurred to me that if simply asking had worked for the coyotes, perhaps it would work as well for the dogs. I sat

Coyotes, Kittens, and Conversations

down with them, and as they jumped all over me I said, "I give you guys plenty of treats. When I pull food from the dumpster for the chickens you get the first shot at it. I think that's a pretty good deal. Please don't eat the eggs."

The next day, the dogs stopped eating eggs.

That's when I started to think I was crazy.

I have read accounts of scientists who administered electric shocks to cats at intervals of five minutes, each shock sending the animals into convulsions. The cats who survived were removed from their restraints, then brought back another day for further shocks, until they had been given as many as ninety-five shocks within a three-week period, or until they died. I have seen accounts of scientists who attached electrodes to seven-day-old kittens, then shocked them up to seven hundred times per day for the next thirty-five days, always during the nursing period. The scientists noted that "the behavior of the mother cat merits attention. When she eventually discovered that the experimental kittens were being given electric shocks during the feeding process or whenever it was close to her body, she would do everything possible to thwart the experimenter with her claws, then trying to bite the electric wire, and finally actually leaving the experimental kitten and running away as far as possible when the electrodes were on the kittens' legs. Her attitude toward the experimental kitten when the electrodes were removed was one of deep mother love. She would run over to the kitten, try to feed it or else comfort it as much as possible." After the thirty-five days, the kittens were allowed to rest, and then the experiment was repeated on the same beleaguered felines.

I have read accounts of scientists who irradiated dogs; the dogs who survived were fed a diet that was abnormally high in fat and cholesterol, and then given drugs to suppress thyroid action. Those who survived were given injections of pitressin, which raises pressure in the arteries. Those who survived were given electric shocks. Those who had made it this far were immobilized with their heads held rigidly in stocks, and leather thongs fastened around their bodies, given further electric shocks. Most didn't survive this. One was able to strangle himself in the harness. Another was not so lucky. After appearing "to be in temporary respiratory distress, presumably as a consequence of active struggling against the stock," the creature was given artificial respiration so the experiment could continue. The dogs were shocked for weeks on end. One of the dogs survived the shocks for seventy-seven weeks, which encouraged the scientists to begin shocking him ninety times per minute. The dog died one hour and fifteen minutes later.

How about this? Scientists raised dogs in complete isolation for their first eight months, then reported that the dogs were frightened of nearly everything. Shocking, but there's more. The scientists stated that when the dogs were placed on electrified grids, they froze and made no attempt to escape. The scientists held flaming matches under the dogs' noses, and "jabbed them with dissecting needles." Still the dogs froze. The scientists pursued the dogs with electrically charged toy cars, which delivered 1,500 volts to the animals on contact. The scientists reported that the dogs, raised in isolation, did not seem to understand the source of their pain.

What does a person do with this kind of information? How do you grapple with the knowledge that, in the pursuit of data—and ultimately in an attempt to make ourselves "lords and possessors of nature"—members of our culture will give electric shocks to kittens and will mercilessly torture dogs? It seems impossible to form an adequate response.

Six nights ago, I dreamt of fishing. In this dream I began to reel in a huge fish. I pulled and pulled, and when it came close enough to see from shore it sped toward me and leapt onto the beach. Its bulk scared me—it was as long as my outstretched arms, and nearly half that distance from dorsal fin to belly. Its cold eye seemed to follow my every movement. Its jaw worked for breath. I wanted to throw it back; I couldn't stand having it next to me. Nor could I bear the thought of killing it. It had swallowed the hook. I had no choice: placing one foot on the fish's head, I pulled on the line. At last the hook came loose with the familiar crunch of cartilage. I still wanted to throw the fish back. Dying now, it was even more hideous. As I searched for a hatchet to finally kill this creature of the deep, a man approached, and said two words: "It's cod." I awoke perplexed, and then realized he meant for me to eat it, take it in.

That is what we all must do.

I called my friend, Jeannette Armstrong. A traditional Okanagan Indian, she is an author, teacher, and philosopher. She travels extensively working on indigenous sovereignty and land rights issues, and helps to rebuild native communities damaged by the dominant culture. I told her about my interactions with the coyotes and said, "I don't know what to make of this."

She laughed, then said, "Yes, you do."

A few weeks later we took a walk, and sat on the steep bank of a river. I leaned against the reddish dirt and played with the tendril of a tree's root that trailed from the soil. In front of us an eddy whirled in circles large enough to carry whole watersoaked trees in lazy circuits. Each round, the logs almost broke free only to fall back toward the bank and slide again upstream. Beyond the eddy the river moved slow and smooth, and beyond the river we could see cottonwoods and haystacks dotting broad meadows, interspersed with fields of alfalfa hemmed by barbed-wire fences. In the distance, the plains gave way to mountains, low and blue.

Jeannette said, "Attitudes about interspecies communication are the *primary* difference between western and indigenous philosophies. Even the most progressive western philosophers still generally believe that listening to the land is a metaphor." She paused, then continued, emphatically, "It's not a metaphor. It's how the world is."

I looked at the river. It would be easy to observe the eddy and make up a half-dozen lessons I could learn from it, for example, the obvious metaphor of the logs traveling in circles, like people trapped in a confining mindset that doesn't allow them to reenter the free flow of life. There's certainly nothing wrong with fabricating metaphors from the things we find around us, or from the experience of others—human or otherwise—but in both of those situations the *other* remains a case study onto which we project whatever we need to learn. That's an entirely different circumstance than listening to the other as it has its say, reveals its intents, expresses its experience, and does all this *on its own terms.*

Certainly it would be a step in the right direction if our culture as a whole could accept the notion of listening to the natural world—or listening at all, for that matter—even if they thought that "listening" was merely a metaphor. I once heard a Diné man say that uranium gives people radiation poisoning because the uranium does not like to be above ground. It wants to remain far beneath the surface of the earth. Whether we view this statement as literal truth or metaphor, the lesson is the same: digging up uranium makes you sick.

But to view this metaphorically is to still to perceive the world anthropocentrically. In this case the metaphorical view expresses concern for the people poisoned by uranium. The Diné man's observation, on the other hand, is a comment on the importance of maintaining the order of things.

I told Jeannette about this, then sat silent while I considered a pair of conversations I'd previously engaged in, one a couple of years before, and one much more recently. In the former conversation I'd been sitting on the floor of my living room, speaking with a scientist friend of mine who insisted that the scientific method—whereby an observer develops a hypothesis, then gathers data to rigorously test its feasibility—is in fact the only way we learn. One of my cats walked into the room, and my friend said, "Hypothesis: Cats purr when you pet them." She scratched her finger on the carpet, and the cat trotted over to her. She ran her hand along the cat's back. The cat purred. "Hypothesis supported," she said. "Sample size, one. Where's another cat?"

I knew I disagreed, but it took me a while to articulate my reason. Finally I said that whether we are electrifying a kitten or petting a cat, if the purpose is specifically to collect data we're still objectifying the cat. "What if," I said, "I pet her because I like to, and because I know she likes it? I can still pay attention, and I can still *learn* from the relationship. That's what happens with my other friends. Why not with the cat, too? But the *point* is pursuing a relationship, not gathering information."

She hesitated, looping strands of hair around her index finger, as she often does when she contemplates something, and then she said, "I guess that would change the whole notion of what knowledge is, and how we get it."

I nodded. The cat, for her part, reached up on her hind legs to push her head against my friend's arm. Absentmindedly, my friend stroked the cat's back.

The other conversation was shorter, but then trees can be rather taciturn. I was walking the dirtroad that leads to my mailbox, which intersects with a paved road. I noticed an old pine tree just on the corner, as I had noticed it many times previous, and I thought, "That tree is doing very well."

Immediately I heard a response that did not pass through my ear but went directly to the part of my brain that receives sounds. I heard a completion of my sentence that changed its meaning altogether: "For not being in a community." I looked around, and though there were other trees nearby, this was not a full tree community. The tree's nearest neighbors included the mailboxes and a telephone pole coated with faded creosote. I began to think about this lack of community, and from there began to think of all the times I had moved, from Nebraska to Maine and back to Nebraska, then Montana, to Colorado for college, Nevada, California, months spent living in my truck, back to Nevada, Idaho, Washington. I thought about the people I had left behind, my grandmother, my brothers, one sister and then another, friends. The irrigation ditch behind my old house. The aspen trees outside the front window, the Russian olives, the immense anthills in the pasture. These were my associations, not what I heard the tree "say." That's the crucial difference. The tree merely expressed one phrase. Everything else came afterward. Try it yourself. Listen to someone, and pay attention to where your thoughts take you. It actually *feels* different to hear than to think.

I told Jeannette about these two conversations. We talked some more, about the river, about her activism and my own, about what it will take for humans to survive. As we talked, a mosquito buzzed around her face, then stopped to perch on her arm. She waved it away.

I told her about the dogs, and how they had stopped eating eggs as soon as I asked. "I can't believe how easy this is."

"Yeah. That's what we've been trying to tell you now for five hundred years."

On November 29, 1864, approximately seven hundred soldiers, under the command of Colonel John Chivington, approached a Cheyenne encampment near Sand Creek, in Colorado. The dawn's early light revealed to the soldiers about a hundred lodges scattered below.

Chivington knew that in an attempt to demonstrate that they were no threat, the Indians of this village had voluntarily turned in all but their hunting weapons to the Federal government. He knew that the Indians were considered by the military to be prisoners of war. He knew further that nearly all of the Cheyenne men were away hunting buffalo. His response to all of this: "I long to be wading in gore."

As was true of Descartes centuries before him, Chivington was no lone lunatic, but had an entire culture for company. This highly respected man—a former Methodist minister, still an elder in good standing at his church, recently a candidate for Congress—had already stated in a speech that his policy toward Indians was that we should "kill and scalp them all, little and big." It would be comforting to think that such a murderous impulse would stamp the man an outcast. We would be wrong. *The Rocky Mountain News,* the paper of record for the region, had ten times during the previous year used editorials to urge "extermination against the red devils," stating that the Indians "are a dissolute, vagabondish, brutal, and ungrateful race, and ought to be wiped from the face of the earth." The paper worked closely with the governor, who proclaimed it was the right and obligation of the citizens and the military of the region to "pursue, kill, and destroy" all Indians. Chivington and his troops did not act alone.

Two white men who happened to be visiting the camp spied the soldiers, and tied a tanned buffalo hide to a pole, then waved it above their heads as a signal that this was a friendly village. Black Kettle, the Cheyenne's principle leader, raised first a white flag and, fearing the worst, a United States flag (given to him by Abraham Lincoln) in a desperate attempt to convince the soldiers not to attack.

There is an awful inevitability about what happened next. Soldiers opened fire. Indians fled. Chivington ordered his artillery to shoot into the panicked mass of women and children. Troops charged, cutting down every nonwhite in their path. Women scratched at the creek's sandy bank, trying to scoop out shelters for themselves and their children. As one soldier later reported, "There were some thirty or forty squaws collected in a hole for protection; they sent out a little girl about six years old with a white flag on a stick; she had not proceeded but a few steps when she was shot and killed. All the squaws in that hole were afterwards killed, and four or five bucks outside. The squaws offered no resistance. Every one I saw dead was scalped. I saw one squaw cut open with an unborn child, as I thought, lying by her side."

Picture the scene: a happy Chivington wades in gore. Mutilated Indians lie still in the cold November morning. In the distance, you can see a group of Cheyenne women and children trying to escape on foot. Far behind them, a group of soldiers charges on horseback. A movement in the dry creek bed to your left catches your eye. In the middle distance you see a child. As a soldier later recalled: "There was one child, probably three years old, just big enough to walk through the sand. The Indians had gone ahead, and this little child was behind following after them. The little fellow was perfectly naked, travelling on the sand. I saw one man get off his horse, at a distance of about seventy-five yards, and draw up his rifle and fire—he missed the child. Another man came up and said, 'Let me try the son of a bitch; I can hit him.' He got down off his horse, kneeled down, and fired at the little child, but he missed him. A third man came up and made a similar remark, and fired, and the little fellow dropped."

Now picture another scene, this of the soldiers riding home, victorious. You know that they scalped every body they could find, even digging up those which by accident had been buried with their heads full of hair. You see so many scalps that, as *The Rocky Mountain News* will soon report, "Cheyenne scalps are getting as thick here now as toads in Egypt. Everybody has got one and is anxious to get another to send east." You know also that the soldiers cut off fingers and ears to get at the jewelry of the dead. But now you look closer, and closer still, and you see that the soldiers "cut out the private parts of females and stretched them over the saddle-bows, and wore them over their hats while riding in the ranks."

Now picture, if you will, a third and final scene. Congress orders an investigation into what Chivington calls "one of the most bloody Indian battles ever fought," and what Theodore Roosevelt later calls "as righteous and beneficial a deed as ever took place on the frontier." The investigating committee calls a meeting with the governor and with Chivington, to be held at the Denver Opera House. Open to the public, the meeting is well-attended. You are in the back. You smell sweat, smoke, and you cannot be sure, but you think liquor. During the meeting someone asks whether, as a solution to the obvious Indian problem, it would be better to civilize or exterminate them. The crowd explodes. As a senator later wrote, "there suddenly arose such a shout as is never heard unless upon some battlefield—a shout almost loud enough to raise the roof of the opera house—'EXTERMINATE THEM! EXTERMINATE THEM!'"

Chivington did not act alone.

Chivington was neither reprimanded nor otherwise punished, and parlayed his fame into fortune as an after-dinner speaker. The University of Colorado named a dormitory after his second-in-command.

That these Indians were killed was in no way surprising. They were never considered human. The women were "squaws" and the men "bucks." The children? They counted even less. They should be killed because, as Chivington was fond of saying, "Nits make lice."

My father never beat anyone who didn't deserve it. My brothers were often beaten because the horse tank was only two-thirds and not completely full, or because they received sub-par grades, which meant anything below an A. As teenagers, my sisters were awakened for a beating because the dishes were not clean enough. I remember that one sister was beaten because a litter of puppies fell into our swimming pool and drowned: instead of fishing them out, she called a brother to do it; she was beaten for not doing it herself, and also because the puppies were worth money.

The bombastic stupidity of his reasoning was irrelevant to what he was going to do. On feeling an urge to beat someone, he found an excuse to do it. In another sense, however, his nonsensical reasons were the point, perhaps more than the physical violence itself. Had he provided valid reasons for his violence—were such to exist—we victims could have maintained a semblance of control by fulfilling his requests. Joe could improve his grades; my mother (and presumably my sister and myself) could be better lovers; my sisters could make damn sure the dishes were always spotless. On the other hand, had he not given any reasons we could more readily have seen his violence for what it was: utterly senseless. Yet by fabricating nonsensical reasons for his actions, he was able to rationalize them to himself, and was able to get us to play an active role in our own victimization. We would meet demand after demand. The demands were insatiable, and ever changing. Today, it was spelling, tomorrow, dead puppies, the day after, dirty dishes. He shifted, we shifted. It was simply an impossible situation.

Taking a Life

"Today we took a little snake. I had to apologize to her for cutting her life off so suddenly and so definitely; I did what I did knowing that my own life will also be cut off someday in very much the same fashion, suddenly and definitely."

Jack Forbes

By now you've probably spotted a contradiction in my story. I suppose there's a chance you can accept the possibility of deals made with coyotes and dogs, and maybe you can even allow that stars helped me out when I was a child. But what about the chickens and ducks whose lives were bartered away in my bargain with the coyotes? Carried away by coyotes, or carried by me to a chopping block, how would that make a difference to them? They seem to be getting shafted either way.

I do not know how they felt about dying. But I know what I have experienced. I know that there have been times when killing a bird has been traumatic and messy—much more so for him or her than for me. Some birds have fought me, and to this day I am haunted by the screams of one rooster who had been silent until the moment I placed his head on the chopping block.

But there have been times the death—the killing—has not seemed so awful. I have had brief glimpses of death, and killing, as something that is not always frightening. It can be accepted and even celebrated, with respect, and in full cognizance of the loss, as a requisite part of a beautiful dance which necessarily ends in death for all of us. It is the bird's death now, and my death later, that allows the dance to continue.

I remember one death in particular. It was the first after I made the deal with the coyotes. I had about a dozen ducks, and too many drakes. At one male to a half-dozen females the hens often approach the drakes, then plop down and raise their tails to be mounted. At a ratio of one-to-one the sex is neither willing nor gentle. Drakes fight each other, but the hens get the worst of it. Hens are frequently chased by drakes until they are cornered, mounted, and then mounted again. Favored hens have no feathers on the backs of their necks from being grasped so often in the bills of drakes. At these ratios, no one seems happy.

I had to do something about that. At the same time, I was running out of food. Because I eat meat I feel it's my responsibility to acknowledge the death it requires. Besides, I don't want to support the practice of factory farming. So I raise birds, I buy part of a cow from a local rancher, I fish, and I've also gone hunting, although the only thing I ever "got" was lost.

I was splitting wood early one afternoon, and noticed the drakes were especially aggressive. Having gained confidence from two previous successful instances of interspecies communication I said aloud, "If one of you is rough with a female again in the next thirty seconds, I'm going to kill you and eat you." I was not *chastising* the birds. There were simply too many drakes, and one had to die. I am fully aware as I type these words, as I was fully aware then, that I was displacing responsibility for my own choice to kill a duck "on the next offender."

About fifteen seconds later a drake tore into a female. He was one of my favorites. There were other ducks who were normally rougher, some male muscovies (a breed of duck) especially, and a part of me hoped that one of them would have been the odd duck out. Of course another part had hoped that none of them would be aggressive, which would have allowed me once again to displace responsibility, this time for not killing any of them. This reluctance to kill is the reason I had not yet kept my end of the bargain with the coyotes.

I turned to the duck and said, "You're the one." Next I set aside my ax to fetch the hatchet. Normally when I pick up the hatchet the birds will run toward me, because I use it mainly to split nuts for them, break open melons, and pulverize huge globs of dough from the pasta factory. But this time the duck I was going to kill, a beautiful, large, white Pekin, ran past me into the coop. At the time I put the birds in at night (I no longer do that), and they were generally loathe to enter it during the day.

I waited for him to come out. He didn't. I considered going in after him, but knew the fact that I had readied myself to kill him did not mean that he had readied himself to die.

Retreating to my library, I thought about all that had happened, and I remembered something I'd read in Barry Lopez's *Of Wolves and Men:* "One of the central questions about predators and their prey is why one animal is killed and not another. Why is one chosen and another, seemingly in every way as suitable, ignored? No one knows."

He continues, "The most beguiling moment in the hunt is the first moment of encounter. Wolves and prey may remain absolutely still while staring at each other. Immediately afterward, a moose may simply turn and walk away . . . or the wolves may turn and run; or the wolves may charge and kill the animal in less than a minute. . . . I think what transpires in those moments of staring is an exchange of information between predator and prey that either triggers a chase or defuses the hunt right there. I call this the conversation of death. . . ."

I checked outside, and the duck was still in the coop. I returned to the book, to read of wolves signaling prey, and prey signaling back: "The moose trots toward them and the wolves leave. The pronghorn throws up his white rump as a sign to follow. A wounded cow stands up to be seen. And the prey behave strangely. Caribou rarely use their antlers against the wolf. An ailing moose, who, as far as we know, could send wolves on their way simply by standing his ground, does what is most likely to draw an attack, what he is least capable of carrying off: he runs."

Lopez calls this conversation "a ceremonial exchange, the flesh of the hunted in exchange for respect for its spirit. In this way both animals, not the predator alone, choose for the encounter to end in death. There is, at least, a sacred order in this. There is nobility."

The duck was still hiding out in the coop. I would wait until he was ready.

He never came out that afternoon, and I didn't shut him or any of the others in that night. The next morning I arose late. He was out and about. When he saw me he waddled back to the coop. I decided to go inside, too.

While I ate breakfast I thought about death, and the conversation of death. This set off another series of associations that were broadly about violence, and the way in which so often we conflate violence and sex, especially in popular culture. Horror movies, for example, may seem prurient in that they frequently show a whole lot of unnecessary tits and ass, but the underlying message is violent. In these dime-a-dozen flicks, if two people have sex, you can usually count on one of them (most often the woman) buying it soon after, often in a fashion with strong phallic overtones. Because both sex and violence in these films are too often random, gratuitous, and devoid of deep emotional significance for the participants and the audience alike, the acts are desacralized, robbed of their inherent meaning.

Not only horror movies follow this equation.

Suddenly it occurred to me that the problem is not that sex and violence are conflated in these films, and in the culture at large. In fact they share something: both are deeply relational in that they inherently create or magnify at least some degree of relatedness. I would say that the predator-prey relationship is even more fundamental, and in a sense even more intimate, than a sexual relationship. But by deafening ourselves to the emotional consequences of violence we have become confused by its relationship to sex. We have come to believe that violence equals aggression, and we have come to base our model of sexuality on our model of violence. This goes a long way toward explaining the prevalence of rape scenes in horror movies, art films, and blockbusters alike, the woman pushing at her attacker's chest, until, by the end of the scene she has her arms wrapped around him, pulling him close to her. By enacting this transition, the filmmakers convert an act of aggression into an act of consensual sexuality. The ubiquity of rape in real life attests to the desire of many members of our culture to attempt this same transition.

But violence does not equal aggression, and our sex need not follow our mistaken model of violence. There are, after all, different kinds of violence. There is the necessary violence of survival, the killing of one's food, whether that food is lettuce, onion, duck, or deer. Then there are senseless forms of violence so often perpetrated by our culture: child abuse, rape, military or economic genocide, factory farms, industrial forestry, commercial fishing. But violence *also* can be like *sex:* a sacramental, beautiful, and sometimes bittersweet interaction.

Death is, and must be, deeply emotional. To intentionally cause death is to engender a form of intimacy, one that we're not used to thinking about. To kill without emotion and without respect, or to ignore the intimacy inherent in the act, is to rob it of its dignity, and to rob the life that you are ending of its significance. By robbing death and life of significance we reduce ourselves to the machines Descartes dreamed about. And we deny our own significance.

I went outside again, and this time, though the chickens pecked and scratched busily at the driveway's gravel, all the ducks and geese were back in the coop, and silent. I waited inside a few moments, and they came out. I walked to the duck and picked him up easily. He rode smoothly, cradled between my right arm and chest. On the way to the chopping block I picked up the hatchet. I laid him down, and *he stretched out his own neck.* I swung the hatchet, not hard enough, alas, and reached back to swing again. He was wounded. His eyes caught mine, and I will never forget that look. They were soft, like we were lovers, and they said, "This hurts. Get it over with." I swung again, and he was dead.

As often happens when you kill a bird, his nervous system caught fire. His wings flapped explosively, as if now, for the first time, he was flying.

I carried him to a post and hung him by his feet so he would bleed while I heated water. I scalded him and removed his feathers, then eviscerated him. As promised, I carried his head, feet, and guts, along with his feathers, into the forest to the east, and placed it all at the base of a tall, shapely pine I now call the coyote tree.

I returned to the tree a couple of days later. The remains of the duck who had taught me about violence, sex, intimacy, and the acceptance of death were gone. Instead of the bare mound of feathers I had seen in the woods each other time the coyotes had eaten a bird, atop the feathers this time was a pile of coyote shit.

I smiled, because I could think of no better way for the coyotes to "sign" our agreement. There was the poop; they had closed the deal.

I was now, of course, thoroughly convinced that I was crazy.

Cultural Eyeglasses

"All through school and University I had been given maps of life and knowledge on which there was hardly a trace of many of the things that I most cared about and that seemed to me to be of the greatest possible importance to the conduct of my life. I remembered that for many years my perplexity had been complete; and no interpreter had come along to help me. It remained complete until I ceased to suspect the sanity of my perceptions and began, instead, to suspect the soundness of the maps."

E.F. Schumacher

ISOLATION DOES STRANGE THINGS to a person's mind. This is true for any social creature, human or otherwise. Monkeys taken from their mothers at birth, placed alone in stainless-steel chambers, and deprived of contact with other animals ("human and sub-human" alike, according to the researchers), develop irreversible mental illnesses. As one of the experts in this field, Harry Harlow, put it: "sufficiently severe and enduring social isolation reduces these animals to a social-emotional level in which the primary social responsiveness is fear."

Harlow and another scientist, Stephen Suomi, wondered if they could induce psychopathology in primates by removing baby monkeys from their natural mothers and placing them in cages with "cloth surrogate mothers who could become monsters." They created a cloth frame "monster mother" that would "eject high pressure compressed air" and "blow the animal's skin practically off its body." They created another "that would rock so violently that the baby's head and teeth would rattle," and finally, a "porcupine mother" that on command would "eject sharp brass spikes over all the ventral surface of its body." In the former cases, the baby simply clung tighter, because, as the scientists reported, "a frightened infant clings tightly to its mother at all costs," and in the latter case the monkey waited until the spikes retreated, then returned to cling to what it perceived to be its mother.

Harlow and Suomi finally discovered that the best monster mothers they could devise were simply the products of their own experiments: the monkeys they had raised in isolation. These monkeys—depressed, made permanently psychopathological by artificially removing them from the social embeddedness in which they had evolved—were too fearful to interact normally with other monkeys, and were incapable of normal sexual relations. Undeterred, the scientists impregnated them through the use of what they called a "rape rack." When the babies were born, the mothers had no idea what to do with them. Many of the mothers ignored their infants, while others, in the words of Harlow and Suomi, "were brutal or lethal. One of their favorite tricks was to crush the infant's skull with their teeth. But the really sickening behavior pattern was that of smashing the infant's face to the floor, then rubbing it back and forth."

About two weeks ago I received in the mail the Executive Summary of the Third National Incidence Study of Child Abuse and Neglect. This comprehensive report estimated that in 1993, approximately 614,000 American children were physically abused, 300,000 were sexually abused, 532,000 were emotionally abused, 507,000 were physically neglected, and 585,000 were emotionally neglected. 565,000 of these children were killed or seriously injured.

What is the relationship between these numbers and our culturally induced isolation from the natural world and each other, from the social embeddedness in which we evolved?

When I was a child, I sometimes used to lie in bed and look at the ceiling. By softening my gaze, I could cause the spackling above to take form. I saw tin cans, demons, books, knives, flowers, faces. I made up mysteries, which I tried to solve with clues I gathered from above. It is possible to find patterns where none exist.

When Descartes said, "I suppose, then, that all the things that I see are false," he was on to something. Each day we are bombarded by so many pieces of information—as I write, there is the sound of the space heater, the black on grey of the computer screen, the plastic of its housing, the pictures of the earth on the wall behind, and below them a pair of newspaper clippings ("Defiant activist defends guerrillas," and "Mother bear charges trains"), the clucking of chickens and chatter of geese outside, the quick movement of a tiny spider on the ceiling, the weight of my clothes, the smell of dust on the back of a cat who just came inside: all these and thousands more in only this one moment. It's never possible to know for certain the "true" source of any given interpretation, the dividing line between our association (i.e., projection) and reality. The question quickly becomes, What *is* real? It is always possible to consciously or unconsciously "see" almost anything we want. I can look at the ceiling and see an image of the Virgin Mary, or I can look at the ceiling and see that the spackler did a damn good job.

Perception is of course intimately tied to preconception. I have, as is true for each of us, a pair of cultural eyeglasses that will determine to greater or lesser degree what will be in focus, what will be a blur, what gives me a headache, and what I cannot see. I was raised a Christian—the mythology resides deep in my bones—and I know the story of Jesus nearly as well as I know my own. Until my late teens I couldn't see some of the darker acts perpetrated in the name of Christ. I still feel a twinge each time I say, "I am not a Christian," a slight apprehension that I may have gone too far. Sometimes I look up, a small part of my upbringing still telling me that my blasphemy will call forth a bolt of lightning from the sky.

Blasphemy is more complicated than the simple act of cursing God. It is an attempt to remove our cultural eyeglasses, or at least grind the lenses to make our focus broader, clearer. There are deep strictures against removing these eyeglasses, for without them our culture would fall apart. Question Christianity, damned heathen. Question capitalism, pinko liberal. Question democracy, ungrateful wretch. Question science, just plain stupid. These epithets—blasphemer, commie, ingrate, stupid—need not be spoken aloud. Their invocation actually implies an incomplete enculturation of the subject. Proper enculturation causes the eyeglasses to be undetectable. People believe they are perceiving the world as it is, without the distorting lens of culture: God (with a capital G) *does* sit upon a heavenly throne; heaven *is* located beyond the stars that make up Orion's belt (and, so I was told, you can *just* see heaven's brilliance if you look closely enough); a collection of humans, each acting selfishly, *will* bring peace, justice, and affluence to all; the United States *is* the world's greatest democracy; humans *are* the apex of creation.

A couple of years ago, mining prospectors in Venezuela shot down about seventy Yanomame Indians who were opposing the theft of their land. Each of the newspaper articles I read about the murders mentioned that the Yanomame could only give approximate numbers of the dead, because they could not count past two. The implication was that because the Indians could not count, they must be unbelievably stupid—perhaps even subhuman. The belief that underlies this implication probably accounts for the fact that the eventually-apprehended mass-murderers were only sentenced to six months in jail. But—and I'm telling this story to point out how deeply embedded and utterly transparent the cultural assumptions are—the truth is that even something as simple as one plus one equals two carries with it powerful and hidden presumptions. I hold up the first finger of my left hand, and the first finger of my right. I put them together. Am I now holding up two fingers? No. I'm holding up the first finger of my left hand, which has the almost invisible remnant of a small wart between the second and third knuckles. And I'm holding up the first finger of my right, which has a tiny freckle near its base. The fingers are different. Arithmetic presumes that the items to be counted—the digits—are identical. Before you dismiss this as so much hair-splitting, consider that Treblinka and other Nazi death camps had quotas to fill—so many people to kill each day, each shift. Guards held contests among the inmates in which winners lived, and a preset number of losers didn't. But they're just so many numbers, right? Not if you lose. It's easier to kill a number than an individual, whether we're talking about so many tons of fish, so many board feet of timber, or so many boxcars of *untermenschen*.

None of this is to say that I have anything against counting; it is merely to point out that even the simplest of our actions—one, two, three—is fraught with cultural assumptions. Nor is this to say—and here is one place where Descartes and our entire culture have gone wrong—that there is no physical reality, or that physical reality is somehow less important than our preconceptions. The fact that Descartes' views—like yours, like mine—are clouded by projection and delusion doesn't mean that nothing exists, or that, as Descartes put it, "nothing has ever existed of all that my fallacious memory represents to me." It simply means we don't see clearly.

The truth is that the physical cannot be separated from the nonphysical. Although it's certainly true that cultural eyeglasses worn by death camp attendants made it seem to them that Jews,

Gypsies, Slavs, Russians, homosexuals, communists, intellectuals, and others were killable, it is also true that no matter how strong our social imperatives, physical reality cannot be denied. Perception is connected to preconception. Conception is connected to perception. This was one reason for widespread alcoholism among members of *einsatzgruppen*—Nazi mobile killing units—and one reason many death camp attendants got drunk before the selections. Not even the lens of Nazism was distorted grossly enough to entirely eradicate the truth.

No anesthetic was necessary for the people who ordered the killings; they had the misleading language of technocratic bureaucracy to distance them from the killings. Thus "mass murder" becomes "the final solution," "world domination" becomes "defending the free world," the War Department becomes the Department of Defense, and "ecocide" becomes "developing natural resources." No one needs to get drunk to do any of this. A good strong ideology and heavy doses of rationalization are all it takes. But it may require little more than a simple unwillingness to step outside the flow of society, to think and act and most importantly experience for ourselves—and to make our *own* decisions.

Let me put this another way. Had Descartes been in the hold of a ship tossing violently in a storm, the contents of his stomach lurching toward his throat with every swell, his famous dictum may not have come out the same. By the same token, had he shared his room not with a stove but a beloved, he may not in that moment have believed that thoughts alone verify his existence, nor that "body, figure, extension, movement and place [were] but the fictions" of his mind.

The point is that physical reality does exist, and it's up to us to detect its patterns. And it is our job to determine whether the patterns we perceive are really there, or whether they're the result of some combination of projection and chance. It's also up to us to determine for ourselves how closely the patterns we've been handed by our culture fit *our* experience of the world.

A frenetic monotony describes our culture's eradication of every indigenous culture it encounters, and an even more frenetic monotony cloaks our inability to recognize this. Throw a dart at a map of the world, and no matter the territory it strikes, you will find the story of cruelty and genocide perpetrated by our culture.

I throw a dart. It lands low and to the right. Tasmania. A little research reveals that our culture arrived in 1803, and the massacres began soon after. In early 1804, weaponless Tasmanians, waving green boughs in a gesture of peace, approached a regiment of British soldiers at Oyster Bay. As the commanding officer later stated, the Tasmanians would be of no use to the British. The soldiers opened fire, killing fifty, including women and children. British encroachment on the island continued through the decades, leading to the Black War, which lasted from 1824 to 1831. One of the many weapons used to civilize these savages was the penis. Rape of Aboriginal women was widespread among settlers and soldiers. There was not a single instance of rape committed by an Aborigine against a white woman. When war had not eliminated the Tasmanians, a bounty was placed on their heads. A settler reported, "It was a favourite amusement to hunt the Aborigines; that a day would be selected and the neighbouring settlers invited, with their families, to a picnic. . . . After dinner all would be gaiety and merriment, whilst the gentlemen of the party would take their guns and dogs, and accompanied by two or three convict servants, wander through the bush in search of blackfellows. Sometimes they would return without sport; at others they would succeed in killing a woman, or, if lucky, a man or two." Bounty and sport still not sufficing to exterminate the natives, Governor George Arthur mobilized all available settlers and convicts to form what became known as "The Black Line" stretching from one side of the island to the other. The settlers systematically beat their way across the territory, trying to drive the Aborigines before them. Although the last full-blooded Tasmanian male died in 1870, neither the Tasmanian race nor culture have been entirely eradicated. Nine Tasmanian women were abducted and raped by seal hunters, and two more went voluntarily. All Tasmanian Aboriginals are related to them.

Had the dart landed a little higher, we would have been in Australia, where between 1790 and 1920 the population of Aborigines fell from 750,000 at the first arrival of Europeans to 70,000 some hundred and thirty years later. We would read in scientific journals the reason for this decline: "the races who rest content in . . . placid sensuality and unprogressive decrepitude, can hardly hope to contend permanently in the great struggle for existence with the noblest division of the human species. . . . The survival of the fittest means that might—wisely used—is right. And thus we invoke and remorselessly fulfil the inexorable law of natural selection when exterminating the inferior Australian." We would read reports of settlers burying live Aboriginal infants up to their necks, then forcing parents to watch as contests were held to see who could kick an infant's head the farthest.

And then we would pass on, back to our lives, back to watching our televisions, back to listening to our music, back to this book, and we would say, "I did not do this. This was not my doing."

I throw the dart again, again, again. Each time a thousand horrors. Each time enslavement, rape, murder, genocide. The dart strikes Africa, where somewhere between thirty and sixty million people (who, according to those responsible were "bestial and sordid," and "the very reverse of human kind," and who would each have otherwise "idly spent the years of a useless, restive life") died after having been captured for the slave trade. Another twelve to fifteen million survived to spend the rest of their lives working the plantations and mines of the New World. The dart strikes New Zealand, where "taking all things into consideration, the disappearance of the race is scarcely subject for much regret. They are dying out in a quick, easy way, and are being supplanted by a superior race." The dart strikes Hawai'i, where a missionary stated that a ninety percent reduction in the population was like "the amputation of diseased members of the body."

The dart strikes my home. I live about a mile from Hangman Valley, near Spokane, Washington, and thrice that far from Fort George Wright Drive, one of the city's arteries. Prior to Colonel Wright's tenure in this city, Hangman Valley and the creek that runs through it were known as Latah, which means in the native tongue *stream where little fish are caught*. At the time, 1858, whites had not been able to bring all of the region's Indians to terms. Then Wright had an idea. Under a flag of truce he called the Yakama warrior Qualchan and his wife to Wright's residence, telling them he was going to proffer a peace treaty. Having already put Qualchan's father in chains, Wright arrested Qualchan, led him directly to a tree and with Qualchan's wife as witness hanged him. As Wright noted in his report to headquarters: "Qual-chew came to me at 9 o'clock this morning, and at 9 1/4 a.m. he was hung." The next day Wright similarly hanged six Palouse Indians. He was a hero.

Four years ago a group of students tried to change the name of Fort George Wright Drive to Qualchan. The citizens of Spokane, those who cared at all, were outraged, and a political cartoonist—my next-door neighbor—drew a cartoon with two frames. On the right, a bunch of hippies with cigarettes and beads, captioned "Wrong." On the left, a drawing of the Colonel, captioned "Wright." The road, which I drive often, remains named in his honor.

I had a fairly hard time of it in school. It's not that my grades weren't good, for they were. Instead it's that the questions I cared about often seemed at odds with what I was being taught. When my teachers told me *how,* I wanted to know *why,* and when they gave me abstractions, I asked them to make the lessons real. Not that *how* isn't important, but I sensed even as a child—in a vague, entirely unarticulated fashion—that to ask *how* without asking *why* might be dangerous: only recently have I grown to name my earlier misgivings, and to know that such an imbalance causes nuclear bombs, nerve gas, napalm, and other examples of inexcusable technology. When teachers tired of my questions, which were for obvious reasons often childish, I would be sent to a room by myself with a book. I was supposed to learn the next year's math. But I taught myself snatches of whatever caught my fancy—one month it was a little Latin, another it was Egyptian Hieroglyphics 101, but often it was my favorite invented game; pitching erasers across the room onto bookshelves or into trash cans (bank shots: double score).

In junior high, I nearly failed Algebra on philosophical grounds. I was told, for example, that the quantity x minus y squared equals x squared minus 2xy plus y squared. Because the two sides are equal, I asked, why should I waste my time working with them? Frustrated, the teacher turned aside the question. Day after day I returned with the same question, and day after day she ignored it. Finally she came up with an answer that seems at this distance to characterize much of my early schooling. She said, "Because if you don't, I'll flunk you." I did the manipulations.

I did them well enough to pass through calculus in high school, and then I did what most people who finish calculus in high school do; which is to study science in college. I had learned by this time to keep my mouth shut, at least on occasion, and had even learned to quiet the inner voice always asking why. Still I gained enough of a reputation among my physics instructors to cause some to laugh good-naturedly each time I raised my hand, and say, "Let me guess: Derrick wants to know why we're doing this. He's going to ask how it applies to his own life." I would smile back, and they would tell me (when they could).

But I still didn't fit in. Although the stars had long since stopped speaking to me—as had trees, horses, birds, garter snakes, crawdads—or at least I had long since stopped listening, when I tried to dive into this brave new world of equations I couldn't fully do it. If the statement "Do this or I will flunk you" characterizes my formative schooling, a weekend assignment for an advanced physics class characterizes the later years.

The assignment, interesting enough on its own, was this: If you spin a coin on its edge atop a flat surface, it will follow a looping pattern of small and large circles. Given a host of initial conditions and simplifying assumptions, we were supposed to find an equation that would describe this path. I spent much of the weekend doing page after page of calculus, differential equations, and lots of old-fashioned algebra (Yes, Mrs. Glass, I eventually did learn my algebra), and finally arrived at an answer. The answer—an indecipherable mass of variables, constants, and integrals that covered the better half of a page—is as meaningless to me now as it was at the time. I see no hint of silver in those symbols, no relation to the sound of a coin as it spins, then slows, then collapses on the Formica with its metallic cicada chatter.

Although by that time I was for the most part inured to the abstract nature of much of what I was being taught, this time something snapped. Maybe the sun was shining that weekend, and I watched it too much from the table where I worked, or I lost too much sleep over the assignment. Perhaps the hours I spent on this problem contrasted too sharply with the burgeoning awareness of my own mortality, and the knowledge that, whatever I may do with the rest of my life, the sun would never slant exactly this same way through these same trees, never again would precisely this air course through my twenty-one-year-old lungs. If I had possessed then the confidence and knowledge I have now—confidence in the validity of my own experience—I would have strode into class on Monday, pulled a coin out of my pocket, spun it on the teacher's desk, and said, "There's your answer."

Of course, if I then possessed the confidence and knowledge I have now, I probably would have flunked the class.

Most everyone I knew hated being at the Colorado School of Mines. Nearly all of us viewed it as a four- or five-year ordeal, something to be endured, like a mule endures the whip. A friend was fond of recalling that he first heard AC/DC's *Highway to Hell* while driving to register for classes. I'm certain the thought that college could be an enjoyable learning process never occurred to most of my peers: we merely wanted to survive it. This attitude was actively encouraged by many of the professors. I remember one class, a required part of everyone's sophomore core, that fully two-thirds of the 300 or so students each semester flunked or dropped. There was another class—quantum mechanics, an advanced physics elective no one in his (the student body was overwhelmingly male) right mind ever took—in which five of six students failed and the other received a "D."

There is only one reward that would cause so many people to endure such an unpleasant and extended trial: money—or rather the promise of money. Students and faculty alike were explicit about this. At the time, graduates from the Colorado School of Mines were virtually guaranteed high-paying jobs with major petroleum or mining transnationals. Headhunters for these corporations knew that Mines' students, having survived these four (or more likely five) years, would have what it takes to thrive in the corporate world.

I differed from many of the students in two significant ways. The first is that until my parents divorced, my family had been wealthy, so I already had an intimate knowledge of the truism that money does not equal happiness: thus I did not have the same burning drive—"When I get out of here, the first thing I'm gonna do is get a red Porsche. And then a black Mustang"—as many of my fellow students.

The other difference, an advantage that in many ways counterbalanced the disadvantage of my dimmed enthusiasm for money, was the long, intimate practice of denying my feelings. If there was one thing I could do well—one area in which my confidence soared—it was in the ability to endure. I was at the time proud of, though also troubled by, my capacity to not show emotion.

I can remember a day in fifth grade, a bright blue January day in Montana, the sun so piercing you had to squint even to look at its reflection in the dulled metal of the monkey bars. Sitting here in front of this computer, twenty-six years and one month later, I can see the short grass of the football field bend in waves before the cold wind, and still feel that wind on my neck. I was standing alone that particular day, that particular recess, and I was crying—something I rarely did. It was something I was not to do again for many years, until I was a junior in high school and a puppy died in my arms. My tears that cold day were not from sorrow, something I dared not feel for fear the sorrow would never end, but instead the tears came from resolve. I had seen—I had felt—the damage that my father's anger could do. I had told my mother that I couldn't say "I love you" because those were words my father often repeated—like a mantra—after he beat someone. So I resolved that cold day in fifth grade to never again feel anger, to never again feel anything.

I was well prepared for school.

The monotony of our culture's genocidal impulse extends not only across space, but also through time; the God of our culture has always been jealous, and whether going by the name of God the Father, Yahweh, Jesus Christ, Civilization, Capitalism, Science, Technology, Profit, or Progress, He has never been less than eager to destroy all those He cannot control.

The Old Testament seems at times little more than a glorification of this genocide. I open to Numbers, and read, "If thou wilt indeed deliver this people into my hand, then I will utterly destroy their cities." I turn a few pages and read again, "And the Lord our God delivered him [Sihon] before us; and we smote him, and his sons, and all his people." A few pages later: "And when the Lord thy God shall deliver them before thee: thou shalt smite them; *and* utterly destroy them; thou shalt make no covenant with them, nor shew mercy unto them. . . ." It never stops.

Follow the rise of civilization, and necessarily you follow the outward path of an expanding circle of death, from the destruction of the barbarians of northern Greece to the rape of the Sabines, from the eradication of Europe's indigenous peoples to the enslavement of Africans, from the conquest of the New World to the intentional introduction of syphilis to the Pacific Islands. The story is the same. The murder of men, women, and children.

Think for a moment about the toddler shot in the aftermath of Sand Creek—"Let me try the son of a bitch. I can hit him." Multiply this child by a million, and place him in the once-forested hills of the Middle East, the once-forested hills of northern Greece, the once-forested hills of north Africa, place him anywhere on the globe, and you will see him being murdered to serve our God: "Some Christians encounter an Indian woman, who was carrying in her arms a child at suck; and since the dog they had with them was hungry, they tore the child from the mother's arms and flung it still living to the dog, who proceeded to devour it before the mother's eyes."

One more example among millions: "At about 1:00 p.m., the soldiers began to fire at the women inside the small church. The majority did not die there, but were separated from their children, taken to their homes in groups, and killed, the majority apparently with machetes. . . . Then they returned to kill the children, whom they had left crying and screaming by themselves, without their mothers. . . . The soldiers cut open the children's stomachs with knives or they grabbed the children's little legs and smashed their heads with heavy sticks." This last example occurred in the 1980s. Troops equipped and trained with United

States assistance took part in a systematic program that killed 10,000 people a year in Guatemala, and intentionally dispossessed more than 1,000,000 of that country's 4,000,000 Indians.

Every morning when I wake up I ask myself whether I should write or blow up a dam. Every day I tell myself I should continue to write. Yet I'm not always convinced I'm making the right decision. I've written books and I've been an activist. At the same time I know neither a lack of words nor a lack of activism kills salmon here in the Northwest. It is the presence of dams.

Anyone who lives in this region and who knows anything about salmon knows the dams must go. And anyone who knows anything about politics knows the dams will probably stay. Scientists study, politicians and businesspeople lie and delay, bureaucrats hold sham public hearings, activists write letters and press releases, I write books and articles, and still the salmon die. It's a cozy relationship for all of us but the salmon.

I don't like it. I do not wish to merely describe the horrors that characterize our culture; I want to stop them. Sometimes it seems to me terribly self-indulgent to write, to shuffle magnetically-charged particles on a hard drive, when day after day it's business as usual. Other times it seems even worse, as if the flow of words were not merely self-indulgent, but an act of avoidance. I could be blowing up dams. I could be destroying the equipment used to deforest our planet. I could be physically stopping perpetrators of abuse. How many social critics, I often wonder, how many writers, really want to stop the cycle, bring down this culture of death? How many have found a way to make a comfortable living while comforting themselves with beautiful descriptions of nature and the occasional outburst of righteous indignation?

The world is drowning in a sea of words, and I add to the deluge, then hope that I can sleep that night, secure in the knowledge that I have "done my part." Sometimes I don't know how we all live with ourselves. What can I say that will give sufficient honor to the dead, the extirpated, the beaten, the raped, the little children—"I can hit the son of a bitch. Let me try him"? I don't know.

In the ten minutes I have stared at this computer screen, trying to fashion a conclusion to this section, more than sixty women have been beaten by their partners, and twelve children have been killed or injured by their parents or guardians. At least one species of plant or animal has been permanently eradicated from the face of Earth, and approximately a square mile of the planet has been deforested.

In the time it took me to write this last sentence, another woman was beaten by her lover.

My mother has often stated she wishes my father were dead. This seems reasonable to me, not only because of the pain he caused her and her children, but also because it would stop at its source the rolling wave of pain he leaves in his wake.

My own wish for him would be that he live in the full understanding of the damage he has caused. Better minds than my own have pointed out that this is the psychic meaning underlying the Christian notion of Hell. Remove Hell from its literal interpretation, which trivializes the profound psychic content in order to create yet one more means to control people ("Give up your land-based religion and accept Jesus Christ as your personal savior or you'll roast in hell"), and what remains is precisely what those like my father—those who would destroy—lack, which is an honest appreciation of their actions. Another way to say this is that for someone who is destructive, for someone who is controlling, for someone who is civilized (and in more general terms, for *anyone*), Hell is the too-late realization that everything and everyone are interdependent. This realization is our only salvation.

Today I am in an airplane. As often happens when I fly, I am thinking about death. As we pass over waves, mottled and unmoving at this distance, or tiny specks of houses, house upon house in straight rows or loops that curve in patterns predictably similar from city to city, I sometimes picture—when the plane drops or skips from turbulence—the craft breaking up, or a wing tearing off, or an engine disappear. Then I picture the plane falling. I wonder how I would spend those last moments, and I perform anew the calculations to reveal how much time I would have before I hit the ground. Let's say we're at 32,000 feet. *Distance equals half the acceleration times time squared. Acceleration equals thirty-two feet per second per second. Time squared equals two thousand. The square root of two thousand is about forty-five.* Forty-five seconds to live.

Below us, there are dry hills, gray, with white roads crawling over them.

Out of nowhere I think of my grandmother. The last words my mother said to her had been "I love you." If this plane fell from the sky, I wonder, would those be my last words? Would I look one last time at the backs of my hands, and say, "My god, how good to be alive"? Or in the shock of it all would a stream of oaths fall from my mind, perhaps stopping breathless on my lips, held back by the same shock and terror that created them?

In these times, times I consider my own death, I often remember that strong white Pekin, and I pray that whenever my own death comes, whether I fall to the earth before I finish this sentence, or gently fall asleep fifty years from now, that I may approach it with the same grace and magnanimity that I first observed in that duck.

I am not a Buddhist. Yet there is a Buddhist story that I hold dear. A monk walks in a forest, and chances upon a tiger. The tiger chases him, and the monk runs until he comes to a cliff. With the tiger on his heels, the man grasps a vine and clambers down. Another tiger appears at the bottom. As the man hangs there, a mouse crawls from a crevice just beyond his reach and begins to gnaw the vine. Death above, death below, and death in between. He sees a big ripe strawberry near his mouth. It is delicious.

In this moment, flying miles above the strawberry fields of California's San Joachin Valley, I think that I would change the ending of this story. Instead of giving the doomed man a strawberry, what if we leave him alone with the two tigers, the mouse, and the fraying vine? For the last time, his arms grow tired, he feels a familiar ache deep in his muscles. For the last time he catches his breath, feels a rasping in his throat and lungs. He feels this, and a thousand other things. It is all delicious.

My god, I think as the plane hits another patch of turbulence, how good it is to be alive.

. . .

The dog who used to eat eggs suddenly died. One day we walked to get the mail, both dogs dashing in circles around me and causing me sometimes to stumble or slow, and always to smile. When we got home, I noticed that Goldmund, the large one, was wobbly on his feet. I went to the barn to collect eggs. By the time I came out, he couldn't stand. I ran inside to phone the vet, then to phone my mother to come help. When I returned he could not sit up. I held him while he screamed, not so much out of pain, it seemed, as out of confusion and frustration that his body—which until moments before had served him well—was no longer familiar. My mother arrived. We drove to the vet. Goldmund moaned on the way, and screamed on the table as they tranquilized him. They took his blood. He died that afternoon, of a stroke, caused by a congenital condition that turned his blood to sludge.

The other dog, Narcissus—a black lab/spaniel mix who somehow ended up smaller than either—was disconsolate. The dogs had been inseparable from the moment I brought them together a couple of years before from two ads for free pups in the newspaper. Narcissus wouldn't eat, and barely left the barn.

I went to the Humane Society, and got another puppy. I knew that dogs are often territorial, having frequently heard Narcissus keen a battle cry as he chased away strays or tangled with the coyotes. It took him less than a minute to warm up to the new one, a border collie cross I named Tupac Amaru.

Amaru is as smart as Narcissus is courageous. I asked him only once to stop biting tires, and only once to stop eating eggs. After the latter I continued to see footprints in the mud or snow near the pfitzers, but instead of eating the eggs, he brought them for me to find: Each day I picked them up from where he gingerly placed them in front of the bushes. I asked him to stop bringing the neighbor's garbage bags into my yard and scattering the trash about. He stopped. Only later did I discover he was now hauling the bags into a thicket, where I couldn't see him, and scattering the garbage there. When I found that spot he took the bags to another. Like Narcissus and Goldmund before, the two walk with me to get the mail. Amaru knows which mailbox is mine; he stands on hind legs to put his paws on the box. He has yet to figure out that mail isn't delivered on Sundays or national holidays.

Soon after I got him, Amaru began to kill birds. Once every two weeks, or three, or four, I would find a chicken in the yard, uneaten and generally unbruised, with some feathers missing from its neck, but dead. I tried telling Amaru, again and again in that stentorian voice, "No! Don't kill the chickens." Each time he would roll on his back, and each time I would think the problem was solved. Then a couple weeks later I'd find another dead chicken, unbruised and missing feathers from the neck. I asked him to stop, but this time it did no good. The killings continued.

I caught him in the act several times. It was never so frenetic as I would have imagined, nor even as frenzied as it usually was when I killed a bird. Amaru would be lying calm in the driveway, the chicken's neck in his mouth. He held it, not chewing or biting hard enough to break skin. On seeing him I would yell, "Cut it out." He would turn his face to me, startled, then he would stand and slink away, shooting me a sidelong glance. The chicken, unharmed, would look startled, too, and a bit befuddled. She, or occasionally he, would eventually stand, stretch, and walk sedately away as though nothing had happened.

Time and again I witnessed these scenes, and time and again I yelled at him to stop. I don't consider myself stupid, and I'm not always such a slow learner. It dawned on me that Amaru might be trying to teach me something.

I had not yet repeated the experience where I killed the willing duck, and although some animals had seemed to approach their deaths with nearly that level of grace, quite often they scrapped with me for their lives. I remember a big white muscovy who'd been especially rough with females and some of the other males who gave me a sound thrubbing with his wings as I carried him to the block. I have three circular scars where a rooster dug his spurs a half-inch into my forearm as I tried to kill one of his sons.

Was it possible that the dog was attempting to show me which animals were okay to kill? Or maybe it had nothing to do with me. Perhaps the animals were frightened into passivity by the gaping maw of a creature twenty times their size. This might be possible, but I still thought of the willing duck, and of others almost like him. I have read tales, many of them contemporary, of elk or deer giving themselves willingly to feed traditional indigenous peoples. Is it possible that Amaru was attuned to something I only picked up rarely?

The coyotes returned about this time, and took a chicken. It was the first they had taken for more than a year, and I must admit that they had kept their end of the bargain better than I had, with my dislike of killing. The day before, I had been writing, and heard a squawk. I looked outside, and saw Amaru chasing a young red rooster. Forgetting any possibility of learning from him, I yelled for him to stop, then continued work. The next day I was again writing, and again heard a squawk. I looked outside to see a coyote trotting away. A quick check of the chickens revealed that the coyote had taken the same rooster Amaru chased the day before.

At what point do the lenses fall out of your cultural eyeglasses? At what point do mechanistic explanations wear thin? I had twenty-five birds at the time, which means even if we throw away the coincidence of coyotes appearing on that day, we still have only a one-in-twenty-five chance they would take the same bird Amaru had chosen. Four percent. The bird had not strayed particularly far from the house—the coyote came right up outside my window. Nor was he weak. He was young, firm, and healthy.

Pushing this further, let's see what we can make of this: mornings when I wake up from a dream about chickens, I know that one has died or disappeared. Am I seeing a pattern where there isn't one? It could be a coincidence. It could also be that there is a mechanistic explanation. I wondered if I might have heard their struggles—if they indeed struggled—in my sleep, and incorporated that knowledge into my dreams. But it has happened, too, that I have dreamt of chickens, then found a dead chick—as happens now and then—in the duck pool, which is far from my bedroom window. Does this mean that I heard the thrashing of chicks no larger than a plum? Once I dreamt of chickens when I was five hundred miles from home. The next day I called my mother, who was taking care of the animals for me, and she said that a chick was missing, and that another was dead. What is the mechanistic explanation for this? There isn't one. Oh, no, here we go again! Crazy Derrick insisting that there are other modes of communication to which we don't pay close attention. It seems possible that Amaru *does* hear something, and so do the coyotes. Whatever they are hearing tells them it is acceptable, even proper, to kill this particular bird and not another. I hear the same language when I dream.

I asked Jeannette once where dreams come from and she said, "Oh, everyone knows the animals give them to us." I don't know if I would agree with her, but I do know that her explanation makes more sense than that given by a physicist friend of mine, who states emphatically that they are the meaningless firings of random neurons.

Amaru finally quit chewing on chickens. The last two times he did it, he left them on the front porch, alive, unbruised, although a little worse for wear. Each time I carried them straight to the chopping block and killed them. I do not know why he quit after this. He may have given up trying to teach me how to listen, or he may have decided I now understood enough to learn on my own. It is also possible that he simply outgrew his puppyish enthusiasm for killing chickens.

Cranes

"God does not send us despair in
order to kill us; he sends it in order
to awaken us to new life."
Hermann Hesse

THE BEST THING THAT happened during my years at the Colorado School of Mines is that I began to fall apart. My high school tears over the death of a puppy didn't mean I was back in touch with my emotions. Emotions are never so simple, rolling like waves, only to recede and return, recede and return, until eventually they can no longer be denied. The walls I had meticulously constructed during childhood began to crack during college and the years after, finally collapsing and taking me down with them.

One part of this transition involved high jumping. I had always, since I was a child, loved that sport more than all others. In fourth grade I made myself a pit and standards out of inner tubes, an old mattress, packing blankets, two-by-fours, nails, and a bamboo pole that I had begged from a florist. I quit jumping when the mattress rotted, but jumped again in ninth grade, before dropping the sport until college.

In my sophomore year of college, I took a handball class, because it happened to fit my schedule. There were too many people for the number of courts, so each day the teacher, who was also the track coach, made the others run laps. It didn't take me long to gravitate to the high jump pit. The coach caught me. I thought he would yell at me for not following his instructions, but he asked me to go out for the team. This scared the hell out of me, and I said no. During the next class period I was again assigned to run, and so again I jumped. Again he asked, and again I said no. We repeated this little dance of wooing and retreating until finally I had the confidence to say yes.

Confidence is central to high jumping. If you believe you'll make it, you probably—unless the jump is very easy—won't. You must *know* you'll make it, enough that all consciousness of self vanishes.

After I'd been jumping a couple of years, I noticed a seeming contradiction in my coach's behavior. He routinely yelled at distance runners, and I'd seen him as a football coach slam his clipboard to the ground, but with me he was nothing but gentle, never once raising his voice. I asked why; not that I wanted the other, but simply because I was curious.

"Everyone knows that if you yell at a high jumper he'll just start crying, and then he can't do anything."

He was right. Had he yelled at me, I would have become self-conscious.

The blurring of boundaries between self and other in high jumping probably provides a key to my early love for the sport, a bridge between the walls I erected to protect me from emotions raised by my father's abuse and the dismantling of those walls years later. In both cases—abuse and high jumping—those boundaries disappeared. As a child, they disappeared because I was of necessity hyperaware, always alert to sounds, sudden movements, the slightest change in musculature or vibes that might indicate the possibility of an attack, that might give me an additional half-second to prepare for my father's violence by psychically absenting myself. Instead of remaining present to my own experience, I was present to my anticipation of his experience. My own self—whatever *that* means—was silent and submerged.

When I jumped, those boundaries between self and other once again became obscure. This time, though, the blurring was accomplished not by hiding the self, but expanding it. On the best jumps, those where I approached that ragged edge of control where instinct and euphoria set me free from time and consciousness, the self grew and dissolved until there was no meaningful separation between me and the rest of the world. The bar and the standards, the pit, the slight breeze in the late April afternoon, the sun, the grass, me, we all worked together.

Because all sports are artificially separated from life, and because high jumping is especially circumscribed—you jump, you sit for half an hour, then you jump again—it became safe for me to feel my emotions in that area. Moreso even than feeling them, I allowed them to overwhelm me, giving up control until I no longer *felt* the exuberance, joy, anger, but instead became them.

I was an excellent jumper, made for the sport both physically and emotionally, but I took to throwing tantrums when I missed important jumps. I'd curse and hurl my sweats, or sometimes pull my shoe partway off and kick it as far as I could—thirty yards was my best. Each time I did this, my coach pulled me aside and put his arm around my shoulder. He'd softly say, "Real athletes don't need to do that." What he didn't know, and what I couldn't articulate, was that I was secretly overjoyed to be showing any emotion at all, no matter how unsportsmanlike it seemed to him.

Maybe I was just growing up. Whatever the case may be, it seemed that the experience of unimpeded emotion when I jumped made it harder for me to ignore my feelings elsewhere.

Just as the return of warmth makes frostbitten fingers feel like they're on fire, this period of gradual return was in many ways the most difficult of my life, more difficult even than childhood. I was beginning to feel things again. My first new look at the unhappiness I saw blissfully accepted by those around me was shocking. I became at first deeply confused, and then just as deeply convinced that awareness, and feeling, led inevitably to decreased happiness. Scientist that I was, I came up with the following: *Happiness equals one over the quantity one plus Awareness.* (Yeah, I know, I was a geek.) Trying this equation on my fellow students, I received nothing but confirmation: *Thank God I'm a happy idiot; You think too much; Who cares?* and the ubiquitous *Of course I hate it here, but when I get out I'm gonna get a red Porsche.*

A friend asked, "If increased awareness means less happiness, why bother?" No answer.

Three or four nights later I had a dream. I was driving. To my right I saw baby cranes—blue-green, all legs, beak, and wings—standing in a field. They took off and crashed, took off and crashed. I stopped the car and got out. "That looks like it hurts. Why do you do it?"

One of the cranes looked me square in the eye. "We may not fly very well yet, but at least we aren't walking."

I awoke, happy. From that moment, there has been no turning back.

This past weekend I taught at a nature-writing workshop. As part of a book signing, I read the first twenty pages of this manuscript. Because I had never before shared them publicly, I was excited and more than a little nervous. Afterward, someone said, "I just really wish a healing energy for you."

I appreciated her words, and told her so, but was also in some vague way annoyed. I knew that if one week from now, or ten, or a hundred, her impulse were still to feel sorrow for me, and to primarily wish me healing, then either I did not do my job as a writer, or she was a bad listener. Immediately after she left, I wished I had pointed to the sky and repeated to her the Buddhist saying "Don't look at my finger, look at the moon."

My family is a microcosm of the culture. What is writ large in the destruction of the biosphere was writ small in the destruction of our household. This is one way the destructiveness propagates itself—the sins of the fathers (and mothers) visiting themselves unto the children for seven generations, or seven times seven generations. The death of my childhood may have been dramatic, but in a nation in which 565,000 children are killed or injured by their parents or guardians each year, my childhood does not qualify as remarkably abnormal. Another way to say this is that within any culture that destroys the salmon, that commits genocide, that demands wage slavery, most of the individuals—myself included—are probably to a greater or lesser degree insane.

I wish that my childhood would have been different. I do not, however, regret what happened. This does not mean that I would gladly go through it again. But mythologies of all times and all places tell us that those who enter the abyss and survive can bring back important lessons. I have no need to merely imagine the unimaginable. And I will no longer forget. I have learned that whether I choose to feel or not, pain exists, and whether we choose to acknowledge them or not, atrocities continue. I have grown to understand that in the shadow of the unspeakable I can and must speak and act against our culture's tangled web of destructiveness, and stop the destruction at its roots.

The Safety of Metaphor

"The most striking difference between ancient and modern sophists
is that the ancients were satisfied
with a passing victory of argument
at the expense of truth, whereas
the moderns want a more lasting
victory at the expense of reality."
Hannah Arendt

ON PLANES AND BUSES, in classrooms, stores, libraries, I began to ask people if they thought it was possible to communicate with nonhumans. They said *yes,* and *yes,* and they said *My friends think I'm crazy, but . . .* and they said, *It changed my life, let me tell you about it. . . .* The daughter of a rancher said her parents gave stillborn calves to coyotes in exchange for the coyotes leaving the rest of their herd alone. A man who worked on the Alaska pipeline said he'd always carried a rifle in the backcountry, and had killed many bears, until one day a native friend said, "Mike, you don't need to shoot them. Apologize to them for being in their home, and walk away." The next time he saw a bear he raised his rifle, then caught himself and lowered it. He said, "I'm sorry," and raised his hand in greeting. Now, I don't know if this account was a cousin of the old fish story, but he said that the bear stopped, squinted, raised one paw in response, then left. Regardless, he never shot another bear. A third-generation pig farmer said that when he picks up piglets to cuddle, they relax silently into his arms; when he picks them up to castrate them, they scream—first to last— even before he reaches for them. Story after story, they pile up, dozens upon dozens of conversations, with or without words, conversations with pets, bears, coyotes, rivers, trees, owls, hawks, eagles, mice.

A friend said, "That's all very nice, but do you have any scientific verification?"

I have plenty of empirical data, but that just means I'm relying on direct experience, not abstract theory. Strictly speaking, scientific verification is impossible, because science is by definition the study of objects, and a conversation is an interaction between two or more subjects. In science, you repeat an experiment in a controlled environment, and you eliminate variable after variable until any moderately careful person can make the same thing appear. But conversations only happen once. So try this: "How are you?"

I'm fine.
Now say it again: "How are you?"
I'm tired.
"How are you?"
"None of your business.
Now again: "How are you?"
The book is green.

Do you get it? Because I'm a willful subject, my answer could be anything.

While it's reasonable to expect repeatability from a machine—I'm writing this while flying in another airplane, and I hope that when the pilot manipulates the plane's controls, the rudder and flaps respond predictably—no sensible person would demand strict repeatability in everyday life. I would at least hope not, for the sake of that person's companions. Similarly, it is scientifically impossible to rigorously verify the subjective existence of anyone other than the experimenter him- or herself: one of the beauties of the Cartesian notion that subjective existence is held only by an elect few is that it's impossible to disprove; just ask my high school friend Jon, who was unable to prove that he existed even when he socked me one.

So, scientific verification of interspecies communication is out, although results of experiments can of course be factored in, weighted the same as other anecdotal evidence, experiments being merely one form of anecdote, with specific underlying and formative assumptions. If you put me in a cage in a lab, stick needles in me or cut off my body parts one-by-one, then "sacrifice" me when you're through, the conversations we have in the meantime will perforce be different than if we meet in other circumstances.

I also know that the nature of physical reality is not determined by popular vote. Many people sharing the same delusion does not make the delusion true, whether we're talking about interspecies communication, modern science, Christianity, or capitalism. Think about how many people voted for Ronald Reagan, Bill Clinton, or Augusto Pinochet, for that matter. Look how many people—including some presumably intelligent ones—spend their lives producing nuclear weapons. Look how many people think money is wealth, and how many believe that land can be bought and sold. It doesn't matter if it isn't true. Remember, this is a game of make-believe. It's a pretty good game, very well constructed; in fact it's so good we've forgotten that it *is* just a game.

All this goes to say that while the stories I've heard about interspecies communication are interesting and believable, science will never give them a stamp of approval. This says a lot more about the presumptions and limitations of science than it does about reality.

Nonetheless, I can and must, like a filter-feeding barnacle, continue to absorb or reject whatever material flows my way. And I can use this material to attempt to deconstruct, or at least review, the belief structures that have been handed down to me by my culture.

When a magazine offered me the opportunity to interview Jim Nollman, I immediately agreed. Nollman has spent the better part of his adult life playing music with whales and dolphins, and studying the different ways they interact with each other and with us. He has written three books that play with the subject of interspecies communication, and has founded a nonprofit organization dedicated to it.

I must admit I wasn't sure that Nollman would be able to contribute much to my overall sense of mental well-being (remember, we're still talking about *talking* with animals). The first major public performance of his work was a Thanksgiving Day radio broadcast of the folk song "Froggy Went A Courtin'," recorded live at a factory farm, with thousands of turkeys gobbling simultaneously at each refrain. The *Washington Post* called him "a harmless crank." Nollman claims the turning point of his life came while performing a duet with a turkey in southern Mexico. I was beginning to feel better already. Perhaps instead of gaining understanding I would find the two of us sharing the same asylum. I was looking forward to my interviews with Napoleon Bonaparte, Jesus Christ, and Marie Antoinette.

Since Nollman lives on an island in Puget Sound, I flew to Seattle to work with my friend George first. When George was driving me to the ferry, we talked about interspecies communication, and he told me about a woman who has extended conversations with wild ravens in their own tongue.

"I've seen it for myself," he said. "It's really unnerving to be talking to her in English, and all of a sudden have her step aside and caw to a raven. It was weird. The bird cocked its head, sat there, then cawed back at her. She changed her inflection. Then the bird, then her."

"What'd they talk about?"

"I don't know. I never asked."

We also talked about intraspecies communication. He said, "These days I can't talk to environmentalists anymore than I can talk to industrialists. They're both playing the same game. Industrialists lie by diminishing the severity of the situation, pretending against all evidence that there isn't a problem. 'We can keep cutting down the forests,' they insist, 'I don't see any damage.' Meanwhile, environmentalists also diminish the severity by pretending the problem can be solved. 'If we just revoke Boise Cascade's charter, or Plum Creek's, we can save the old growth. If we can just reform the Forest Service, if we can just take back Weyerhaeuser's illegally gained lands, the old growth can be saved.' Well, the old growth is *gone*. We've killed it coast to coast. To pretend otherwise is ridiculous."

I nodded, and we drove in silence. The silence lengthened. I didn't know what George was thinking about. I often don't. I looked outside, to the grass off the interstate's shoulder, then back to George. I told him that while I had once seen a newspaper report that humans are causing the greatest mass extinction in the history of the planet, it had been relegated to two-column-inches on page twenty-four of the B-section.

"We should be happy the paper mentioned biodiversity at all," George chimed. "I mean, a newspaper is a corporation, and it's foolish to expect corporations to do what's best. No one expects it from Union Carbide or Westinghouse. Isn't it a bit naive to expect the corporation known as *The New York Times* to be different? 'All the News That's Fit to Print'? The function of a corporation is to make money, whether it manufactures bulk industrial chemicals (most of them toxic), or bulk industrial opinions (most of them just as toxic). And ethics just don't fit."

He had a point. Newspapers lying to serve their own interests go back as far as newspapers themselves. The turn-of-the-century historian Henry Adams put it as clearly as possible: "The press is the hired agent of a monied system, and set up for no other purpose than to tell lies where the interests are involved."

Newspapers manifest the culture as a whole. Just as it is true that any father who would crush a child's will would not be able to speak of it honestly, so, too, a culture that is snuffing out life on the planet would necessarily lie and dissemble to protect itself from the truth. Environmentalists lie, industrialists lie, newspapers lie. Parents lie, children lie. We all lie, and we are all afraid. Afraid to not know what is going on, and even more afraid of finding out. The opposite is true as well. Honest discourse is the first and most important step in stopping destruction.

George and I had lunch, and he dropped me off at the ferry before continuing northward to give a talk in Bellingham. "It's for a Christian television show," he said, "and that's a hopeful sign. Ten years ago you had to put on an owl suit to get mainstream media to pay attention. Now, all I had to do was write a book, and I'm having rational discourse with Christians."

The ferry ride to Friday Harbor was chilly, and a cold headwind brought the blood to my cheeks. As we weaved between islands, I stood to watch the waves roll beneath the ferry, went inside to warm up for a while, then returned to stand behind the railing above the ship's square bow.

Jim was waiting for me near the dock, and he drove me in his old yellow pickup to the home he shares with his wife and their two daughters. He showed me his garden, a beautiful patchwork of herbs, fruit trees, berries, and vegetables, set off from the pathways that weaved through them—like the Sound through the islands—by small boulders he'd moved for borders. He took me to a one-room cabin across the garden from his house.

We talked about his garden, how every day he walks the paths for an hour or so, stands in front of the bushes and talks to them. He observed that whenever his family leaves, the plants look listless on their return, even if they've been well taken care of.

"The plants know when we're here," he said, "or when we're

not here. How do you verify something like that? It's pointless to even try."

He continued, "I know this about my garden in the same way I know my hat is made out of cloth. To be able to surrender to the knowledge that the garden and I are connected nurtures my soul. I wish more people could know this connection more often, and I believe people did know it before we became so dependent on machines and jobs and time."

Away from the Sound, the afternoon grew warm, and in the sunny cabin, with its wide windows and the line between sun and shadow sliding slowly across the floor, it became warmer still. Jim said, "People laugh up their sleeves at anything that defies the industrial explanation of our lives, anything that is spiritual. But these experiences are grace. Interacting with nonhumans doesn't have anything to do with gathering information; it has to do with being blessed. And wanting to be blessed. It has to do with that intersection of communication and communion."

I nodded in agreement, and then changed the subject. "Do you ever wonder if you're projecting?"

"There was a time, when I was thirty-five or forty. I was working intensely with orcas, alongside scientists, and I worried about that all the time. But I don't really care anymore. I'm content to set up situations where 'those things,' whatever they are, are likely to happen. The meetings themselves are so remarkable—whether they involve 'interspecies communication' or not—they justify themselves."

The tape recorder hummed and ticked on the table between us. Jim continued, "I couldn't do what I do if I had to count on results, because too often I don't have any, in terms of what our culture or magazines or editors would believe. In the late 80s I was doing a film every summer, and we'd have these incredible interactions with whales, but the filmmakers never got them. It's like they never happened. Finally I had to walk away."

I looked at him, puzzled, and he continued, "I had to find a new reason for my work, for my art, or I would have had to stop doing communication with nonhumans. Then I realized that art doesn't really need to have a reason to exist. It's like what John Cage said, 'Art is whatever you can get away with.'"

I liked so much of what he'd said earlier, but I found myself on a slippery slope of damp squib. I tried to pin him down. I had to know if he thought these experiences were as real as the hat on his head.

"Being an artist, everything is just metaphors." He paused. "It's safe. If I came out and said these things as pure energy, I'd get in trouble. That doesn't happen if you talk about them as metaphors."

"But are they true?"

"It doesn't matter. It just matters if they're interesting. If you're going to last, you can't take any of it very seriously, yourself, the universe, anything."

"Why not?"

"You won't have a voice. I wouldn't be able to publish. I wouldn't be able to speak. This summer I get to work with some world-famous marine biologists; we'll be doing stuff with hump-back whales. Ten years ago these guys wouldn't have touched me with a ten-foot pole, and now they'll work with me straight on. And you know why? Because I've never made any sweeping statements. I've never said that whales are intelligent. I've never taken a stance."

I guess, I thought, *I'll have Marie Antoinette all to myself: this guy isn't going anywhere* I *want to go.*

"Everything we're talking about here," he continued, "is very threatening, to the culture, and to people's basic ideas about how the universe works. The trick is to talk about it without shutting people down. How do you breach their defenses? What is your schtick to be able to get them to listen, and to make it so you can continue? I'm trying to change the culture, trying to change the way people perceive their place in the world, but I'm also trying to make a living. How do you do that? It would be very easy for me to get lumped into a box, as somebody who just plays music with whales. And I don't want to get lumped there."

I understood where he was coming from, but the same phrase kept popping into my head: *We're screwed.*

I stepped away from the conversational fire, and asked, knowing well the answer, why the notion of communicating with coyotes, whales, plants, is threatening to the culture.

"If the Earth is dead, it feels no pain. If the Earth weren't considered dead, we couldn't build the Empire State Building, because we couldn't bring ourselves to hurt the planet so much just to make a big building. The entire culture is based on the belief that the earth is inanimate."

I stepped even further away, and, because the seminal experience of his life *had* come in a barnyard in Mexico with a turkey, asked what has caused him to continue to listen to the natural world, at least metaphorically.

"We need to distinguish between listening and hearing. I believe I listen better than many people, but I still don't hear very well. I have a lot of friends around the world who are able to actually *hear* the natural world. Still, whether or not we hear, listening is important. Until we start to listen—and, I hope eventually hear—the natural world for ourselves, nonhumans will be regarded as objects. Just the act of trying to listen can change a lot of our perceptions about nature, and that can change the way we live."

We talked through the afternoon, and eventually I turned off the recorder. After dinner, and after going with him and his wife to a reading in town, I returned to spend the night in the cabin. There, I fell asleep listening to the rustling of the stalks in his garden. About three, a cock began to crow. I shut the window and covered my head with a pillow to stifle the noise, then fell back asleep.

The next day, riding the ferry back, I stood on the bow and watched the houses float by on islands like so many pieces of beached wood. I wondered how much this trip had really helped. I had no need to be convinced of the metaphorical efficacy of listening to the natural world. The mess of houses, seaplanes, and boats—never mind the floating styrofoam and tiny oil slicks—were sufficient evidence that we're not listening. But this had more to do with listening to our own detritus.

None of this is to diminish the importance of listening as metaphor. Nor is it to diminish the importance of listening to our trash, which clearly is just as crucial to our survival. If we were paying any attention, would we be making plutonium, jet skis, mink coats, protein drinks, breast implants, satellite surveillance systems?

The Safety of Metaphor

The problem with viewing this metaphorically is that metaphors don't take down dams. Metaphors are not inescapable. "That's a nice metaphor," says the vivisectionist, the politician, the factory farm owner, the scientist, "but you're wrong."

"It's a nice story," say the rest of us, "but now it's time to get back to work."

I went inside the ferry and sat down. I was no longer that interested in the question of my own sanity. Compared to what we've done, and what we continue to do, even to this little corner of the planet, the whole notion of making a deal with coyotes no longer seemed so crazy. Questioning my own sanity amid all the unspoken insanity of our culture seemed like the craziest idea I'd *ever* heard.

Of course I also realized I was making an unfair leap of logic: the fact that some people make satellite surveillance systems doesn't mean coyotes understand a damn thing. They might, but there's no connection.

I went back outside, and found the fins of orcas gliding above the Sound's smallish waves. At first only a few people saw the black triangles, but more and more noticed, until virtually everyone was leaning against the ferry's railings, gasping in unison as we saw the black and white and black of their bodies, all of us straining to see this bit of nature gliding through the pollution of this well-traveled stretch of water.

Most everyone I know speaks openly about the clear and present collapse of industrial civilization in one-on-one conversations. This is true not only for my friends, who are mainly writers, activists of one sort or another, or revolutionaries, but also for people I encounter on buses or planes, in airports, and so on. It's also true that almost without exception the people I know most intimately speak of the certainty that unless it is stopped, our culture will destroy every living being on the planet. Once again, they say this only in private.

I once stood behind a woman and her little boy in line to board an airplane. He looked up at her. "What if the plane crashes?"

"Shhh," she said. "we don't *talk* about that."

There is a sense in which Nollman was right. The price of

admission to public discourse is an optimistic denial pushed to absurd lengths. I live less than three miles from the Spokane River, which begins about forty miles east of here as it flows out of Lake Coeur d'Alene. Lake Coeur d'Alene, one of the most beautiful lakes in the world, is also one of the most polluted with heavy metals. There are days when more than a million pounds of lead drains into the lake from mine tailings on the South Fork of the Coeur d'Alene River. Hundreds of migrating tundra swans die here each year from lead poisoning as they feed in contaminated wetlands. Some of the highest blood-lead levels ever recorded in human beings were from children in this area. Yet just last summer the *Spokesman-Review*, the paper of record for the region, wrote that concern over this pollution is unnecessary because, in their words, "there are no human bodies lining the Spokane River."

The resemblance between this behavior—a steadfast refusal to acknowledge physical reality—and my own denial as a child is frightening. I see myself at the kitchen table, bringing the spoon to my mouth with a mechanical precision that would have made Descartes proud. I see my father by my bed, a dark figure on a background nearly as dark, and in that one so-brief instant of awful recognition, I feel my consciousness slip away—*This cannot happen. This cannot happen to me*—quickly, like running footfalls down a distant corridor, or like the last bit of water sucking down an open pipe. As my consciousness disappears, so, too—poof—does my father. Poof, no more father, no more rape. Poof, no more clearcuts, no more lead, no more crash. Suddenly for all our claims to rationality, we are, each and every one of us, as much out of our minds as we are out of our bodies. Poof.

Just today a friend told me she used to date a man who hunted. She hated the fact that he killed.

"Do you eat meat?" I asked.

"Yes," she replied, "but I don't have to see them die." A moment's pause, and she added, "I can't believe I just said that." Another pause, and we both laughed.

Poof.

A few weeks ago I participated in a conference of about twenty-five environmentalists and small farmers. For three days we attempted to name values we hold in common and in opposition to each other. The purpose was to begin a dialogue between these two beleaguered groups, which may lead to better working relationships as we both try to stop the destruction of family farms and farming communities by transnational agribusiness corporations.

One of our exercises was to pretend that the year was 2018, and that somehow our culture had undergone a revolution in values such that we were now living sustainably. We wrote what we believed sustainable communities and farms would look and feel and smell like, what technologies would be used, and so on.

I don't know whether it broke my heart more to perform the exercise or for the group to share the results. This was due in part to the fact that no mention was made, either in the setup of the exercise or in the answers, of the nearly insuperable physical difficulties we face—for example, the fact that those in power control guns, tanks, airplanes, biological and nuclear weapons, as well as all major media outlets, and have shown themselves time and again more than eager to use these various tools to destroy any perceived threat. Nor did anyone mention the probably unconscious and certainly irrational imperative that drives all of the destruction. My discomfort arose primarily because even when we spoke of technology, no one mentioned the crash. We spoke much of "appropriate" or "friendly" technologies, but we did not define either one, nor did we mention how or why people would implement these technologies. Finally, I could hold back no longer.

"Everyone here knows industrial civilization isn't sustainable. We all know that any technology that relies on the use of nonrenewables is by definition not sustainable. We also know that by definition, any technology or activity that damages any other community—human or nonhuman—isn't sustainable. Finally, everyone here knows that there's no way within the next twenty years we'll make a transition to a technologically sustainable culture. The best we can hope for is that we begin to throttle down our overblown technology, to bring ourselves to a soft landing instead of a full crash."

Everyone seemed to agree, and it came clear to me that while these thoughts had probably occurred to nearly everyone in the room, no one else had been willing to speak until someone broke the ice. Poof.

When dams were erected on the Columbia, salmon battered themselves against the concrete, trying to return home. I expect no less from us. We too must hurl ourselves against and through the literal and metaphorical concrete that contains and constrains us, that keeps us from talking about what is most important to us, that keeps us from living the way our bones know we can, that bars us from our home. It only takes one person to bring down a dam.

There are times the lies get to me, times I weary of battering myself against the obstacles of denial, hatred, fear-induced stupidity, and greed, times I want to curl up and fall into the problem, let it sweep me away as it so obviously sweeps away so many others. I remember a spring day a few years ago, a spring day much like this one, only a little more sun, and warmer. I sat on this same couch and looked out this same window at the same ponderosa pine.

I was frightened, and lonely. Frightened of a future that looks dark, and darker with each passing species, and lonely because for every person actively trying to shut down the timber industry, stop abuse, or otherwise bring about a sustainable and sane way of living, there are thousands who are helping along this not-so-slow train to oblivion. I began to cry.

The tears stopped soon enough. I realized we are not so outnumbered. We are not outnumbered at all. I looked closely, and saw one blade of wild grass, and another. I saw the sun reflecting bright off the needles of pine trees, and I heard the hum of flies. I saw ants walking single file through the dust, and a spider crawling toward the corner of the ceiling. I knew in that moment, as I've known ever since, that it is no longer possible to be lonely, that every creature on earth is pulling in the direction of life— every grasshopper, every struggling salmon, every unhatched chick, every cell of every blue whale—and it is only our own fear that sets us apart. All humans, too, are struggling to be sane, struggling to live in harmony with our surroundings, but it's really hard to let go. And so we lie, destroy, rape, murder, experiment, and extirpate, all to control this wildly uncontrollable symphony, and failing that, to destroy it.

Claims to Virtue

"Exploitation must not be seen as such.
It must be seen as benevolence. Perse-
cution preferably should not need to be
invalidated as the figment of a paranoid
imagination; it should be experienced as
kindness. . . . In order to sustain our
amazing images of ourselves as God's
gift to the vast majority of the starving
human species, we have to interiorize
our violence upon ourselves and our
children, and to employ the rhetoric of
morality to describe this process."
R.D. Laing

FOR YEARS I'VE BEEN haunted by a fantasy involving someone like Jesus. This person—woman or man, it doesn't matter—comes into a community and talks about love. She, or he, tells people they should treat each other with respect, and that this respect must extend to humans and nonhumans alike. A crowd gathers as this person says they should do unto others as they'd have others do unto them, and they begin to murmur quietly as they hear that they should share with each other everything they own. The discomfort of especially the crowd's children grows more noticeable as this stranger tells them they should love each other, love the land. (He or she says nothing about loving the enemy.) The children hide giggles behind their hands, and now even the adults bite the insides of their cheeks. Finally, after much hesitation, one of the community members responds, "Friend, we respect what you have to say, and thank you for telling us, but can't you tell us something we don't already know?" The stranger looks closely, and seeing the obvious well-being of the people, realizes that her (or his) words are redundant. The stranger merges into the community, and all continue with the dailiness of their lives.

The reality of our Judeo-Christian culture is of course far different. A primary purpose of Judeo-Christianity has not been to move us toward a community where the teachings of someone like Jesus—simple and necessary suggestions for how to get along with each other—are made manifest in all aspects of life, but instead to provide a theological framework for a system of exploitation. Easy as this is to say, not many people say it (at least in public). It is more convenient for exploiter and exploited alike to pretend their parasitic relationship is Natural, ordained by God. It is easier to believe in a logic that leads directly from original sin to totalitarianism—*Because human beings are selfish, evil creatures, they must be controlled; therefore might, guided by an all-seeing God as interpreted by an elite priesthood, makes right—*

than it is to take responsibility for one's own actions, and to fight for egalitarianism. It is easier to listen to the voice of God than it is to listen to the voice of one's conscience, suffering, and outrage. And it is easier to follow the well-worn yet faulty logic leading once again from original sin this time to apocalypse— *Because human beings are evil, and have sinned, they must die. All beings on earth die. Therefore, all beings on Earth must be evil, and must have sinned. Death is the flower of sin. To avoid death requires the annihilation of evil: therefore, all things on Earth must be annihilated*—far easier than it is to accept one's death as natural. It is all so easy, so sanctimonious, to shift responsibility for your own choices and their consequences onto the divine plan of some invisible God.

If you feel like raping a woman, don't just do it; have your God decree that under some circumstances such behavior is not only acceptable, but righteous, your God-given right: "And seest among the captives a beautiful woman, and hast a desire unto her . . . then thou shalt bring her home to thine house. . . . If thou have no delight in her, then thou shalt let her go wither she will; but thou shall not sell her for money, thou shalt not make merchandise of her, because thou hast humbled her."

Rape alone is problematic as a method of social domination, in that it only temporarily provides the rapist control; to extend this over time, to permanently "make merchandise of her," you must have your God issue a series of decrees hemming women in, binding them to you as your property. Have your God say (while hoping no one notices your own lips moving) that because Eve listened to the serpent—remember, my father never beat anyone who didn't have it coming—every woman "shall welcome [her] husband's affections, and he shall be [her] master." Have your God say any woman who has sexual intercourse freely will be put to death (her body not being her own). Any man, too, who has sex with another man's wife shall die, because he has diddled with another man's property, although no punishment shall be meted out on the man who has intercourse with an unmarried woman (but we'll put her to death for good measure). Small wonder that one of the daily Orthodox prayers reads: "I thank thee, O Lord, that thou has not created me a woman."

The deal is off with the coyotes. They're back, they're eating chickens, and they'd better watch out. If it's war they want, well, it's war they'll get.

It lasted two years, and they kept their end of the bargain far better than I kept mine. I probably only killed six or seven birds the whole time. But I don't care, damn it. They're my birds, to kill or not, and the coyotes are eating them. I talked to a friend, the guy who used to kill bears in Alaska.

"New coyotes, new deal."

The next day I awoke early from a dream, walked to the window to look out on a cold February dawn. I saw a coyote trotting away, empty-handed, as it were, and I opened the window. I shouted, as I had two years before, "Please don't eat the chickens, and I'll give you the head, feet, and guts when I kill them."

It didn't work. The coyotes came back with a vengeance. Week after week. A chicken. A duck. I'd dream of chickens, and another bird would be gone.

I pictured this new batch of coyotes, tough young dogs wrecking the neighborhood. If they were people, they'd lean against buildings, smoke cigarettes, and make rude comments to passersby. Or maybe these were the pups of the ones I'd made the deal with, ungrateful wretches no longer satisfied with crumbs from my table but determined—damn them—to take everything I owned. Worse yet, these might be the original coyotes, sick of my promises—*Next weekend. I'll kill one and give you the guts. I swear. I mean it.* Maybe they just came to take what they thought was their due.

Sometimes I'd see them, and wish I was holding a gun. I would've shot them where they stood. Or at least that's what I told myself; had the gun been in my hand instead of safely stowed in the closet, I don't know if I would have followed through.

Over the years I've known many people with no such hesitation about coyotes; ranchers, for example—those who shoot first, and rarely ask questions later. I didn't want that; I just wanted them to stop taking chickens.

Finally I called a friend and asked her to help me put up a fence. It took us the better part of two weeks to get around to it, in which time the coyotes took a couple more chickens. Because I didn't want to confine the birds, the completed fence ran around only half my property, cutting off easy access from the woods to the east and forcing the coyotes to cover a long stretch of open ground if they wanted a clean shot at a meal. I figured, rightly enough, that the dogs could (and would be happy to) patrol the open area. The only birds who got it after that were the ones who squeezed through the fence to forage in the woods. I figured they were asking for it.

The return of the coyotes caused me to reevaluate all I had experienced. I wondered again if I had been projecting, if other interpretations better described the two-year respite from their raids. That didn't seem likely. It seemed more to the point to re-evaluate what defines a conversation. I'm aware that at least some of the conversations so far—the original one with the coyotes, many of the conversations with the dogs, and the conversations of death with birds—have been one-sided, by which I mean I have simply made requests to which they have acceded: the coyotes quit eating chickens, the dogs quit eating eggs, and the birds gave me their lives and flesh. What have I given in return? Knowing the one-sidedness of these earlier interactions, can I even say that the ending of the "deal" with the coyotes was the end of the conversation? That would certainly imply a perverse definition of *conversation*, the word being reduced to *do as I say*. Where does mutuality fit in, the simple pleasures of neighborliness?

I remembered a brief conversation I'd had with Jeannette after the coyotes came for the rooster Amaru had singled out the day before. I asked her if Amaru was trying to tell me which animal to kill. She was silent for a long while, and finally she said, "I think there might be other lessons to learn."

We've all read about the agricultural revolution about ten thousand years ago—when large groups of people in the Near and Middle East shifted permanently from hunter-gatherers to husbandry. Many anthropologists and historians, as well as religious scholars, suggest that this transition was the *felix culpa,* or fall from grace, which led to the life of toil described in Genesis. Everything I've read suggests that members of hunter-gatherer cultures—even those alive today, who've been driven to the least hospitable regions of the planet such as deserts and dense jungles—work far less to support themselves than people living any other lifestyle. They work three to five hours a day. I've also read they feel closer to the rest of the world than we do, that they usually don't see the world as a dangerous place of eternally warring opposites: me against you, man against woman, man against nature, God against all.

Instead hunter-gatherers see the world, and I realize I'm grossly generalizing, as a ribbon of cooperation: you and I cooperate, and that process of cooperation helps define our community; men and women cooperate; humans and nonhumans cooperate to allow the world to continue; the gods cooperate with all.

I used to understand all that in my head. Now I understand it in my body; I've gained a visceral understanding of how this transition caused us to view the world as a competitive place.

Take a quail. I see coveys of them nearly every day. If I were a hunter-gatherer, or merely hungry, I would probably eat some. But I do not own them, and even if I killed one to eat, it would not be mine. The thought of ownership does not occur to me. The quail are simply my neighbors, and I say hello to them just as I do to the deer I see occasionally, or the hawk that often floats above the house, the trees outside the windows, and the magpies that have for years made great mounding nests in the trees' lower branches. In each of these cases, after we say our brief hellos, we continue with our days, just as happens when I nod and smile to the retired doctor (not the neighbor who drew the cartoon of genocidal Colonel Wright, but another one) who lives across the way. If a coyote eats a quail, as I suspect happens often, or one of the marmots who live among the rocks, I am simultaneously sorry for the end of a life and glad for the coyote. It's not personal. In fact it can and will be me some day. That's life.

The chickens are different. They're mine. I raise them from eggs I collect and put into an incubator, or I buy them at Aslin Finch Feed Store for ninety-seven cents each. I rear them in my bathtub until the weather turns warm enough to let them outside. I dig through dumpsters to find food for them. I sell the eggs. I eat the meat. These chickens belong to me—they do not belong either to the coyotes or to themselves. A coyote who kills a hen is costing me six eggs a week at a dollar fifty a dozen, and when she kills a rooster she's taking meat I could have put into a stew.

If I perceive chickens as my private property, it makes sense that I would build a fence around them to prevent coyotes from stealing them. I see now the line of thought and experience that leads ineluctably from this perception of private ownership— the word *private* coming from the latin *privare*, to deprive, because wealthy Romans fenced off gardens to deprive others of their use—to the protection of this perceived ownership at first through fences, then through the creation of a theology and politics to justify my perceptions, and finally through a whole system of police, prisons, and the military to enforce my rights when others are so stupid or blind as to not acknowledge my ownership.

I see also a parallel and complementary line of thought that doesn't merely protect my belongings, but proactively and permanently prevents others from stealing them. Instead of building a fence, why don't I, as I mentioned before, just kill the coyotes? It would be easier, and would eliminate the worry. I'd be in chicken heaven, or at least chicken-owner heaven. Of course coyotes are sneaky, so unless I kill them all I'll eventually be forced to invent better ways to kill them. Others, too, may steal the birds. There are hawks, snakes, skunks, raccoons, and rumor has it, a mother bear and cubs can be found. Now that I think about it, even though my retired-doctor neighbor and his family seem very nice, they do sometimes look enviously at the big black hen. I've got to stop them all. Today I own chickens, tomorrow I eradicate coyotes, and the day after I knock off the retired doctor and his family. And it's not only the chickens. I need gasoline to run my truck—I can't dumpster dig without a truck—and gas has to come from somewhere. I heard that Saddam Hussein wanted to cut off access to United States' oil in the Persian Gulf. The dirty bastard. We've got to stop him, too.

Shit. I don't have money to build a nuclear bomb, and there's no room in my refrigerator for that economy-size canister of anthrax. As for the latter, I'll have to get a bigger refrigerator. I'll have to start saving for the warhead. The tree outside my window is awfully big, and I just realized I own it, too. I wonder how much I could get for it.

It's not unheard of for old trees—big pines, firs, and cedars a thousand years old—to scream audibly when they're cut down. I've heard from loggers that the screams are disturbing at first, but as with anything else, you get used to it.

We've had a long time to get used to the screams. Just as our civilization's expansion is marked by a widening circle of genocide, so too forests and all of their inhabitants precede us. Deserts dog our heels.

The need to deforest started in what used to be the Fertile Crescent of the Middle East, Mesopotamia. The land was fecund, as land so often is before we get our hands on it. Cedar forests stretched so far that no one knew their true size, and sunlight never penetrated far enough to touch the humus that has long since baked, crumbled, and blown away. Forty-seven hundred years ago Gilgamish, ruler of Uruk, a city near the Euphrates River, decided to make a name for himself by building a great city. Armed with "mighty adzes," and more importantly with a justification—the promise of "a name that endures"—that would allow him and his cronies to deafen themselves to "the sad song of the cedars" as they cut them down, Gilgamish entered the forest, briefly reflected on its beauty, vanquished its protector, and took what he needed.

There goes the neighborhood! It's not unlike the times my father found fault with one of us—he was right, end of conversation. So too the transformation of wild nature to usable resource marked the end of our conversation with wild nature. The rest has been a steady journey to an all-too-familiar destination, one devoid of life.

The story of this journey is as monotonous in its own terrible way as the story of our culture's genocidal practices, which is not surprising, considering, as we shall eventually see, that they spring from the same hollow impulses. Soon after Gilgamish was history (i.e., dead), the ruler Gudea of the nearby city of Lagash took up the mantle, and built his own city, cutting trees to build temples, and once again, to build a name. Name after name rulers are recorded, building up like silt in streams from the eroded hillsides they left in their paths. And nations, too, rise with the fall of forests and fall when they are gone. Troy, Greece, Lebanon, Rome, Sicily, the trees were cut for the greater good, for ships, for commerce, for this reason or that. Always a reason, always deforestation. France, Germany, Britain, the United States, a sandy thread of dead and dying forests that leads to South America, Siberia, Southeast Asia, and now back to my own home, where the last of the American forests fall.

It is not possible to commit deforestation, or any other mass atrocity—mass murder, genocide, mass rape, the pervasive abuse of women or children, institutionalized animal abuse, imprisonment, wage slavery, systematic impoverishment, ecocide— without first convincing yourself and others that what you're doing is beneficial. You must have, as Dr. Robert Jay Lifton has put it, a "claim to virtue." You must be convinced—as the Nazis were convinced that the elimination of the Jews would allow the Aryan "race" to thrive; as the founders of Judeo-Christianity were convinced their misogynist laws were handed down not from their own collective unconscious but from the God they could not admit they created; as my father was convinced he was not beating his son but teaching him diligence, respect, or even spelling; as politicians, scientists, and business leaders today are convinced they're not destroying life on earth but "developing natural resources"—that you are performing a service for humankind.

Forests have fallen as surely to these claims to virtue as they have to axes, saws, and fellerbunchers. By looking at the successive claims used to rationalize the deforestation of *this* continent, perhaps we can begin to see not only the transparent stupidity of them but further still to the motives that underlie the destruction.

Early European accounts of this continent's opulence border on the unbelievable. Time and again we read of "goodly woods, full of Deere, Conies, Hares, and Fowle, even in the middest of Summer, in incredible abundance," of islands "as completely covered with birds, which nest there, as a field is covered with grass," of rivers so full of salmon that "at night one is unable to sleep, so great is the noise they make," of lobsters "in such plenty that they are used for bait to catch the Codd fish." Early Europeans describe towering forests of cedars, with an understory of grapes and berries that stained the legs and bellies of their horses. They describe rivers so thick with fish that they "could be taken not only with a net but in baskets let down [and weighted with] a stone." They describe birds in flocks so large they darkened the sky for days at a time and so dense that "a single shot from an old muzzle-loader into a flock of these curlews [Eskimo curlews, made extinct by our culture] brought down 28 birds."

The early Europeans faced much the same problem we face today: their lofty goals required the destruction of these forests and all life in them, but they couldn't do it without at least some justification. The first two claims to virtue were the intertwining goals of Christianizing the natives and making a profit. These embodied a bizarre yet efficient exchange in which, as Captain John Chester succinctly put it, the natives gained "the knowledge of our faith" while the Europeans acquired "such ritches as the country hath." Both the natives and the "ritches"—including the forests of New England—were quickly cut down.

Soon the claim to Christianization was dropped, and the rationalization became "Manifest Destiny," the tenet that the territorial expansion of the United States was not only inevitable but divinely ordained. Thus it was God and not man who ordered the land's original inhabitants be removed, who ordered the destruction of hundreds of human cultures and the killing or dispossession of tens of millions of human beings, who ordered the slaughter of 60 million buffalo and 20 million pronghorn antelope to make life tougher. Thus it was God and not man who ordered that the native forests of the Midwest be felled by the ax.

Manifest Destiny as a claim to virtue soon evolved back into the ideal of making money. An enterprise was deemed as good as it was profitable, while domination and control remained safely unspoken. The forests of the Northwest were described by a corporate spokesperson as "a rich heiress waiting to be appropriated and enjoyed." To be honest, not even this claim was new in any meaningful sense, but a mere recycling of the words of our Judeo-Christian fathers—"And seest among the captives a beautiful woman, and hast a desire unto her . . . then thou shalt bring her home to thine house"—with a substitution of trees for women, whipsaws for penises, and the immutable laws of economics for the immutable laws of God.

That brings us to today. As the effects of industrial forestry on this continent become increasingly clear—fisheries vanish, biodiversity goes monotone, communities fall apart, and rich biomes become tree farms—corporate profitability loses its effectiveness as a claim to virtue. Another claim—jobs—has arisen, but this has no ring of truth in an era of automation, downsizing, and the Asian lumber mill. The search for a different justification begins anew.

Recognizing that the forests of this country are in a state of ecological collapse, the timber industry and the politicians and the governmental agencies that serve it have begun to claim the way to improve the health of these massively overcut forests is, unsurprisingly enough, to cut them down. The government has provided, in the words of one of the industry's Senators, "exemptions from environmental laws for logging needed to improve forest health." The Forest Service has disallowed citizens from purchasing federal timber sales to leave the trees standing, because "then the trees won't get cut down." A clearcut is then rationalized by declaring that "while insect and disease populations are currently at endemic levels, there is a potential for spruce bark beetle populations to reach epidemic proportions." In other words, we must cut these admittedly healthy trees because they might get sick someday. The timber transnational corporation Boise Cascade has run advertisements likening clearcuts to smallpox vaccinations.

It's all insane. It doesn't take a cognitive giant to see that if logging were "needed to improve forest health" there'd be no need to exempt it from environmental laws. The most difficult and disturbing task is to understand how and why, after millennia of deforestation, the destroyers and defenders alike accept each new, ephemeral, transparently false claim to virtue at face value. One reason, of course, is that the pattern itself is horrifying, too terrible to think about. A second reason is that if we allow ourselves to recognize the pattern and fully internalize its implications, we would have to change it. And so we propagate, or at least permit, the myths. It's called passing the buck.

Rational discussion presupposes rational motivations, yet claims to virtue are always attempts to place rational masks over nonrational urges. This means that to focus on the claims without broadening the debate so that it includes a consideration of the underlying urges is to be irrational and ultimately to fall into the same pattern of destructiveness. Another way to say this is that while the claims themselves possess the veneer of rationality, the process is not rational, and cannot be resolved by rational discussion. It can seem rational, but only within a severely distorted, nonrational framework—and then only so long as one doesn't question the framework itself.

Take the doctors at Auschwitz. As has been made clear by Lifton, the physicians working there would not have been effective cogs in the Nazi machine without first being quite certain they acted in the best interests of the world, and even in some cases of the Jews themselves. Some exhibited genuine concern for the well-being of the Jews, but only within the strict confines of the Auschwitz reality. In other words, while refusing to question the justice, sanity, or humanity of working prisoners to death or gassing them in assembly-line fashion, and refusing to question the abysmal conditions under which prisoners were housed, they often did what little was left to alleviate suffering.

One of the most common ways they did this was by preventing outbreaks of typhus, tuberculosis, and other communicable diseases by injecting patients with phenol. Children, adults who had long been on the medical block, and others who were ill or had the potential to become ill were selected for injection. The physician or technician filled the syringe from the phenol bottle and thrust the needle into the heart of the patient, emptying the contents of the syringe. Most patients fell dead almost immediately, although some lived for seconds or even minutes. Just like the Forest Service and timber companies, these physicians were preventing outbreaks by killing their patients. This could be rationalized by saying that dead and burned prisoners were no longer infectious risks to the living. Rationale aside, it was murder.

Paradoxically, the way out from these destructive frames of

mind is to step in—experience, not thought or rationalization, is the only cure-all. Instead of hiding behind notions of racial purity or pretending to prevent epidemics, notice that at this moment *I am lifting this boy's arm. He is six. His skin is pale. His eyes lock on mine: he is terrified. I am inserting the needle between his fourth and fifth ribs. It slides in easily. He winces, stifles a sob. I depress the plunger. He stiffens, and before he can fall off the stool my attendant carries him to the back door. The attendant returns, and ushers a woman through the front door. She takes her place on the stool. I begin to lift her left arm. Her eyes, too, lock on mine. I realize, in that instant, that I am the last thing she will ever see.*

Trust experience. Descartes' inversion of what is to be believed makes no sense to me, not to any of my senses. Thought divorced from experience is nonsense. I know from my own childhood this divorce can be essential to survival, but paradoxically, it is this same divorce on the part of perpetrators that gives rise to these awful claims to virtue.

I was not at Auschwitz. I wasn't there for the first clearcut, or the second, or the thousandth. I can read about death camps, and I can read about the forest that was turned into this book, but if the story is to mean anything to me, if it is to change my life, it must lead back to my own experience. And it does. From a rocky knoll not far from my home, the knoll where the coyotes came to remind me of our deal, I can see clearcuts white on green on a snowy winter's day. Entering the region's forests I am sure to encounter more stumps, slash piles, and dead hillsides than trees ancient enough to scream as they go down. There's a place I know near Spokane—by no means unique—where clearcuts wrap around a mountain, drop into a valley, climb a nearby ridge, and cut a swath deep into the next watershed. Recently I walked those clearcuts, past whitened slash piles of wood cut a dozen years ago and past the green limbs of this year's cut, and in ten consecutive miles I never once came within twenty yards of a live tree.

Do not, however, for a moment believe me. I could be conjuring this clearcut as easily as Gilgamish conjured his claim to virtue. Go look for yourself. Listen to the wind pick up soil that has baked and crumbled. Listen to distant trees speak as they sway, and listen, finally, if you can hear them above the whine of the chainsaws, to their screams as they are felled.

The relationship between Judeo-Christianity and exploitation is not so straightforward as I may have made it seem. It would not have been enough for the religion's founders to have simply made up a God and, as with a hand puppet, put words into the Deity's mouth. To become deaf to the clamoring of one's conscience and to the pleas of victims requires more than fabrication: it requires a belief stronger than experience, unshakable by the spilling of blood.

This doesn't mean that those who exploit don't consciously fabricate or lie, for they clearly do. Like the layers of an onion, under the first lie is another, and under that another, and they all make you cry.

In 1939, Germany invaded Poland. Hitler's justification was that Polish troops had already attacked. This was a simple and conscious lie. Beneath and behind this lie, pushing it into action, was the notion that in order to fulfill its destiny the Aryan "race" needed room to expand. I don't know to what degree Hitler believed this; already we are sliding out of the realm of the conscious lie and into the realm of semiconscious justification for unspoken (and often unspeakable) urges. Pursuing this further we find the belief that Aryans were superior to Poles or other Eastern Europeans, and so more deserving of land. Beneath this belief there were undoubtedly others equally absurd, nesting like so many Russian dolls.

Another example: The United States Forest Service regularly uses the presence of *armilleria* root rot as an excuse to cut trees. This is often a conscious lie: examination by plant pathologists routinely reveals *armilleria* at or beneath endemic levels. In any case, *armilleria* is a secondary pathogen, which means disturbances, such as cutting trees, actually increase its prevalence in the remaining roots. So the conscious lie becomes self-fulfilling, and the rot becomes pandemic. And then comes another lie, the only way to improve the health of the forest is to cut it down. Beneath all of these lies is the notion that we can manage the landscape without destroying it. And underneath this? The God-given mandate, the evolutionarily-ordained duty, the economic policy, all driven by the notion that we are not normal citizens of this planet, that instead we are the most important creatures—really the only ones who matter—on Earth.

Back to Judeo-Christianity, and the relationship between this religion and exploitation. Many of the men who drafted the Bible, and the men who later helped shape the Christian worldview, probably believed, sincerely, that it was their God-given right to rape a woman and their holy duty to silence all women. Don't take my word for this. Let the fathers speak for themselves. Tertullian stated that women were "the devil's gateway," and was in agreement with Ambrose that all evil stems from women. Origen, the father of the Alexandrian church, so hated the flesh that he castrated himself to become, in the words of St. Matthew, one of the "eunuchs for the kingdom of heaven." He stated, "What is seen with the eyes of the creator is masculine, and not feminine, for God does not stoop to look upon what is feminine and of the flesh."

Examples of Christian misogyny are legion: St. Chrysotom said, "What else is woman but a foe to friendship, an unescapable punishment, a necessary evil, a natural temptation, a desirable calamity, a domestic danger, a delectible detriment, an evil of nature;" St. Thomas Aquinas, "The voice of a woman is an invitation to lust, and therefore must not be heard in church." St. Augustine got right to the point: "I know nothing which brings the manly mind down from the heights more than a woman's caresses."

This notion that sexuality and women—in fact the earth and all direct experience—bring men down from what is considered most important—the heights to which manly men may attain—is a central theme of our culture. The denigration of the flesh is essential to science, where a body is considered "nothing but a statue or a machine," and where direct experience is considered "mere anecdotal evidence" or noise to be ignored while we search for the real signal. And of course it is fundamental to Christianity: I recently came across a paragraph in the book *Porneia: On Desire and the Body in Antiquity*, which details some of the methods used by early Christians to try to control the erotic. It states:

"Ammonius used to burn his body with a red-hot iron every time [he felt sexual desire]. Pachon shut himself in a hyena's den, hoping to die sooner than yield, and then he held an asp against his genital organs. Evagrius spent many nights in a frozen well. Philoromus wore irons. One hermit agreed one night to take in a woman who was lost in the desert. He left his light burning all night and burned his fingers on it to remind himself of eternal punishment. A monk who had treasured the memory of a very beautiful woman, when he heard that she was dead, went and dippled his coat in her decomposed body, and lived with this smell to help him fight his constant thoughts of beauty." Clearly, these men suffered.

It would be comforting, as always, to believe these are the words of a few sad men. We would, as always, be wrong. Origen, St. Augustine, St. Thomas Aquinas were influential men. And they articulated—as did Descartes, Bacon, Hitler—deep cultural urges in ways that obviously resonated with a great many people.

Take Martin Luther, who wrote, "I would have such venomous, syphilitic whores broken on the wheel and flayed because one cannot estimate the harm such filthy whores do to young men who are so wretchedly ruined and whose blood is contaminated before they have achieved full manhood." If his message hadn't resonated, would Luther be known as the father of a church? Would any of these men be esteemed, even beatified? No, their words would have been ignored instead of being translated into action.

By the time Luther gave voice to his hatred, in the sixteenth century, women had been getting burned at the stake for nearly seven hundred years, since the council of Salzburg in 799 C.E. approved the torture of witches. Of course the legalized murder of women goes much farther back. Millions of women—up to twenty percent in many communities—were tortured and killed on the pretense that they were witches, and that they had committed crimes against men.

The extremely influential and popular tome *Malleus Maleficarum*—which in 180 years went through thirty-five editions in four languages—detailed many of these crimes. Women were murdered, for example, because they did "marvellous things with regard to male organs." It goes on to tell us that women "collect male organs in great numbers, as many as twenty or thirty members together, and put them in a bird's nest, or shut them up in a box, where they move themselves like members, and eat oats and corn, as has been seen by many and is a matter of common report." According to the women's executioners, these women copulated with devils, traveled on clouds, stole milk, rode atop he-goats or broomsticks and so should be tortured and killed—remember my father never beat anyone without good reason.

Not only women have suffered at the hands of Christians. As mentioned before, hundreds of millions of indigenous peoples everywhere have been tortured, mutilated, and murdered to further the glory of Christ. "They built a long gibbet, low enough for the toes to touch the ground and prevent strangling, and hanged thirteen [Indians] at a time in honor of Christ Our Saviour and the twelve Apostles. . . . Then, straw was wrapped around their torn bodies and they were burned alive." The same is true, in smaller numbers, of the Christian treatment of Jews. Inquisitions, pogroms, and mass exterminations are Christian traditions as well and deeply celebrated as communion. Muslims, too—no mean misogynists themselves—have fallen before the avenging sword of Christ Our Savior. In order to free the Holy Lands of the unworthy, Crusaders repeatedly pillaged their way across eastern Europe and into the Middle East. To bring this discussion full circle, back to a Christian hatred of women, because non-Christian women were at the time of the Crusades considered particularly vile (sexual contact with them causing "an enormous stench to rise to heaven"), and most especially because defeats on the field of battle were inevitably attributed to a lack of chastity on the parts of Crusaders, rape played a smaller role than it normally has in the forward march of civilization. Instead, the Crusaders, as after the battles of Antioch, "did no other harm to the women they found in [the non-Christians'] tents—save that they ran their lances through their bellies."

The belief that men own women continues to permeate our culture. Even today politicians and others cite the Bible frequently to support their view. Recently the local newspaper ran a multipage profile of a young woman who, according to the profile's first sentence, is a "role model for the entire city." This is not only because as a Christian she decided to abstain from sex until she married, but because she decided until that time never to be alone with a man. When the man who eventually became her husband asked her father, a Christian pastor, for permission to court his daughter, her father refused. The suitor took her acquiescence to her father's wishes as a positive sign: "I knew that how she respected and honored her father was how she would respect and honor me." He asked again in six months, and this time her father agreed to turn his daughter over to the clearly like-minded suitor. After the article ran, the newspaper received many letters praising this woman and her family. Not a single letter commented on the woman's ownership by successive males.

More recently, a drunken woman was raped by two men after having danced an impromptu striptease at a party. The newspaper responded with an editorial entitled, "Act provocatively and you provoke," with the subtitle, "Sometimes, women lead men into temptation." The primary author of the editorial was a self-described fundamentalist Christian. The editorial's last line is, "If a woman demands the right to be a promiscuous fool . . . she shouldn't expect society to embrace her as a victim when she gets burned." The newspaper also published a rebuttal by a solitary dissenting member of the editorial board. Although his editorial did not ascribe blame to the woman (hedging bets, however, by stating that "ultimate accountability for this woman's behavior occurred when she was raped by the men she teased"), he did state that "because two men couldn't control themselves, a rape occurred," implying that rape is a crime of sexual passion, not violence and subjugation. Taken together, the editorials, both written by men, reinforce the Biblical notion that a woman's body is not her own, to do with as she pleases, and also that for men, rape is desirable, a temptation.

How does this come about? How is it that Jesus was a fair feminist for his day—treating women with a deference remarkable for his immersion in a deeply patriarchal culture—yet the religion that bears his name shows no such respect? How is it that pagans, Jews, Muslims, heretical Christians, Indians, Africans, Polynesians, Asians, women, men, children, salmon, forests, have been murdered by the *millions* in the name of a man who said that people should love their neighbors and love their enemies?

At least part of the answer is that the words of Jesus are ultimately irrelevant to the course of historical Christianity. Far more important to this course are deeply hidden urges that grope not only for expression but also for sufficient pretext to allow fulfillment without acknowledgment, and hence without accountability.

Few people would be senseless enough to believe that my father beat my sister because she found dead puppies in the swimming pool, or for any reason other than those emanating from my father's damaged psyche. He blamed it on the dead puppies simply to confuse us all, himself especially, and to drown out the horrific experience of beating his own child.

Few would be ignorant enough to believe Hitler's justifications for murdering millions of people in Europe and Africa. We can see—probably more easily than he—through and beyond his words to his intent, made deathly clear in the showers at Treblinka and on the stone cold killing fields of the Soviet Union.

By the same token, it isn't difficult to honestly evaluate the insanity and hatred that characterized the witch trials, that conceptualized, then created a suitable political, social, philosophical, and theological context for the torture and murder of women because they were alleged to "do marvellous things with regard to male organs."

How then do we so blind ourselves to the same impulses that surround us today, that are central to, and propel our culture? Do you think today's destruction of the salmon is so much less than last century's destruction of the passenger pigeon? Do you think the enslavement of 150,000,000 children is so much less than the race-based slavery of not-so-long-ago? Is the ongoing genocide of indigenous peoples so much less than the Final Solution, so much less than Manifest Destiny? It is safe to speak of Hitler because he is dead, and because you and I were not there to participate. My father is safely out of my life. None of this emerged in the midst of the beatings.

This fear and hatred of life, shape shifter that it is, stays always one step ahead of our discernment, slipping each time we nearly understand it to faster, more efficient ways to control and then destroy the objects of our hatred, and with them ultimately ourselves.

The patriarchal family gives rise to a patriarchal God, who can be internalized to wield Fatherly control even when the father is absent. When threats wear thin the patriarchal God sends a Son to prove His love. My father always knew exactly how far to push with violence before relenting to confuse with signs of affection, and to get us to agree that our suffering, compared to his own, was nothing. So, too, with Christianity. And now what? Christianity—by now entirely divorced from the teachings of its nominal founder—inevitably gives way to science, an infinitely stronger tool to control and destroy not only humans but the entire planet.

Those who wish to destroy will do so. It really is that simple. Remove the words, and the acts are there. Beatings, rapes, enslavement, sanctified murders in autos-da-fé, or industrialized death-dealing with Zyklon B, chainsaws, driftnets, mink coats, time cards, clocks, protein drinks, satellite surveillance systems, and the soul-murder of lives wasted in quiet desperation.

In the beginning is the urge. In the people who would destroy it is always there. Like poisoned water, it is heavy; like poisoned water, it is ungraspable; like poisoned water, it always seeks for cracks to seep through, to exploit, to wear away, to open; like poisoned water it emerges, and when the vessel breaks, as so often it does, like poisoned water it comes out raging its mantra of death.

Seeking a Third Way

"For those in whom a local mythology still works, there is an experience both of accord with the social order, and of harmony with the universe. For those, however, in whom the authorized signs no longer work—or, if working, produce deviant effects—there follows inevitably a sense both of dissociation from the local social nexus and of quest, within and without, for life, which the brain will take to be for 'meaning.'"
Joseph Campbell

THE MESSAGE FROM THE stars that sustained me as a child—that the cruelty we take for granted is not natural—sustains me to this day. For I know that beneath the fear and hatred, beneath the urge to control and destroy, far beneath the scarred shells that protect and define us, people are good. Deep down our needs are simple: apart from food, shelter, and clothing there are the needs to love and be loved, for community, to be open to the world at large and for it to be open to us, to affect and be affected, to understand and be understood, to hear and be heard, to accept and be accepted. It is only when we fear that these needs won't be met that we grasp at them, and in the grasping lose any chance of satisfying them. Love controlled is not love; just as sex demanded is rape and acceptance expected is subservience. But if we fear, then demand we must, for to fear these needs will not be met is to fear for our lives as surely as if our lack of love and acceptance were instead the absence of food and water. With these deep needs unsatisfied we waste away, shrivel, and die as from hunger or thirst. We die, but we go on surviving. The search for that which should have been there all along continues, but we can no longer receive it, nor even recognize it.

And so we grasp all the more recklessly, demand all the more strenuously, never now slaking thirst nor sating hunger. The circle of necessary control grows wider, the hold grows tighter, until the objects once loved are hated for the shreds of their remaining independence, the perceived unwillingness to conform to the precise and impossible accommodation of our ever-changing wishes which could grant us satisfaction, give us peace. We sense that this control of others is futile, perhaps, and yet we act upon the unacknowledged belief that to realize this control and quiet our fears we must affect all those we encounter that do not reflect our imagined dominance, silence them, deny their subjective existence, and ultimately, kill them. At this point there can be no respite for the hungry and thirsty save death, which will

come too soon for those controlled and never soon enough for those who control.

Fearing death, fearing life, fearing love, and fearing most of all the loss of control, we create social rules and institutions that mirror our fears and reinforce our destructive behaviors. Having surrounded ourselves with images of ourselves, and having silenced all others, we can now pretend that the false-front world we've created is instead the world we've been given. We can pretend the world is a very dangerous place, where dogs eat dogs, where children and others must be beaten into submission, where a fierce struggle takes place in which only the strongest, meanest, most unethical and hateful survive, and ultimately where we die alone and afraid. Any threat to this illusion must be annihilated before it reminds us of what we've lost, what we've destroyed, and of what could have been. And so we kill all witnesses: the vast flocks of passenger pigeons; the islands of great auks; the massive herds of bison; the great forests; each and every nonhierarchical and peaceful indigenous culture; each and every new child, wild and beautiful and free and creative as she is; even our own consciences and direct experiences of the world.

No matter how we try, we cannot eradicate every vestige of life and love. Each new child—human, plant, animal, stone, or star—offers a new possibility, and each new encounter an opportunity for communion, however great or slight. Just yesterday I drove to the grocery store to pull boxes of scraps from the dumpster. As I worked I noticed a man sitting on a curb, watching. His clothes were old, ill-fitting, and torn, his shoes falling apart. I couldn't tell his age; the bottle, in a brown paper bag, from which he drank may have aged him ten years, or maybe twenty-five. I finished the boxes, and got in the truck. We made eye contact, and nodded. He stood and walked toward me. "Do you get food out of there?"

Homeless people ask me that all the time. Had I pulled anything of value, I would have given it to him.

"Sometimes. Today I just got lettuce leaves."

He thought for a moment, looked away, then looked back to me. He reached in his pocket and said, "Can I donate a couple of bucks so you can get some food?"

Communion. "No thanks," I said, "The lettuce is for my chickens." I smiled, and he smiled back. "Thanks," I said, "Thanks so much."

Things don't have to be the way they are.

It's two days later. Two young chickens died the night before last, most likely from cold and damp. I was awakened near dawn not by dreams of chicks, but by the barking of my dogs. I stumbled to the window and pulled the drapes in time to see them chasing a slender slip of reddish-tan through deep grass and into the woods. I went back to sleep, and they awoke me again not long after. Again I looked outside, and this time saw the dogs not running, but standing and barking. I followed their gaze to see a coyote—I assume the same one because it had the same reddish coat—standing twenty feet away, not moving. We made eye contact for one long moment, and still dopey from sleep I could think of nothing more profound to say than, "Hey, why don't you stay away from the chickens?" The coyote continued to stare, as now did the dogs, perhaps all three stunned by the brilliance of my morning wit. My mind slogged through mud as I tried to assemble another comment. Finally the coyote turned and walked slowly into the trees, and the dogs, too, turned to mind to their morning. I crawled back into bed.

When I awoke for the day I went outside and into the rain. The chicks were huddled, trilling, under a makeshift shelter that keeps them dry, and normally warm as well. Closer inspection revealed two dead chicks far underneath the mass. I took them to the coyote tree, and returned to my desk. A little later I heard Narcissus give his battle cry, taken up now by Amaru, who is learning the same pitched yell. Running outside I saw again the same coyote, again standing to stare. Again I called the same feeble question, "Why don't you stay away from the chickens?" This time the coyote turned, walked to a fence post, lifted his leg, then trotted into the bushes.

I have a strong suspicion of what the coyote may have meant by this, but I don't know for sure. I do know that my efforts at interspecies communication are doomed so long as I expect others—by which I mean everyone else on the planet—to learn my

language, and I remain unwilling to learn theirs. In the ways of these other languages I remain embarrassingly ignorant. Though I own no television I know commercials for products I will never use better than I know birdsongs I hear at dawn and dusk. Play me three notes of *Stairway to Heaven* or *Freebird* (or even, embarrassingly enough, the theme songs to *Green Acres* or *Gilligan's Island*), and I can name that tune, but play me a symphony of bird songs I hear each day, and I've got no clue as to their origin or meaning. How could I possibly expect to integrate myself as a citizen into the community I at least *call* home if I can't be bothered to learn even their spoken or sung languages? And if I can't be bothered to discover who is speaking when the birds of morning begin their song, how can I expect to understand the language of gesture, or, beyond that, intent? How can I hope to grasp, accept, or appreciate what may be said by trees or grass or stones?

I had another dream of fishing recently, this time fishing from a boat on a rolling ocean. Once again I caught a huge fish, and once again it rushed me. This time, instead of leaping next to me the fish wrapped the line—strong as steel cable—around the boat, and then dove. It began to pull me down. I awoke, moaning and frightened.

Perhaps this dream, too, is about what we must do. We need not only eat whatever fish the Dreamgiver and the world offers, but we need to let it eat us as well. We need to let the world hook us as we have hooked it, and to let it play us and reel us in. Perhaps in taking the world into our bodies we also need to dive into the body of the world, to dive down deep and let it pull us deeper still, until at last we not only consume but are consumed, until at last we are no longer separate—standing alone and lonely on the darksome heights to which only men aspire—but instead, simply living in commune with the rest of the world.

Only recently—especially after teaching at a university for a few years—have I come to understand why the process of schooling takes so long. Even when I was young it seemed to me that most classroom material could be presented and assimilated in four, maybe five, years. After you learn fractions and negative numbers in first or second grade, what new principles are taught in math until algebra in junior high? It's the same with science, art, history, reading, certainly writing. Nearly everything I learned those years—and this was true for my friends as well—was gleaned through books and conversations outside class. It's true to the point of cliché that most of the "crap" we learn in high school, as Simon and Garfunkel put it, is a bland stew of names, dates, and platitudes to be stored up the night before each test, then forgotten the moment the test is handed in.

During high school, I believed the primary purpose of school was to break children of the habit of daydreaming. If you force them to sit still long enough, eventually they tire even of sinking turn-around fadeaways at the buzzer to win NBA championships. Having sat in the back of the class lining rockets over the left field fence for the better part of thirteen years, I was ready to move on.

I've since come to understand the reason school lasts thirteen years. It takes that long to sufficiently break a child's will. It is not easy to disconnect children's wills, to disconnect them from their own experiences of the world in preparation for the lives of painful employment they will have to endure. Less time wouldn't do it, and in fact, those who are especially slow go to college. For the exceedingly obstinate child there is graduate school.

I have nothing against education; it's just that education—from the Greek root *educere*, meaning *to lead forth* or *draw out*, and originally a midwife's term meaning *to be present at the birth of*—is not the primary function of schooling. I'm not saying by all this that Mrs. Calloway, my first-grade teacher, was trying to murder the souls of her tiny charges, any more than I've been trying to say that individual scientists are necessarily hell-bent on destroying the planet or that individual Christians necessarily hate women and hate their bodies. The problem is much worse than that, it is not merely personal nor even institutional (although the institutions we've created *do* mirror the destructiveness of our culture). It is implicit in the processes, and therefore virtually transparent.

Take the notion of assigning grades in school. Like the wages for which people later slave—once they've entered "the real

world"—the primary function of grades is to offer an external reinforcement to coerce people to perform tasks they'd rather not do. Did anyone grade you when you learned how to fish? What grades did you get for pretending, shooting hoops, playing pinball, reading good books, kissing ("I'm sorry, dear, but you receive a c–"), riding horses, swimming in the ocean, having intense conversations with close friends? On the other hand, how often have you returned, simply for the joy of it, to not only peruse your high school history textbook, but to memorize names and dates, and, once again for the joy of it, to have a teacher mark, in bright red, your answers as incorrect?

Underlying tests as given in school are the presumptions not only that correct answers to specific questions exist, but that these answers are known to authority figures and can be found in books. Tests also generally discourage communal problem solving. Equally important is the presumption that a primary purpose of school is to deliver information to students. Never asked is the question of how this information makes us better people, or better kissers, for that matter. Systematically—inherent in the process—direct personal experience is subsumed to external authority, and at every turn creativity, critical thought, and the questioning of fundamental assumptions (such as, for example, the role of schooling on one's socialization) are discouraged.

If you don't believe me, pretend for a moment you're once again in school. Pretend further that you have before you the final test for a final required class. If you fail this test, you fail the class. While you may have enjoyed the process of schooling, and may even have enjoyed this class, you enjoyed neither enough to warrant repetition. Pretend the test consists of one essay question, and pretend you know the instructor well enough to understand that if you mimic the instructor's opinions you'll get a higher grade. If you disagree with the instructor—pretend, finally, that you do—you'll be held to a higher standard of proof. What do you do? Do you speak your mind? Do you lead with your heart? Do you take risks? Do you explore? Do you write the best damn essay the school has ever seen, then return next year to retake the class? Or do you join with thousands—if not millions—of students who face this dilemma daily and who astutely bullshit their way through, knowing, after all, that C stands for Credit?

Grades, as is true once again for wages in later life, are an implicit acknowledgment that the process of schooling is insufficiently rewarding on its own grounds for people to participate of their own volition. If I go fishing, the time on the water—listening to frogs, smelling the rich black scent of decaying cattails, holding long conversations with my fishing partner, watching osprey dive to emerge holding wriggling trout—serves me well enough to make me want to return. And even if I have a bad day fishing, which, as the bumper sticker proclaims, is supposed to be "better than a good day at work," I still receive the reward of dinner. The process and product are their own primary rewards. I fish; I catch fish; I eat fish. I enjoy getting better at fishing. I enjoy eating fish. No grades nor dollars are required to convince me to do it. Only when essential rewards disappear does the need for grades and dollars arise.

It could be argued that I'm missing the point, that the product of the years of homework and papers and tests are not the physical artifacts, nor the grades, nor the bits of information, but instead the graduates themselves. But that's my point exactly, and we must ask ourselves what sort of product is that, from what sort of process.

A primary purpose of school—and this is true for our culture's science and religion as well—is to lead us away from our own experience. The process of schooling does not give birth to human beings—as education should but never will so long as it springs from the collective consciousness of our culture—but instead it teaches us to value abstract rewards at the expense of our autonomy, curiosity, interior lives, and time. This lesson is crucial to individual economic success ("I love art," my students would say, "but I've got to make a living"), to the perpetuation of our economic system (What if all those who hated their jobs quit?), and it is crucial, as should be clear by now, to the rationale that causes all mass atrocities.

Through the process of schooling, each fresh child is attenuated, muted, molded, made—like aluminum—malleable yet durable, and so prepared to compete in society, and ultimately

to lead this society where it so obviously is headed. Schooling as it presently exists, like science before it and religion before that, is necessary to the continuation of our culture and to the spawning of a new species of human, ever more submissive to authority, ever more pliant, prepared, by thirteen years of sitting and receiving, sitting and regurgitating, sitting and waiting for the end, prepared for the rest of their lives to toil, to propagate, to never make waves, and to live each day with never an original thought nor even a shred of hope.

In *Letters From an American Farmer,* Michel Guillaume Jean de Crévecoeur noted: "There must be in the Indians' social bond something singularly captivating, and far superior to be boasted of among us; for thousands of Europeans are Indians, and we have no examples of even one of those Aborigines having from choice become Europeans."

Benjamin Franklin was even more to the point: "No European who has tasted Savage Life can afterwards bear to live in our societies." It was commonly noted that at prisoner exchanges, Indians ran joyously to their relatives while white captives had to be bound hand and foot to not run back to their captors.

It is small wonder, then, that from the beginning, whenever we have encountered an indigenous culture, we have had the Lord our God—replaced now by economic exigency—tell us that "thou shalt smite them; *and* utterly destroy them; thou shalt make no covenant with them, nor shew mercy unto them." What seems at first aggression is in fact self-preservation, a practical staunching of what would otherwise be an unmanageable and embarrassing flow of desertions.

The same self-preservation motivated my father's actions when I was a child. To preserve the person that he had become, he had to smite and utterly destroy all who reminded him of what could have been, and of the person he once was, far beyond conscious memory, before his parents, too, out of self-preservation destroyed him. So he lashed out with fist, foot, voice, penis, all so he could forget, all so we could never know, ourselves, that alternatives to fear existed. Had he been able to destroy the stars to so destroy me, he would have done it. Had he been able to destroy the stars, as even now we are destroying the seas and forests and grasslands and deserts, he would have succeeded, I am sure, in destroying me.

In the eighteenth century, de Crèvecoeur wrote, "As long as we keep ourselves busy tilling the earth, there is no fear of any of us becoming wild." Though the wild outside diminishes each day, as do intact cultural alternatives, the fear of these alternatives remains. The fear shall remain so long as we live the way we do, and so long as there are alternatives we must avoid. The alternatives shall remain so long as there is life. We should not be surprised, then, that our culture as a whole must destroy all life and that we as individuals must not dwell upon the horrors we visit not only upon others but upon ourselves, that we dwell instead upon the daily earning of our bread, and beyond that pile upon ourselves project after project to keep ourselves always occupied, always unconscious of the fact that we do not have to live this way, always blindered to alternatives. For if we looked we might see, if we saw we might act, and if we acted we might take responsibility for our own lives. If we did that, what then?

One method Nazis used to control Jews was to present them a series of meaningless choices. Red identity papers were issued to one group, while another received blue. Which will permit my family to survive another selection? Are identity papers with or without photographs safer? Should I declare myself a shoemaker or clothier? When the line splits, do I step to the left or the right? In making these choices victims felt the illusion of control over their destinies, and often failed to reject the entire system. Resistance to exploitation was diminished.

Not only Jews have faced false choices. My sister: should I fish puppies out of the pool, or should I call my brother? My brother: should I park close to the house or to the street? Myself: should I continue to eat or should I freeze in place? My mother: should I throw water, or should I pull him into the other room?

Last fall I attended a debate, of sorts, between two people running to be Manager of the Washington State Department of Natural Resources. Although one was female and the other male, they were, as is so often true of political opponents, for all prac-

tical purposes indistinguishable. Talking of the public forests, the first spoke not of salmon, lynx, or grizzly, but of "managing an asset portfolio." The second never mentioned the words "forest" or "wildlife," and in fact mentioned no creatures save cows. Because so much money is involved in the "managing of this public resource," he said, these forests should be considered "a big business to be run by a CEO."

That evening—as the moderator, a representative of the region's corporate newspaper, asked his final question, "Do environmental regulations work, or do they go too far?"—I thought of the words of Meir Berliner, who died fighting the SS at Treblinka, "When the oppressors give me two choices, I always take the third." I thought also—as I reflected on meaningless talk of shuffling numbers on abstract ledgers—of the real-world effects of these people's decisions. I wondered, if wolves, elk, owls, or salamanders could right now take on human form and speak through me or anyone else here, what would they say? If the children who will inherit the consequences of our actions were here tonight, those of the seventh generation, as the Indians say, or even of the second or third or fourth, how would they respond?

When the moderator opened the evening to the public, I raised my hand. I said, "A comment, and then a question. The comment: I have to say that if bobcats, wolves, trees, and salmon could vote, they wouldn't vote for either one of you." Everyone gasped, as though I had pulled a gun. "Now a question: Pretend we're children two generations hence, and defend your actions to us. Tell us why we shouldn't hate you for destroying our world." Another gasp, as though I had fired it through their hearts. A friend of mine, sitting next to me, who is a longtime environmentalist, slid slightly away from me on the metal chair beneath him.

Notwithstanding the knowledge that every creature—except for the more wounded among us—tries to move in the direction of life; and not withstanding the white-haired and wizened woman who approached me—after the politicians addressed neither comment nor question—to thank me and say she wished she would have said the same; and notwithstanding the knowledge that there can be no more important comment to make nor question to ask, I felt intensely alone. I had broken the most basic commandment of our culture: *Thou shalt pretend there is nothing wrong*. I had rolled a grenade across the dance floor.

I drove home alone, crying. When I got there, I walked into the frosty October night, and found my feet carrying me to the coyote tree. Wrapping my arms around it, I sobbed into its cobblestone bark, feeling the grooves and rough corners with my outstretched fingers. Soon I stopped holding it, and it held me. I walked home; no longer crying yet chest heaving still. I needed more. I stepped to the huge ponderosa that stands outside this window, the ponderosa where each spring magpies add to their tumbled nest, and removed my clothes. I folded myself into the arms of this grandfather tree, this fatherly tree, and it held me as my own father never had. I cried again, into its bark, and never felt the cold. Comforted and safe now, I put on my clothes, and went inside; strengthened and emboldened by the huge beating hearts of these trees, I was ready to continue the fight, to nevermore accept only the two proffered choices, but to seek out a third, and follow it to the end.

Somewhere along the line, my schooling fell short. Not only did it fail to permanently eradicate my perception of an animate world, it also left me ill-prepared for a life of gainful employment.

Through college I worked as a physics assistant for the National Oceanic and Atmospheric Administration (NOAA). I learned how to program computers, assist in experiments, and align lasers. I also learned that if you pour liquid nitrogen out of a thermos on a hot July afternoon, it evaporates before it hits your bare feet yet still feels deliciously cool. Most important, I learned that I would never again sell my time.

I've never understood the stereotype of inefficient or lazy federal workers. The scientists with whom I worked were smart, resourceful, and dedicated. If one of my supervisors called in sick, I could usually count on him showing up later, unwilling to miss the day's experiment.

Their love for their work struck me, because I sometimes called in sick when it was a nice day, rationalizing the lie by telling myself I was sick of work, which was true enough.

For nearly as long as I can remember, I've had the habit of

asking people if they like their jobs. Over the years, about 90 percent—with the exception of my bosses at NOAA—have said no. As I sat bored those days at my computer, I began to wonder what that percentage means, both socially and personally. I wondered what it does to each of us to spend the majority of our waking hours doing things we'd rather not do, wishing we were outside or simply elsewhere, wishing we were reading, thinking, making love, fishing, sleeping, or simply having time to figure out who the hell we are and what the hell we're doing. We never have enough time to *catch up*—I never knew what that meant, but it always felt as though I were running downhill, my body falling faster than my legs could carry me—enough time to try to understand what we want to do with the so very few hours each of us are given.

Two incidents stand out in my transition from lackadaisical employee to not being an employee at all. The first took place during my junior year in college. One of my classes took a field trip to a Hewlett-Packard plant, where hundreds of employees designed and assembled calculators and computers. The factory was a vision of hell—a clean, well-lit, unionized, well-paying, reasonably quiet, yet horribly repetitive hell—as people, mainly women of color, soldered circuits on boards, or used huge magnifiers to inspect the work of others. I couldn't imagine anyone choosing to spend a life this way, and wondered what they ignored in order to maintain composure and even sanity amid the boredom. I assumed that a purpose of the trip was to convince us to finish our degrees, thus guaranteeing we would never enter this circle of hell except as overseers. For me it didn't quite work that way, because the alternative seemed little better. Our guide was an engineer who didn't assemble but designed circuit boards, and I will never forget the pride with which he showed us his cubicle—perhaps eight feet by ten—and said, "After three years I've been given a window." The window was tall and narrow, and didn't open. The grass was green, the sky pale blue, the clouds white, the day warm.

The next morning, class began at eight. The instructor was an ancient, foul-tempered moose of a man who made it his practice to ask questions seemingly out of the air, and then whirl to demand an answer from a student caught unawares. That morning I was his victim. He said, "So," followed by a long pause as he paced the front of the classroom, "what did you learn yesterday?" He trailed off, then twisted impossibly quickly for a man his size, age, and health. He pointed and called my name.

Because this was a required class, and because my grades weren't high enough to guarantee safe passage, and because I knew from experience that disagreement was not agreeable to him, under normal circumstances I would have simply brownnosed my way out of his spotlight. But I was, as always, slow in the morning, and I'd been caught off-guard, so I told the truth, "I learned I wouldn't want to work for Hewlett Packard."

The class laughed. Dr. Kline didn't. He smiled absently, and entered into his lecture as though he hadn't heard me. I thought I was safe. Then he stopped mid-sentence, turned, pointed again, and said, "That's okay, Derrick. They wouldn't hire you anyway." I realized my error then, and realized it again when I received my next test back.

The other incident I remember just as clearly. I sat at the computer at work, debugging. I was bored. It was afternoon. I was twenty-two. It was June. Along the front range of the Rocky Mountains in Colorado, thunderheads move in almost every afternoon between May and early July. They materialize, darken the day, spit a few drops, open the sky with lightning, then disappear like so many dreams.

Turning away from the computer I saw through my own narrow window (at least it opened) the green, the blue, the flashes. I looked to the clock, the screen, the window. An hour passed, then two. I looked again at the clock and saw it had been only twenty minutes. I willed the second-hand, the minute-hand, the hour-hand to move faster, to deliver me to five o'clock when I would be released as from my prison term. Then suddenly I stopped, struck by the absurdity of wishing away the only thing I've got. Eight hours, eighty years, it was all too similar. Would I wish away the years until the day of my retirement, until my time was once again my own? At work I tried to keep busy to make the hours pass quickly. It was no different when watching television, socializing, moving frenetically—there are so many

ways to kill time.

I remember staring at the computer screen—light green letters on dark—then at the clock, and finally at my outstretched fingers held a foot in front of my face. And then it dawned on me: selling the hours of my life was no different from selling my fingers one by one. We've only so many hours, so many fingers; when they're gone, they're gone for good.

I quit work two weeks later—having sold another eighty of my hours—and knew I could never again work a regular job.

A couple of years ago I decided to clean the barn. I'm a sloppy housekeeper, and an even sloppier barnkeeper. All the animals, who freely wander in and out, share the barn with piles of beekeeping equipment and extra hive bodies, firewood, books, magazines, tools, nesting boxes for the hens to ignore, and boxes of food pulled from dumpsters (for birds).

If ever a place was described in the mythology of mice as the Garden of Eden, this was it. Mice especially love making nests in hive bodies. They chew holes in the honeycombs, bring in straw and piles of pasta for warmth and food, then urinate everywhere so the boxes reek and are sure to be rejected later by bees. Mice don't seem to mind the smell. Perhaps they think the same thing about our habitations.

Moving hive bodies, I found many nests of baby mice: pink, hairless, wriggling. Dogs, cats, and chickens huddled round as I picked up each box, then darted in to snatch mice that were old enough to run and simply swallow those too young to move.

I had conflicted feelings about the killing. I don't like to kill, especially when it doesn't lead directly to food, but I must admit I've picked up from bees a certain antipathy toward mice. Not only do mice destroy stored equipment, they sometimes, especially in winter, move into occupied hives. They've been known, albeit infrequently, to kill entire colonies, or drive the bees away.

The discomfort with killing them arose from the fact that my dislike of mice is general, not individual. The babies being swallowed two or three at a time by the dogs, or pecked at, aligned, and swallowed whole by chickens had never harmed me, bees, or anyone. I've not before hesitated—or at least not hesitated long—

to kill or drive away mice I've found inside beehives. That never seemed unjust. But as I was cleaning I kept feeling I was doing something wrong.

My suspicions were confirmed when I arose the next morning. The countertop in my bathroom was covered with mouse droppings, probably fifty pellets where in the several years before there had never been any.

The message seemed unmistakable, but in the two years since, I've not been able to take the communication further. I've heard other stories of animals defecating to communicate displeasure, of travelers returning home from a too-long vacation to find one pile of cat manure in the center of the bed, or of people who quit feeding squirrels on their porch, only to have the squirrels first beg, then scratch at the windows, and finally leave a neat row of pellets along the railing where once peanuts were placed.

Perhaps the question of further communication is not so important. Do I really want to carry on an extended conversation with a mouse? I don't even like mice. Perhaps a better, or at least more immediate, question has to do with out status as neighbors. I have to admit the mice didn't ruin *all* the stored boxes, or even that many. Perhaps in the years before I went on my cleaning frenzy, we were simply coexisting, the ruined boxes my tithe to them, and the occasional nests I found and destroyed in the process of doing my work their tithe back. If I had an arrangement with coyotes whereby they relented from taking "my" chickens in return for a tithe, perhaps the mice, too, considered themselves to have entered into an arrangement with me.

All of this is speculation. What I know is what I experienced: I made an unprecedented incursion into the place they live, into their home, if you will. That same night they made a similarly unprecedented incursion into the place I live, into my home. Was this a reprimand? A warning? A simple statement of frustration, sorrow, and anger? Or was this, as mechanistic explanations would require, simply random?

I learn and forget repeatedly that my claims to ownership— especially with regard to living beings—are inevitably illusory. Do I own the barn, and with it the right to end all life that enters? Do I own the beeboxes, and so is it acceptable for me to

feed every baby mouse I encounter to *my* chickens, ducks, dogs, cats? It strikes me that ownership as practiced by our culture is an expression of a will and capacity to control, and even to destroy. It's my barn, so I can do whatever the hell I want with it. The mice are in my barn, so they're mine, too, to trap, poison, feed to chickens, or simply stomp on, if I so choose. The land I live on is mine, so I can poison it with herbicides, pesticides, and Kentucky bluegrass, or I can cut the trees, sell them for two-by-fours, and put up condos if I've a mind to. If I had a wife, she would just as surely be mine, as would any children we might have.

What if we stand the notion of ownership on its head? What if I do not own the barn, but instead it owns me, or better, we own each other? What if I do not view it as my right to kill mice simply because I can, and because a piece of paper tells me I own their habitation? What if, because their habitation is near my own, I am responsible for their well-being? What if I take care of them and their community as the grandfather ponderosa outside this window takes care of me, and as before that the stars soothed me? This relationship of mutual care doesn't mean that none shall die, nor even that I won't kill anything, nor eventually be killed; it simply means we will treat each other with respect, and that neither will unnecessarily shit where the other bathes. The bees, too, stand in my purview, and so it becomes my responsibility to make sure, to the best of my abilities, that they can sustain their community. The same can be said for the communities of wild roses, native grasses, trees, frogs, mosquitos, ants, flies, bluebirds, bumblebees, and magpies that, too, call this their home. We all share responsibility toward each other and toward the soil, which in turn shares responsibility to each of us. What if all of life is not what we've been taught, a "solitary, poor, nasty, brutish and short" competition to see who may own or kill the others before the others can own or kill them? What if we don't need to live our whole lives alone? What if life is a web of immeasurably complex and respectful relationships? What if the purpose—even the evolutionary purpose—is for each of us to take responsibility for all those around us, to respect their own deepest needs, to esteem and be esteemed by them, to feed and feed off them, to be sustained by their bodies and eventually to sustain them with our own?

I recently drove cross-country, and I spent a lot of time listening to the radio to pass the miles. I came across a talk show about disciplining children. Caller after caller described the necessity of, in the words of the host, "wearing out the belt." A seven-year-old girl, according to one typical caller, no longer had to be "whipped," as he put it, because she was conditioned to "fall right into line" whenever he mentioned the belt. This caller was proud of his youngest daughter, five, whom he has had to whip only a few times, because, as he said, "She's smart, and she sees what happens when her sister gets out of line."

The host laughed as he read a news report of a woman upset because when she arrived at the day care to pick up her three-year-old son, she found him crying, his mouth taped shut. The host expressed agreement with a district attorney who would not press charges.

I heard only one caller speak out against the violence. He said that as a Christian he had no choice but to step in whenever he saw someone publicly strike a child. "Violence against children is wrong," he said, because "it springs from anger, and anger goes against the teachings of Jesus."

The host, also a self-described Christian, disagreed (for the only time on the show), asking sharply, "What business is it of yours?"

Hearing that, I thought back to an interaction I had with a woman and a child several years ago. I was at a social services office, waiting with a friend while she straightened out a problem with her medical coupons. The office was crowded, the wait long, the room hot, and tempers short. The conversations I overheard were sharp and tense. A television blared in one corner of the room, making patience or sustained thought nearly impossible.

Finally my friend's name was called. I wandered around the room until a quick movement caught my eye. I turned in time to see a four-year-old slap an infant.

Both mothers reacted instantly, grabbing the four-year-old and shouting, "Bad girl! You're a very bad girl!"

All conversation stopped, as though someone had hit a pause

button. When talk resumed, I no longer heard the women, but only saw them shaking the girl and shouting. I began to tremble.

I wanted to run to the women and ask them to stop. I don't know why I didn't. The child was frozen. Perhaps she was used to this and benumbed. Some of the other children seemed terrified. Most adults seemed oblivious. Perhaps they, too, were used to it.

The women continued to shout, and continued to shake the girl. I made my way outside and sat on the curb.

A few minutes later the mother of the four year old emerged, pushing a stroller in which there was another infant. The four year old held tight to the stroller.

My friend followed them out the door, and it happened that we walked in the same direction as the woman and children.

The mother continued to berate the child. Another woman in the parking lot pounded on her hood, laughing and shouting, "You tell her."

Why doesn't anyone stop this, I wondered. Why don't I?

For two blocks I walked behind the woman. Over and over she said, "You're a bad girl!" I knew if the child heard it often enough she would believe it. My hands were shaking. I thought I would throw up, and wanted to do something. I didn't know what to do.

Suddenly I became very calm. I knew what was necessary. Without thinking, I walked to the woman and said, "I saw what happened, and what she did wasn't that bad."

"She struck an infant."

"Don't you realize that every time you say these things, you're doing the same to her?"

The woman's jaw dropped. For a moment she stood in the middle of the street, naked and vulnerable. Then her defenses returned and she shouted at me, "This is none of your business."

I thought, of course this is my business. The child doesn't belong to you; she belongs to herself. She deserves to be treated with respect, honor, love, and tenderness. We all do. I couldn't say any of this, though, because the woman was now jerking away, pulling the child behind her.

. . .

Seeking a Third Way

Clearly, most of us working to protect the natural world hope our society will soon change direction. Without a fundamental shift in the way we act, the best of our efforts will in the long run add up to nothing, only affording a few more generations of lynx, bobcat, grizzly bear, and so on, the opportunity to live out harried lives before we ultimately exterminate them. Most everyone I know doesn't believe a cultural change of heart will happen voluntarily, which means that many of us are simply doing what we can to protect the few remaining pockets of biological and societal integrity until the system collapses. If after that those humans who survive are of good heart, and are willing to listen to the natural world, they may be able to relearn how to live with what the land gladly offers. If that happens, there may be hope for the continuation of life on the planet.

The bottom line with regard to what will survive seems to be this: if the urge to dominate as manifested by our culture is instinctual, there is no hope for humans, and not much hope for any other large forms of life. Those humans who come after will continue in this path we have followed, a path determined for us long before the rise of our species, long before the appearance of mammals, reptiles, fish, mold, bacteria, or even proteins. If what we're doing is natural, our path became biologically overdetermined when the rules for the game of life were set up: those capable of dominating will; those incapable will be eliminated. According to this perspective, the destruction of dodo birds, to choose just one example, may have been regrettable, but we simply couldn't help ourselves, and in any case they were unfit for survival. As for indigenous peoples, they, too, are "inferior" and must make way as we "invoke and remorselessly fulfill the inexorable law of natural selection." *I'm sorry*, we'll say, *but that's the way the world goes.*

An imposing body of literature supports this view of humans as inherently destructive, and a complementary view of nature as a cutthroat competition for survival. The Bible, of course, and the mainstream of Christianity are explicit in their condemnation of humanity as sinful, and mortal existence as a vale of hardship and tears. Science, too, gets in its licks, phrased now in terms of Natural instead of Divine Law.

Here's an example: I just read a popular book called *Demonic Males*. The authors state that because rape occurs in orangutans, rape and other violence by human males is, to use their word, "natural." While stating that parallels between human and non-human behaviors "justify nothing," they also state that "rape as an *ordinary* part of a species' behavior implies that it is an evolved adaptation." Recognizing the ubiquity of rape within our culture (but inaccurately extending it cross-culturally), they give their evolutionarily-ordained reasoning for rape: "By a logic that challenges our strongest moral principles it could pay the woman to acknowledge the rapist's power and form a relationship that, while initially repellent, she comes to accept." We need to remind ourselves that they are attempting to "justify nothing" as we read that "a demonstration of power implies that the female's safest future is to bond with the violent male." The authors have assumed not only the "true nature" of what we perceive as rape in orangutans, but also that orangutans are what Descartes would have called "beast-machines" driven by instincts—with no great measure of volition or cultural imperative—such that all actions performed by them become, by definition, natural, or rather Natural. While mentioning the human cultures (indigenous and non-indigenous) in which rape has existed, they ignore the many cultures in which rape was—beyond nonexistent—inconceivable until the members of these cultures were taught by example what it means to be civilized.

Wars of extermination somehow become Natural as well: the authors conclude that "neither in history nor around the globe today is there evidence of a truly peaceful society." But to make this statement, the authors are forced to ignore scores of peaceful cultures. They must ignore the difference between feuds and raiding parties, forms of ritualized violence where humiliation is the goal, and genocide. These are crucial differences. To ignore the qualitative and quantitative differences between counting coup and, not only using, but having *invented* something like napalm is to be entirely deaf to any reasonable sense of morality.

Take the Semai, of Malaya, to provide just one example among many: "As long as they have been known to the outside world," one anthropologist who lived with them wrote, "they have con-

sistently fled rather than fight, or even run the risk of fighting."
The Semai never strike their children, nor strike each other. When
they speak in Malay, they translate the verb *to hit* as *to kill*. If two
people quarrel, the worst they may do is call each other "cock-
roach," or some other name. The quarrel goes no farther, but is
taken to a third party for resolution. The Semai believe that to
make another person unhappy is to increase the probability that
the other will suffer an accident. This is something they try to
avoid under all circumstances. These characteristics have caused
many Westerners to label the Semai as "timid," or "weak." The
authors of *Demonic Males* ignore them altogether.

Such obviously selective scholarship in defense of the status
quo perplexes me as much as any other manifestation of our
culture's destructiveness. The question I keep asking myself—as
I watch the *Spokesman*'s editors insist that any concern regarding
lead pollution is unnecessary because "there are no human bodies lining the Spokane River," or as the authors of *Demonic Males*
deftly ignore the hundreds of human cultures that are based on
cooperation and peacefulness—is this: Are these people evil, or
are they stupid? We stumble over ourselves to avoid the truth, to
avoid the many grenades that are slowly wobbling across the floor.
The answer seems to be that in making ourselves blind we become evil *and* stupid. We are afraid what it would mean were we
to see.

Although the authors state that "patriarchy is worldwide and
history-wide," and comes out of men's "evolutionarily derived
efforts to control women," it took me only an hour to find a
description of the Paliyans, indigenous forest hunters of India,
for whom "independence of authority is a treasured right. Neither spouse can order the other, and neither, by virtue of sex or
age, is entitled to a greater voice in matters of mutual concern."
It took me another fifteen minutes to find that the Bushmen
live—or rather used to, before they were civilized—such that
"the status of husband and wife are on terms of equality, which
precludes any prediction that a husband or wife will follow the
lead of the other." And then I read the words of the Jesuit priest
Paul Le Jeune, who wrote in the seventeenth century that "the
Savage tribes . . . cannot chastise a child, nor see one chastised."

"How much trouble this will give us," Le Jeune lamented, "in carrying out our plans for teaching the young!" When Le Jeune upbraided an Indian man for the sexual freedom his wife enjoyed (he was not sure he was the father of her child), the Indian responded, "Thou hast no sense. You French people love only your own children, but we love all the children of our tribe."

The examples are there, if only we look.

And while it is certainly unfair to single out the authors of *Demonic Males,* they serve as important examples. These authors are not *exceptionally* bad scholars. They have simply said what people want, and perhaps need, to hear. Our culture has never lacked for apologists, and, as was true of Chivington, Descartes, St. Paul, St. Crysotom, and Martin Luther, the authors of *Demonic Males* are not alone. As is true for much religion and philosophy, a primary purpose of anthropology has been the legitimization of behavior patterns. Among many others, the anthropologists E.E. Evans Pritchard("men are always in the ascendancy"), E.R. Leach ("male domination has always been the norm in human affairs"), Claude Lévi-Strauss ("women are commodities"), and Steven Goldberg (*The Inevitability of Patriarchy*) have attempted to naturalize male domination. Like the authors of *Demonic Males,* the Jewish symphony members who ignored their burning synagogue, me as I gave away memories of my own experiences, or my mother as she obscured signs of sexual abuse in order to get through the day, our society simply ignores any evidence that could potentially threaten our view of the universe. Unstated always, and ignored as surely as the evidence itself, are the ulterior motives that hide beneath. It should not be terribly surprising that people would ignore the world to rationalize exploitation. In order to exploit, we must deafen ourselves to the voices of those we are victimizing. The justification of this exploitation would demand that we continue with our selective deafness, selective blindness, and selective stupidity.

But maybe I'm proceeding as selectively as the authors whose work I have maligned. Perhaps I, too, am trying to impose an order on the universe to match the needs of my interior life. Stars speak? Cradle me? Coyotes agree to deals, and ducks offer their lives to me? Mice retaliate on my bathroom counter, and we all participate in a dance of courtesy and the giving of gifts? There is no blood in this, no sharpness of tooth and claw. Perhaps my efforts at ordering the universe are as pathetic as those I criticize. Maybe, after all these years, I'm still a frightened little boy trying desperately to find love (or at least safety) in a violent household—in a violent universe—where none exists, and so I project, ignore evidence, do everything I have accused others of doing; I will do anything to avoid that one most basic truth of all—that I am entirely alone.

I do not know the interior nature of the universe, nor the essential truth about evolution. But if there is one thing I know about natural selection it is this: creatures who have survived in the long run, have survived *in the long run*. It is not possible to survive in the long run by taking from your surroundings more than you give back, in other words, one cannot survive in the long run through the domination of one's surroundings. It is quite clearly in the best interest of a bear to make sure that the salmon return and that berries ripen. They can eat them, but they cannot hyperexploit them and still expect to survive. Insofar as competitors enrich and enliven the natural community in which they live, it is in the bear's best interest to see that they, too, thrive, which it does by doing nothing—by simply being a bear. The same can be said for deer, who couldn't survive without wolves or other predators, and for wolves, who couldn't survive without deer. The same can be said for all of us—human and nonhuman alike—that we cannot long survive unless we cooperate with those around us.

It seems likely that no one living today will ever experience a fully natural interaction with either another human or nonhuman. All observations, including my own, are made as through a glass darkly, because we now live in a world of refugees.

The Yanomame Indians are a violent and misogynistic group of people, but how much of that violence has developed in defensive response to marauding Europeans? We shall never know what they were like before, nor will we know anything about peaceful groups. After encountering the Arawaks, Christopher Columbus wrote: "They have no iron or steel or weapons, nor are they capable of using them, although they are well-built people

of handsome stature, because they are wondrously timid. . . . [T]hey are so artless and free with all they possess, that no one could believe it without having seen it. Of anything they have, if you ask them for it, they never say no; rather they invite the person to share it, and show as much love as if they were giving their hearts; and whether the thing be of value or of small price, at once they are content with whatever little thing of whatever kind may be given to them." The Arawaks were exterminated for their kindness.

These are some observations that are worth our consideration. We know that groups of Yanomame who were better hidden from European influence are less misogynistic and less violent than their troubled cousins. Our violence has reversed the rule of co-operative natural selection, such that those who fight possibly survive, and those who don't fight will most likely die. The inverse is true as well: those who survive learn how to fight, or more precisely, those who survive learn by painful experience to deafen themselves to their own suffering, and the suffering of others. The deafness facilitates the perpetration of extreme violence since extreme violence and survival are now associated. The violence leads only to further deafness, each furthering the other in a spiral of attenuated feelings until at long last we mimic "beast-machines"—horribly frightened, and not so very rational after all.

I do not know what my brothers would have become without exposure to my father's violence. Nor do I know the same about my sisters or my mother. Nor also do I know what it would have been like to have a father whose parents had not transformed him through their own violence. With no notion of what a peaceful family or a peaceful culture or a peaceful culture might have to offer, I am now a refugee from my own childhood. The millions of rape victims around the world are refugees from a worldview that was not inevitable, but chosen. We all—human and nonhuman alike—are refugees from the war zone that is civilization.

We would not expect studies made of Russians fleeing the advance of Nazi panzers in World War II, or later suffering under the eyes of *einsatzgruppen,* to adequately reflect ordinary—

nonstressed—human behavior, so why do we assume that anthropological studies—by definition performed by members of the dominant culture or those at least partially assimilated, under rules devised by the dominant culture, for the benefit and perpetuation of that same culture—reveal any more about the ordinary—nonstressed—state of humans? The same can be asked about studies of nonhumans. What makes us think, as we systematically destroy their homes and exploit them, that they will act around us as they ordinarily do—perhaps fearlessly, perhaps cooperatively—or even that they are any more capable of acting as they would have before?

What happens to those who are so stupid—or perhaps so principled—that they do not modify their behavior to protect themselves in this war zone? The dodos, a product of their benign environment, were fearless when they first encountered Europeans. We cured them of that fearlessness by destroying them, as we cured the Arawak people, the passenger pigeon, the Eskimo curlew.

The violence of civilization provides us with two options. We can distance ourselves from the world of experience, sense, and emotion, or we can die. I've tried the first, and I'm not ready for the second. We need a third option.

Breaking Out

"The world of the concentration camps . . . was not an exceptionally monstrous society. What we saw there was the image, and in a sense the quintessence, of the infernal society into which we are plunged every day."
Eugène Ionesco

I'M NOT SUGGESTING THAT there is no selfishness in the world, nor that the world would be a better place if we'd "stop acting so selfishly." We *would* be better off if we were to act in our own best interest. No one benefitted from my childhood. No one benefits from rape. Hitler benefited no one, not even himself. Who benefits from the production of plutonium? Who benefits from the production of weapons of mass destruction? Who benefits from the use of pesticides? Who benefits from the eradication of indigenous peoples? Answer: no one you know, or would care to meet. To believe we're acting out of self-interest would be to buy into the presumption that our way of living serves us well, and that the destruction is merely an unfortunate by-product, a grotesque trade-off made by the rest of the world.

There's a sense in which the last part of this equation is true: the hyperconsumerism that marks our way of life is predicated on the exploitation of human and nonhuman "resources" worldwide who pay with their own misery—remember the 150,000,000 children enslaved; the billion chickens per year crammed into metal cages—to create monetarily cheap consumables. But the second half does not equal the first: the consumer lifestyle does not lead to living well, and it is not in anyone's best interest. This is not to say that, all other things being equal, and remaining snugly within the constricting framework of our culture, I would rather be poor than rich. But that is part of the problem: by systematically eliminating alternatives— try to withdraw from the cash-and-wage economy and live in the United States as a hunter-gatherer—we've confined ourselves in a kind of prison.

Just as at Auschwitz, or in other situations of perpetual trauma, circumstances can be created in which people are so oppressed and their options so narrowly circumscribed that it pays to exploit others, to make certain that they themselves get the easier job or the last scrap of potato, to make certain they can hop like a frog longer than the people who must be killed that day (or in our case, receive a pink slip). In a concentration camp, it is better (in terms of maintaining physical life: spiritual life is an entirely different question) to be the killer than the killed, better to be a collaborator than a resister, a guard than a collaborator, a supervisor than a guard, and better still to be the boss. But of course it would be better to not be in the camp at all.

Our way of life presupposes that it's in our best interest to coerce others into doing what we want them to do. This presupposition is manifested in our economics—by definition, the purpose of capitalism is to amass enough wealth to put others to work for you—and it's enshrined in our scientific explanation of the world. As the influential sociobiologist Richard Dawkins puts it: "Natural selection favours genes which control their survival machines [*survival machines* and *lumbering robots* are, sadly enough, two terms Dawkins uses for humans and other living beings] in such a way that they make the best use of their environment. This includes making the best use of other survival machines, both of the same and of different species." But this presupposition—that it's in our best interest to exploit others—is valid only for the extremely confining and specific circumstances of people living under constant threat of trauma, those who cannot afford to build and maintain relationships. Do we "make the best use of" our friends? If so, what does that say about our friendships? I remember once hearing an economist speak about "the way people are." He evoked his teenage years when he shared milkshakes with friends, two straws to a glass, and each would pull on the straw for all he was worth, trying to get the most shake. My own teenage experience was far different; my friends and I would generally insist the other take the last of whatever we were sharing. The relationship, and my friend's feelings, were always more important than the material at hand. To take more than my share would have meant the end of a friendship.

Part of the reason we've been able to convince ourselves that by exploiting others we're acting in our own best interest is that we've accepted a severely constricted definition of self. My father may have gotten off during his visits to my room late at night, but what did that do to his soul and to our relationship? Is it in a father's best interests to terrorize his son, to establish control through a hierarchy based on size and strength? It's all very well and good for the authors of *Demonic Males* to theorize that "it could pay the woman to acknowledge the rapist's power and form a relationship that, while initially repellent, she comes to accept," and that "a demonstration of power implies that the female's safest future is to bond with the violent male," but in the real world, where real men rape real women, where real fathers rape real children, where the real activities of our culture are destroying the real world, who are the real beneficiaries? "Like successful Chicago gangsters," Richard Dawkins has written, "our genes have survived, in some cases for millions of years, in a highly competitive world. This entitles us to expect certain qualities in our genes. I shall argue that a predominant quality to be expected in a successful gene is ruthless selfishness. This gene selfishness will usually give rise to selfishness in individual behavior." How pathetic this is, that in an attempt to rationalize our actions, we have at last given up claims that our destructive, irrational, behavior is even in our best interests as human beings, and have sunk to redefining our very selves as nothing more than "survival machines," "lumbering robots" driven to insane action by the "selfish" desires of our genetic material. The Christian hatred of the body merges here with Cartesian solipsism to conjure ourselves entirely out of subjective existence.

It is time to return to the real world. If my brothers were to die, I would feel pain and loss: they are a part of me as surely as my hands, my fingers, or the hours of my life. If my mother were to die, or my sisters, I would feel pain. Each of my friends is a part of me, connected by bonds at least as strong, though not so visible, as skin.

I love the land where I live, the trees—the coyote tree, the grandfather ponderosa, and others—the dogs, cats, birds, coyotes, spiders, ticks, even the mice. How can we be so poor as to define ourselves as an ego tied in a sack of skin, or worse, as lumbering automatons pressed into service by gangsterish genes? We are the relationships we share, we are that process of relating, we are, whether we like it or not, permeable—physically, emotionally, spiritually, experientially—to our surroundings. I am the bluebirds and nuthatches that nest here each spring, and they, too, are me. Not metaphorically, but in all physical truth. I am no more than the bond between us. I am only so beautiful as the character of my relationships, only so rich as I enrich those around me, only so alive as I enliven those I greet.

The boundaries of the concentration camp are not made up of landmines and electrified wire. There are no guards posted to shoot us if we stray. We need not take the whip from the hands of the guards, nor use it to strike those beneath us. It's all much simpler than that. We need only walk away, and re-enter the world in all its unity.

No one emerges from trauma unscarred. Having been severely traumatized, it becomes the work of at least a lifetime to denormalize the trauma—to recognize it for the aberration it is—and to begin to reinhabit your body, your senses, your mind, to reinhabit relationships, to reinhabit a world you perceive as having betrayed you.

Only recently have I learned that not everyone awakens in the night to listen for the sound of the door creaking open, or at four in the morning stares hard into the darkness of a room intentionally blackened, searching for the black-on-black of a silhouette. Throughout my twenties, I checked the room each night, and though I never found anyone hiding under the bed, or in the closet, I continued to enact the fear I learned as a child. Even now I often put my clothes hamper in front of the door, not expecting it to stop anyone, but instead mechanically manifesting my childhood prayer: *Do not let him come for me when I sleep. Do not let him catch me unready. Let me be awake always, so when he comes, I can go away.* A few nights ago I dreamed my father was raping me, saying again and again as he interminably came, "I am going to make you like me. I am going to make you normal."

I have my poison; you have yours. *Name it. Walk away from it.* But it's terrifying. There are landmines. I can see them, having grown up with them. There is barbed wire. I do not like this concentration camp, but I believe the world is no different.

. . .

Having passed through trauma, we have a choice we must revisit for the rest of our lives: attempt to denormalize the trauma, or try to make the trauma feel normal. If the barriers are too frightening, the landmines too real, we can try to rationalize, to normalize what happened to us. This also helps rationalize what we're doing to others. This process of normalizing is central to the fabrication of claims to virtue. It is also central to the way Western science and religion manifest themselves.

Examples of this normalization are as near as today's paper. A local couple is on trial for animal abuse. After receiving complaints for a number of years, sheriffs raided their puppy mill. The officers found a dog with exposed bone where a fractured jaw had healed, several with protruding intestines, and several more with neck lacerations from constricting collars. There was one mother trying to feed nearly forty puppies. Thirty-five of the adult dogs had to be killed. The couple's defense in court? They owned those dogs. They cited Psalms 8: "Thou madest him [man] to have dominion over the works of thy hands; thou hast put all *things* under his feet: All sheep and oxen, yea, and the beasts of the field; The fowl of the air, and the fish of the sea, *and whatsoever* passes through the paths of the seas." The emphasis—that beasts of the field are *things*—is in the original.

The judge evidently had no choice but to find them guilty of some of the charges. He then delivered an attack which the newspaper called blistering. He did not attack the defendants but instead "overzealous animal rights activists" who called for justice in the first place.

What do you do, how tired do you get, when each day you struggle against an entire culture based on the normalization of trauma-inducing behavior? There is no sanctuary.

Last winter, ice came in a rain that froze the instant it touched any solid surface. Then more rain, more ice, until the night shone, every blade of grass, every needle on every pine tree a prism for the moonlight that eventually poked through the clouds.

A crust covered the snow and an inch-thick sheath of ice dressed trees, wires, and rocks. Branches fell. Entire trees snapped under the weight, cracking like rifle reports in the deathly-still night. Cars couldn't negotiate the black-ice. Power failed all over town. When clouds returned, the night was as dark as dark can be, as night was before the dawn of our culture. Then the moon reemerged, its light refracting through the thousands of tiny spears.

It was cold. I sat near the fire until something—someone— called me outside. I felt the same urgency I'd felt the day I first looked out to see the coyote sneaking up. I knew this call was not from the coyotes, though I didn't know who it was.

I began to walk toward the mailbox, but my feet carried me in the opposite direction, into the forest. I was walking toward the coyote tree. I walked faster, each step making two sounds as first I broke through the ice, then packed the snow underneath. Doubled grasses swayed or snapped as I brushed against them, and trees were breaking, perhaps four to the minute, like a desultory firefight. I began to run.

I got to the coyote tree. The break was jagged and fresh, no ice. I kissed and stroked the wound, then put my arms around the standing trunk, pressing my face into its smooth coldness. I kissed it. I didn't know what else to do. Stroking the ice-covered bark, I said, "It will be all right. You'll be okay." I didn't know if this was true. I also said, "I love you."

What is the appropriate response to a friend's injury, when to remedy the injury or even ameliorate the pain is beyond your power? I held the tree that night, and held others, and tried to give back at least a little of what over the years they have given me.

During the massacre at Sand Creek ("I can hit the son of a bitch. Let me try him") two women and their children were able to escape, but they soon realized that they were lost. They took refuge in a cave too shallow to hold off the cold. Late at night a large wolf entered the cave, and lay next to them. At first they were frightened, but at least they were warm. The next day the wolf walked with them, resting when they rested. Finally one of the women said, "O Wolf, try to do something for us. We and our children are nearly starved." The wolf led them to a freshly killed buffalo. They ate. Walking with them for the next few weeks, the wolf found food for them when they were hungry, and protected them from both humans and nonhumans. At last he led them to their people, the Cheyenne, and after receiving food, he disappeared.

Things don't have to be the way they are.

The story I've recounted is merely an anecdote told by a nonscientific people. Who are the witnesses? They are irrational people making nonscientific observations.

If we decide the story is a metaphor, we need not call them liars, but we also need not reconsider our worldview. The women and children *took on the qualities* they observed in wolves, huddling together in a shallow cave, perhaps even finding an old wolf skin to wrap around themselves to stay warm. They stalked buffalo, and found a fresh kill. Maybe they even chased away wolves. They avoided white men as the wolves, too, had learned to avoid them, and eventually found their way home. Our perception of physical reality must be based on solid scientific evidence, not fairy tales.

I once asked a scientist friend of mine what it would take to convince her that interspecies communication is real. She said, "If an animal were to act against its nature after you asked it to, I'd reconsider."

Leaving aside the question of what defines an animal's nature, I asked, "Like a pack of coyotes not eating chickens?"

"Not good enough."

I suppose that was a polite way of saying she didn't believe me. I told her how the Chipewyan Indian children frequently found wolf dens in order to play with the pups, and told her that we don't even have to take the Indians' word for it: the eighteenth-century explorer Samual Hearne, the first white man to explore northern Canada, described it: "I never knew a Northern Indian [to] hurt one of them; on the contrary, they always put them carefully into the den again; and I have sometimes seen them paint the faces of the young wolves with vermillion, or red ochre."

She didn't say anything, so I pulled a book off the shelf and told her about an incident at a wildlife refuge in New Jersey. A population explosion of whitetail deer prompted managers to allow hunting there. Many people opposed the hunt, so some areas of the refuge remained off-limits. "A funny thing happened," stated a manager, "and I would not have believed it had I not seen it happen. For a couple of days prior to the hunt, we spotted numerous deer leaving the area to be hunted, swimming the Passaic River into the area that was closed to hunting. It was as though someone had tipped them off. And hunting season hadn't even begun." I told my friend that every experienced hunter I know often witnesses this same thing: bucks feed openly in fields a few days before the season opens, then disappear before the shooting begins.

She continued to look at me, her face blank, and I could tell she was losing patience. I pushed ahead, and told her about the Gaddy Goose Refuge. In the mid-1930s, a North Carolina farmer named Lockhart Gaddy began feeding Canada geese at his farm. Soon, there were so many that tourists began to visit. The geese felt safe: at neighboring farms they wouldn't allow anyone within a quarter-mile of them, but at Gaddy's they allowed tourists to touch them. Both birds and visitors continued to increase until there were nearly 30,000 Canada geese, and as many human visitors. In 1953 Gaddy died of an apparent heart attack while feeding the geese. His wife, Hazel, said there was silence among the 10,000 birds there at the time. Gaddy was buried on a mound fifty feet from the goose pond in a grove of trees. Witnesses commented that on the day of the funeral the geese were silent. After it was over, they paraded to the grave, walking all around and over it time and again. The number of geese visiting the refuge continued to increase until Mrs. Gaddy's death in the early 1970s. A relative of the Gaddys' took over, but the geese apparently communicated to one another that the Gaddys were no more, and by 1975 the refuge had to be closed because the geese were gone. Although large V-shaped formations continue to fly overhead during their autumn migration, they never land anymore.

"Nice story," she said. "What's your point?"

I closed my eyes and thought, then told her the story of the wolf taking care of Indians after Sand Creek.

Exasperated, she said, "This is not evidence. These are just stories. They don't mean anything. Give me hard science. Give me something reproducible." A long silence between us. She crossed her arms and looked down. She reached with her right hand to stroke her chin. Finally looking back up, she said, "You know, there is nothing you can say that would convince me."

I was exasperated, too. I was angered by her dogmatic faith masquerading as skepticism. I thought about saying a lot of things, but instead grabbed some other sources, and said, "Okay, I'll give you the only sort of reproducibility our culture can create with regard to human-wolf relations. 1630: 'It is ordered [in the Colony of Massachusetts Bay], that there should be 10 shillings a piece allowed for such wolves as are killed.' 1645: 'Mr. Bartholomew, John Johnson, Mr. Sprauge, Mr. Winsley, & Mr. Hubbard are chosen a committee to consider the best ways and means to destroy the wolves which are such ravenous cruel creatures, & daily vexations to all the inhabitants of the colony.' 1854: 'All hands were preparing meat in pieces about two inches square, cutting a slit in the middle and opening it and putting a quantity of strychnine in the center and closing the parts upon it. . . . One morning after putting out the poison, they picked up sixty-four wolves. . . . The proceeds from that winter's hunt [sic] were over four thousand dollars.' 1872: 'Before proceeding to skin the dead wolves, the Mexicans [hired by an outfit in Kansas] captured this old fellow [a wolf "who was exceedingly sick"] and haltered him, by carbine straps, to the horns of the buffalo carcasses, near which he sat on his haunches, with eyes yellow from rage and fright. . . . Man never appreciates the wonderful command that God gave him over the other animals until surrounded by the wild beasts of the solitudes, in all their native fierceness.' 1871: 'Not far above this [temporary village built by wolf and buffalo hunters] was a road going thro the swampy creek valley, about 75 yards wide, and this had been artistically and scientifically paved with gray wolf carcasses.' 1900: 'I can not believe that Providence intended these rich lands, broad, well watered, fertile and waving with abundant pasturage, close by mountains and valleys, filled with gold, and every metal and mineral, should forever be monopolized by wild beasts and savage men. I believe in the survival of the fittest, and hence I have "fit" for it all my life. . . . The wolf is the enemy of civilization, and I want to exterminate him.'"

We stared at each other for a long moment, then she looked away. I should have stopped, but I didn't. I told her that after killing all but one of the pups in a den, government officers would chain the last one to a tree, and then shoot all the adults who tried to rescue the frightened pup. After being trapped, wolves would be collared with a leather belt, tied to a stake, and—jaw wired shut—either left to die of dehydration or to be dismembered by the hunters' dogs. Wolves were lassoed and then dragged to their death. I told her that even today, wolves are shot from airplanes, poisoned with strychnine, cyanide. Killed.

Is it any wonder, I asked my friend, that we do not observe them coming to us in the dark, that they do not feed us, care for us, and lead us home? Is it any wonder they run frightened from us?

It should be clear by now, I said, after all these years, all these extinctions, all these lost opportunities for redemption and community, that somewhere along the line, to switch from Latinate to Anglo-Saxon roots, we fucked up. And today? We're still fucking up. We still believe we stand alone atop the world. But it has to stop. At some point we will finally have to look around and see if anyone is still able, and willing, to lead us home.

She shifted uncomfortably in her chair. I wondered if I had said too much.

I majored in economics at graduate school. The main lesson I learned was about the primacy of process, that when I act from indirect intentions, roadblocks arise, requiring force of will to maintain my course in direct proportion to that course's distance from my heart.

Here's what I mean: I went to graduate school not because I particularly cared about economics, but so I could continue high jumping. When I'd graduated from college, I'd felt as though a part of me had died too soon. I'd only jumped for two and a half years, and with just another year I thought I could qualify for, and maybe even win, the Division II national championship.

But even that possibility didn't motivate me as much as the unfettered joy of the sport. I loved the utter loss of self-consciousness as I stood up, the glide of the approach, the softness of takeoff—more an inevitability, a falling upward, than a thrust—the eerie, erotic smoothness of clearing the bar. The sport was a perfect fit for me. This doesn't mean I didn't work at it, for I did, but there is a difference between work for the sake of love, which provides its own motivation, and work for the sake of another end.

There's a Chinese term that encapsulates my high-jumping experience: *wu-wei,* which means *not doing,* not in the sense of *doing nothing,* but of *not forcing.* Not only were my best jumps unforced, but the flow of high jumping—from accidental discovery by the handball teacher, to his patient nurturance, to winning our conference championship—contrasted painfully with the larger, and largely forced, process of schooling.

The Roman philosopher Seneca wrote of a similar process of assistance or resistance: "The fates guide those who will; those who won't they drag." If earlier the fates had guided me into jumping, they now began to drag me away. Soon after signing up for classes, I discovered that the School of Mines had switched athletic associations, and the new association did not allow graduate students to compete. On hearing this I considered dropping out, but because I'd already jumped high enough to qualify for many regional and national meets, I kept attending school with the thought of jumping independently.

The fates didn't allow this, either. A few weeks later I injured my jump foot. Neither the trainers nor school doctors could find anything wrong, so I dealt with the injury the way I dealt with all pain, by walling it off. The positive form of the self's disappearance in jumping returned to its shadow as I forcefully separated myself from my body signals. I hopped to my mark on one foot, turned off the pain, ran the approach, jumped, allowed the pain back in, and hopped out of the pit. I kept hoping that if only I could deafen myself sufficiently to the pain, I could will myself over the bar, and was surprised at how poorly this worked. I kept jumping, and, as I later found out, kept rebreaking my foot—for X rays later revealed it to be broken—with every jump I forced myself to do.

Nor did classes work out. I majored in economics because it

was the easiest thing offered at the School of Mines, and because I'd enjoyed the half-dozen or so classes I'd already taken. I could only enjoy them, though, because I didn't take them seriously. While the goal of economics—as is also true of physics—consists of equations ostensibly created to describe real-life events, it does so poorly. In order to make equations manageable (thus allowing the pretension that life is manageable) economists must disregard or fudge variables that may be difficult or impossible to quantify. Thus today I can look in an economics textbook and see that $Wh \equiv B + M$, which means that wealth by definition equals bonds plus money, because, as the authors state, "bonds and money are the only stores of wealth." This example is not unfair: corporate accountants do not factor human happiness into their bottom lines, or the suffering of enslaved children. The voices of wild wolf and caged hen do not enter these equations. Like our science and our religion, corporate economics deafens us to corporeal life.

What's more ludicrous is that the equations fail to describe even our economic system. The equations I learned were based almost exclusively on the model of something called "the free market." It was hard for me to waste time learning equations based on something that doesn't exist: even Dwayne Andreas, former chief executive officer of the agribusiness transnational Archer Daniels Midland, admits, "There is not one grain of anything in the world that is sold in the free market. Not one. The only place you see a free market is in the speeches of politicians." You see the same thing in economics classes.

For our economics textbooks to have been accurate, they would need to be printed in blood. The blood of indigenous peoples destroyed so their land could be taken, bought, and sold. The blood of salmon, beaver, and buffalo commodified and killed for the money they have come to represent. The blood of all of us whose lives are diminished in the act of commodifying others. The blood of slaves and wage slaves who spend their lives toiling so their owners may have the leisure that is the birthright of every living being. The blood of the land itself, poisoned by "externalities," those cumbersome details too dark or difficult or inconvenient to take their place in the economic equations that guide so much of our lives. The blood of everyone who is silenced by economic theory. In the same vein as our science and religion, the most obvious function of our economics is the erection of a sociopolitical framework on which to base a system of exploitation.

I hung on through fall semester, and bailed in early spring. High jumping was a bust. The classes were meaningless, and were no longer fun. I remember a class in managerial economics, the textbook for which was Machiavelli's *The Prince.* The instructor told us our grade would be based on presentations, and because the business world is, as he put it, "a world of cutthroat competition," students were encouraged to sabotage other students' work. He gave the example of someone stealing the bulb from a slide projector when the presenter had left the room. Because the presenter had another bulb in his pocket, he received an A. I did not last the day; after hearing that story I packed away my notebook, slipped out the door, and went to the registrar's office to drop the class.

Economics

"The theories of Milton Friedman
gave him the Nobel Prize; they gave
Chile General Pinochet."
Eduardo Galeano

THE WORD economics comes from the Greek *ta oikonomika,* which means *the science of household management.* It is how one takes care of one's house. The word has suffered devaluation, and now means the management of money.

The word *ecocide* comes from Greek as well, *oikos,* meaning *house,* and *cidium,* meaning *to slay or destroy.* Ecocide is the destruction of a house.

It doesn't make much sense for me to raise chickens. Why should I go to the trouble of incubating chicks, keeping them in my bathtub, dumpster diving for food, and conversing with coyotes, when I can go to Albertson's and buy a package of drumsticks for less than a buck a pound?

Not much that we do in our personal lives makes much economic sense, just as most things we do for money make no sense in personal terms. It makes little economic sense for me to write this book: my pay will probably hover around a buck an hour (enough, at least, to buy a pound of chicken). From a fiscal standpoint, I'd be better off working at McDonald's. High jumping didn't pay. Friendships don't pay. It makes no economic sense to make love: it takes time, uses calories, and costs money if you use condoms or pills.

I suppose if we stretch the definition, making love can be made to fit into certain economic categories: my friend tells me the price for sex on East Sprague here in Spokane is fifty bucks for a lay, forty bucks for a blow, and a hundred for the woman to do whatever you want for an hour.

It could be argued that by moving swiftly from lovemaking to buying sex I am blurring distinctions that shouldn't be blurred. But that's what happens to any process when we turn it into an economic exchange, whether we're talking about a trick on East Sprague, a pound of chicken at Albertson's, or a book at Hastings or Borders. The complex and often murky processes—lovemaking in the first place; the gathering, raising, or killing of food (as well as more broadly our relations with other species) in the second; and in the third the process of exploring and articulating what it means to be alive and human—have been telescoped into commodities that can be quantified and transferred. *I'd like three books, two packages of chicken McNuggets, and a blow to go, please.* That which it is possible to reduce to a commodity and sell, is. That which can't, is either (by definition) devalued, ignored, or simply destroyed.

Let's get back to East Sprague, and to what must be lost in transition from intimate to commercial. Love is certainly lost, but what else? Perhaps nothing. Perhaps the transition merely demystifies—removes the shroud of projection, of unnecessary and cumbersome mystery—to reveal what, at base, is really there: friction on skin, stimulation of nerve endings, lubrication, seminal emission. Nothing else. Perhaps our economics reduces it as surely and cleanly as does our science to what is reproducible and quantifiable in any laboratory, to what is real: we have time of erection, cubic centimeters and chemical content of semen, chemical content of the woman's lubrication (if you pay fifty). With the right equipment we could track the chemicals in the man's brain as he comes, and those in the woman's brain as she thinks of something else.

Here's the problem: in this tidy world of economic categories, there's no room for love, joy, mystery, for the sometimes confused and confusing, sometimes clear and clarifying, sometimes beautiful, sometimes magical suction of body on body, skin on skin, soul on soul. The process of lovers entangling and moving together figures little in the exchanges on East Sprague.

But I suppose even within the context of a relationship we could twist sexuality to make it fit within economic categories: I give pleasure in order to receive an equal amount of pleasure. It's an economic exchange as surely as if money changed hands, with the currency now caresses. But as was the case for the two friends sucking on straws, this description of economic selfishness does not describe the process as I experience it. My experience—and this is true not just about sexuality—is quite the opposite of what our economic philosophy would suggest. The purpose—and this, too, is true for all of life—is in the giving, sharing, and receiving wrapped inextricably into a single thread.

Our economics, as is true of our science, represents the triumph of product over process, and form over content. It is the triumph of selective deafness and blindness over conscience and relationship. I don't care how miserable was the chicken's life nor how poisonous the hormones, just give me cheap and juicy drumsticks. I don't care that the prostitute is probably poor and was sexually abused as a child, nor that the encounter will be devoid of emotional content, just get me off. My shoes were made in an Indonesian sweatshop? I don't have the money to buy socially and ecologically friendly shoes that cost twice as much. It doesn't matter that the production of my toilet paper came at the expense of clearcut mountainsides, sedimented streams, and rivers poisoned with dioxin; I cannot afford, once again, to buy the unbleached and recycled stuff that goes for fifty cents a roll.

One of the problems with our economic system is that money is valued over all else. That is enough to guarantee widespread misery, degradation, and ultimately the destruction of most, if not all, life on this planet. It is axiomatic that people will not pay for that which they can get for free. This means that with certain notable exceptions—professional athletes, many of the self-employed, creative workers such as artists, scientists, members of the helping professions, and so on—most people will not get paid for doing what they would otherwise do, what they love: why should someone pay if you will do it anyway? Another way to say this is that as with grades, if implicit motivation is there, there's no reason for external reward. The counter of this is also true, that oftentimes monetary rewards substitute for implicit motivation. What this means is that so long as money is valued—and in fact necessary—a great percentage of people will end up spending a great deal of time doing things they don't want to do.

Prior to contact with our culture, it was common for members of indigenous cultures throughout the world to live "a careless life." Indeed, the Khoikhoi were said to "scarcely admit either force or rewards for reclaiming them from that innate lethargick humor. Their common answer to all motives of this kind, is, that the fields and woods provide plenty of necessaries for their support, and nature has amply provided for their subsistence, by loading the trees with plenty of almonds . . . and by dispersing up and down many wholesome brooks and pure rivolets to quench their thirst. So that there is no need of work. . . . And thus many of them idly spend the years of a useless restive life."

Because our cash economy is predicated on the idea of a society composed of atomistic individuals pulling in selfish directions, it can do no other than reward selfish behavior. Communal behavior is not rewarded in this system, which means the cash economy can do no other than destroy communities. It damages relationships, too, not only because relationships consist of processes, not products, and are thus invisible to the system, but also because any relationship based on atomistic individuals pulling in selfish directions is not a relationship at all. And our cash economy can do no other than destroy life on the planet, because life has neither value nor voice, whereas resources, for example two-by-fours, while still voiceless, have value. Given the system of rewards, it is a surprising testament to the tenacity of life that any viable natural communities persist. It is an open question as to how much longer they will do so.

Our economics promises a life of increasing ease, which would put us back where we started so many rapes, clearcut forests, and extirpated species ago. For those of us rich enough to reap its benefits, our economic system offers a life devoid of experience; as though life, and experience, were a hassle. I can buy fast food. I can buy fast sex. I can buy fast ideas. It is as though our goal were to pass our days comfortably in an embryonic hot tub, television turned on for community so we need never relate to another living being, umbilical cord attached so we need neither chew nor swallow. This kind of withdrawal makes sense for a traumatized people who believe that they've been forced to inhabit a treacherous world filled with selfish individuals. But if the world is not as they believe, then how sad that we avoid relationships to avoid the hassle.

Had I been satisfied to buy shrink-wrapped drumsticks at

the grocery store, I may never have begun a conversation with coyotes, nor had the honor of meeting that brave Pekin who taught me about death. I would never have dug in a dumpster for the birds, nor felt the communion of generosity with that homeless man. I may not have paid attention to the complaint of the mice, nor the contempt of the lone red coyote. I may never have begun this exploration, with the richness of understanding it has brought to me.

It's true as well that had I not attended the School of Mines, I would not have high jumped, and had my father not abused me, I may never have been sufficiently alienated from our culture to see it for what it is. Negative experiences can lead to joy and understanding. Life is untidy. When we reject this messiness—and in so doing reject life—we risk perceiving the world through the lens of our economics or our science. But if we celebrate life with all its contradictions, embrace it, experience it, and ultimately live with it, there is the chance for a spiritual life filled not only with pain and untidiness, but also with joy, community, and creativity.

Last December I saw an advertisement outside an electronics store. There was a little boy, delirious with delight, surrounded by computers, stereos, and other gadgets. The text read: "We know what your child wants for Christmas." I stared at the poster, then said to no one in particular, "What your child wants for Christmas is your love, but if he can't get that, he'll settle for a bunch of electronic crap."

Don't look at my finger. Look at the moon. The point of this book is not to excoriate our culture. To believe that any one thing is "the problem" would be to believe that if we simply reform our economic system, everything will be okay, or if we reform science, or Christianity, or if I simply wait for my father to die, then everything will suddenly be fine.

But it won't be fine. We need to look deeper. Ours is not the only deathly economics to evolve, and Christianity is not the only body-, woman-, and earth-hating tradition. Women have also been raped, killed, and mutilated to serve Allah. The Hindu code of Manu V decrees that "A woman must never be free of subjugation," and there have been many indigenous cultures as virulently misogynistic as our own. Other systems of knowledge have blinded people to physical reality and have deafened them to the suffering of others as surely as Western science. Other cultures have screwed up the environment, though none with the intensity, scope, enthusiasm, or finality with which we have approached this task.

But not every culture has done these things.

Don't look at my finger. Look at the moon.

We need to look beyond, to the urges that inform, to the hidden wounds and presumptions that lead first to the conceptualization and later implementation of our economics, our science, our religion, our misogyny and child abuse. An economics like ours can emerge only from a consciousness like ours, and only a consciousness like ours can give rise to an economics like ours. To change our economics, science, religion, or our intimate relations with humans and nonhumans, we must fundamentally change our consciousness, and in so doing fundamentally change the way we perceive the world. Try to see the patterns. Look. Look again, and look a third time. Listen.

Make no mistake, our economic system can do no other than destroy everything it encounters. That's what happens when you convert living beings to cash. That conversion, from living trees to lumber, schools of cod to fish sticks, and onward to numbers on a ledger, is *the* central process of our economic system. Psychologically, it is the central process of our enculturation; we are most handsomely rewarded in direct relation to the manner in which we can help increase the Gross National Product.

It's unavoidable: so long as we value money more highly than living beings and more highly than relationships, we will continue to see living beings as resources, and convert them to cash; objectifying, killing, extirpating. This is true whether we're talking about fish, fur-bearing mammals, Indians, day-laborers, and so on. If monetary value is attached to something it will be exploited until it's gone. This story is oft-repeated and oft-ignored. Take the great auk, also called the spearbill in tribute to its massive bill, and called by the Spanish and Portuguese *pinguin,* which means *the fat one,* in reference to the soft jumpsuit of blubber that enveloped it. This flightless bird was common throughout Europe, existing side-by-side with humans as far south as the Mediterranean coast of France. By the year 900, the great auk was no longer perceived as a neighbor; it had become a commodity. It was slaughtered commercially for the oil derived from its fat, and for its soft elastic feathers. By the mid-seventeenth century, hyperexploitation had killed all but one of the great auk nesting sites in Europe, and that was destroyed before 1800.

In North America, too, humans coexisted with great auks for thousands of years, perhaps thousands of human generations. But they didn't develop an economics requiring the objectification of all others, and so the relationship continued. Humans smoked auk meat to eat through winter; they ate their eggs; they rendered fat into oil which they stored in sacks made from the birds' inflated gullets; they dried the contents of eggs, then ground them into flour from which they made winter pudding. Humans did all this, season after season, generation after generation, causing no appreciable harm to the birds. I do not know what these humans gave to great auks in return, but I would stake any hope I have for continued human existence on the belief that the humans gave something back to these stately black birds, with their powerful lungs and wings made for diving and undersea propulsion. Perhaps all they gave back was the right for them to be.

The earliest description we have of a North American encounter between Europeans and great auks ends, as these encounters always do, in tragedy for the natives: "Our two barcques were sent off to the island to procure some of the birds, whose numbers were so great as to be incredible. . . . In less than half-an-hour our two barcques were laden with them as if laden with stones." The next year another chronicler noted, "This island is so exceedingly full of birds that all the ships of France might load a cargo of them without anyone noticing that any had been removed." Having been noticed by members of our culture, the fate of the great auk was sealed.

They were slaughtered for their meat, which was sold. They

were slaughtered for their oil, which was sold. They were slaughtered for their feathers, which were sold. Their eggs were taken for markets in Boston and New York. Wrote an Englishman: "These Penguins are as big as geese and . . . they multiply so infinitely upon certain flat islands that men drive them from hence upon a board into their boats by the hundreds at a time, as if God had made the innocency of so poor a creature to become such an abundant instrument in the sustenation of man."

At last, around the turn of the nineteenth century, bans were placed upon the killing of remnant auk populations. The bans, being as nominal as environmental restrictions are today, were of course ignored, and the last known rookery was destroyed in 1802. But one colony, a tiny one of perhaps 100 individuals, remained, near Iceland. Word of this colony finally reached Europe, and collectors quickly offered a local merchant high prices for eggs. By 1843, most of the birds were gone, and on June 3, 1844, three fishermen killed the last two auks, and smashed the last auk egg.

It would be easy for me to hate that local merchant and his three hirelings for what they did to the world in general, and to me in particular, when they eradicated these creatures. But as with Chivington, Hitler, Descartes, Bacon, the authors of the Bible, "free market" economist Milton Friedman, and so on *ad nauseum,* these men were not alone. They had, and continue to have, an entire culture for company. A bureaucrat with the Canadian Department of Fisheries and the Ocean stated the matter perfectly. His honesty is frightening: "No matter how many there may have been, the Great Auk had to go. They must have consumed thousands of tons of marine life that commercial fish stocks depend on. There wasn't room for them in any properly managed fishery. Personally, I think we ought to be grateful to the old timers for handling the problem for us."

Any being that sparks economic interest is doomed. Eskimo curlews, passenger pigeons, puffins, teals, plovers, all these and more were exterminated or diminished by the insatiable lust for killing that our economics both rationalizes and rewards.

Sea mink, exterminated for their fur. Beavers, decimated. Wolverines. Fisher, marten, otter. Buffalo, wood bison, pronghorn antelope. Salmon: "A ball could not have been fired into the water without striking a salmon." Cod: "So thick by the shore that we hardly have been able to row a boat through them." Halibut. Herring: "I have seen 600 barrels taken in one sweep of a seine net. Often sufficient salt cannot be procured to save them and they are used as manure." Capelin: "We would stand up to our knees in a regular soup of them, scooping them out with buckets and filling the wagons until the horses could scarcely haul them off the beaches. You would sink to your ankles in the sand, it was that spongy with capelin eggs. We took all we needed for bait and for to manure the gardens, and it was like we'd never touched them at all, they was so plenty."

You or I could catch all the fish we could ever eat, cut all the trees we could ever use, kill all the animals whose skins we could wear, and we still would not destroy the planet. Or rather, we could kill all that is given to us only so willingly as we give back. What the hell use would it be for me to overfish West Medical Lake, where just tonight I caught my dinner? Why would I possibly take every fish? They would rot. It makes more sense to leave them so I can come back next week or next year, or never. Why should I stop them from living out their lives in their own manner?

Right now in the Bering Sea forty-five trawlers, each larger than a football field, drop nets thousands of yards long and catch up to 80 tons of fish per day. These ships can remain at sea for months, catching sea lions, seals, pollock, whales, halibut: anything that crosses their paths. Most of what they catch is not worth any money, so it is simply shredded and dumped back in the ocean. If none of the eighty tons of fish could be converted to cash, no sane people would ever want to kill so many, which is itself powerful support for the thesis that our economic system makes us crazy, or at least manifests prior insanity, or both.

But money doesn't rot. It doesn't swim away to live another day. It doesn't fight back. It doesn't disappear to the bottom of the ocean. It doesn't get eaten by other fish.

Like the Christian heaven far from Earth, and like the roboroaches made more pleasing by the removal of their wings and the insertion of electrodes to facilitate their control, money perfectly manifests the desires of our culture. It is safe. It neither lives, dies, nor rots. It is exempt from experience. It is meaningless and abstract. By valuing abstraction over living beings, we seal not only our own fate, but the fates of all those we encounter.

The Goal Is the Process

"It's life that matters, nothing but life—the process of discovering, the everlasting and perpetual process, not the discovery itself, at all."
Fyodor Dostoyevsky

WHAT'S THE POINT? Is it to accumulate wealth? If you were to ask 10,000 people if their main goal is to accumulate wealth and material possessions, the overwhelming majority would say *no*. But if the answer to this question were to be based not on their words, but on how they spend most of their waking hours, the answer would be a resounding *yes*.

What if the point of life has nothing to do with the creation of an ever-expanding region of control? What if the point is not to keep at bay all those people, beings, objects, and emotions that we so needlessly fear? What if the point instead is to let go of that control? What if the point of life, the primary reason for existence, is to lie naked with your lover in a shady grove of trees? What if the point is to taste each other's sweat and feel the delicate pressure of finger on chest, thigh on thigh, lip on cheek? What if the point is to stop, then, in your slow movements to-gether, and listen to birdsong, to watch dragonflies hover, to look at your lover's face, then up at the undersides of leaves moving together in the breeze? What if the point is to invite these others into your movement, to bring trees, wind, grass, dragonflies into your family and in so doing abandon any attempt to control them? What if the point all along has been to get along, to relate, and experience things on their own terms? What if the point is to feel joy when joyous, love when loving, anger when angry, thoughtful when full of thought? What if the point from the beginning has been to simply be?

When I went to graduate school that first time, I spent many evenings talking to an instructor in the English department. He mentored me for a year of independent study in creative writing, and we became friends. It was not uncommon for us to talk in his office till dawn. He was a Christian, and one night spoke of his belief: "Your faith must be strong enough that you can walk the path blindfolded."

Without thinking, I responded, "No. Wherever you put your

foot, there is the path. You become the path."

We looked at each other, stunned. At the time I had no clue as to the meaning of what I had just said, but I knew it was true.

Many years later, I taught at Eastern Washington University. The class was organized in a nonlinear fashion, similar to this book. In class we talked about anything: love, sex, death, abuse, money, fear, drugs, games, aspirations, god (with both a large and small *g*). We played hide-and-go-seek in an empty building. We played duck, duck, goose. We played capture the flag. We learned how to dance. Anything to help imbue our writing and our lives with feeling.

One quarter I had a student—a good writer and thinker—who often asked, especially when we greatly deviated from the subject of writing, "What's the point?" I usually had no answer, and so merely smiled and shrugged. Sometimes I said, "To have fun," and sometimes, "I don't know."

On the last day of class I stood at the chalkboard while they called out memories of the class time we'd spent together. I wrote them down as fast as I could, covering board after board. Finally we began to slow, and I heard the same student ask, "What's the point?"

I turned around, and the class laughed. I laughed, too, but before I could shrug a woman slammed her hand down on her desk and cried, "I get it! The point is that he can't tell us the point. The point is that we have to get it ourselves!"

I walked to the empty seat next to hers, sat down, placed the chalk on her desk, and said, "There's nothing else I can teach you. Thank you. Have fun."

I was raised a fundamentalist Christian. Many of my best memories happened because of our belief that one should not participate in secular activities on Sabbath, that is, from Saturday sundown to Sunday sundown. No shopping, no television, no movies, no sports (although made-up games *were* acceptable in my family). No books were allowed that weren't either about the Bible or nature.

The observance of Sabbaths was admittedly a little too legalistic in its implementation. We often counted the minutes till sundown on Sunday so we could watch the end of a baseball game or pick up a novel, and my siblings often left early for movies on the rationale that the theaters were in the shade of a mountain, and therefore the movie did not technically begin till after the sun had gone down on the spot where they sat.

Fortunately my family did not adhere to the dictionary definition of *secular,* which is *pertaining to the world or to things not spiritual or sacred.* It is a horrifying definition. But the natural world was considered sacred enough in my family to permit me to take long, rambling walks among Creation, for which I am thankful. In retrospect my childhood Sabbaths became a time to think and not think, a time to wander, a time to sit. They became a blessing, a joy, a refuge.

I often spent Sabbaths in the pasture, looking at ants and grasshoppers, or wading through the irrigation ditch catching crawdads and garter snakes. I would like to say my intentions were always benign, but they were not. Most times I was content to watch, but sometimes I mixed ants from different hills to watch them fight, or threw caterpillars in to watch the ants swarm. Often I caught grasshoppers to feed to the toads who lived in our window well.

Each spring brought new shoots of plants to nibble and taste, new tiny toads who danced in the grass, chest-deep water (icy cold from mountain glaciers) in the irrigation ditch, clumsy wasps on fresh spring wings, the reawakening of anthills, the return of robins and meadowlarks, the reemergence of my old friends the venerable window well toads.

Summer. Russian olives turned silver and cottonwoods dropped their fibrous snow. Flower followed flower, each one feeding bees and wasps and beetles for a week or two, then drying, losing petals, closing in on itself, and hardening to a seedpod. Willow, dandelion, sweet clover, alfalfa. Thunderstorms day by day, then no moisture at all, until grasses yellowed to brittle stalks in the heat of August. The irrigation ditch drained to pools, puddles, mud, dust, and the crawdads went away—I never knew where—for another year.

Sundays during fall I took long lone tramps with rations of peeled raw potatoes and apple bits my mother had cut for me.

Always I looked at bugs: at ants and their hills, more frenetic now; at wasps turned desperate and ill-tempered by the shortening of days and almost certainly the knowledge of their own impending deaths. I loved to look at the hard double, treble, or quadruple barrels of mud dauber nests; it never occurred to me to break one open to see inside, instead I just ran my fingers along them. In boggy shadows, armies of spiders dashed from plant to plant in miniature forests of mint.

And winter. Sundays then were mostly spent inside, with books, or talking to my pet turtle. Sometimes I went out, to be with the horses or cows, insects no longer being available. I looked close at the bark on trees, knobby or smooth, and felt the trees' cold-stiffened limbs. Warm winter days I got down on my knees to look at the still-living sheaths of last year's—and next year's—grasses, and moved the gritty soil between tongue and foreteeth, tasting sharpness, sweetness, and the gifts of next year's life.

It is spring. Today I took two chicks out to the coyote tree. Both of them so young to die, four days old, or perhaps five. One of them hatched with a crossed beak and only half a head, and had struggled from the beginning. It learned how to eat, how to drink, and then how to die. The other, in all seeming respects normal, thrived three days, began to cry on the fourth, and died later that night.

I carried them in the warm spring noontime. I walked past nuthatches beginning to nest in the birdhouses I attached to stacks of dead beeboxes—*I think I'll choose this one. No this one. But this one is so near to all these twigs.* I walked into the rocky woods to the east, past the fine white feathers of a goose dead a couple of weeks and through a broad meadow jumbled with volcanic rock, buttercups, and camas. I arrived at the coyote tree, half-mast relic struggling to survive, her top lying jagged and still green in the slough near her base. I touched her trunk—*How are you?*—and placed the dead chicks among the feathers of past offerings. I said to each chick, quietly, *Now you get to be wild. Go, little one, go.* I touched the tree one more time and climbed back to the rocky meadow.

In addition to the flowers, yellow, purple, I saw also surveyor's

The Goal Is the Process

153

stakes and the yellow of their flags. They're going to build here. Hundreds of houses and thousands of apartments. They. Developers, I guess you'd call them. I don't. Nor do I call them speculators (*speculate: to meditate; to contemplate; to consider a subject by turning it over in the mind and viewing it in its different aspects and relations*). Killers is probably the best name for them, because that's what they do. Developers. My dictionary defines *develop* as *to cause to become gradually fuller, larger, better.* A child develops into an adult; a caterpillar develops into a butterfly; a baby nuthatch—tiny, featherless—develops into an adult who can survive the winter by eating insects and insect eggs that if left alone would develop into adult insects, and a baby hummingbird—even more tiny and just as featherless—develops into an adult that can fly south, past pesticide-laden fields of monocrops, clearcuts, and poisoned waterways, to a warmer home for the winter, and then find her way back next year to make her so-tiny nest in the same boughs of these same pine trees, saying, like the nuthatch, *I think I'll choose this one.* But a beautiful rocky meadow, ripe with flowers, full of the coyote tree's struggle to survive, full of the dailiness of tiny flies and anthills and coyotes and deer and baby pine trees and the decaying feathers of chickens and ducks and geese and the falling snags of pine tree elders who died in last decade's fire: all this fullness does not develop into green-lawned and sterilized houses, or white box apartments.

I sometimes wonder if the coyote tree gave up last winter, if she used the ice storm as an excuse to leave behind a life she knew would no longer be so rich. Did she know what was coming? Do the salmon, too, and the frogs, and the salamanders, do they all know, and are they giving up to become ghosts because they no longer enjoy, no longer can tolerate what we have become?

Two weeks ago I had a dream, the worst of my life. I heard the voice of the Dreamgiver, resonant and caring. It said, "You work so hard to make a better future. Would you like to know what lies ahead?" I nodded ever-so-slightly. Then—how do I say this?—I saw nothing but black, nothing at all, and I heard nothing but my own screams, of horror and despair. I know from this dream that it is possible, in fact quite likely, that the future will be far worse than I can imagine, worse even than I can dream.

Perhaps bull trout, blue whales, and manatees wish as little as I to see this future.

It will not long slow the machine, but if I am not going to blow up dams, which for today I am still too frightened, too bound, too small in my own person to yet do, the least I can do is remove these stakes. I removed them, each and every one, and removed the flags from bushes and dead trees and the limbs of tall standing pines. After removing all these, I returned home to where the baby chicks, out of the bathtub where they stay through the chill of the too-early-spring nights and into the sunshine of the yard, were doing their dances of joy, leaping into the air and dashing back and forth, glad to be alive, glad to peck at the soft dust beneath their feet.

Heroes

"If I were permitted to write all
the ballads I need not care who
makes the laws of the nation."
Andrew Fletcher

STORIES TEACH US OUR social roles, and the people we look up to as heroes help validate who we are and what we feel. They help determine whom we become. When I was young, I watched the movie *Lawrence of Arabia* more times than I could count. Early in the film, Lawrence snuffs a match with his fingers. Another character tries this, and yelps that it hurts. At eight years old, I identified with and was profoundly encouraged by Lawrence's response: "Of course it hurts. The trick is not minding that it hurts." Among all the storybook characters I encountered, I unconsciously sought out one who supported my perception of reality, which was that in order to survive, one must not mind the pain. Other people, with different perceptions of reality, will choose different heroes. The heroes chosen, both personally and culturally, say much about who we are.

I went with Jeannette Armstrong to New Zealand. She is working on a book about what community feels like to indigenous people. She wants to understand how some indigenous communities have survived the dominant culture's onslaught while others have not. The Maori culture has. She asked me along because of my facility for asking questions, and because I do not understand community in my bones, and never will. As water may be transparent to fish, and as air is normally transparent to us, community is transparent to her. Similarly, although her culture has been devastated by civilization, my immersion in this culture gives me understanding and perspective forever denied her. I might think of questions she would not.

While there, we were to stay in *mareas,* or Maori common houses, and speak with Maori activists and artists. I was anxious about the sleeping arrangements, because the Maori, as is true for most indigenous peoples the world over, often sleep in huge rooms on pads strewn about the floor. I am a painfully light sleeper. With this in mind, I warily gauged each person's potential for thunderous snoring. I need not have worried: with the exception of the first night, when I covered my head with two pillows, a duffel bag, and a backpack, and still heard the rhythmic rumbling of the fellow next to me through my earplugs, I slept comfortably, well, deeply, and securely. The act of sleeping communally engenders communal intimacy.

The first evening, we went to dinner at *Tapu Te Ranga,* a marae built by the Maori writer Bruce Stewart. Probably sixty people were preparing or eating stews of seafood and greens, the latter picked from a nearby ditch. I was one of the few nonindigenous people there.

As we stood in line, Jeannette introduced me to another Maori writer, Witi Ihimaera. He looked at me closely, then said, "You're not indigenous. Are you white?"

"It's the culture of my birth."

"What do you mean?"

"I mean, I see it for what it is."

He looked to Jeannette and I followed his gaze. Her face was hard to read. He looked back to me and asked, "What are you, then? Do you want to be indigenous?"

I laughed. "No, and I couldn't be if I wanted. I suppose I'm a nonwhite white."

He nodded, then said, more a comment than a question, "And you're a writer."

I nodded in return, then reached to fill my bowl with stew.

He continued, "Then I have a question for you. If someone were to help you see and experience something powerful and inexplicable, something considered impossible by most Westerners, would you write about it?"

"That depends on whether the people who helped me gave their permission."

He smiled, somewhat formally, then asked, "What if they weren't authorized to do so? What if they gave the experience to you as a gift, yet their tradition as a whole was not open to outsiders?"

I thought for a long time. Finally I answered, "There is so much in this world that belongs to all of us, so much I can experience and learn for myself, that I can't see why I should write about something another considers secret."

He smiled again, even more formally, and before turning away said, "Ah, so you *are* a nonwhite white."

I didn't know what to make of this conversation. On one hand I admired his directness, but it also seemed that he'd been trying to put me into a box, and had, disquietingly for him, been unable to do so. Watching him later I realized that he had precisely three boxes in which to place people: good indigenous, wounded indigenous, and white. There seemed room neither for bad indigenous people nor for whites who can't be lumped as either "Indian wannabes" or as those who mine indigenous traditions the way multinationals mine their land.

I need to be clear about this. Although there is much I admire about many indigenous cultures, and much I despise about my own tradition, it would serve neither me nor the world for me to turn my back on the dominant culture and attempt to be something that I'm not. I'm white, of Danish, French, Scottish descent. I'm civilized. I'm not and will never be from an indigenous culture. That doesn't mean I cannot establish a relationship with the land where I live, based not on indigenous beliefs and practices but instead on my own primary experience. Nor does it mean I cannot help bring to a final halt the pervasive destructiveness of our culture. On the contrary, it seems traditional indigenous people generally have their hands full maintaining their cultures under the social, ecological, economic, religious, and military stresses placed on them by our culture, which means it falls primarily to those of us born in the dominant culture, those of us who know it most intimately, to eat away at it from inside, to break it down, and ultimately to destroy it before it takes down with it the rest of the planet in its final act of other- and self-consumption. Our culture has created this mess, and it seems only appropriate that in attempting to rectify it we begin by looking inside.

I wasn't thinking about this when Witi walked away. Instead, I was both intimidated and put off by this first major interaction with a Maori person, and was thinking that I faced a long and trying week.

But not all Maoris were like Witi, and having once been interrogated I seemed to vanish from his notice. Other Maoris made me feel welcome. Having witnessed my discomfort, several came to make conversation, and later, during a reading, an elder poet pointedly brought his eyes to meet mine whenever he spoke of family, greeting, community, and love.

One of the people who made me feel most welcome was Bruce Stewart. He is a large man, with round belly and wide white beard. His long hair is pulled back in a topknot. He is stunningly gentle, and just as stunningly honest. He's the only writer I've encountered who has been able to fashion a story about a fart into a piece of literature: in his story *Thunderbox* a teacher asks her students to write a paragraph about honesty, and instead of giving the teacher the platitudes she'll reward ("My father is the most honest person I know. He donates money to the poor every Christmas. And God knows, and God blesses him abundantly and he is very rich"), the story's protagonist is starkly honest ("When I let off a good loud fart everyone knows who it belongs to"), and for this he gets into trouble. I felt a certain kinship to Bruce and his fictional characters. Often when I speak out at public meetings, my comments—as at the debate between candidates for Commissioner of Public Lands—often have the same effect as an explosive fart at a genteel dinner party: noses wrinkle, people look and lean away, and nearly everyone tries to ignore the deep breach of etiquette.

Bruce welcomed me with a warm hug and by bringing his nose to touch mine in a traditional Maori greeting. We talked, about the marae, a beautiful huge house built almost entirely from discarded materials, about his work running a nursery for endangered plants, and about what it will take for us to survive. But he was too busy for us to talk extensively then, and he, Jeannette, and I agreed to talk later in the week.

Jeannette and I stayed a few nights at another marae in Wellington, and when we returned to Tapu Te Ranga it was nearly empty: Bruce was there, and his wife, their many children, her sister, and perhaps a dozen others. One of his children, a tiny boy, wandered in and out during our conversation.

I asked Bruce, "What will it take for us to survive?"

He motioned us to follow, and led us outside to a beautiful

vine reaching out to shade a planked walkway. Large white flowers hid in the recesses of the foliage. He said, "This vine no longer has a name. Our Maori name has been lost, so we'll have to find another. Only one of this plant remained in the world, living on a goat-infested island. The plant could go any day. So I got a seed and planted it here. The vine has grown, and although it normally takes twenty years to bloom, this one is blooming after seven."

He continued, "If we are to survive, each of us must become *kaitiaki*, which to me is the most important concept in my own Maori culture. We must become caretakers, guardians, trustees, nurturers. In the old days each *whanau*, or family, used to look after a specific piece of terrain. One family might look after a river from a certain rock down to the next bend. And they were the kaitiaki of the birds and fish and plants. They knew when it was time to take them to eat, and when it was not. When the birds needed to be protected, the people put a *rahui* on them, which means the birds were temporarily sacred. And some birds were permanently *tapu*, which means they were full-time protected. This protection was so strong that people would die if they broke it. It's that simple. It needed no policing. In their eagerness to unsavage my ancestors Christian missionaries killed the concept of tapu along with many others."

I looked at Jeannette. Her face was hard. Bruce continued, "To be kaitiaki is crucial to our existence. So while I am in agony for the whole planet, what I can do is become kaitiaki right here. This can spread, as people see this and say, 'We can do that back at home.' Perhaps then everyone can, as was true in our Maori culture, become caretakers of their own homes. Children will say to their parents, or to others, 'I'm sorry, but you can't do that here.'

"I'm more of a practical man, so rather than write papers about being kaitiaki, I just do it. I don't trust words. I'm frightened of the intellectualism that can insulate us from action and turn the problems and solutions into puzzles or fantasies. As Maori we already have the words, the concepts. But we can't rest on what our ancestors gave us. The work has got to be done."

I thought about the question I ask myself each day, about

whether I should write or blow up a dam, and asked, "Where do writers fit in?"

"Part of this work must be done by artists, philosophers, educators, and others who can articulate and perpetuate the Maori way of living, people who can help us untangle ourselves from the *pakeha*, the Europeans. And as a pakeha yourself there are many important things that you, too, can articulate. From your knowledge and from where you live. But I hope to think any piece of art spurs us into action. I want to believe in sustainability. Now. Not in the future. Not some distant day. Now. Great artists, such as Witi Ihimaera, describe that way of life and help us live it."

He stopped, stared at me intently, then said, "I'm sixty, so I only have ten or twenty years left. I don't have time for a lot of words; I want to use those years for action."

He looked away, then continued, "I hope before I die that I can hear kiwi again. Thousands of people come here, and I ask them, 'Hands up those of you who've heard a kiwi in the wild.' A bit less than one percent raise their hands. Kiwis have not always been so rare. Years ago I heard hundreds of kiwis all around me, in parts of Fjordland where predators hadn't reached. Because people hear the ruru in television advertisements, or kiwi on the radio, they think these birds are still common; it's not until they stop and listen that they realize they haven't heard a living ruru for a long time. The truth is that New Zealand has the most endangered birds in the world. The birds can't handle the rats, opossums, and cats—the worst of the introduced predators. People must begin to feel the responsibility of that very quickly."

He paused, then began again to speak, at first slowly, then with greater urgency, "We need different heroes. One day in the native bush in Fjordland I stumbled across a tombstone. Scraping off the moss I made out 'William Doherty, 1840.' Doherty died trying to save birds. Seeing that rats were making their way into Fjordland he started to move some of the birds onto an island where they could be safe, and he died rowing back. He deserves to be recognized as a hero, as a man 150 years ahead of his time."

Bruce was on a roll now, and spoke so quickly I could barely understand his New Zealand accent, "Actually, he wasn't ahead of his time. That was the time, then, and he could see it. I want to create a monument for him, do a garden in his honor using endangered native plants. We need heroes who leave threads for the rest of us to follow."

He looked out the window, and his speech slowed. "We also need patches of native bush full of native birds and animals, cathedrals where man is not as important as he makes himself out to be, where he instead recognizes himself as a small part of the big family. If we were to make those spaces of harmony available within walking distance from every house, so everybody was a kaitiaki, we would change the world. That's the plan I'm working on. If everyone nurtured a seedling and planted it they would be building their new church. And I'm in a rush."

Yesterday I received my monthly electric bill from the Washington Water Power Company. The envelope also contained a flyer for an event entitled *Stars: A Celebration of Heroes* that the utility will be putting on to benefit local charities. The headliner for the evening is General H. Norman Schwarzkopf.

The flyer doesn't mention that in 1992, an international war crimes tribunal found Schwarzkopf and his fellow defendants guilty of nineteen counts of War Crimes and Crimes Against Humanity for their roles in what is inaccurately known as the Persian Gulf War, a "war" in which 148 United States soldiers died (many from so-called friendly fire) and between 250,000 and 500,000 Iraqis, mostly civilians, lost their lives as well. Schwarzkopf was in charge of the American assault. In this war, American troops used plows mounted on tanks to bury Iraqi soldiers alive in their trenches: after one wave of bulldozers incapacitated the defenders, another filled the trenches with sand. In at least one verified incident, American soldiers slaughtered thousands of unarmed Iraqi soldiers walking toward American positions, hands raised in an attempt to surrender; the Americans used anti-tank missiles to blow apart ostensible prisoners. Two days after the cease-fire was declared, Schwarzkopf approved the combined arms slaughter of Iraq's Republican Guard Hammurabi Division as it retreated from the front ("Say hello to Allah," an

American said as his laser-guided Hellfire missile destroyed an Iraqi vehicle). In clear violation of international law, American forces used napalm, fuel-air explosives (which release a cloud of highly volatile vapors that mix with air and detonate, creating overpressures of up to 1000 pounds per square inch—"Those near the ignition point are obliterated," notes a CIA report blandly), and cluster bombs (some of which, called "Bouncing Bettys," rebound off the ground to explode at stomach level, and others of which spew almost 500,000 high-velocity fragments—"specially formulated metal shrapnel to maximize damage to both man and machine"—per acre, and which were overwhelmingly used against taxis, buses, trucks, and Volkswagen Beetles; less than ten percent of the destroyed vehicles in one section of what has been called the "Highway of Death" were associated with the military. Most were, as one GI described, "like a little Toyota pickup truck that was loaded down with the furniture and the suitcases and rugs and the pet cat and that type of thing."). The United States Air Force intentionally bombed a baby milk powder factory, a vegetable oils factory, a sugar factory, the country's biggest frozen meat storage and distribution center (three times in one day), grain silos across the country, twenty-eight civilian hospitals, 52 community mental health centers, a major hypodermic syringe factory, 676 schools (including eight universities), many marketplaces and apartment buildings, and civilian highway traffic (Najib Toubasi, to provide one example out of tens of thousands, was driving a bus filled with 57 civilians when it was struck by two bombs: "People were running away and the planes followed them and strafed them with machine guns. . . . I was wounded in my right leg. I was holding on to a woman with my right hand and a child in my left hand. We were running across the desert. The woman got hit, and the child was screaming, 'I don't want to die! I don't want to die!'"). Many of these attacks took place after the cease-fire was declared. Americans intentionally bombed the Amariyah civilian bomb shelter, twice. The first bomb opened a hole in the shelter's roof, which enabled the second bomb to be dropped cleanly through the hole to blast its way to the bottom of the shelter, where it killed all but seventeen of the 1500 mostly women and children hiding there—

"Nearly all the bodies were charred into blackness; in some cases the heat had been so great that entire limbs were burned off."

I will not be attending the event billed "An Evening to Honor the Heroes Among Us."

"Not everything the Maori have done has been beautiful," Bruce Stewart said, "and I can't let my love for my own people blind me to that. Before the Maori arrived, there were other groups who lived here, called the Maoriori and the Patipiahiti. These groups were extreme pacifists, and very evolved in their thinking. It is said that whenever any scuffle broke out among these people, at the first sign of bloodshed all fighting must cease. The Maori then came, and slaughtered these earlier, more peaceful people. We need to not only cherish and maintain what is best from our Maori culture, but we also need to face the parts we do not find pleasant. And we need to see our way to re-evolve a culture as beautiful and advanced as the one once here."

Jeannette looked at him closely, seemed to study his features. There was a long silence, then she asked, "What would you wish to save?"

Bruce said, "It frightens me that being Maori is becoming a matter of wearing greasepaint and singing action songs for competitions. It hurt me to learn that computers are now used to judge singing contests, and it disturbs me that dances once held in circles are now held in rows, with people facing each other like in combat. I'd like to see the circle come back, and the drum, and I'd like for people to once again dance for their own spiritual well-being, rather than for competition.

"Still, because the culture is hard to annihilate altogether, some good things remain, such as the familyness and the maraes. I'm especially glad that people are starting to get back to the concept of nonownership of the *whenua*."

As was true for so much of my time speaking with Maoris, I got lost in the vocabulary. I raised my eyebrows.

He saw me, stopped, then said, "The English word would be *earth*. But English, which is very exacting when it comes to legal deals and dollars, is imprecise when it comes to things like earth. In English, earth can be called soil, which has connotations of being unclean, as in 'The clothes are *soiled.*' And it can be called dirt, which of course has similar connotations. That could never happen in Maori.

"*Whenua* also means placenta, and so is associated with female energy. That caused problems when the Christian missionaries came. The Maori recognize two types of energy, the *tapu,* or male energy, and the *noa,* or female energy. We view these energies as opposites. When the opposites are in balance harmony is reached, called *waiora,* the two waters. But the missionaries said the tapu was good and the noa was evil.

"My point is that the Maori still have these concepts; we just need to reclaim them, and to live them more. In this way the young give me great hope. They are searching for truth and wanting to live it. It does wonders for mothers, for example, to take their children down to the gardens and speak Maori while they plant their food."

We were back inside now, and Jeannette looked at the walls of the room where we sat, and to the beautiful wood that made up the textured ceiling.

Bruce noticed her look, and said, "This place arose from the need to be sustainable, and not just on the dollar or food levels. Maraes are our art galleries, our museums, our places of history, our universities, our preschools. They are the places where we are buried. They become our whole life.

"People say they don't have the money to build them, but I don't think that's the problem. The problem is that most people don't have the will. This whole place is assembled from the wastes of the city, and is a statement on the use of materials. In the old days they just flattened old buildings with great big donkey-knockers on cranes. I used to get in there and grab all this beautiful timber, some of which you can't find anymore because the trees are gone. And most of this place is made of car cases that originally came from tropical rainforests and were just going to be dumped. I love these car cases; they're so beautiful, I haven't got them covered. I'd love to be carried to my gravesite on a car case."

He paused for a long time, and had I been able to think of a question, I might have asked it. I'm glad I didn't, because finally he said, "But this place is more than a statement. It represents my mum. It *is* my mum. When I was a child, racism was lovely and loud and blatant. When I was just starting school I was wounded deeply by the other kids, who would point and call, "Maori, Maori, Maori." Suddenly I knew I was something that wasn't good. I didn't know what it meant; I just knew the kids were pointing at me. Many things like that happened. And now I'm glad they did, because eventually instead of trying to become a pakeha, which I did for a lot of my life, I started to get angry. I used that anger to do this work.

"Then the anger turned over to love. And that's because of my mum. She loved me without question, even when I was hard on her. I won a lot of prizes in school, and my mum was proud of me; she helped me a lot. But on prize-giving night in sixth form, when I was seventeen, I made myself sick because I didn't want anyone to see my mother. I had kept her a secret for a long time because I thought her darkness made her ugly. What sort of a system would make a boy ashamed of his mum?

"My mother never said a word. Just loved me. That's why I say she's my greatest teacher. I never heard her running down the pakehas, which probably she should have. She realized what was happening; that's why I have a pakeha name. She told me, 'If people go down a list and see a Maori name, straightaway you're not going to get this little privilege.' Bruce Stewart looked good on the list.

"My mother died when I was 17, that same year. I saw her with all my schoolmates, and she asked me for a kiss. I said, 'Not in front of my friends.' And I never saw her again.

"I went through a lot of grieving, and later went into the bush, and spent many lonely years, savoring and trying to understand. And one of the things that emerged is this house, which is designed as the mother. My mother, and the great mother."

He paused again for an even longer time, but I had learned my lesson, and just waited. A deep sigh, and he continued, "As we built this marae, we realized that we were actually building ourselves. People who've done a lot of work here have changed. We rescue a piece of beautiful wood out of an old building, and as we restore it and put it in place, we rescue and restore ourselves."

Another sigh, and I knew he was finished. There was another question I had to ask: "Do the trees and grass speak to you?"

"They don't at this stage," he answered. "I wish they would. They did to the old people. I think a lot of things spoke to the old people. I'm just taking it a stage at a time by instinct.

"The most important thing for me is to go down to the nursery and walk amongst all those little trees. Some of them you have to wait for the seed, and get it at the right time; some seeds have to hibernate for two or three years before they can grow."

He became once again more animated. "Little nurseries like this are springing up everywhere. And they're done not by the government but by ordinary people. That's why they work. People come here when we're planting, to get their little seedlings. And you see the children come back. The children are more aware than their parents, and the younger children know more than the older ones.

"The biggest thing that stops us is ourselves. When ancient Maori warriors were defeated, they were ready to go again two weeks later, because they were warriors—made up of battling stuff. And along the way they tapped unseen forces. We can still do it. All of us.

"We are suffering from a great illness, and the way to get better is to serve others. We should all be in service. It makes us well. I serve the birds and trees, the earth, the water.

"Anybody can do it. They can do it in their way. It's action time."

I looked at Jeannette. She looked at me. We smiled. I turned off the tape recorder. That was enough for one day.

Metamorphosis

"Between living and dreaming
there is a third thing.
Guess it."
Antonio Machado
(translated by Stephen Mitchell)

WHEN I MOVED INTO this house, lawn surrounded it on three sides. One of my great pleasures these last eight years has been to watch Kentucky bluegrass give way as wild plants moved in to take its place. The first year saw an explosion of thistles, all green and spikes and purple flowers. I feared they might take over, their thorns keeping me from stepping out the door. I needn't have worried; they thinned out two years later. Then vetch, dalmation toadflax, scotch broom, each of these noxious weeds moved in and moved just as quickly out, each one preparing the ground for what was to come next, and each one teaching me that noxious weeds are at least sometimes a sign that disturbed ground is trying to heal itself. I realized, too, that as with everything else, our lawns manifest our cultural desire: they are static, they are artificial, and they are kept sexually immature. Yet with the lawn now gone, the natural scenery changes every day, as new flowers bloom and old ones form seedpods, then die. It changes every season. It changes every year. Each spring and summer different flowers, grasses, bushes, trees. Mullein ("nature's toiletpaper"), Queen Anne's lace, native grasses of a dozen different types and names, wild roses, pine trees.

This summer a nine-year-old boy has taken to visiting me—or more accurately visiting the birds, dogs, and cats—nearly every day. One day I asked him if he knew the name of a huge bush that over the past several years had sprung seemingly from nowhere to hide a good portion of my gravel driveway. He asked, "Does it have purple berries?"

I looked at him, then looked at the bush, then back at him. "I don't know. I never looked that closely."

We walked to the bush, and it did. Huge sprays of them. I don't know how I missed them before. He said, "I don't know the name—Grandma would—but I know those berries make great paintballs. When you throw them, the juice makes an awesome stain."

I made a mental note. He continued, "The seed for this bush probably came from one of those other three bushes back there."

He saw my incredulous look—I've lived here nearly a decade, consider myself reasonably attentive, and never noticed the bushes—and he said, "I was trying to see where the geese go on their paths through the wild roses, and I saw a bush there, there, and there." He pointed to each bush, clearly visible from where we stood.

There is a lot to learn.

This summer I was fortunate enough to witness an outbreak of aphids on a maple tree outside my door.

Because summers in Spokane are hot, then dry, then even hotter, several years ago I planted a half-dozen deciduous trees on the south side of the house. They've grown and spread to the point now that they make passable shade for the dogs and birds. Maybe in another few years they'll cool the house as well.

About six weeks ago, I noticed some aphids on the leaves of the maple tree's lower limbs. I watched them shake their tiny bodies as they seemed to settle into more comfortable positions from which to suck the tree's juices. A few days later I noticed more aphids, and then more, until nearly every leaf revealed a score or more of the little buggers. The leaves were covered with honeydew—a sweet substance exuded by aphids—which dropped to splatter where the tree overhung the porch.

Were I an employee of the Forest Service, I probably would have declared a forest health crisis, and used the opportunity to cut down not only that tree, but all trees of merchantable value within a couple miles. Were I otherwise a typical resident and consequently more interested in chemical control than observing processes, I would have sprayed the tree with an insecticide. As it was, I asked my mom what I should do. She said I should spray the tree with water to wash off the aphids. I thanked her, then did nothing at all. How much richness, I wondered, do we deprive ourselves of by accepting the default decisions handed to us by our elders? It should be said that my mom's plants are healthier than mine.

Each day I watched closely, rooting unsuccessfully for the

arrival of ladybugs to trim the aphid population. The tree started dropping leaves. My mom again suggested the cold water wash. I again demurred.

A week passed and no ladybugs arrived, but the tree began to buzz with wasps, yellow jackets, hornets, and flies, all coming to lap up the honeydew. The tree dropped more leaves.

About a week later I saw first one ladybug, and then another. Other bugs arrived, too, at first singly, and then whole hordes of quarter-inch-long orange-and-black torpedo-shaped insects that sent me scurrying to the library to see what they were. I found out that they, too, were ladybugs in the larval stage.

Many times I witnessed what may have been the conversation of death as larvae passed their mandibles over first one and then another aphid before grasping a third or fourth to pull from the leaf. Or maybe what I witnessed was no conversation at all, especially one of mutual choice, because I also saw the front legs of aphids moving frantically as the bodies disappeared into the mouths of their captors.

Watching, it was hard for me to maintain the level of abstraction that had allowed me to root for the arrival of ladybugs. I am also aware that nonarrival would have meant the eventual death of the tree: just because a herbivore does the chomping doesn't make it any less a killing.

A friend asked if after watching the doomed aphids struggle, I still thought the world was cooperative, and I said that I didn't know. But watching the profusion of bugs—wasps and flies who continued to arrive to eat the honeydew, caterpillars who arrived to carve flesh off leaves, a dozen species of spiders who came to eat anything they could get their palps on—I told her what I did know. The tree had made it clear to me that the price of diversity is death: without the death of the leaves there are no aphids, without aphids there are neither wasps nor ants nor spiders nor ladybugs nor their voracious larvae.

There is something else I wanted to understand. What does the ladybug larvae think as it passes over one aphid for another, and what thoughts race through the aphid as it races across the leaf? What does the maple tree think and feel as the first leaves begin to drop? Does it feel pain and resentment, or anticipation

at the new community being built up? Does it feel as though it is giving an offering? Maybe it doesn't feel any of these things. Perhaps all. Or maybe it feels something entirely different and unfathomable to anyone not a maple tree.

As the larvae fatten and get ready to pupate, they search for the undersides of leaves or boxes or pieces of wood from which they can hang and metamorphose: become tubby and hard and sexually mature. They don't form cocoons, but hang exposed, and I have seen a larva bite into a pupa. I have seen them also now change slowly into adults.

Looking more closely around this land, I can find the chrysali of moths and butterflies. They hang from eaves, limbs, overhangs where I've sloppily stacked boxes of beekeeping equipment. I wonder what their metamorphosis feels like to them: what it feels like to go to sleep an infant and wake up an adult, with new wings, a different body, and an entirely different set of motivations.

I remember my own growing pains as a teenager, the ache of bones stretching me eight inches in one year, and I wonder if these insects, too, feel deep pains from their process of maturation. There is no faster nor more radical transformation I know in nature than the process of pupating, and I wonder if the level of pain corresponds.

Transitions by definition involve pain, loss, sorrow, and even death. But I wonder—staring at a stumpy black-and-orange blob, legless, headless, eyeless, that will soon be a ladybug—if perhaps during the transmogrification these creatures are aware. Perhaps they sleep, and dream. I wonder if they dream of flying. I remember my dream of cranes, and wonder if someone will appear to them, too, to say, "We may not yet fly very well, but at least we aren't walking."

Again I look over the tree—the aphids are gone, but the spiders and ladybugs remain, cleaning up after the party, as it were—and again I wonder if these dormant pupae feel, and if they dream, or if perhaps they sleep dreamlessly as one way of life passes and another takes its place.

Insatiability

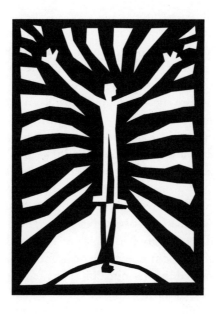

"We need everything that's out there. We don't log to a ten-inch top or an eight-inch top or a six-inch top. We log to infinity. Because we need it all. It's ours. It's out there, and we need it all. Now."

Harry Merlo
Chief Executive Officer
Louisiana Pacific

EVERY DAY NOW I hear heavy machinery as it comes closer to my home: the clank of treads, the rumble of diesel engines, and the scrape of steel blades on volcanic rocks. I don't know how much longer I can take it. I may soon flee, run down the path followed by so many before me—Indians and wolverines, buffalo and beavers, even my own ancestors, the indigenous of Europe: outcasts and refugees, each and every one. The dispossessed.

I don't know how much longer we can keep running. For the indigenous of Europe, there was always north, and east, directions they could go to try to maintain their way of living for another generation before falling to a people bent on subduing the planet and all its members. No matter that my ancestors' flight pushed them into the homes of others, disrupting and making refugees of community after community as each tried to avoid their inevitable extermination. For the first Americans to be contacted by Europeans, in the Caribbean, there were other islands to which they could escape, and for those met later there was always west. Never mind, again, that one dislocation leads to another, and an expanding wave of refugees thus always precedes the march of our culture. At least back then there was someplace to go.

Where can we go from here? There is nowhere left to hide. And where we do try to hide, there we will always be found. Found also will be excuses to continue to pick away at whatever autonomy and integrity—ecological and otherwise—remains, to grind away until we've nowhere and nothing left.

As if we need another example, we can find one without looking so far as the now-melting icecap in Antarctica, or the plummeting populations of krill and penguin, nor toward the other pole, where transnational oil companies melt the tundra and destroy caribou calving grounds to extract oil and make a buck. I can open my window, or simply listen with window still closed to hear the encroachment of bulldozers: the sound of money being made. Or to choose one more absurd and wasteful example among too many—one or more for every place and person and creature on earth—I can look at Mount Graham in Arizona.

For years the San Carlos Apaches have been staving off attempts by members of the dominant culture to build a huge astronomical observatory on one of their most sacred sites, Mount Graham. The mountain is also home to the gravely endangered Mount Graham red squirrel. Leading the fight to defend this mountain is an organization called, appropriately enough, the "Apache Survival Coalition." Leading the fight to build the observatory are the University of Arizona, the Max Planck Institute, and the Vatican, the unholy trinity of academia, science, and Christianity, supported by the full power of the state.

The land originally belonged to the San Carlos Apaches, or rather they belonged to it. The San Carlos Apaches buried their dead there. They prayed there. They communed there with Ga'an, or spirits who also call this mountain home. The mountain is central to their moral and physical universe, which cannot be separated.

The land was not lost through immediate conquest: the Indians retained it when Congress formed their reservation in 1871. But the mountain was lost two years later as President Grant unilaterally abrogated the treaty, giving the land to Mormon settlers. Still the Apaches prayed there, and still the other residents continued with their lives: the Mount Graham red squirrel, Mexican spotted owl, Apache trout, twin-spotted rattlesnake, Sonoran mountain kingsnake, white-bellied vole, and so on, all now in danger of extinction (the mountain is home to at least eighteen species and subspecies of plants and animals found nowhere else on the planet).

After the Mormons came logging trucks: the land not taken by settlers was put under the care of the Forest Service, which led predictably to roads and clearcuts. Still some wildlife persisted, and still the San Carlos Apaches prayed.

Then came vacation homes and a Bible camp. Still the ecological, spiritual, and cultural backs of the mountain and its people had not been broken.

A new irrationale was conjured to justify the further burdening of the mountain and its people: the telescope. In 1984, the University of Arizona, the University of Ohio (which because of student pressure has since withdrawn from the project), and the Vatican came together to build a world-class observatory on Mount Graham. It hardly seems necessary at this point to go into the details of the last thirteen years: it's a story we've heard too many times. It's the story of study after study showing damage to indigenous peoples and to wildlife, and the suppression of these studies. It's the story of men with money intimidating scientists to fabricate more studies—fraudulent but effective barriers to truth—that find precisely what men with money wish to hear. It's the story of politicians waiting with open hands for their votes to be purchased. It's the story of willful, fatal, and all-too-familiar ecological ignorance on the part of those who run the country: Manuel Lujan, Secretary of the Interior, said about protecting the Mount Graham red squirrel, "Nobody's told me the difference between a red squirrel, a black one or a brown one."

It's the story of routine deceit by the government: when part of the way through the project, University of Arizona researchers realized the site where they'd already installed multiple telescopes was not optimal (thirty-eighth out of fifty-seven sites studied), they requested permission from the government to place more telescopes elsewhere on the mountain: at first federal bureaucrats demurred, but pressure and money convinced them to sign on, and so on December 3, 1993, the Forest Service sent a letter by regular post to several San Carlos Apache people asking for input on the proposed site addition. When those opposed to the observatory hadn't responded by December 6 (they had yet to receive the letters) the Forest Service declared the public input requirement fulfilled and quietly issued permission for the University of Arizona to build on the new site. Before dawn the next morning, the University began cutting ancient trees. The documents do not record whether the trees screamed as they were felled.

It's the story of the silencing of native voices: contrast the words of San Carlos Apache medicine man and spiritual leader Franklin Stanley, Sr—"We have listened to you tell us Mount

Graham is not sacred. But those who say that do not know, and they have not talked to the spiritual leaders, like myself. . . . Nowhere else in this world stands another mountain like the mountain that you are trying to disturb. On this mountain is a great life-giving force. You have no knowledge of the place you are about to destroy"—with the words of Charles W. Polzer, S.J., Curator of Ethnohistory at the Arizona State Museum in Tucson, brought in by the Vatican to dispute the sacrality of Mount Graham—"Had Mount Graham been a sacred locale for the Apache nation, military records would clearly mention it as the focal point for punitive raids."

The story of Mount Graham is also the story of routine genocide: Father George V. Coyne, Director of the Vatican Observatory and former housemate of Polzer, stated that the Apache cosmology is "a religiosity to which I cannot subscribe and which must be suppressed with all the force that we can muster." It is the story of absurd claims to virtue overriding all reason, ethics, and evidence: Coyne said the Vatican is involved in this project in order to seek out extraterrestrial beings which "might be brought within the fold and baptized," and defined the protocol necessary on contact: "First of all, one would need to put some questions to him, such as 'Have you ever experienced something similar to Adam and Eve,' in other words, 'original sin'? And then you would have to ask, 'Do you people also know a Jesus who has redeemed you?'" Presumably if they do not, they will be given the same choice as has been given to countless indigenous peoples here on Earth. It is the oft-repeated story of the silencing of all dissenting voices, and the consistent, persistent, incessant wearing away at all that is not Western. It is the destruction of every vestige of ecological or spiritual integrity.

The name of the observatory, by the way, is the Columbus Project.

One afternoon, in the living room of some Maori activists, I was asked if I work on these issues so that indigenous people will like me. There was silence for a moment as I thought about the question—it had never occurred to me. Three other people in the room—two women and a man—interjected that they didn't think the question was fair. Another silence, and Jeannette said she thought it was important.

The question had not been asked in the same inquisitional tone as had Witi's; it seemed that Paulo, the questioner, was genuinely curious as to my motives.

Why does anybody work on these issues? As much to the point, why do so many people ignore them? I can't answer the second, but I know that for most of my friends the answer to the first is that they can't imagine their lives without it: working to slow the destruction or proactively shut down the machine is as natural and unquestioned to them as eating, breathing, sleeping. Many perceive the pain of denuded forests and extirpated salmon directly in their bodies: part of their personal identities includes their habitat—their human and nonhuman surroundings. Thus they are not working to save something *out there,* but responding in defense of their own lives. This is not dissimilar to the protection of one's family: why does a mother grizzly bear charge a train to protect her cubs, and why does a mother human fiercely fight to defend her own? Some arrived at this place primarily through intellect, following a single strand of personally perceived destructiveness back to its source, and others arrived primarily through their emotions, feeling in their bones the outrage, sorrow, shame, and pain of residing in a sea of horrors, and only later brought it up to their minds. People in both categories find it incomprehensible that so many people don't act.

Each year come Super Bowl time, I wonder why so many people can become so excited over a game, yet so few will pause to mourn the passing of the salmon, and almost none will work to stop their steady slide toward extinction. Imagine a moment of silence for the environment before the Super Bowl!

An activist friend once told me of a conversation she'd had with her grandmother, a devout Catholic. The two were watching a television program about prisons. My friend commented that yes, jail food did in fact taste terrible. Her grandmother was shocked and asked how her darling granddaughter could possibly know.

"I've been arrested several times, Grammy."

Silence. I can only imagine the possibilities running through the grandmother's head. Finally my friend continued, "For sitting down in front of bulldozers that were cutting logging roads into ancient forests."

"Why would you do something like that?"

My friend thought a moment, then said, "What would you do if someone was going to run a bulldozer through St. John's cathedral?"

Her grandmother looked at the television, looked out the window, then looked back to her granddaughter. She said, "Next time, don't take on those bulldozers sitting down. You stand up for yourself."

I told Paulo that sure, I wanted him to like me, but only because I liked him, not because he's indigenous. I also said I didn't much care if he liked me for my work; if he did like me I hoped it was because, as I said, "I'm a dang nice guy." I told him also that I'd been doing the work long before I met him, and that I would certainly continue whether he approved or not. Finally, I told him I had reasons entirely independent of him or anyone else for hating what civilization is doing to the world.

I briefly dated a woman who thought my activism was a form of acting out, and who said I despised the culture because it was safer to do so than to despise my father. I thought, and still think, that there was a shred, and only a shred, of truth in what she said, the shred being that he *does* provide me an avenue of understanding into many of the culture's otherwise incomprehensible actions. But on the main she was wrong.

I do despise my father for his own detestable activities. I am quite clear on this point. In the parlance of chemistry, I believe he was a catalyst for my activism. A catalyst is a substance that hastens a reaction. My father initiated the reaction, but the activities of our culture make the "sins" of my father seem minor—were they not properly understood as the micro version of our culture's macro activities. Discrete catalysts can be found for many other activists as well. The Forest Service clearcut behind the activist Barry Rosenburg's home sealed his decision to devote his life to the forests. The Plum Creek clearcut that destroyed Sara Folger's water supply pushed her in the same direction. But as in chemistry, the catalyst is only the beginning of a process.

Insatiability

The question I should have asked that ex-girlfriend before we stopped dating is why more people aren't activated by the ubiquitous catalysts they encounter daily. To return to chemistry, there is something called an *activation energy*, which is the amount of energy that must be present before a certain reaction can proceed. What, I should have asked, is your own activation energy? What's your catalyst? How much—and what—will it take for you to begin to act?

I never got to ask. We broke up, and lost contact, before I could articulate this response.

Violations come not only in paroxysms of rage, spasms of violence and violent orgasms. They come more often with constant erosion, as at Mount Graham, as everywhere, with an incessant imparting of the full knowledge that there is nothing, no one, nowhere, no thought, no action, that the violator will not seek out and attempt to control.

All through college I maintained some minimal contact with my father. I'm not sure why. I never called him, but he called me, once a month, or every other month. I spoke civilly to him, not bringing up the past.

Nor did I bring up the present. These evasions of all that was important gave our conversations a surreal, ungrounded feeling that I still can't quite wrap my mind around. What *did* we talk about? I couldn't bring up the present because he hadn't changed at all—he was still attempting to control me—and I couldn't bring up the past because I hadn't changed enough—I wasn't strong enough to stand up to his denial. The smell of his abuse still clung to my skin and to my clothes. It hung in the air around me.

He kept "spies" on me all through high school, college, and after. One morning in high school I nearly got in an automobile accident, and that night received a call from him asking if I was all right. Fellow students in high school—acquaintances, and even people I didn't know—upbraided me for mistreating my father. During college I was forced to ask many of my instructors not to reveal information about me to anyone without my written consent. I've since found they were bound by law to do this anyway, but the law never prevented my father from calling, nor did it prevent the instructors from talking to him.

The last time I saw my father was on the night of my senior collegiate conference championship. I had attempted to prevent him from finding out I was a high jumper; my attempt was unsuccessful. Four weeks before my final meet he called and asked if he could fly down to attend. I said no. He asked again. I said no. He asked a third time. I told him that if he attended, I would leave.

As I mentioned earlier, the only thing that got me through college was high jumping. I loved it as I had loved nothing before. Every waking, and even dreaming, moment during my senior year was focused on winning that meet. The meet came. Two of us were ranked even odds to win. My main competitor was from Pueblo, where the meet was held, and had a huge contingent to cheer him on. He was a flashy jumper, all movement and rotation and explosive energy, while I was faster, and more fluid. During warmups, each time he jumped, the crowd of maybe a thousand erupted. To silence the crowd, I made sure to begin my approach even before he cleared the pit.

The competition was close, but, breaking my own school record, I won. I still remember my exhilaration as I began my descent on the winning jump without having felt the bar on the back of my legs, meaning I'd made it. We said good-bye after a good season, and I took a lap to cool down. A line of people streamed onto the field to congratulate me, and I began, still in something of a daze, to shake hand after hand. I heard someone say my name, and looked up to see my father.

I walked away. I found out later he had tried to approach me before the competition, and had been prevented by security. I thought about this incident on the way home, and over the next days and weeks. Had he come to the meet, I thought, then sat in the back, leaving quietly after it was done, my frustration at having my desires trampled would have been mixed with a certain respect and understanding of his desire to silently be a part of my life. But that wasn't what was happening. I understood— knew in my heart and bones and muscles, and most especially in my anus and mouth and penis—that the primary reason he came was because I asked him not to. There could be no area in my life, whether high jumping, school, automobile accidents, my body, my emotions—or even, had he known, the stars—that he would leave alone.

Violence, and evil, doesn't always come dressed in black, and it doesn't always look like Charles Manson. Nor does it always come to us as obviously and arrogantly as the breaking of my sister's hymen, the blackening of my brother's eye or the discoloration of my mother's back. Often it comes to us with a simple plea to be reasonable. *Why can't I come to your track meet?*

Just this week, steelhead—oceangoing rainbow trout—were listed as an endangered species in the region. Once, they swarmed the rivers thick as the now-extirpated salmon. They are now following their larger cousins to extinction, to the final and perhaps only refuge from our culture.

The *Spokesman-Review* predictably wrote an editorial stating that we all need to approach this reasonably, emphasizing that no one wins if recalcitrant parties dig in their heels. The author mentioned Indians in particular, and made a sidelong reference to the "crazy ideas" of environmentalists and scientists whose plans for saving steelhead impede the commercial activities that are driving them to extinction.

What if we said *No?* What if we were to be unreasonable? What if we forbade those who will destroy from determining for us what is and what is not within the bounds of acceptable behavior. Within Nazi Germany, the reasonable thing to do, of course, was to go along. Even within the ghettos, the reasonable action was to obey and cling to daily existence. But you know what? The percentage of people who survived the clearing of the Warsaw Ghetto was higher for those who took up arms in resistance than it was for those who, reasonably, went along.

I've not seen my father since the night of the track meet, and with one exception, I have not spoken to him since. But still, many years later and many states away, he knows who my friends are, he knows the names of people I've dated, often knows what I am doing: I checked one day into a hospital, and received a call from him the first night. After I checked out a nurse told me that through my stay he had regularly spoken with both nurses and doctors.

I'm not suggesting my father is the culture. He clearly is not. He is one sad, pathetic, fearful, controlling, violent person. He was merely my own personal catalyst for the life of activism I've chosen. But he is not alone.

I open my window, and the sounds of bulldozers treble in volume. I think about the coyote tree, dying steelhead, being reasonable, and what it will take for us to survive. I don't know how much longer I can take this sound, nor especially the knowledge of what it means, but I don't know where to go.

Last spring, at the workshop where I first read the opening pages of this book, and where a woman later approached to wish me healing, we all performed an exercise entitled "Peacemaking and Voluntary Simplicity." We sat in a large circle, candles burning in the center of the room, each person speaking in turn as a "talking stick"—a piece of wood with a feather on one end dangling from a leather thong—was passed hand to hand. As the stick made its way around, I considered what I was going to do or say. My first inclination was to not touch the stick: the person in charge of the exercise was not traditional Indian, and had the night before shown herself willing to exploit indigenous traditions. My second inclination was to simply tell the truth, that I was uncomfortable with our unauthorized use of a symbol belonging to a tradition that has explicitly declared itself off-limits to us.

As the stick came closer, I found myself increasingly agitated, at least as much by what was being said as by the cultural appropriation. Person after person stepped close to the edge of outrage, then stopped to turn their anger and shame regarding our culture on themselves: "Sometimes I find myself getting angry at the heads of corporations or at politicians who design and implement murderous policies. But then I always have to realize that I am part of the problem, because I, too, drive a car. I realize that most of all I need to have compassion for politicians. They must suffer, simply being who they are."

What about compassion for the murdered? The comments around the circle took me back a few years to a panel discussion I heard at an environmental law conference. The panelists were

Buddhists, addressing much the same topic, and saying much the same thing. There was talk of compassion for wounded wretches who wound us all, of taking pleasure in the dailiness of our lives, of living simply, but not much talk about how to slow or stop the destruction. Afterwards, a woman from the audience stood to ask her question: "Everything you say makes perfect sense, but what do you do if you are standing in front of someone who is aiming a machine gun at a group of children, or is holding a chainsaw in front of a tree?"

This is the point at which virtually all of our environmental philosophizing falls apart. It is *the* central question of our time: what are sane and appropriate responses to insanely destructive behavior? In many ways it is the *only* question of our time. Future generations will judge us according to our answers. So often, environmentalists and others working to slow the destruction are capable of plainly describing the problems (Who wouldn't be? The problems are neither subtle nor cognitively challenging), yet when faced with the emotionally daunting task of fashioning a response to these clear and clearly insoluble problems, we generally suffer a failure of nerve and imagination. Gandhi wrote a letter to Hitler asking him to stop committing atrocities, and was mystified that it didn't work. I continue to write letters to the editor pointing out untruths, and continue to be surprised each time the newspaper publishes its next absurdity. At least I've stopped writing to politicians.

It is desperately true that we each need to look inside, to make ourselves right—as a poet friend of mine writes, "The Old One says you must put your house in order before you can have guests"—but it's also true that because we are embedded in and dependent upon this planet, and because we owe the planet our lives for having given us life, and because (one hopes) a deep spring of love lies hidden within us, this making ourselves right, this inner work, if it is to mean anything at all, must of necessity lead us to effective action, to actions arising from the love and responsibility we feel toward our neighbors.

The members of the panel on Buddhism blew it. Each in turn stated that the most important thing is to have compassion for the killer, to try to see the Buddha-nature in each of us.

That was a very fine, enlightened position, I thought, but one that helps neither the children nor the trees, nor for that matter the murderers. Nor, in fact, does it help the bystander. Enlightenment as rationalization for inaction. Pacifism as pathology. As Shakespeare so accurately put it, "Conscience doth make cowards of us all."

I mentioned this to George, who has been a Buddhist since his early teens. George's response was even more direct than mine. "That's bullshit," he said. "There's a story that the Buddha killed someone who was going to later be a mass murderer. He did it so that he, instead of the murderer, could take on the bad karma caused by killing. And also, presumably, to save the innocent lives. The appropriate response is to stop the murderer by any means possible, as mindfully and compassionately as you can. If you must use force do so, and if you must kill, do that, too, the whole time being fully aware of the implications of what you're doing."

I related to George a story I once heard of a samurai whose master had been killed, and so who was bound to track down the murderer. For years he followed him, until finally he cornered the man in a room. The samurai raised his sword, and from terror the other man spat in the samurai's face. The samurai held the sword poised, shaking now with anger. Finally he sheathed his sword, wiped his face, and walked away. He could not kill the man in that moment, because had he done so it would have been for the wrong reason.

The stick was close now, only two people away. I didn't know what to do. I thought of a conversation I'd had with Jeannette and one of the Maoris. I said that I feel bad whenever I drive, because I'm adding to global warming. The Maori nodded agreement. So did Jeannette. Then she added fervently, "But you didn't set up the system. Do what you can, but don't identify with the problem. If you internalize what is not yours, you fight not only them but yourself as well. Take responsibility only for that which you're responsible—your own thoughts and actions. You didn't make the car culture, you didn't set up factory farming. Do what you can to shut those things down."

The stick came to me. I took it, despite my earlier misgivings, and suddenly calm, said, "There can be no real peace when living with someone who has already declared war, no peace but capitulation. And even that, as we see around us, doesn't lead to further peace but to further degradation and exploitation. We're responsible not only for what we do, but also for what is in our power to stop. Before we can speak of peace, we have to speak honestly of the war already going on, and we have to speak honestly of stopping, by any and all means possible, those who have declared war on the world, and on all of us. Those who destroy won't stop because we live peacefully, and they won't stop because we ask nicely. There is one and only one language they understand, and everyone here knows what it is. Yet we don't speak of it openly."

I took a breath, then continued, "I have to be honest here. During the reading last night I told you of my childhood, but I didn't tell you this: If I were once again a child, with only the options open to me as a child—in other words no running away to fend for myself—but also knowing what I know now of the futility of trying to talk my father out of his violence, I know I would have killed him. How else do I protect the innocent, the little boy who was me? Pacifist as I am—I've never been in a fistfight, nor even shouted in anger—I still would have killed him. And I don't think that would have been wrong."

I looked at the faces around the room: some people were stunned, some looked away, a few disappeared behind a mask of impassivity, many looked intrigued, and quite a few nodded, eyes fierce with solidarity of understanding. I continued, "The point is that we're all in a room with a cannibal, with a mass murderer, and we need to figure out what to do about it."

It is night. I sit in front of the computer, typing. The lamp—a halogen bulb atop a long pole, with an inverted bowl beneath to reflect light toward the ceiling—is on. The center of the bowl is semi-clear plastic, through which I see the husks of moths fatally attracted by the bulb. I try to keep the lamp off when bugs are in the room, and if I see one spiral toward the light I extinguish it. But I'm usually too late, and I hear the flutter of wings until all is still. The smell of burnt moth floats down.

No wings flutter against the plastic housing now. I look outside, to see a small moth beating itself against the window, trying to get in. All night they try to fly in one direction, and during the day they try to fly out the other. It breaks my heart to see tiny wasps and black bees trying to find their way home, held back by a barrier they neither see nor understand. Plastic makes it worse. A few of my windows have clear plastic taped over them to decrease heat loss during the winter. Over the years the plastic has developed holes, too small for a finger but large enough for an insect. In they go, and it is nearly impossible for them to find their way out. I sometimes try to lead them, but that is maddening: they move toward the hole, then slip past the paper I'm using to guide them, and retreat back to the plastic, back to where they will soon die alone, of hunger, of thirst. Even to the end, I don't think they understand.

Violence

"We kill when we close our eyes to poverty, affliction, or infamy. We kill when, because it is easier, we countenance, or pretend to approve of atrophied social, political, educational, and religious institutions, instead of resolutely combating them."
Hermann Hesse

IT'S A BEAUTIFUL SPRING day, and the geese are sulking. Actually, only two of them are, two males. With the arrival of spring the birds have been especially amorous, with the geese seemingly interested in anything that moves. A third male goose is especially interested in one of the ducks (a large one, at least); she seems to return his affection, often sidling up to him and plopping down with a loud and presumably erotic (to him) quack. She lifts her tail invitingly, and he clambers up on her back.

The two males have been upset with me lately, puffing themselves up and hissing whenever I approach, then braying excitedly when I'm done with my chores and leave. I know it's not just me they're upset at, because they've been chasing everyone except Amaru, the larger of the dogs. The other day they nailed (I believe *goosed* is the technical term) the largest of the roosters, and one of the geese has repeatedly gone after a sick hen with a bad leg.

The hen spent most of the winter sitting atop the firewood piled inside the barn, venturing out only rarely. Early this spring she stopped going outside at all. I needed to leave for two weekends straight, and I told her that if she weren't better by the time I got back, that I would kill her. I got back, and still she sat in the barn, looking miserable.

The next morning as I showered, I steeled myself to the notion that if she were still inside by the time I got dressed and went outside, that I would kill her. I went to the barn, and couldn't find her. A search of the yard revealed her stretched out by the pumphouse, giving herself a dust bath. She has gone outside every day during the two weeks since, and seems to be walking better.

The male geese don't like her. Thrice now I have gone outside and found them bullying her. Today was the worst. I was working, and heard an odd flapping outside. I looked out the window, and saw one of the males standing on her back, pulling at her head with his mouth. I've seen enough birds mating (or attempting to mate, when it comes to *that* form of interspecies communication) to know that though this resembled an attempted mounting, it was not. He was simply attacking her. His best buddy stood beside him. I ran outside, realized I wasn't wearing shoes (don't run around a chicken yard without shoes), ran back in, found only sandals, ran back out, grabbed a piece of wood, got the goose off her, and chased him around the yard, losing my sandals twice and using the long piece of wood as an extension of my arm to force him into a corner. Finally I caught him, held him, and told him that if I ever caught him doing that again, I would eat him for dinner.

It is the next day, and I have been thinking more about the goose and hen. Two nights ago I dreamt of chickens, and was surprised to find none missing. Later in the day, though, one of the ducks disappeared. Obviously the Dreamgiver knew something I didn't. That makes me wonder if the goose, too, knows more than I. Perhaps he merely wants to put the hen out of her misery.

If the goose attacks her again, and if I kill him, would I be killing for the wrong reason? Or am I, to ask the same old question, simply projecting my feelings onto the situation? Was the goose merely being a goose? Maybe. But there's a third male goose, not a member of this duo, who does none of these things. He usually hangs out with his duck-buddy, wandering about eating cantaloupe rinds and lettuce heads.

Perhaps, once again, this is all displacement of responsibility. If I want to have goose stew, maybe I shouldn't rationalize, but just grab a hatchet and kill one. But I don't know.

I killed the goose. After I warned him, he killed the wounded hen, then a rooster, then another hen. Still I hesitated.

A few days later I returned from errands to find yet another hen dead, with the skin ripped from her skull. She looked as though she'd been scalped. The goose's face was bloody, and blood flecked red across his white breast. I said to him, "That's it," and picked up a stick. I used it again to corner him. He must have known the stakes were higher this time, because he kept ducking under the stick and racing away. I finally caught him, and held his large body close, one wing trapped against my chest, the other under my right arm. I remember his eyes were wide, and I could see the black of pupil, blue of iris, white of fear, red of lid, white of feathers, and red of hen's blood.

I dropped the stick, and on the way to the chopping block picked up the hatchet in my left hand. I laid down his head. He did not stretch it like the Pekin of so long ago, but held his neck in a tight s that afforded no room to strike. Finally, more through random movement than cooperation, he straightened his neck enough that I could hit it cleanly. I broke his neck, but did not cut all the way through; I struck again and his head came free. Blood exploded from his neck, his mouth gaped and closed, gasping for breath, his chest heaved, pushing air past taut vocal cords to give voice for the last few times of his already completed life. His wings moved hard against my breast and arm, and finally I released them to spread. Blood covered the block, and the dogs—who had long ceased hurting the birds—approached to lap it up.

I hung him to bleed, then scalded and picked him. I eviscerated him and put him into the refrigerator to cool. The next day I would make a stew.

That night my friend Julie Mayeda took me to dinner. We went to a Thai restaurant, where I ordered chicken and she seafood, and we both tried not to think about the lives represented in our meals. I couldn't get over the look in the goose's eyes. It wasn't so much the fright, but simply the knowledge in my *own* body that his eyes were now closed, his body now dead. His running as I chased him had been the last his feet felt of the ground that had always been his home, the hatchet descending was the last thing he saw. Julie and I talked of the existential confusion caused by someone's presence one moment and absence the next. The goose was here this afternoon, now he is not. All that remains is meat—no longer even flesh, really—in the refrigerator.

Midway through the evening it occurred to me that this had been the hen's last day, too. Since I hadn't killed her, I felt myself not quite so existentially involved. I mentioned this to Julie, who responded, "But that's not right. If you . . ." She trailed off.

I nodded agreement to her unsaid statement. Neither of us

spoke. We poked at the meat on our plates, the remains of some creature's existence. I said, "Had I killed the goose last week, the hen would be alive."

"I didn't want to say that."

"But . . ." I paused, and took a bite of chicken. "It's true."

I realized I was responsible that day not for one but two deaths, one through the use of a hatchet, the other through inaction. By not killing the goose, I killed the hen as surely as if it had been me and not the goose who tore the skin from her scalp.

The hardest part for me is always that moment of inevitability, the microsecond after the decision has been made, but before the hatchet begins to fall. At every moment up to then I can let go my hold on the bird, and allow her or him to return to scratch and peck at the dirt, but from that instant the bird, though still fully alive for the time it takes the blade to fall upon its neck, is as good as dead.

I feel the same each time I hook a fish, and I felt the same the one time I had a deer centered in the sights of my rifle. It was standing in a thicket, and had I been able to discern antlers amongst the tangle of tiny boughs, my finger would have pulled the trigger, and that animal's life would have ended. It is an awful power to hold another's life in your hands.

This morning I killed a baby goose. Born blind and deformed, it would never have walked. Before I killed it I cradled it in my palms, holding it secure so it could at least once in its life feel the warmth of the sun on the still sticky down of its back. Its head wobbled, and it cried as loud as it could, as loud as any just-born goose can. I stroked her or his neck, and said good-bye.

When I was younger, I would turn off my feelings before I killed a fish, or a bird, or a grasshopper, or fly. I would look with almost disinterested eye at the bluegill on a stringer or the chicken on a chopping block. Something did stir, but it was too deep, and I knew also that if I allowed it to well up I would never go through with what I intended.

I no longer go away—allow my body to become what Descartes called "a statue made of earth"—while my arm raises and brings down the hatchet. I know that the answer—to what question I've no idea—is not to shy away from death, or even from killing, and especially from feeling. Death is everywhere, and will seek me out no matter where I hide, now and again in the causing, and later in the receiving.

This understanding came to me, oddly enough, when I was using the toilet. I realized that every time I defecate, I kill millions of bacteria. Every time I drink I swallow microorganisms, every time I scratch my head I kill tiny mites.

Because life feeds off life, and because every action causes a killing, the purpose of existence cannot be to simply avoid taking lives. That isn't possible. What is possible, however, is to treat others, and thus ourselves, with respect, and to not unnecessarily cause death or suffering. This seems so obvious I'm embarrassed to write it, but it's so frequently and savagely ignored—consider factory farms, the mass rapes and child abuse endemic to our culture, the one hundred and fifty million children enslaved, *ad nauseum*—that I've no real choice.

Viktor Frankl died yesterday. Although most famous for his book *Man's Search For Meaning,* in which he described his experiences as a prisoner at Auschwitz, and articulated his understanding that those who found meaning in their lives and in their suffering were better able to survive the horrors of the camp, I mention him because of something he said toward the end of his life: "There are only two human races—the race of the decent and the race of the indecent people."

He is right, of course. To restate this in terms of this book's exploration: there are those who listen and those who do not; those who value life and those who do not; those who do not destroy and those who do. The indigenous author Jack Forbes describes those who would destroy as suffering from a literal illness, a virulent and contagious disease he calls *wétiko,* or cannibal sickness, because those so afflicted consume the lives of others—human and nonhuman—for private purpose or profit, and do so with no giving back of their own lives.

There are those who are well, and those who are sick. The distinction really is that stark. Attending to this distinction leads again to the central question of our time, restated: How can those of us who are well learn to respond effectively to those who are not? How can the decent respond to the indecent? If we fail to appreciate and answer this question, those who destroy will in the end cause the cessation of life on this planet, or at least as much of it as they can. The finitude of the planet guarantees that running away is no longer a sufficient response. Those who destroy must be stopped. The question: How?

On December 17th of 1996, members of the Tupac Amaru Revolutionary Movement (MRTA) took over the Japanese ambassador's house in Peru and seized some 500 hostages. They released women and children immediately, and for humanitarian reasons released all but seventy-two of the remaining hostages over the next several weeks. Their primary demand for the release of the final group, which included several Supreme Court members, a former chief of Peru's secret police (responsible for the torture and murder of countless civilians), and regional executive officers for many Japan-based transnational corporations, was that imprisoned MRTA members be freed.

Because of my obvious interest in the relationship between unarmed and armed resistance to the violence of the culture, I spoke with Isaac Velazco, an MRTA member since 1984. In 1988, Velazco was arrested and beaten. He escaped, and fled to Germany.

I asked him why the MRTA formed. He said, "Tupac Amaru formed because there is nothing resembling democracy for the majority of Peru's citizens. For the perhaps three million privileged Peruvians there is a democracy; but their democracy is our dictatorship, a continuation of the often irrational destruction that's been going on in Peru for five hundred years.

"Prior to the arrival of Europeans, Peru was home to one of the most advanced cultures of America, where, with collective ownership of the means of production, the problem of hunger was solved. Yes, the Incas subjugated other peoples, sometimes violently, and they were sometimes met with violent resistance. But better scholars than I have shown that even the ruling classes showed respect for the land, and for children. They made sure everyone was fed through a sophisticated network of storehouses.

Contrast that to today, when one hundred and eighty of every thousand children in Peru die of curable diseases before they're five, and adults die as slave laborers washing gold in the jungles of Madre de Dios. An FAO report suggests poverty will be eliminated in Peru before 2025, not because of improving conditions, but because we'll all be dead of starvation. Our country is turning into a huge concentration camp."

I asked what the MRTA wants for Peru. He replied, "I am not sure what you mean. We *are* Peru. We want nothing *from* Peru. There are others who want plenty from Peru: our oil, wood, fish, gold. Our lives. Capitalism is taking away what is elemental to our lives: our land, rivers, forests are being violated by institutions and individuals who have deafened themselves to the meanings they have for us. The majority in Peru have traditionally lived by hunting and fishing, and small-scale agriculture, by growing bananas, manioc, and fruits. These people are not reaping the benefits—whatever they may be—of neoliberal 'development.' They—we—are being killed. We want to stop this annihilation of our people, and we want our people—the vast majority who are denied a voice in our so-called democracy—to be heard.

"Truth, as someone once said, is revolutionary. This is one reason those in power routinely lie. The takeover of the ambassador's house, and the consequent attention focused on the appalling conditions in Peru's prisons, conditions which up to then had been for the most part ignored, points out that when those in power lie, the only way to conduct a meaningful dialogue with them is to have in your hands a way to force them to be accountable. Even then you can be sure they will remain true only so long as you continue to hold them tightly in your hands."

I asked how he became politicized.

"Because each of us is born into already-extant political systems, we are born politicized: we each must either accept (sometimes by default) or reject the political system into which we've been born. Those born and raised farther from the centers of political power are less likely to be influenced by the entire politics of servitude and slavery.

"I have long opposed capitalism and its effects on my people. I tried unarmed resistance, but soon grew to see that as useless.

To witness the murder of one's comrades, without a weapon to defend themselves, is a quick way to be convinced of that approach's futility. Almost all MRTA members have had that experience, through the disappearance of their parents, the torture of their brothers, the rape of their sisters; others have suffered the violence in their own flesh, directly."

If the government were to disappear, I asked, and the MRTA were to govern, what would they do? "Our goal is to build a society that respects the autonomy of each region. We'd continue our current program of respecting each village's grassroots organizations, we'd assist them in electing their own representatives, and together we'd develop the production of food and other necessities. We need to produce and distribute our own food. We already know how to do that. We merely need to be allowed to do so."

I asked whether writing helps bring about social change. "In our villages a high percentage of people do not read or write. But it's important that ones like you, who know how to do it, write so sensitive persons of the middle and upper classes may understand it's possible to live in a world where the lives—and the ways of living—of all beings are respected. This in no way implies it is incompatible to write *and* take up the rifle. Many poets and sensitive or conscientious intellectuals have done exactly this in Peru and other places."

The standoff at the ambassador's house ended on April 22— Earth Day here in the United States—of that next spring. It ended the way stand-offs between "decent" and "indecent" people so often do: with the slaughter of the decent by the indecent. A single incident stands out: as Peruvian soldiers burst into the Japanese ambassador's residence, one of the MRTA members ran into the room where a number of the hostages were being held. He aimed his automatic rifle at them, stopped, stared, turned, and walked back out of the room. Moments later he was gunned down trying to surrender.

I cannot get this image out of my mind. Again and again I picture him aiming the rifle, stopping just before the moment of inevitability, and walking away. I picture him dead. I can think of nothing that better illustrates why the world is dying, or rather being killed, and why the best, most heartfelt efforts of those of us struggling for justice and sanity so often end in betrayal, loss, and sometimes bloodshed—inevitably our own blood and the blood of those we are trying to protect.

Something that should be abundantly clear by now is that while many of us enter into this struggle because we care about life and about living, the truth is that our enemies, those who are destroying life on this planet, the "indecent race," the cannibals, have shown themselves time and again to be willing, in fact eager, to kill to increase their power. It's that simple.

The siege at the ambassador's house lasted a little over four months. During those four months prisoners seized by the MRTA played chess, gave and received cooking and music lessons, sang Happy Birthday to each other, and compared their imprisonment to "a cocktail party without liquor." On release, most of the prisoners the MRTA voluntarily let go shook the hand of Nestor Cerpa, head of the MRTA commando that undertook the action, and wished him well. Many asked for his autograph. After their release, some expressed solidarity with the MRTA. These expressions lasted long enough, and came in the face of a repressive enough government force, to make the Stockholm syndrome unlikely.

During those same four months, members of the MRTA imprisoned by Peru continued their existence in "President" Fujimori's prison tombs ("President" is in quotes because, as often goes unreported in the corporate press, Fujimori disbanded the legislature, overturned the constitution, and enacted a self-coup in 1992). "They will rot," said Fujimori, "and will only get out dead." During those four months, Victor Polay—founder of the MRTA—and other prisoners at Callao Naval Base continued to be confined to tiny cells twenty-five feet underground; they were allowed to walk outside, hooded and alone, for thirty minutes each day. In those four months, prisoners in Yanamayo (12,000 feet) and Chacapalca (more than 15,000 feet, and an eight-hour drive from the nearest village) suffered bitter cold, once again in solitary confinement, in rooms with paneless windows. During those four months, more MRTA members—or more likely peasants or Indians unfortunate enough to have caught the attention of secret police—were captured, tortured, and in at least one case, murdered. The survivors will probably be sentenced, by faceless military judges in trials lasting only minutes, to life imprisonment in these "prison tombs."

During those four months, those responsible for the death squad killings of thousands of Peruvians continued to lead comfortable lives, their anxiety eased by a general amnesty issued June 16, 1995 by Fujimori, which quashed all investigations or indictments of human rights violations occurring after May 1980. The hostages released by the MRTA who expressed solidarity received death threats from Peru's secret police. At least one radio reporter who criticized the military was kidnapped and tortured.

In those four months, the Peruvian government, central to the region's drug trade, continued to traffic in cocaine; in 1996, one hundred and sixty-nine kilos of cocaine were found in the presidential plane, one hundred and twenty kilos were found in one Peruvian warship, and sixty-two in another. Also that year, Demetrio Chavez Petaherrera, one of the biggest drug kings in Latin America, testified in a public hearing that since 1991 he's been personally paying Peru's drug-czar Vladimiro Montesinos (an ex–CIA informant long linked to drugs, death squads, and the torture of civilians) $50,000 per month in exchange for information on United States Drug Enforcement Agency activities. A few days afterwards, Petaherrera was taken to Callao and tortured until he recanted. And Fujimori's brother, Santiago, his nephew, Isidro Kagami Fujimori, and other of his relatives continued to traffic cocaine through any number of dummy corporations. Some of the profits from this trafficking go to purchase black-market helicopters used to kill civilians.

The children of Peru continued to starve, the forests continued to fall, and the fisheries continued to be depleted. In other words, Fujimori continued his policy of committing genocide and ecocide to benefit transnational corporations. In other words, it was business as usual in the civilized, industrialized world.

Fujimori and the military, while pretending to negotiate in good faith, dug five separate tunnels beneath the compound. Two of the miners hired to dig the tunnels died, and the rest disappeared: their families have no idea what happened to them. Members of the security forces—trained in the United States at taxpayer expense, and wearing taxpayer-purchased flak jackets (one of their American instructors called the assault and subsequent massacre "money well spent")—prepared for an assault, and listened to the routine inside the compound through a pin-sized microphone smuggled in when a hostage requested a guitar (as well as microphones hidden in the chess set, and in other amenities brought in to help the hostages pass the time). The CIA helped Fujimori prepare the slaughter.

During or after the assault, all the MRTA members were summarily executed. Military microphones picked up the sounds of two of the guerrillas—sixteen-year-old girls—begging soldiers not to shoot. They were, of course, immediately murdered. Other rebels, including Nestor Cerpa, were shot at point-blank range in the forehead. At least one of the rebels was led away to be tortured before his murder. One of the soldiers who participated in the slaughter said, "The order was to leave no one alive. For us, the instruction was to leave no prisoners." Relatives who went to claim the bodies of the dead were beaten and arrested at a military hospital. Nestor Cerpa's aunt was allowed to view the bodies. All but two had been cut into pieces and placed in plastic bags. She counted thirty bullet holes in her nephew's head. The dismembered bodies of most of the rebels were scattered in unmarked graves, and some relatives who visited marked graves were arrested.

To stop the genocide and ecocide that characterizes—and has always characterized—our culture requires that we learn to fully internalize the implications of one very important fact: we and they—those who are destroying the world—are operating under two entirely different and utterly incompatible value systems. As Frankl said, there are those who are decent, and those who are indecent. We value life, and the living, and they value control and power. On the largest scale it really is that simple (on an individual scale it is much more complex—human rights and environmental organizations are rife with petty power struggles, and there probably exist at least a few in power who retain some level of decency). Time and again we show ourselves willing to die or to live to support ecological and economic justice and sanity, and time and again our enemies—the indecent ones, the destroyers—show themselves willing to lie and to kill to maintain control. Throughout the entire siege, members of the MRTA treated their captives with humanity and grace. In response they were lied to and betrayed. I know of no longterm activists who have not repeatedly experienced this same pattern of lies and betrayal, although for many of us in the more privileged sectors of the world, the full consequences of our enemies' behavior are yet to be brought home with such force and finality as is normally reserved for the colonies.

I have thought long and hard not only about the siege but about what we can learn from it. Isaac Velazco's words roll round and round inside my head: "When those in power lie, the only way to conduct a meaningful dialogue with them is to have in your hands a way to force them to be accountable. Even then you can only be sure they will remain true so long as you continue to hold them tightly in your hands." This statement, and the massacre, have many implications. The first is that, ultimately, negotiations are bound to fail. You cannot negotiate with someone who systematically lies to you. If you win your points during negotiation, the agreement will be broken. Indians have seen this, as have forest activists, toxics activists, nuclear activists, antiwar activists, and so on. This is not to say we shouldn't negotiate. But to expect to be dealt with fairly by those who have shown no scruples about lying and using naked force to take what they want is to engage in magical thinking. It is delusional. It is, to speak of this as we would a dysfunctional family, like playing the part of codependent partner in a parasitic and abusive relationship. It is to participate in our own victimization.

The bitter truth that most of us are unwilling to face is that our enemies are institutionally and oftentimes individually psychopathological. They have the cannibal sickness. The lives of those they kill simply do not exist in the minds of the killers. This is true for victims whether the Forest Service and the timber industry speak of board feet rather than living forests, agribusiness corporations speak of 10,000 "units" in confinement instead of living hogs, or the corporate media reports that

United States warplanes caused "collateral damage" in Iraq—the deaths of tens of thousands of men, women, and children in apartments, buses, and bomb shelters. Thus after the assault, Fujimori stated that he was "very sorry for the loss of three human lives," meaning the two soldiers and one hostage who died in the assault (the hostage who died was a Supreme Court Justice who had voted against Fujimori's amnesty of death squad leaders; reports vary as to whether he died of a heart attack or a bullet wound; the Peruvian Human Rights organization DeRechos alleged that he was murdered by the military). The other lives that Fujimori caused to prematurely end were evidently something less than human. Representatives of the various transnational corporations with an interest in Peru's resources stated they would change none of their genocidal and ecocidal policies. Most of the transnationals fully supported the decision to use force. A representative of Mitsubishi said there was "no other way" to end the crisis. A representative of Mitsui Metal and Smelting said it was "very regrettable" that one Peruvian hostage died. He did not regret, of course, the killing of the MRTA members. What was there to regret?

Those of us in the United States, those who are at least somewhat privileged—probably white, perhaps male, possibly rich or at least not so hungry as the children of Peru—must recognize that in a world of shrinking resources it is only a matter of time until the guns are turned on us. Someone once asked John Stockwell, an ex–CIA agent whose conscience forced him to speak out against the agency, why he had not yet been killed. He said, "Because they are winning." We who are relatively privileged need to ask ourselves what we are willing to give up, what amount of security we are willing to sacrifice to change the status quo. In the wake of this action by the MRTA, and the consequent murder of those involved, we—each of us—need to question what we can do to help change things for the better, and stop the mindless destruction.

During those four months, fourteen members of the MRTA held the attention of the world, and they held back, if only for a brief time, and if only in the so-very-tiny space of one house in one city in one country in South America, the steady march of our culture as it relentlessly destroys everything it encounters. For that brief time the world was shown an alternative of determined and fully human resistance, of people fighting for their right to be *on their own terms.* What if there were fourteen more, or fourteen more than that, or fourteen hundred more than that? What if we each individually began to organize, knowing full well the stakes and the potential consequences—both good and bad—of our actions? What if we each in our organizations at long last said to those who run the country, those who run the companies, those who help further the destruction, run the machine, "You shall not pass. This is where I live, and this, if necessary, is where I shall die." And what if we meant it?

We are losing a one-sided and defensive war. If we learn nothing else from the bravery and deaths of the fourteen tupacamaristas, it is that we must take the offensive, we must struggle—never for a moment letting go of the life-affirming values we believe in—and bring that struggle to their doorstep instead of ours. We must learn also that resistance is never futile, and that we have no option as human beings but to struggle as though our lives depended on it—which of course they do—to ensure that each and every one of us is granted the right to be. Our goal must be nothing less than the rediscovery of what it means to be a human inhabitant of this world into which each of us is born. The planet is waiting for us to rediscover it, waiting to be allowed nothing more than the simple right to be. It will grant the same favor in return—anything else will bring about our completely unnecessary demise.

The Parable
of the Box

"Tell me whom you love and I will tell you who
you are."
Arsene Houssaye

SOMETIMES IN THE DARK gray of false dawn I awaken with a start. In the confusing moments between dreaming and waking I occasionally trick myself into believing none of the problems we've been discussing exist. No genocidal impulse. No wage slavery. No anthropogenic climate change. No ecological collapse. No tyranny of money. In those brief moments I believe I can walk to the Spokane River and once again see rapids get "lashed into whiteness" by uncountable salmon, salmon that—in this nightmare of the waking world—I have never seen, and never will. In those moments the awful reality of what we have done and continue to do seems so nonsensical as to be implausible. It makes sense in those moments, for example, to ask whether I dreamt or read that the government of the United States (it, too, a figment of this dreamscape) smuggled crack cocaine into slums (crack and slums are in these moments figments as well)—raising a generation of American addicts and enriching gangs that control their lives—then used profits from drug sales to kill peasants in Central America. This is all too stupid, too cruel, too absurd. It couldn't be real.

No matter how hard I try, the morning inevitably intrudes on these reveries, and I awaken. But later, all through the day and into the evening as I now write these words, the problems I describe become no less absurd, no less cruel, no less stupid.

A parable of this stupidity centers around a box. The box is full of salmon, and a man sits atop the box. Long ago this man hired armed guards to keep anyone from eating his fish. The many people who sit next to the empty river starve to death. But they do not die of starvation. They die of a belief. Everyone believes that the man atop the box owns the fish. The soldiers believe it, and they will kill to protect the illusion. The others believe it enough that they are willing to starve. But the truth is that there is a box, there is an emptied river, there is a man sitting atop the box, there are guns, and there are starving people.

In the 1930s, anthropologist Ruth Benedict tried to discover why some cultures are "good," to use her word, and some are not. She noticed that members of some cultures were generally "surly and nasty"—words she and her assistant Abraham Maslow recognized as unscientific—while members of other cultures were almost invariably "nice."

Benedict is of course not the only person to have made this distinction. The psychologist Erich Fromm found that cultures fell, sometimes easily, into distinct categories such as "life-affirmative," or "destructive." The Zuñi Pueblos, Semangs, Mbutus, and others that he placed in the former category are extraordinary for the way in which they contrast with our own culture. "There is a minimum of hostility, violence, or cruelty among people, no harsh punishment, hardly any crime, and the institution of war is absent or plays an exceedingly small role. Children are treated with kindness, there is no severe corporal punishment; women are in general considered equal to men, or at least not exploited or humiliated; there is a generally permissive and affirmative attitude toward sex. There is little envy, covetousness, greed, and exploitativeness. There is also little competition and individualism and a great deal of cooperation; personal property is only in things that are used. There is a general attitude of trust and confidence, not only in others but particularly in nature; a general prevalence of good humor, and a relative absence of depressive moods."

Readers may more closely recognize our own culture in Fromm's description of the Dobus, Kwaikutl, Aztecs, and others he put into the category of "destructive." These cultures, he said, are "characterized by much interpersonal violence, destructiveness, aggression, and cruelty, both within the tribe and against others, a pleasure in war, maliciousness, and treachery. The whole atmosphere of life is one of hostility, tension, and fear. Usually there is a great deal of competition, great emphasis on private property (if not in material things then in symbols), strict hierarchies, and a considerable amount of war-making."

Fromm also defined a third category, "nondestructive-aggressive societies," which included Samoans, Crows, Ainus, and others who are "by no means permeated by destructiveness or cruelty or by exaggerated suspiciousness, but do not have the kind of gentleness and trust which is characteristic of the . . . [life-affirmative] societies."

Given the ubiquity of this culture's destructiveness as well as its technological capacity, there has never been a more important time to ask Ruth Benedict's question: Why are some cultures "good" and others not?

Benedict found that good cultures, which she began to call "secure," or "low aggression," or "high synergy cultures," could not be differentiated from "surly and nasty" cultures on the basis of race, geography, climate, size, wealth, poverty, complexity, matrilineality, patrilineality, house size, the absence or presence of polygamy, and so on. More research revealed to her one simple and commonsensical rule separating aggressive from nonaggressive cultures, a rule that has so far evaded implementation by our culture: the social forms and institutions of nonaggressive cultures positively reinforce acts that benefit the group as a whole while negatively reinforcing acts (and eliminating goals) that harm some members of the group.

The social forms of aggressive cultures, on the other hand, reward actions that emphasize individual gain, even or especially when that gain harms others in the community. A primary and sometimes all-consuming goal of members of these cultures is to come out ahead in their "dog eat dog" world.

Another way to put this is that social arrangements of nonaggressive cultures eliminate the polarity between selfishness and altruism by making the two identical: In a "good" culture, the man atop the box from the parable above would have been scorned, despised, exiled, or otherwise prevented from damaging the community. To behave in such a selfish and destructive manner would be considered insane. Even had he conceived such a preposterous idea as hoarding all the fish, he would have been absolutely disallowed because the box was held at the expense of the majority, as well as at the expense of future generations. For him to be a rich and influential member of a good culture, he would have had to give away many or all of the fish. The act of giving would have made him rich in esteem. But he would never have been allowed to strip the river. There would have been no fear with regard to the "gift" of fish, for social arrangements would have made him secure in the knowledge that if his next fishing trip failed his more successful neighbors would feed him, just as this time he had fed them.

It all comes down to how a culture handles wealth. If a culture manages it through what Benedict called a "siphon system," whereby wealth is constantly siphoned from rich to poor, the society as a whole and its members as individuals will be, for obvious reasons, secure. They will not need to hoard wealth. Since this generosity is manifested not only monetarily but in all aspects of life, they will also not need to act out their now-nonexistent insecurities in other ways. On the other hand, if a culture uses a "funnel system," in which those who accumulate wealth are esteemed, the result is that "the advantage of one individual becomes a victory over another, and the majority who are not victorious must shift as they can." For reasons that should again be obvious, such social forms foster insecurity and aggression, both personal and cultural.

One of the primary problems with our system of social rewards is its tautological nature. We grant communal responsibility and esteem to those who have accumulated and maintained power; but the primary motivation for those who are responsible for decisions affecting the larger community lies in the accumulation and maintenance of power. The good of the community does not matter. In time, the community takes on the character of these esteemed leaders. This happens primarily through direct decisions, the inculcation of citizens to emulate those who receive this respect, and the institutionalization of the leaders' drive for power. Institutions—be they governmental, economic, religious, educational, penal, charitable—will mirror their founders' proclivity for domination. It's inescapable. The system of rewards guarantees that responsibility for community decisions falls to those least capable of making decisions that will benefit the community, to the indecent, to the *wétikos,* the cannibals, to those who would destroy. The French anarchist Sebastien Faure located two principles that govern all politics within our system:

first, the acquisition of power by all means, even the most vile; and second, to keep that power by all means, even the most vile.

At some point in the ceaseless expansion of our culture's realm of control, the notion of a community was replaced by the acceptance of communal control by distant and increasingly unresponsive institutions. The larger the institution, the more accumulated power it takes to reach the top. It would follow that the primary motivations of those at the top are founded in the acquisition and maintenance of power, which means the more likely that the institution will manifest this particular form of destructive (and psychotic) behavior.

I received peculiar confirmation of this self-evident tendency a few years ago—as well as additional confirmation that the political is the personal—when I came across a study of the sexual habits of politicians. The study grew out of psychologists Dr. Sam Janus's and Dr. Barbara Bess's work with drug addicts. Realizing that a good portion of their clients supported drug habits through prostitution, their emphasis shifted toward the study of prostitutes. Eventually their work focused on "elite prostitutes" who "catered to an entirely different type of client." Finally, they realized that the "missing link in understanding the function of the prostitute in contemporary society" consisted of an examination of the women's customers.

The psychologists conducted extensive interviews with eighty high-priced prostitutes about their 7,645 clients. They found that sixty percent of the clients exercised some form of political power, while the remainder were mainly wealthy businessmen. The authors required two independent sources for each report on the sexual habits of the clientele before accepting it. The results are disturbing: "Very seldom (only about 8 to 10 percent of the time) does a politician ask a call girl for straight intercourse," instead primarily requesting "games of humiliation and dominance." The authors report that "the women whom we interviewed reported that their clients went much further than that, often demanding them to act out complicated scenes of torture and mortification of the flesh, involving floggings, lacerations, mock crucifixions, and mutilation of their genitals." The authors conclude, and I quote this in full because it stands so central to our culture: "To understand why so many politicians are not merely promiscuous but are addicted to sadomasochistic practices for which they need the expensive services of a 'paraprofessional sex therapist' requires a deeper look into the psychodynamics of the power seeker. These are characterized by a strong need to dominate which co-exists in precarious equilibrium with an equally intense need for submission. This psychological pattern is manifested outwardly by a drive to subjugate and control others (but always in obedience to some higher ideal), and in private by imperious demands for violently aggressive sex which upon orgasm abruptly becomes transformed into an equally sharp state of infantile dependence."

What is writ large in the destruction of the biosphere is writ small on the bodies of women, and inscribed on the psyches of these, our leaders, the men who will determine for us whether we as a species survive.

In 1994, the Mayan Indians of Chiapas, Mexico, began a revolution, calling themselves Zapatistas. The revolution was their response to extreme poverty caused by control of their homeland by distant economic interests. ("Where I live, everyone dies of illness—they die without anyone having to kill them.") Soon after the beginning of the insurrection, an advisor to Chase Manhattan Bank wrote a memo advising, "While Chiapas, in our opinion, does not pose a fundamental threat to Mexican political stability, it is perceived to be so by many in the investment community. The government will need to eliminate the Zapatistas to demonstrate their effective control of the national territory and of security policy."

What is writ small in the bedrooms of politicians is writ large across the south of Mexico, and anywhere else that anyone resists the control of their lives by those who would destroy.

It is 5:30 in the morning. A few moments ago I awoke with a start. This time I am not confused. I have never been more clear. I know the nightmare can have only one conclusion, and I know also that the nightmare cannot be defeated on its own terms.

It is not possible to fix this culture, to halt or even significantly slow its destructiveness. Nightmarish shape shifter, as I hope by now I've made clear, this culture's destructive urges can yoke all circumstances to its advantage. A parable of this adaptability begins with a single person. He or she wakes up from the nightmare to reject the behavior modifications of our culture. He or she becomes the catalyst of a popular movement advocating cooperation, sharing, and love. Call this person Jesus, or Spartacus, or Martin Luther King, or Gandhi, and this movement the Zapatistas, or the Anabaptists, or any number of names. The response by authorities, those atop the box and the soldiers who also dream the nightmare, is swift and certain. First, the authorities eliminate the offending person or group, "to demonstrate their effective control of the national territory and of security policy." This elimination has been the fate of all who effectively oppose the perceived divine right of the wealthy to control the lives of those they impoverish or enslave: Jesus, Martin Luther King Jr., the Anabaptists, the Arawaks, the Khoikhoi, the San, and tens of millions of other individuals and groups; if we go back far enough, it happened to the ancient indigenous Europeans and Middle Easterners.

The next and most important step in the nightmare's process of adaptation must be to coopt and subvert the message, as Christians have done with the story of Jesus, as corporations and mainstream environmental groups do with peoples' desire to live on a healthy planet, as the New Age movement does with Indian symbology.

Here is the real lesson of the story of Jesus, the main myth of our Christian culture: oppose us and we will kill you, speak to us of love and we will nail you to a cross. We will deify your image and ignore your words. Within the span of three generations, your precious people will be killing each other in your name.

The real gods of our culture—those who are esteemed, granted great social power—are not those who try to implement egalitarianism, who try to put in place a "siphon system," who try to make ours into a "good" culture; the real gods are those who gain and wield control through the use of force. The real gods are the emperors, the kings, the presidents, the wealthy—the Roosevelts,

Rockefellers, Bushes, Kennedys, Weyerhaeusers—those who enrich themselves by despoiling land, people, everything and everyone within their reach. The nightmare cannot be defeated *on its own terms.*

This does not mean that Jesus, Spartacus, and the Arawaks lived and died in vain. They merely came too soon for their words and actions to alter the destructive course of this culture: they intersected this cannibal culture before it had sufficiently destroyed its ecosystemic base, and entered its endgame. Although I cannot predict the future, I do know that any culture that consumes its natural environment base will eventually collapse under the weight of its own strengths. Until then, what we each need to do is awaken to our own personal role in this nightmare, to loosen the delusion's hold. Once we have awakened, once we know that the man does not sit atop the box through divine right, once we recognize that cultural convention is merely cultural invention, once we know that it does not have to be this way, that not all cultures have as their trajectory centralized control and ultimate annihilation, it is time to start the real work, time to devote our lives to saving what few fish remain, time to make sure that no one ever again sits atop the box.

Violence Revisited

"What I fear is being in the presence of evil and doing nothing. I fear that more than death."

Otilia deKoster

I'M NOT SUGGESTING, BY the way, that a few well-aimed assassinations would solve all of our problems. If it were that simple, I wouldn't be writing this book. But to assassinate Slade Gorton and Larry Craig, for example, two Senators from the Northwest whose work may be charitably described as unremittingly genocidal and ecocidal, would probably not slow the destruction much more than it would for me to write them each a letter. For that is where the analog between my family and the culture begins to fall apart, or at least lose simplicity. Although my father is not unique within the culture, he was alone within the family, in that he was a discrete package of violence, which means that his removal would have stopped the horrors. Once his violence had been eliminated, the rest of us could have attempted to pick up the pieces of our shattered lives and to heal, both physically and psychically. Although his removal would not have guaranteed our emotional survival, it would have helped promote it. But Slade Gorton and Larry Craig are not discrete packages of violence. They are neither unique nor alone within the culture, but are merely tools for enacting genocide, ecocide, and other atrocities, as surely as are dams, corporations, chainsaws, napalm, nuclear weapons, Colonel Chivington, the *Malleus Maleficarum,* and claims to virtue.

If I were to kill Slade Gorton and Larry Craig—and remember as you read this the difficulty I have killing fish or birds, and the surge of emotion I feel at the killing of an aphid by a ladybug larva, and know that to kill a human being would be extremely difficult for me, if not impossible—they would simply be replaced by two more people with the same worldview. The genocidal and ecocidal programs originating specifically from the damaged psyches of Gorton and Craig would die with them, but the shared nature of the destructive impulse would continue, making their replacement as easy as buying a new hoe.

I recently shared a heated argument on this subject with my

Buddhist friend George. I suggested, sort of contradicting the previous paragraph, that there are some cases where assassination is appropriate. Hitler, for example. Had the German resistance succeeded in killing Hitler in their July 20, 1944 bomb plot, or better, long before, the lives of literally millions of Jews, Gypsies, Russians, Slavs, homosexuals, communists, intellectuals, and so forth would have been spared. The generals had planned to negotiate a peace with the Allies, which means that millions of soldiers would also not have lost their lives; the same would have been true for millions of civilians killed by United States and British terror bombings, and millions more killed by German and Soviet programs of systematic terror.

George argued, rightly enough, that killing Hitler would have done nothing to eradicate the underlying anti-Semitism, as well as the culture's broader urge to destroy, and that Hitler merely manifested this urge brilliantly enough to capture the hearts of those who voted him into power and to hold the loyalty of the millions of soldiers and citizens who actively carried out his plans. In essence, George was merely pointing out, once again rightly enough, that Hitler didn't act alone.

"But," I said, "What about Anne Frank? She would still be alive." I recalled a photograph I'd seen of an unknown member of the French Resistance murdered by the Gestapo in September 1944. The photograph showed only his back, and the razor marks of his torture. He would have lived. "It's fine," I continued, "to talk about historical forces, but what about this person, or this person, or this person, each an individual, each dead because we hesitated to kill Hitler?"

"What are you going to do?" George asked, "Kill everybody who helped him? And what about Suharto in Indonesia, Mobutu in Zaire, Hussein in Iraq, Schwarzkopf and Bush for that matter? What about Reagan? His policies were every bit as genocidal as Hitler's. Are you going to kill each of them? And if you do, what about you?"

"If I would have killed Hitler, the Gestapo would have killed me. Not my first choice for how to die, but I would have needed to prepare for that possibility."

"That's not what I mean," he said. "If you kill Hitler, or if you kill all of them, what does that make you?"

Silence stretched between us. I thought of the story George told about the Buddha committing murder, but in this moment that didn't seem to help. Finally, I said, "A killer."

I thought again of the immense gap that separates those who do not destroy from those who do. That gap is one of the reasons for the success and contagion of the cannibal sickness, because cannibals have fewer problems killing than noncannibals, and especially because the cannibals have trapped us in an alley with two dead ends. If we fail to fight them we die, and if we fight them we run the risk of becoming them.

Another problem with violence is its finality.

When I'm on the road, I always carry a baseball bat in the back of my truck to use each time I see a snake. If the snake is sunning herself, I stop the truck and use the bat to shoo her to safety. Sometimes, if the snake is especially sluggish, I loop her over the bat and carry her out of traffic. If she's already dead I don't use the bat at all, but carry her to my truck, then take her to some quiet spot where she can lie to decompose with dignity.

But most often when I stop I have to use the bat not to save the snake but kill her. Too many times I've seen them live and writhing with broken backs, flattened vertebrae, even crushed heads.

Early this spring I came across a garter snake sunning at the edge of a road. He didn't move as I approached. I nudged him with my toe and he still didn't move. Peering more closely, I saw that his head looked strange in a way I couldn't quite put my finger on. I prodded him again. Still nothing. The closer I looked the more I thought his back must be broken.

I got the bat and struck him.

But I was wrong. He wasn't injured. Only cold. When I smashed his head he writhed for all he was worth on the pavement. Of course now I had no choice but to finish killing him.

I cannot now pass that spot without thinking of the mistake I made, and especially of the finality of that mistake. I can go on, and I can shoo snakes off the road in the future. But this one is dead. I do not like the fact that my wrong decision cost this snake his life.

Recently I came across three quotes that reveal much about our culture. The first, from the October 26, 1939, issue of the newspaper *Daily Sketch*, describes our economics in a nutshell: "New York Stock Exchange had a boom yesterday following Von Ribbentrop's speech at Danzig. Wall Street interprets the speech as meaning a long war. Stocks rose almost to the highest levels of the year."

The second, from Winston Churchill, describes in a nutshell our future: "It is probable—nay, certain that among the means which will next time be at their disposal will be agencies and processes of destruction wholesale, unlimited and perhaps, once launched, uncontrollable. . . . Death stands at attention, obedient, ready to shear away the peoples en masse; ready if called on to pulverize, without hope or repair, what is left of civilization. He awaits only the word of command."

The third, from Albert Einstein, describes our capacity to destroy: "I know not with what weapons World War Three will be fought, but World War Four will be fought with sticks and stones."

When as a teenager I first heard about Mutually Assured Destruction—the American and Soviet policies of building massive arsenals of nuclear weapons, guaranteeing that if either side struck all life on the planet would be destroyed—it became clear that something is fatally wrong with our culture. Even though at the time I considered myself conservative—as late as my freshman year in college I voted for Ronald Reagan—I understood that to build enough bombs to kill everyone on the planet hundreds of times over made no sense. Who gains from such an irresponsible and stupid undertaking? Even to construct enough bombs, nerve gas, containers of anthrax bacilli, or what have you, to kill everyone just once would be monstrously insane (to construct *any* weapons of mass destruction is monstrously insane). What seemed even more insane was that most people didn't seem to share this perception of runaway lunacy, but went about their business as though this capacity for destruction—we're talking about killing everybody on the planet, here—was nothing out of the ordinary. I couldn't wrap my mind around it. Because I wanted to believe what I had been told, that our country was doing the right thing, the best thing, the most civilized thing, the *sane* thing, I began to read history books, speeches, even policy documents. It still didn't make sense. I read the commentary of political columnists who stated they would rather see their daughters dead than married to communists, and I wondered why no one challenged this thinking. Even as a teen I wondered how these people maintained credibility after giving voice to sentiments so unthinkable, shameful, hateful, controlling, and just plain stupid. I heard policy makers refer blithely to the deaths of hundreds of millions of people as though they were speaking of wheat falling from an open hand. This made no sense to me. I read an article lamenting that unless we built more bombs—perhaps enough to kill everyone not hundreds but thousands of times over—the United States would soon be conquered by the Soviet Union, the conquest being "done in such a way that at no one point will we feel it sensible to resist at a cost of 100 million lives." One hundred million. My family. The families of my friends. Their friends. Everyone I had ever met. Everyone I had ever seen. All dead, with room for millions more. This made no sense to me.

Don't get me wrong. I was opposed to communism, whatever that was, and believed that the Soviet Union was not only communist (which it was not) but was also, as Reagan put it, an "evil empire" (which it was, though certainly no more so than the United States). Asked to write an essay in praise of the United States for its bicentennial, I attacked the government for failing to "protect our brave allies" in South Vietnam.

But even though I thought "defending" South Vietnam was a righteous undertaking, the way it was done made no sense to me. No, I was not one of those people calling for the defoliation of the entire countryside, believing that all would be fine if we could just nuke the commies out of existence. Instead, I remember reading that the cost to American taxpayers to prosecute the war was between $250 and $350 billion. This money was spent to kill between one and three million people, which means that during the war the government paid between $80,000 and $350,000 to kill a Vietnamese person. This in a country where the per capita income is well under $1000 per year. Not a whole lot of "bang for the buck," as military analysts are wont to say. A cheaper, more effective, and certainly more life-affirming anti-Soviet policy would have been to hand each of our supposed enemies $40,000, then tell them to go home and take care of their families. Forty to eighty years' worth of wages in one pop would buy a hell of a lot of goodwill: had the Soviets offered me an equivalent amount of money to vote for Gus Hall, perennial Communist party presidential candidate in the United States, I would have voted, signed petitions, carried placards, and written letters to the editor. Anything to allow me to permanently stay on the gravy train.

So the goal was never to stop the Soviets. That's what we said, but our actions and inventions pointed to the real goal of our culture.

Incendiary devices causing firestorms that burn to death hundreds of thousands of people in a single night. Bouncing Bettys. Land mines. Atomic bombs. Hydrogen bombs. Neutron bombs. How do we make sense of these?

The military and CIA experts James A. Dunnigan and Albert A. Nofi analyzed military spending, and made comparisons that reveal much about the real intent of our culture: "For what the world spends on defense every 2.5 hours, about $300 million, smallpox was eliminated back in the late seventies. For the price of a single new nuclear-attack submarine, $726 million to $1 billion, we could send 5 to 7.5 million Third World children to school for a year. For the price of a single B-1 bomber, about $285 million, we could provide basic immunization treatments, such as shots for chicken pox, diphtheria, and measles, to the roughly 575 million children in the world who lack them, thus saving 2.5 million lives annually. For what the world spends on defense every forty hours, about $4.6 billion, we could provide sanitary water for every human being who currently lacks it. Looking at it another way, the roughly $290–$300 billion that the United States [spent] on defense in 1990 is greater than the total amount that Americans contribute to charity each year, about $100 billion, plus total federal, state, local, public, and private expenditures for education, roughly $150 billion, plus NASA's entire budget of $7.6 billion, plus federal and state aid to families with dependent children, $16.3 billion, plus the cost of the entire federal judiciary and the Justice Department combined, $5.5 billion, plus federal transportation aid to state and local governments, $17.5 billion. . . . A single Stinger missile costs $40,000, or roughly 30 percent more than the income of the average American family, nearly twice more than the income of the average black American family, and about 400 percent more than the so-called poverty line . . . [and] the price of 2,000 rounds of 7.62-mm rifle or machine-gun ammunition, about $480.00, is slightly more than what the average Social Security beneficiary receives every month." How do we wrap our minds around these priorities?

Or take plutonium. How do we explain the fabrication of plutonium? Plutonium is fundamentally a man-made element. Although traces occur naturally in uranium, its use in nuclear weapons and power have caused it to be "produced in extensive quantities," as my staid CRC Handbook of Chemistry and Physics puts it. *Extensive quantities*, in this case, means about 260 metric tons of plutonium-239, in addition to nearly a thousand tons of plutonium's fifteen other isotopes. Two hundred and sixty metric tons is two hundred and sixty thousand kilograms is two hundred and sixty million grams is two hundred and sixty billion milligrams. The inhalation of a few of these milligrams—a barely visible speck—causes death by internal asphyxiation in a few months as lung tissues scar up from a bombardment of alpha radiation and choke off oxygen supply to the blood. Two hundred and sixty billion milligrams is two hundred and sixty trillion micrograms. The inhalation of a few of these micrograms—by far invisible to the naked eye, as well as undetectable by human taste or smell—likely causes fatal lung cancer in ten or twenty years, as cells damaged by alpha radiation multiply uncontrollably; the incidence of lung cancer among beagles forced to inhale comparable amounts of plutonium was 100 percent. Two hundred and sixty trillion micrograms is two hundred and sixty quadrillion nanograms. The best estimate for plutonium's LD-50, or the dosage at which 50 percent of the victims die, is around ten nanograms.

The intentional fabrication of thirteen quadrillion lethal doses of plutonium seemed nonsensical to me until I was able to begin drawing lines of connecting thought and understanding from point to destructive point of our culture's behavior. The greatest mass extinction in the history of the planet. Ubiquitous genocide leading to the deaths of scores or hundreds of millions of people. Race-based slavery, leading to the deaths of scores or hundreds of millions more. Class-based slavery. Child slavery. Mass rapes. Vivisection. Factory farms. Irrational, deadly, and suicidal military budgets and policies. What picture emerges when you see all these together?

The deforestation of the Middle East, Europe, North America, the Amazon, now Siberia. The depletion of fishery after fishery. Just yesterday I read that scientists now predict that bluefin tuna will go extinct within the coming generation. The elimination of passenger pigeons, Eskimo curlews.

There can be only one end to this, of course. Apocalypse. Götterdämmerung. The destruction of the world in the final war of the gods, gods we have first, as I mentioned before, projected, and then reintrojected. Stasis. Death. The end of all life, if the dominant culture has its way. It's where we've been headed from the beginning of this several-thousand year journey. It is the only possible end for a culture of linear—as opposed to cyclical—progress. Beginning, middle, end. Self-extinguishment. The only solace and escape from separation: from ourselves, from each other, from the rest of the planet. Plutonium. DDT. Dioxin. Why else would we poison ourselves? No other explanation makes comprehensive sense. Apocalypse. "The first angel sounded, and there followed hail and fire mingled with blood, and they were cast upon the earth; and the third part of trees was burnt up, and all green grass was burnt up." American Chestnut. American Elm. Idaho White Pine. Redwood. Tallgrass Prairie. Shortgrass Prairie. "And the second angel sounded, and as it were a great mountain burning with fire was cast into the sea: and the third part of the sea became blood; And the third part of the creatures which were in the sea, and had life, died." Blue Whales. Right Whales. Cod. Halibut. Tuna. "And the third angel sounded, and there fell a great star from heaven, burning as it were a lamp, and it fell upon the third part of the rivers, and upon the fountains of waters; And the name of the star is called Wormwood: and the third part of the waters became wormwood; and many men died of the waters, because they were made bitter." Salmon. Bull trout. Western Cutthroat. Alabama Sturgeon. Western Sturgeon. Snail Darter. Arizona Pupfish. Each of these and so many more, individually, communally, and as species, destroyed not by angels nor by God, but by a culture aspiring toward the conclusion set forth from the beginning.

For me, at least, it was a relief to finally acknowledge and articulate this understanding I long had held in my bones, that underlying all this otherwise incomprehensible behavior is a desire to destroy other and self. The culture's terminus: the destruction of all. It's primary intellectual task: to simultaneously rationalize, justify, and obfuscate the actions leading to this goal.

Clarity. No longer did I have to ignore smoke from next door's burning synagogue, nor try to take at face value the myriad self-contradictory claims to virtue that daily front for destructive behavior, nor find myself befuddled by the false choices that bind us to the annihilation of our planet. Clarity.

Examples abound. They are as near as many children's bedrooms and as far away as the stars the Vatican hopes bring light and warmth to beings who like ourselves have experienced original sin and the murder of the sinless.

Last week I read in the newspaper that the largest white pine in Idaho is dying. Nearly four hundred years old, its time has come, and beetles have arrived to finish it off. The tree stands on Forest Service ground, and the district forester does not want to allow the beetles, nor the tree, their way. Of course he's not talking about saving the tree's life; he wants to cut it down, pulp it, and turn the stump into a display. The reporter noted that despite the size of the tree, it may very well take more paper to justify implementation of the forester's plan than the tree would provide as pulp. A citizen has penned on the marker in front of the old one: "This tree is dying, too bad they cut all the rest." The tree shall not stand alone for long.

Last week I also read, in a different newspaper, that the Forest Service has begun injecting heart rot fungus into healthy trees in order to kill them. Here is the rationale: Logging has damaged forests. In order to justify continued deforestation, the Forest Service and timber industry fabricated the previously mentioned claim to virtue that additional logging is needed to repair the logging-induced damage. Thus, as I alluded to before, dead trees, dying trees, and trees that may someday die—this definition has been intentionally created to encompass all trees—must be cut so that they do not someday become sick. Now, evidently, at least some National Forests are beginning to suffer a shortage of dead, standing trees. Because in a healthy, functioning forest, dead trees remain for decades or centuries to house and feed other members of the community, those other members are suffering. The solution proposed by the Forest Service is of course not to stop cutting trees, which would mean an end, or at least a slowing, of deforestation, but instead to kill more trees. To inject poison into their hearts. Presumably once enough trees have been injected, the Forest Service will declare another forest health crisis and cut down all merchantable timber within a few-mile radius. The only way I can make sense of all this is to invoke our culture's belief in Armageddon—and its associated death urge.

Yet another example. On October 13, 1997, Columbus Day plus one, NASA launched the Cassini Space Probe. The ostensible purpose was to explore Saturn. We could discuss the arrogance, stupidity, and inhumanity of spending $3.4 billion to explore another planet while $285 million would save the lives of 2.5 million children annually on the planet we already occupy. But the death urge is made even more clear by another factor. Because Cassini's propulsion source didn't have the power to send it straight to Saturn, NASA sent it first to Venus, and then, after two swings around that planet, the probe returned home, approaching within 312 miles of Earth's surface. It used the acceleration caused by our gravity to slingshot the probe out to Saturn. Here's the danger: in order to power its instruments, the probe contains 72.3 pounds of plutonium, mainly plutonium-238, which is about two hundred times more deadly than plutonium-

239. Seventy-two and three-tenths pounds of plutonium is almost thirty-three thousand grams, or almost thirty-three million milligrams, or almost thirty-three billion micrograms, or almost thirty-three trillion nanograms.

There are two ways the plutonium could have been delivered to human victims. The first is that the Titan IV rocket carrying the probe could have exploded on launch. NASA estimated the danger of this at one in four hundred and fifty-six, which is bad enough, considering the consequences, but the truth is that a Titan IV rocket has already exploded. Nongovernmental estimates of failure were "between one in ten and one in twenty."

The other way the plutonium could have killed people would have been if on the flyby the probe suffered what NASA scientists dryly called "an inadvertent reentry." If NASA calculations would have been imprecise (a mission to Mars crashed because scientists failed to convert English to metric measurements in their calculations), or if the probe had malfunctioned, it could have fallen into Earth's atmosphere and burned up. As the scientists put it: "If an accident or failure resulted in loss of control of the spacecraft prior to Earth swingby, the spacecraft could conceivably be placed on a Earth-impacting trajectory." If the craft were to "be placed on a Earth-impacting trajectory," the scientists said that "the potential health effects [of plutonium poisoning] could occur in two distinct populations, the population within and near the reentry footprint and most of the world population within broad north to south latitude bands." In other words, the plutonium would have poisoned those near the crash, and everyone else. The scientists stated that "approximately 5 billion of the estimated 7 to 8 billion world population at the time of the swingbys could receive 99 percent or more of the radioactive exposure." These quotes are from NASA's Final Environmental Impact Statement for the Cassini Probe, one of the documents used to justify the launch.

The Cassini Probe was not the first to carry plutonium. It will not be the last. In 2002 the Comet Nucleus Mission will lift off carrying 25.5 kilograms of plutonium. In 2003 the Pluto Flyby will carry the same amount. Five launches to Mars will carry a total of seventeen kilograms, and four launches to the moon will carry another 42.5 kilograms.

Plutonium. Death. We inject phenol into the hearts of Jews and fungus into the hearts of trees. We send plutonium on rockets known to explode. Before members of our culture exploded the first atomic bomb, scientists were not certain that the explosion would not set off a chain reaction that would consume the entire atmosphere. Yet they proceeded. They believed their calculations were correct, they gambled, and they won. Or lost, depending on your perspective. And, as any gambler knows, the roulette ball eventually must land on double-zero. It is simply a matter of playing enough times.

All too often—every moment of every day, really—the intent of our culture becomes blazingly clear in action. In rare moments of often unintentional honesty it comes clear in speech. The detonation of the first atomic bomb was one such moment. Standing stunned before the awesome power he had helped to bring about, Robert J. Oppenheimer, one of the lead scientists of the Manhattan Project, gave voice to words that sum up in one sentence the essence of our culture: "I am become death, the destroyer of worlds." Staring into a blast brighter than the sun, hotter, less useful—useful only to destroy—Oppenheimer was not alone. He had for company not just Descartes, Chivington, and all the rest, but also in this case those of us who see the culture for what it is, and who stand with him, staring into this power, uncomprehending, afraid, and trying desperately to stop the long and binding chain of action and reaction we see unfolding before us.

Every morning now the rumbling of explosions penetrates my dreams. They—those who would destroy the forest to the east—are getting closer, and they've begun to blast. In my dreams I hear explosions, and the sounds of bulldozers that become the clanking of tank treads. Every dream ends with me running away. I awaken to the barking of dogs, and see Amaru staring at the coyote, who sits not thirty feet from him and returns his stare. I open the window, and Amaru, Narcissus, and the coyote all look at me for one frozen moment before Amaru and Narcissus give chase. The rumbling and explosions continue. I arise, shower, and walk to the coyote tree, carrying, as I have been doing lately, an offering of bread. I don't know whether I am feeding coyotes or deer, porcupines or skunks, magpies or chipmunks. But I know that each day the bread is gone. I see at the coyote tree that they—those who are neither developers nor speculators but killers—have returned, and brought with them more stakes, and more ribbons. They have painted the ground, so even pulling up the long wood and metal stakes no longer will slow them. As I stand there, frustrated, exasperated, horrified, the ground shakes beneath my feet from another blast. I feel it in my bones, up my legs and along my spine, and I see it in the swaying of trees, both little and big. I'm at a loss—I don't know what to do.

What do we do with our anger? Pretending not to feel it doesn't help, nor do the inappropriate manifestations that necessarily follow this pretense. Damming the flow merely forces the fury to find side channels for expression, and as with the poisoned water I mentioned earlier, an outlet will always be found.

Here's what has me thinking about this: after too many years of being too sedentary, I'm trying to rekindle my love of basketball. All through high school and early college I used to play several times per week, only leaving the sport when high jumping swept me away. But as I've gotten older—I'm in my thirties now—my springs aren't so taut, and I no longer float over the bar. I no longer jump fences barely breaking stride, as I did in my late teens, nor do I jump them after serious consideration, as I did in my late twenties. Now I look for a gate, or, failing that, crawl under.

So far basketball hasn't been as much fun as I remember. I'm unwelcome on the courts, not because of age or inability (I haven't lost *that* much), but because I'm white.

Spokane's population is as purely white as any I've seen, and most of the local people of color I've spoken with tell stories of hatred and outrage, ranging from pointed looks in public to beatings by police. Nearly every African-American male I've taught at Eastern Washington University had either been struck or cursed by members of the Spokane Police Department. Last year I read that a white teenager attacked a black teenager in a parking lot;

the white teen's mother ran to her car to grab mace and a knife. Returning to the fight, she maced the teen her son was attacking, then repeatedly stabbed him in the groin. Police refused to press charges. The receipt of hate mail by nonwhite students at Gonzaga Law School, here in town, has become something of a yearly tradition. Just across the border in Idaho squats the Aryan Nation's compound, a beacon for racists nationwide. It is against this backdrop that I took my sweats and basketball, my tattered shoes and rusty twenty-foot jumper, to a community gym.

I was one of the few whites in the building. Most of the players refused to acknowledge my presence, and even when I was playing they responded to my "Nice shot," or "Good pull" by looking away. As a teen I played basketball in the downtowns of many cities I visited: Chicago, New York, Watts. Never before had I been treated this way.

I sat out a game, atop a short row of stowed bleachers. The quality of play was good. The team running left to right, consisting of four black men and one white, scored nearly every time down the court. Although the white guy was nowhere near the best on the team, I knew from covering him that he was good—sag on defense and he'll sink a twenty-five footer: move out to guard and he'll glide by for an easy bucket. From the bleachers I watched him take the ball to the hoop and miss a contested layup. Two black men sitting on my left began to shout, "White fuckers ruin everything. Don't give him the ball. He'll just miss." As they were shouting, the white guy made a nice steal and pass to a black teammate, who missed an open layup. The men on my left didn't pause in their shouting, nor presumably perceive the contradiction between what they witnessed and what they said.

I wrote this in a letter to a friend, who wrote back, "Racism is tied intimately to power and class, don't you think? If you feel the world is against you, and you notice that the white man has power and money—which in our culture amounts to the same thing—I believe it would be tough for a person of color not to be racist."

I wasn't happy with this answer. I'd just wanted him to validate my feelings of not having been welcomed, and for him to tell me that of course those comments had been rude.

I wrote him back, and he wrote me again, "Surely you can see why a white man is going to get scrutinized, and any miss is going to be held against him. They probably don't want you there—nothing personal, here, Derrick—because you, or rather what you stand for, which in this case is whiteness, control every other place in town except the basketball court. Whites control the government, the economy, the newspapers, plus the police and the rest of the legal system. And now we want the damn basketball court, too! It's no wonder they want whites to miss."

All I'd wanted is some exercise. But I knew he was right. It's no more possible to remove these basketball players from the racist society that engenders their anger than it is to remove our political leaders from the culture that creates *their* drive for power. My friend John Keeble has said he likes to study members of the Aryan Nations and other hate groups because "at least they admit they're racist, and that they're afraid. The whole culture is racist and afraid, but most of us don't talk about it."

I know all this. And it makes what happened at the gym comprehensible. But I also know it's not okay to displace anger. Nothing excuses rude or violent behavior toward random or semi-random people. My father stealing my childhood is no reason for me to steal someone else's, just as his own parents destroying his was no reason for him to steal mine. The psychological wounds that drive CEOs and politicians do not excuse their genocidal and ecocidal policies. The wounds that drive our culture to these same ends are similarly no excuse.

I mentioned a fantasy before, of Jesus or someone like him not being crucified but accepted. I have another fantasy. I wish that those of us who feel anger—which is most of us—could learn to see our anger for what it is, and turn it toward appropriate sources. Instead of cursing a white guy for missing a layup I wish that the people in the gym would turn that anger toward bringing about change. Instead of complaining about racist basketball players I wish I would turn my own anger also toward change.

I wrote this again to my friend. He wrote back, "If only it were that easy. It'd be great if we could simply pick out the real enemy instead of having the poor fight the poor. But our culture is designed for us not to see that. Instead we find some 'common enemy' to unite against. It's all sleight of hand. 'Look how the welfare bums ruin society.' Or blacks, Jews, the Ayatolla, Saddam, Mexicans, Cubans, commies, homosexuals, feminists, environmentalists, Indians, the white guy who just missed a layup. All of which takes our attention away from the mega-corporations that basically dictate, and destroy, life as we know it."

He's right again, of course. But it's actually even worse than that. Who, exactly, are we supposed to get mad at? Picture this: you're driving down the interstate, and you get passed by a semi of logs going to a Weyerhaeuser mill. You know, from having read Weyerhaeuser's own documents, that the company has clearcut more than four million acres. You know that just in 1992, the company deforested forty-five square miles in Washington, twenty-five square miles in Oregon, and 152 square miles in the southern United States. You know that Weyerhaeuser is a major deforester of tropical rainforests. You know that the company has from the beginning been a strong supporter of the Indonesian military dictatorship that has murdered nearly a million of its own citizens. You've read vice-president Charles Bingham's response to criticism of the company's genocidal destruction of the land bases upon which indigenous peoples (and all of us, for that matter) depend: "I feel no apologies are necessary for offering the members of those ["primitive," his word from a previous sentence] societies a choice." You know that Weyerhaeuser offers similar choices to indigenous peoples across the globe, deforesting its way from continent to continent, consciences cleared all around the boardroom by the multiple claims to virtue of creating profits for shareholders and choices for the newly landless primitives. You know that the choices offered now to "primitive" peoples by transnational corporations differ little in tangible effect from those offered not-so-long-ago by Christian missionaries.

What do you do? Do you follow the trucker to a rest stop, and slash his tires while he uses the toilet? After all, he is wittingly or unwittingly lending his talents and time to an ecocidal project, to an institution actively committing genocide. And slashing his tires *will* slow the destruction, even if only ever so slightly. Or do you drive on, and wave and smile as you pass him? After all, he is simply a working man trying to earn his living, and support his family. The chances are good in any case that he harbors a more righteous and understanding hatred of the company than you do: that has been the case for the independent loggers, drivers, and mill owners I've known who've been forced to contract out to timber transnationals. And slashing his tires will probably not accomplish much more than ruin the day of a semi-random person. Does that help? How do you make sense of this contradiction: that you have nothing against the man personally, and may be able to understand the reasons for his actions, but once again the tangible effects of his actions are to contribute to ecocide—the destruction of one's house—and genocide. Is it a displacement of anger to act against this person?

Or how about this: do you find Charles Bingham's home address, and do you go there, and do you destroy his home as his decisions similarly destroy the homes of humans and nonhumans across the globe? Now that he has no home, and he can move anywhere, do you say to him, perhaps as the police lead you away, "I feel no apologies are necessary for offering the members of this family a choice as to where they will next live"? If you do this, what have you gained, and what has the world gained? Even though the destruction of his home is less of a sin—though more of a crime—than the destruction he causes (for three primary reasons: he has the money to relocate; he does not feel the unity with his land that his victims feel, or he could not commit ecocide; he is not without blame), is it a displacement of anger to act against this person?

Or how about this: do you systematically slash the tires—you and everyone you know—of every Weyerhaeuser vehicle you see? Do you do everything you can to drive Weyerhaeuser out of business? And when you're done with Weyerhaeuser, do you start over with Boise Cascade, then Potlatch, then Louisiana Pacific, then Georgia Pacific, then Daishowa, then Mitsubishi? Do you clearcut your way through timber transnationals with the same relentlessness with which they clearcut their way through living communities? And then do you choose another industry? Is *this* a displacement of anger?

Or do you do nothing? Do you write respectful letters to Weyerhaeuser executives politely requesting they stop deforesting—as Gandhi wrote respectfully to Hitler—and do you request also that Weyerhaeuser's executives stop the genocide they will not, and cannot, even admit? Do you write your congresspeople? Do you contribute twenty-five dollars to the Sierra Club, and go about your day? Do you write articles and books articulating the problems as clearly as you can, and hope it will make some difference? Is all this a displacement of anger? Or is it a denial of anger and a displacement of responsibility? Is all this as much as you can do? If salmon, tuna, or wolverine could take on human manifestation, what would *they* do?

I don't know where to place the anger. If Slade Gorton and Larry Craig, as I mentioned before, are tools for the enacting of atrocity, and if the same can be said, to greater or lesser degrees of culpability, for Charles Bingham, for George Weyerhaeuser, for those who lend their talents to Weyerhaeuser, for the institution of Weyerhaeuser itself, for all other transnational timber and other types of corporations, for all of us insofar as we participate in the economy of death that surrounds us, informs us, engulfs us, that determines for us how we will spend the majority of our waking hours, that determines for us what chemicals we unbeknownst to us ingest with every meal and inspire with every breath, that determines which creatures among us will live—for now—and which will die, then who is it, precisely, who is wielding these tools? Who, or what, is behind it all? Where do we look for ultimate responsibility, and where exactly do we strike out, either in righteous anger at the destruction of all life, or, coolly, calmly, like the Buddha, like the samurai who tracks down the murderer of his master, because it is the right thing to do?

Coercion

"I have never been able to conceive how any rational being could pro- pose happiness to himself from the exercise of power over others."
Thomas Jefferson, Owner of slaves

I HAVE TO ADMIT I'm pretty fucked up. I keep telling myself I'm one of the lucky ones—*the* lucky one—and that's true. I told myself that as I sat on the couch and watched my brothers beaten and humiliated. It could have been me, but it wasn't. As I watched my sisters cringe in the middle of the room, expectant of the next blow, I told myself I was lucky to only be witness and not victim. I still tell myself I'm lucky. My brother's epilepsy, from blows to the head, is among the least of his problems. Having been struck so hard that your brain is damaged in that way, how can you ever create a life? Having been formed in a fire of hatred—or is it love, I never can be sure—and refined in a crucible of violence, how can you even think of carrying on? How can you even think, or more to the point, ever stop thinking? Yes, I *was* the lucky one.

It's hard. Have you wondered that the great scenes of intimacy and ecstasy I've described in this book have had as their other the stars, a tree, high jumping? Have you wondered what high jumping taught me about love? And that the romantic partners I've described in this book have been peripheral to the discussion: I've spoken more of my conversations with coyotes than with lovers. What does that mean? What does it mean that on the night I confronted the politicians I returned to the arms of a tree, and not of a woman?

I have no answers, and feel as though most of the time I don't even have questions. The questions I do have so often seem simple avoidances of what I feel, and of what I am afraid to feel, underneath.

Until the end of my twenties I had nightmares almost every night. A vampire who slashed my face with a razor as I said to him, "You cannot hurt me." A doctor who strapped me seated to a wall, then pulled away the seat and spread my legs to rape me. Dream after dream where I escaped danger, only to find myself back where I began, or to find that those I trusted turned out, too, to be vampires. Or rapists. Or murderers. The nightmares have slowed, to perhaps two or three per week.

I often feel as though I've forgotten how to fall asleep. I can lie there awake for hours. Not scared, always. Just awake. And when I do fall asleep I often reawaken, probably an average of fifteen to twenty times per night. I am likely as not frightened, yet I am able to fall back asleep. I am thankful for that, or I would not sleep at all.

The first woman I ever dated snuck up behind me once to tickle me. Once. I whirled, fists raised, before I even thought, and my own look of horror that reflected back to me in her face has stayed with me ever since. Of course I did not hit her. I have never hit anyone. But no one sneaks up on me.

I sometimes feel as though the tone of this book is not appropriate. I'm not certain the language is raw enough. My language is too fine, the sentences too lyrical, to describe things neither child nor adult should have to describe at all. As for the atrocities that are not mine but are experienced by others—just today I read a report from Algeria that police routinely pump salt water into political prisoners' stomachs until they burst, or have prisoners stand naked before a table, testicles on the flat surface, and. . . . they, too, should not have to be described. But I know also that if I pretend they do not happen by not writing about them, and you pretend they do not happen by not reading about them, the horrors themselves will not go away. Given the numbers, right now somewhere in a torture center in Algeria (or in many other countries) a woman is being gang-raped by guards, and a man is having a hole bored through his leg with an electric drill. Right now in factory farms. . . . It's not the writing that must change, but the reality.

Writing this book is the hardest thing I have ever done, but so long as I allow myself to remain focused on choosing the words precisely, I can keep myself distracted not only from the difficulty but from the feelings. And keeping ourselves distracted from our feelings is the point of so much of what we do, is it not?

This book is as artificial as any other, and is bound by the laws of cultural production. I allow you to know only what I want you to know of what I know. Even I am allowed to know only a small portion of what I know.

I do not know who I am. When my father came into my room, and I went away—poof—what happened to the part who remained behind? Who is he, and what does he feel? What did he feel? How can I ever make right to him what I put him through by leaving? I know I saved myself, and I do not precisely blame myself, but what of the me I left behind?

I have been splintered into a thousand pieces, and I do not know if I shall ever be whole. I do not even know what wholeness means, and looking around it does not seem that many others do, either.

It should be clear by now that a central belief of our culture—if not *the* central belief—is that it is not only acceptable but desirable and necessary to bend others to our own will. This belief in the rightness of coercion motivates us not only collectively but individually, not only consciously but subliminally.

Coercion is central to our religion, whether we offer those different from us the immediate choice of Christianity or death, or the more eternal choice of Jesus or damnation.

Coercion is central to our scientific philosophy, whether we speak of Descartes' dream of possessing nature, Bacon's storming of nature's strongholds to make her our slave, the suggestion in *Demonic Males* that a woman's safest future may be to bond with a violent man, or Dawkins' pathetic description of selfish genes coercing us to coerce others.

Coercion is central to our applied sciences, whether we speak of dammed rivers, "scientific management" of forests, predator "control" projects, or the exploration of the human genome by self-styled "genetic prospectors" seeking to exploit the chromosomal makeup of often-unwilling peoples.

Coercion is central to our economics, whether we speak of the Middle Passage, the modern-day enslavement of one hundred and fifty million children, the forcing of people to enter the wage economy through the removal of realistic options and more broadly the wage slavery that defines capitalism, or the routine use of police and the military to assist the men atop their boxes to accumulate ever-more wealth.

Coercion is central to our legal system, which presents one face to those in power, and a different face to those who fight this power. In the case of the former, coercion is systematized through a body of lawmakers and interpreters which supports and rationalizes the use of force by those in power to gain material possessions or otherwise bend certain others—the powerless, the silenced, the not-fully-human—to the will of the already powerful. Just as my father never beat anyone without good reason, it is more pleasing to the now-silenced consciences of those doing the coercing to arm themselves not just with weapons and claims to virtue but also with a system of legalistic arguments that justify coercion.

The legal system presents a different face to those who infringe upon the right of those in power to use coercion. Thus the crucifixion of Jesus, and of Spartacus. Thus the slaughter of the Anabaptists. Thus the murder of more than 100,000 in the Peasants' Revolt of 1524, and the torture and murder—purely legal, of course, and fully supported by such luminaries as Martin Luther—of their leader, Thomas Münzer. Thus the torture and murder of the mestizo chief Tupac Amaru, who in 1781 led an unsuccessful rebellion that, until it was crushed, abolished all forms of forced labor in liberated territories around Cuzco. Thus the murder of Crazy Horse. Thus the murder of half the Haymarket conspirators in Illinois. Thus the betrayal of Nestor Makhno and other anarchists after the Russian revolution. Thus in 1995, hot on the heels of the Nigerian military memo stating, "Shell [Oil Corporation] operations still impossible unless ruthless military operations are undertaken [against the Ogoni people] for smooth economic activities to commence," Nigeria executed writer and environmentalist Ken Saro-Wiwa.

Coercion is central to our politics, whether we speak of James Madison insisting, during our country's constitutional convention, that the main goal of the political system must be "to protect the minority of the opulent against the majority," or whether we listen to the words of Adam Smith, godfather of modern economics: "Civil government . . . is in reality instituted for the defense of the rich against the poor, or of those who have some property against those who have none at all," or whether we read the words of seminal political theorist John Locke, who observed, "Government has no other end but the preservation of property." Or we can listen to Richard Nixon: "The American national psychology has few doubts that reasonable men can settle all differences by honest compromise. But the reality is that force has always been the ultimate sanction at a conference table. Diplomacy by itself cannot be effective unless our opponents know what pressures we will be willing to bring to bear."

Coercion is central to the raising of our children, whether we speak of grades, desks arranged in rows before a central authority, or the wearing out of the belt. Consider in contrast the Semay of Malaya who "emphatically deny" that they teach their children, but insist "our children just learn by themselves." If a parent tells a child to do something and the child responds, "I *bood* [a word meaning "to not feel like doing something]," the subject is closed. To put pressure on the child is strictly forbidden. Children learn most activities through imitative play that in time becomes adult behavior.

Coercion is central to our relations with other species, whether we speak of vivisection, factory farming, industrial forestry, or commercial fishing. All grossly immoral and exploitative, all most often scrupulously legal.

The rates for rape and other abuses of women make clear that coercion is central to our cross-gender relations.

As water is to fish, as air is to birds, so coercion is to us. It is where we live. It is what we drink. It is what we breathe. It is transparent. So deeply inured are we that we no longer perceive when we are coercing or being coerced. Grades. Wages. Jobs. The sale of fingers one by one and the purchasing of sex in seemingly simple monetary transactions. On a more grand, though no more outrageous, scale, napalm, penitentiaries, deforestation: all these manifest this need to coerce others.

I have been thinking once again about rape. Given the geography in which we find ourselves, this habitat in which we are reared, this landscape of coercion that surrounds us seemingly everywhere we look, everywhere our culture has been able to touch and transform, it is no wonder, it occurs to me at last, that the levels of adult rape, child abuse, and child rape are so high.

But there is another, and much more powerful, point to be made here: given the degree to which coercion suffuses every person and every action born of this culture, and given coercion's so-often utter transparency, it is a testament to the resilient goodness inherent in each and every one of us that these acts of deeply intimate coercion do not occur even more frequently.

But they do not. There still exist many of us who do not rape, who neither strike nor egregiously coerce others. For the time being, goodness and mutuality have not been exterminated. Like the species still surviving the onslaught of our economics, like the indigenous cultures still surviving our religion, our wars, our guns, our liquor, and our money, like the rivers still surviving our concrete, heavy metals, and pesticides, and like the stars that once again have begun to speak to me at night, or perhaps were speaking all along, I understand now that somewhere inside of each of us—some more than others—still survives that person who would not and will not rape, who would not and will not coerce, that person who understands what it means to be alive and to be a part of a relationship, a family, a community both human and nonhuman. Like the women and children lost after Sand Creek, these lost survivors—or those who at least recognize that they are lost, and who deeply do not wish to coerce—merely need someone—human, star, wolf, bee, or anyone else under the sun—to lead them home.

Honeybees

"Happiness is love, nothing else. A man who is capable of love is happy."
Hermann Hesse.

THE EVIDENCE OF INTERSPECIES communication and the fundamental *beingness* of nonhumans is so obvious as to render my previous skepticism embarrassing. To attempt a proof that nonhumans communicate would not only be degrading—imagine a book purporting to prove that blondes can think—it would be silly, like proving the existence of gravity, love, death, or physical existence. It could be written in two words—*pay attention*—or better, in one—*listen*.

One evening last spring I sat on the couch, looking out the window and talking on the phone. The lights were off, inside and out. The window was open. It was that time of day when shapes lose distinct edges, when solid shadows blur into background. The dark contour of a dog lay tucked in a hole he'd dug to fit his body. I mentioned on the phone that when I brought in the chicks for the night, one was missing. The conversation flowed on, I forgot about the chick, and barely noticed when the dark form stood and walked around the house. Moments later it returned, walked toward the window, stooped, left behind a tiny black bundle, and walked away. When I realized what had happened I put down the phone to run outside. The dog had brought the body of the chick.

During the summer I don't put kitty litter in the cat box, relying instead on the cats to go outside. This is fine with two of them, but the third—who had a very difficult time grasping the concept of using the cat box in the first place, often standing in the box to drop her feces on the floor—did not make the transition so easily. She did, however, find a compromise both of us could live with: she defecated outdoors, and urinated in the bathtub. I then unthinkingly and unilaterally abrogated this agreement by putting more chicks in the tub. When I thought about it later, I hoped she would merely use the other shower. She didn't, but just went outside like the other two. When the weather began to cool I forgot to bring in the cat box. Soon I noticed a smell, and saw she was urinating in a corner of the living room. I brought the cat box inside. That first night—and this is really the point of this story—she jumped on my lap as I worked, which each cat often does, sleeping there while I type or sit. That night, however, she jumped immediately back down and ran out of the room. I followed, and saw that she went directly to the cat box, clearly showing me that she, too, could follow the rules, if only I would learn to get them straight.

Just moments ago I received an email from a friend of Jeannette, who had suggested that she send me the following: "Several years ago, two friends living in Naramata, B.C. observed on several occasions in winter a bald eagle circling over a flock of coots in Okanagan Lake. After some time, invariably one coot would rise and be taken by the eagle. Whether this is done to protect the young or other members of the group, or for some unknown reason, apparently this phenomenon is common knowledge to indigenous and non-indigenous people who live close to the earth. We know that in the complex interaction of all beings on earth, cooperation is an important factor."

Once having begun to look, one has no choice but to see these incidents everywhere, for that is where they are.

The neighbors have a new puppy, an Anatolian shepherd the size of a small bear, who only in the last couple of days discovered my walks to the coyote tree, and followed me and the dogs. Today he discovered the chickens, and has delighted in trotting after them to see them scatter, and he discovered too the cats, delighting even more in giving them chase. As I type these words, a cat is up a tree. Time after time I went outside to say, "No. Go home." He ignored me. Sometimes I tried to be more reasonable: "You can stay here if you don't chase the chickens or cats." He still ignored me. Finally, after the cat went up the tree, I lost patience and roughly pushed him toward home. I stomped my foot, and was going to do it again until I realized how silly I must look. Not so much caring—who is the dog going to tell?—I stomped again. He finally left. Now he dozes on the neighbor's porch. I'm sure he'll be back. My point is that the fact that he did not acquiesce to my requests, or that he doesn't yet know much English (I must admit I know very little cat, dog, chicken, goose, duck, or songbird, though I hear them every day), does not mean that conversations between humans and nonhumans do not exist. After years of doubting, I'm finally growing to understand that my skepticism has all along revealed more about my own inability to perceive or even conceptualize fully mutual conversations— and more basically my inability to allow another to have desires distinctly different from my own—than it does about the nature of human-nonhuman relations.

As you've probably guessed, I've always had an affinity for bugs, and for as long as I can remember I've been especially fascinated by bees, ants, and other social insects. When during the spring semester of my sophomore year in college—the same semester I started high jumping—I saw an ad in the classifieds for a bee-hive, I called and bought it immediately.

Soon I found myself wandering down late evenings to the corner of the pasture, to sit next to the hive and listen to the bees' soft sounds as they moved and talked and sang inside their home. Sometimes I rapped gently to hear their buzzing rise in response, but most often I just sat. I put my face to the opening to smell the rich, moist, fecund scent of bees and wax and honey. To this day I know of no smells quicker to soothe.

I'd go down days, too, to watch the guards pace back and forth on the hive's front stoop; I'd watch as they checked every bee that entered to make sure she belonged. Drones—huge, clumsy, powerful males, never once known to do any work around the hive—would take off or land with a distinctive roar. Sometimes I would stand next to the hive and be surrounded by scores of bees who flew in large or small circles around my head, or zoomed far above to tumble back in what I soon learned are called *play fights*. I grew to understand that these were for the most part young bees leaving the hive for the first or second or third time, and circling, spinning, rolling for the joy of sunshine and flight and the rush of air over newly extended wings. Older bees—you can tell because young bees have more hair on their backs, which tends to wear off as they get older—usually paid me no mind, but flew around me as they would a telephone pole or any other obstacle to be avoided as they circled to their cruising altitude above the tops of nearby trees. Coming back home they dropped to land on the stoop, where guards greeted them. Many foragers, too tired from their sometimes several-mile journeys, would miss the entrance and crawl the last few inches home.

Grasshoppers always gathered in front of the hive. I never before knew that these insects ate flesh, but saw now that they often scavenged the carcasses of those bees who died just outside, as well as those who died inside and who were not, for whatever reason, carried away to be deposited elsewhere. So long as the grasshoppers stayed away from the hive's entrance, the bees did not seem to mind. Occasionally a grasshopper would land—most likely accidentally—on the porch, causing the guards to make a quick rush, with a fanning of wings and a raising of abdomens. The grasshoppers always jumped away.

I bought more hives, and loved to lie on my back to watch the bees—not scores now, but hundreds or thousands—flying crisscrosses through the morning or afternoon sky. I'd watch one circle and rise, then orient herself and fly away, her body growing smaller against the light blue of the summer sky. When she blinked out in the distance, I would pick another to watch, perhaps this one coming home, her body growing larger and taking form as she returned with a stomach full of nectar or saddlebags full of pollen.

But all was not contemplation. Beekeeping is some of the hardest work I have ever done. That first year I arranged the hives aesthetically, scattering them about a large marshy pasture. I learned never to do that again: at up to a hundred pounds each, boxes of honey are heavy enough when the truck is parked right there. After the first twenty yards, the boxes seem to gain about a pound a yard for the rest of the haul. By a quarter mile, I was cursing bees, cursing the July sun, cursing aesthetics, and wishing I would have taken up needlepoint. Of course that year was the best harvest I ever recorded, at well over two hundred pounds per hive. I had about fifteen hives by that time. You do the math. Even at this remove, I'm not sure I'm up to it.

When hives are arranged to fulfill more pragmatic considerations, the work is still hard: there is much lifting, obviously, and you also, at least at first, have to worry about stings. When I was a beginner, I suited up each time I worked bees, wearing the hat, veil, and zipped overalls familiar to most anyone who has ever seen a public television program on the honeybee. As I became more familiar with them, and used to the stings, I began wearing far less protective attire, usually just cutoffs and no shirt, baseball cap atop my head to keep bees out of my hair (they don't like brunettes: brown hair reminds them of bears and skunks), and sometimes leather gloves if the bees were particularly feisty. I switched to this outfit because I had learned several important lessons. The first is that in June, July, and August, the sun can be hot, especially when you're covered head to foot in canvas overalls, and most especially when you're carrying hundred pound boxes over an aesthetic quarter mile. The second is that stings really aren't so bad: they hurt less than a pinch (unless you get stung inside your nose or on your anus, each of which happened once, which is once more than I would prefer to remember), and by now they cause me to swell far less than a mosquito bite. Stung on the wrist, five minutes later I would be hard-pressed to tell you which wrist it was.

The third lesson ties into everything I've been writing about in this book. It was the bees who—along with high jumping—provided me my first real somatic understanding of cooperation and compliance: work against bees and they sting; work with them as they work with themselves and they reward you with honey, joy, and sore muscles.

Watching them, listening to them, feeling their stings when they're angry or the delicate touch of their feet (their *pretarsi,* in entomology-speak) when they contentedly walk across the back of your hand, seeing the queen—long and slender—move slowly from cell to cell of the honeycomb as she lays more than her own weight in eggs every day, hearing the drones bumble from hive to hive, looking closely at the excited tail wagging and circular dances of scouts who've found new food and want to share these secrets with their sisters, you learn in time that beehives have their own rhythms and personalities. If you pay attention they begin to share their secrets with you, too. Cold days annoy them, because they have to stay inside. Some hives are always in a bad mood, others always cheerful. Move slowly, respect them, and don't crush them when you disassemble and reassemble their homes, and they will accept you. It's really very simple. Treat them as you would want to be treated, and the chances are good they will respond in kind.

A Turning Over

"This country, with its institutions, belongs to the people who inhabit it. Whenever they shall grow weary of the existing government, they can exercise their constitutional right of amending it, or their revolutionary right to dismember or overthrow it."
Abraham Lincoln

I JUST GOT OFF the telephone with an old friend. We first met in church when we were teens, and stayed in close contact until I left Montana. Since then, our paths have diverged. He has a family, and I do not. He has a wage job, and I do not. He has had to place his art—he's an extraordinary flautist—on the periphery, and daily my art and activism move closer to the center of my life. We only talk a few times a year, but I realized speaking to him that, from different paths, we have arrived at many of the same places.

Dave said to me, "People never get paid for anything of value. I don't get paid for loving Beth, or the children, and I don't get paid for playing the flute."

I didn't say anything. He continued, "I'm tired, Derrick. I work three jobs and I can't get ahead. Beth still works retail, and because she stands all day she needs a foot operation."

A deep breath, and then he said, "I don't know where we'll get the money. I just quit a job that had health benefits, but you know what? Whenever we made a claim, our problem wasn't covered. It all looks so good on paper, but it never works out. I was sorting packages on that job, and carrying them. It was so mind-numbing. I thought I would go crazy. But the other jobs are no better. Remember when I was a courier for the bank? I'll bet I've driven a half-million miles these past ten years. That's 10,000 hours. Or more. And what do I have to show for them?"

I asked what he wanted to do. "I would love to have access to some land, where Beth and I and the kids could just live. But I don't think that's going to happen."

Another long pause, and he said, "Beth's not happy."

"With you, or the job?"

"I don't think she's going to bail. But she's just unhappy. She hates her job, and it spills over."

I wanted to give him a hug over the phone. We had not talked for so long. He said, "I don't know what I'm going to do, Derrick. I don't know what I'm going to do."

For many years I've been trying to figure out why revolutionary movements almost always fail to materially and permanently help the poor. This is true for armed revolutions such as the Russian Revolution, revolutions of the heart such as the teachings of Jesus, and revolutions that attempt to combine the two. When the revolution is over, the new boss—whether he's St. Augustine, Luther, Washington, or Lenin—is inevitably, as the rock band The Who suggested, the same as the old boss.

At first I thought the problem was primarily psychological, that having overturned the old social order, revolutionary leaders were unable to release their newfound power to the people. This means, of course, that the supposed revolutionaries never overturned the old social order at all, but merely inserted new names and possibly new mechanisms for the same old dominance and exploitation. At best they may have instituted social programs and nationalized industries, as Castro did in Cuba, but the repression ultimately remains. I say this not to diminish the importance of instituting social programs, but to point out the tenacity of the repression. It is also true that in many cases the revolutionaries—I'm thinking especially of the founding fathers of the United States and the Bolsheviks, but it's just as true for many so-called anarchists, like Michael Bakunin—never intended to break down the hierarchies, but used the language of independence, democracy, and perhaps economic egalitarianism to make their seizure of power palatable to the mass of people, who would as always gain little from this changing of the Praetorian Guard and who would as always suffer the most in the process.

While psychology explains the failure of many revolutions, it doesn't suffice for all. Even taking into consideration the danger to one's soul of embarking on the path of violent revolution, and considering also that those who preach or foment peaceful or violent overthrow of the established order may not be the best qualified, temperamentally or otherwise, to sustain a new nonhierarchical social order—Jesus was great at railing against the powerful, but had he not been killed, could he have enacted and maintained his egalitarian vision?—I realized there had to be more. People are varied enough in their skills and morals that, given the thousands of historical revolutions, large and small, someone (or more likely some group) somewhere along the line would have been able to pull off a solidly egalitarian revolution. Having been set on this nonhierarchical path, at least some groups would have been able to maintain it. Obviously, many indigenous cultures *have* been able to construct and maintain relatively egalitarian societies, as have some religious groups, but especially within the mainstream of Western Civilization these groups are despairingly rare.

My second thought was that any group that through revolution (armed or unarmed) succeeded in establishing a peaceful, nonhierarchical community would not be allowed to survive, for reasons already elucidated. This is especially true if that community contains anything, such as resources, useful to those in power. Voluminous evidence supports this thesis. Still, this answer didn't seem to suffice, because nearly always, even in those communities and especially states or nations, where the egalitarian power structures have been stressed but not demolished by outside forces, the governmental and economic forms have sooner or later reverted once again to the same old patterns of domination. Why is this?

Perhaps it has to do with the incapacity to attend to our own feelings omnipresent in a severely traumatized people. Perhaps our marvelous capacity to adapt to even the most atrocious situations is the major reason revolutions fail. We're so good at getting along that we do so at the expense of actions that would in a meaningful sense bring a change in those original circumstances that cause our suffering. We shuffle and bow before the established order, knowing that it's better to be alive and humbled—even if we must sell our hours for another's profit—than it is to be dead. Then when some new despot comes along mouthing new slogans of egalitarianism, instead of opposing both the old and new tyrannies, we adapt yet again, perhaps even believing for a time the new slogans. And when the new slogans prove false? Amnesia, that most adaptable of all forms of adaptation.

There is an image that has stuck in my mind since I first encountered it in a book many years ago. Thousands of Jews, fresh from the Warsaw Ghetto, all stand or sit in a large arena, like a courtyard or stadium. They are led off in groups of five or so. The movement of each group down a corridor leads quickly to a new round of rifle fire from the direction of their disappearance. Why don't the remaining people flee? To try to understand, I've turned the question back on myself: staring straight into the maw of global ecological collapse, why do we follow along, equally trusting, equally complacent, down a corridor we know has only one exit, an exit we anticipate all too well? In a less dramatic though no less inevitable manner, why do we walk down paths of wage labor, toiling away our lives for some chimerical goal of fiscal sufficiency? I remember speaking with my students about the doomed Jews from the Warsaw Ghetto, and asking why they thought these people acted, or failed to act, as they did. One of my students gave an insightful answer: "Undoubtedly some were in denial until the end, but I'm sure others realized that even when your external choices have been removed, you at least can still act with dignity." So the mother facing the machine gun holds tight to her child's shoulder, feels one last time the texture of her skin, and in that moment attempts to convey to her daughter an entire lifetime's worth of love. Is that a solution? Not in the larger sense of stopping the Nazis. But it is a beautifully and lovingly adaptive response arising directly out of the circumstances faced by the doomed woman and her family.

Perhaps that explains the behavior of my friend Dave as well. He cannot escape his economic conditions, but these conditions do not disallow a love for his family that gets him through each day. He can hold them, and love them, as meanwhile slip away the hours of his life. The same is undoubtedly true from his wife's perspective.

Maybe this is it, I thought: instead of creating a revolution, rushing and overpowering our armed guards—both tangible and internalized—we adapt as best we can, put our heads down, get through the day.

Then I had another thought: perhaps the problem is that those of us striving for egalitarianism, or just trying to make a fine, noble, and happy life, tire of this struggle more quickly than those whose wounds for whatever reason give them a super-human stamina in their indomitable quest to control and destroy. Perhaps revolutions fail because those in power feel more fear than we feel love. Or perhaps because we ourselves feel more fear than love. I don't like to think this, but evidence suggests it may be at least partly true.

I think also of something George often replies when I become too theoretical, when I ask with too much vehemence why people work jobs they hate, why so many people earn their living by deforesting, or mining, or working other obviously destructive jobs: *Sixty days,* he says. That's how long it takes before people begin to die of starvation. *Sixty days.* Dave can't quit his job because in sixty days his children will die. No longer can Dave kill and eat Eskimo curlews from a flock that one day may have passed directly over the spot where now he lives. No longer do most of us—myself included—have the skills to raise or gather our own food. We are members of only the third or fourth generation in the history of humankind who have not known how to build our own shelters. I say I want a revolution, and that I want to "shut down the machine," but until we find a new equilibrium, how are we going to eat? Sixty days: those two short words, those two altogether too short months, are a primary reason most of us do not rebel. We still have too much to lose.

While all of these are clearly contributing factors to the inevitable failures of revolutions, and also failures to revolt, I recently came across some analysis that finally makes clear the reason for the lack of success. It's not good news. Just as the problems with our schooling are not psychological—only requiring we find better teachers—so too do we not simply need to find better revolutionaries. The problems inhere in the structure and functioning of our society.

The analysis came from a book entitled *Communism in Central Europe in the Time of the Reformation,* by Karl Kautsky. One of the groups Kautsky describes is the Taborites, a group of communists who were never conquered externally, but whose experiment devolved nonetheless into a pseudo-community as selfish, militaristic, and intolerant as surrounding city-states. This selfishness, militarism, and intolerance extended, to provide one example among many, to the extermination of the Adamites, a sect more communistic than they ("Those whom the sword had spared, the fire consumed," comments Kautsky). "The fate of Tabor is of the greatest interest," Kautsky writes, "for it shows what would have been the outcome of the Münzer movement . . . and of the Anabaptist movement . . . if they had remained unconquered." He follows this with a few sentences I disagree with, and then says, "While the needs of the poor engendered the struggle for communism, those of production demanded the existence of private proprietorship."

There you have it. The needs of mass production—a funneling of resources toward producers—is in opposition to the needs of the community—a siphoning of resources toward the poor. In one sentence the failure of egalitarian dreams. So long as we value production over relationship, and in fact over life, so long shall we follow our current path of ever-increasing immiseration for the ever-increasing majority.

Recall that the primary feature Ruth Benedict observed as leading to a "good" culture, one that is peaceful, and one in which the members are almost invariably "nice," is that members of these cultures have set up a "siphon system" to shuttle wealth from rich to poor. This "siphon system" is antithetical to the primacy of private (from the same root as *deprive*, remember) property. Even those revolutions claiming to dispose of private property—Marxist revolutions, for example, which in any case do not even purport to dispose of rigid hierarchy—continue in this insoluble contradiction between the needs of mass production and the needs of human beings.

It really is very simple. What you value is what you create. This is true whether we speak of motorcycles, interstate highways, nuclear power plants, napalm, and indoor sports arenas, or harmonious familial and communal relationships and harmonious relationships between ourselves and our nonhuman neighbors. The inverse is true as well: by looking at what we or anyone else creates, we can determine much more accurately than with words alone what is deemed valuable.

By not questioning the primacy of production, and therefore

the valuing of private property over (human and nonhuman) relationships, most revolutionaries guarantee their revolutions won't change fundamental power structures. For it doesn't matter whether capitalists, the Supreme Soviet, proletariats, the Church, or intellectuals control the means of production, the truth is that this group—fill in the blank—then controls the means of production. The property is just as private whether the owners claim to be capitalists, communists, "horny-handed workers," or anarchists. Wealth funnels toward the producers and away from the community as a whole. "Meet the new boss, same as the old boss."

If we wish to do away with bosses, we need to do away with the primacy of production. We need to learn from egalitarian religious and especially extant indigenous groups that the emphasis of our society must be on process: not on the creation of *things* and the accumulation of monetary or political power, but on the acknowledgment and maintenance of relationships, on both personal and grand scales.

How a group that has as its foundation the maintenance of relationships can stand up in direct conflict to a group based on production is a question to which I don't yet have an answer. It is, however, a question that needs to be asked, and answered, and soon.

It should be apparent that what plays out in intrahuman relationships plays out more broadly in our relationships with the rest of the world. A culture that values production over life values the wrong thing, because it will produce *things* at the expense of living beings, human or otherwise. And it will destroy its ecosystemic base. To argue over whether the Trilateral Commission, Weyerhaeuser, Bill Gates and Microsoft, the Bolsheviks, or a small band of Maoists should control production as the world burns seems a wee bit absurd, and more than a little pathetic.

I'm not saying that Dave's condition as a wage slave is the same as the condition of a woman about to be shot by a Nazi police officer. Nor am I saying that to grow up in a violent household is the same as to be murdered and mutilated by a United States

Cavalry trooper. Nor am I saying that the Holocaust is the same as the destruction of indigenous peoples, nor am I saying that clearcuts are the same as rape. To make any of these claims would be absurd. Underlying the different forms of coercion is a unifying factor: Silence. The necessity of silencing victims before, during, and after exploitation or annihilation, and the necessity at these same times of silencing one's own conscience and one's conscious awareness of relationship is undeniable. These radically different atrocities share mechanisms of silencing; science, for example, has been used as efficiently to silence women as it has Jews as it has trees as it has rocks as it has children, chimpanzees, the elderly, our dreams, our common sense, and our sense of the sacrality of community. The same can be said for the uses of our religion, economics, politics, and so on. The perpetrators of these atrocities share a deeply unifying belief in their own separateness and superiority, and a tightly rationalized belief in the rightness of their actions. The perpetrators share a deep fear of interconnection and of the unpredictability of a life that may end in death tomorrow, or not for a hundred years, but one that will nonetheless end.

The psychologist Erich Fromm changed Descartes' dictum from "I think, therefore I am," to "I affect, therefore I am." If Gilgamish can cut down a forest, if he can make a name for himself, he has affected the world around him. If Hitler can "purify" the Aryan "race," if he can become the progenitor of a thousand-year Reich, he has, too. If my father can make my teenage sister wet her pants from fear and pain, or if he can make me take his penis against my skin—and more broadly if he can destroy our souls . . . you get the picture. Frederick Weyerhaeuser (acting now through the unliving yet immortal corporate proxy that bears his name) deforested first the Midwest, then the Northwest, and now wants the world. Fearful of life, the perpetrators forget that one can affect another with love, by allowing another's life to unfold according to its own nature and desires and fate, and by giving to the other what it needs to unfold. One can affect another by merely being present and listening intently to that other. All of this is true whether we speak of forests, children, rocks, rivers, stars, and wolverines, or races, cultures, and communities of human beings.

In the same speech where he said there are only two races—the decent and the indecent—Viktor Frankl also said, "Every nation is capable [of the] Holocaust." As we have seen, this is true.

My father is not Hitler, he is not the head of Weyerhaeuser, nor is he Gilgamish. But to deny they have anything in common is to refuse to see. To insist that each of these perpetrators is somehow an aberration—to try to remove each individually from the cultural context that creates them all—is to not merely facilitate but to make inevitable the continuation of their atrocities. It is to believe, even as we walk down the corridor toward the sputtering sound of rifles, that miraculously, our turn will never come.

I feel conflicted about my newfound understanding of the flaws of historical revolutions. On one hand it's important to understand the past, so we can at least try not to repeat mistakes. On the other, I'm not sure how understanding what's wrong will help us determine what's right.

In my mind, I keep seeing the face of my high school friend Jon—now an avid pursuer of ever-larger American Dreams—and I keep hearing his voice in my head, sharply teasing, "So, the Russian Revolution was a scam? Our Founding Fathers were hypocrites? Stop the presses! Anybody who doesn't understand that revolutions are like revolving doors, where one boss steps in when another steps out, shouldn't be talking about revolutions. You've got to get what you can in the meantime. Make yourself comfortable."

His voice continues, "How does your analysis help? Instead of new bosses taking over production, you want to stop production altogether? Does the word *starvation* mean anything to you? And what do you think would happen if you walked into an Eagle Hardware Store—motto: *More of Everything*—and announced you wanted the customers, never mind the owners, to give up their jet skis and jacuzzis, their three hundred types of track lighting and economy-size bags of Weed 'n' Feed? Those people would rip you limb from limb, and they'd feel good about it."

He's right. But his voice—as I imagine it—has more to tell: "If, as you say, our religion, philosophy, science, economics, politics, and so on are manifestations of cultural desire, and if"—the voice hesitates, then spits the next words—"*as you say*, that means these fields have as their purpose the rationalization of exploitation, what makes you think we could expect anything different from a revolution that comes from this same culture?"

"Shit," I say out loud.

"Checkmate," the voice replies.

Today I read in the newspaper that across the globe, sea turtles are dying from massive tumors afflicting up to 90 percent of some populations. The tumors, noncancerous growths called fibropapillomas, are killing turtles much faster than turtles can reproduce. The article reports: "The tumors themselves don't kill as much as they smother. Eyes and noses get covered. Lungs and the heart are constricted by the tumors on the inside." Tumors have been seen on turtles from Brazil to Florida, from Hawaii to Indonesia, and can grow to be at least half the size of the turtle him- or herself. The best guess as to the specific cause is fertilizer or manure runoff from factory farms. Changes in water temperature may also be affecting the creatures' ability to ward off viruses.

Also in the newspaper, I read that McDonald's opened its first restaurant in Bolivia, the one hundred and sixth country into which the company has metastasized. I suddenly remembered seeing an ad the company placed in business journals showing a photograph of the globe, with the caption, "Our expansion plan." Just as presumably fertilizer and manure runoff is good news for the fibropapilloma-inducing viruses, the expansion of McDonald's, and more broadly the culture it represents, into ever-new territories must be good news for the global domination virus, or better, dementia.

Finally, I read an editorial stating that attempts to mandate a reduction in the emission of greenhouse gases to ameliorate global warming—which disaster even the editorial admits may result in "melted ice caps, rising seas, swamped coastal cities, floods, storms, diseases, devastated wildlife"—constitute "an unfounded assault on industry." The editorial labeled those who believe global warming is occurring, including the vast majority of climatologists worldwide, as the "Chicken Little crowd" and as a "fringe minority." Jaded though I am to the absurdities to which we are necessarily forced the moment we begin to value production over life, I still had to read the column several times to make myself believe it.

Years ago I asked one of the editors of this paper what is the purpose of his editorials. His reply was the only honest statement I've encountered by him: "To tell people what to think."

The world is burning up. The powers that be obfuscate and lie. What are we going to do?

It was unfair of me to pick on the Cassini probe as an egregious example of our culture's death urge. The truth is that Cassini is not unusual, which I guess was the point all along. We are irradiating the planet. Hundreds of tons of nuclear waste litter the bottom of the ocean, everything from sunken nuclear submarines to thousands of tons of plutonium, ruthenium, americium, cesium 137, radioactive iodine, and other toxic wastes routinely released from, among many others, Britain's Sellafield nuclear reprocessing plant. As author Marilyn Robinson remarks: "The first questions that arise in attempting to understand Sellafield, and more generally the nuclear and environmental policies of the British government, are: How have they gotten away with so much? and Why on earth would they *want* to get away with it?" A few months ago the former secretary of Russia's National Security Council revealed to United States officials that at least one hundred one-kiloton nuclear weapons were missing. Called "suitcase bombs," these warheads are small enough, as the name implies, to be carried inconspicuously in a suitcase. Neither the American government nor the corporate press has made mention of these missing nukes.

When thinking about the risk from Cassini, remember the missing suitcase bombs. Remember also the radioactive tanks at the Hanford Nuclear Reservation in southern Washington: these tanks are leaking into the groundwater, and, soon enough, into the already-beleaguered Columbia River. They also explode with some regularity. No one even knows what's in many of them. Remember that in the 1950s the United States exposed citizens downwind of Hanford to intentional releases of radiation to see what would happen. Remember also that because of nuclear testing—the explosion of hundreds of nuclear bombs worldwide—plutonium residues have been found in the bodies of creatures from pole to pole. Remember also that between 1950 and 1998, the rate for women's breast cancer in this country has gone from one in fifty to one in eight.

I hate to say this, but Cassini is nothing out of the ordinary.

A Life of My Own

"The greatest virtue between heaven and earth is to live."

'The Great Treatise' of the I Ching

WISHING AWAY THE WAGE economy did not make it cease to exist, and my determination to stop selling my hours did not lessen my need for food, nor for a place to stay. In other words, despite my highfalutin philosophy, I still had to find a way to earn some cash.

I was fortunate. There's a world of difference between having the opportunity to take a well-paying job and walking away, and not having been granted that opportunity in the first place. There was a time not long after college when I was poor enough that I collected aluminum cans for money to buy food, but had things gotten really bad, I could simply have taken a job. Or I could have borrowed additional money from my mother (something I have done with too-great frequency). I wasn't going to starve. The same can't be said for the majority of people in the world.

During my parents' divorce, my father essentially got everything but the house. He kept the stock shares, condos in Jackson Hole, and fast food franchises, as well as the other toys and trappings of a truly (monetarily) wealthy person. But the house was valuable, and when after years of working jobs everywhere from race tracks to art galleries my mother sold it, she had enough so that probably she could survive to the end of her days without being forced to reenter the wage economy.

I approached with a plan. I loved working bees, and wanted to borrow enough to become a small-scale commercial beekeeper. That way I could work hard during the season, and use the off-season to read and think and write. She consented.

My time with bees was in some ways a disaster: they all died—twice. It wasn't my fault either time, but that doesn't lessen the sorrow of seeing so many millions of deaths, nor lessen the sense of failure.

It did not begin disastrously, only dishonestly. I bought three hundred hives from a man going out of business in Arkansas. At least that's what he initially told me, and presumably what he continued to tell the bank. His luck had been awful: he'd had eight hundred hives when he'd moved down from Oregon several years back, but he lost hundreds by this means and that. He placed several hundred in beautiful drop sites between rivers and irrigated fields of soybeans: no one told him that rivers in the South flood every winter, and when he went to visit his drops early that spring he found nothing but a few empty hive bodies high in the boughs of trees. Later that year he lost hundreds of stored bee boxes when a pile of oil-soaked rags spontaneously combusted, taking with them his honey house. The bank was after him for his remaining 150 hives, or to my extremely vague understanding, the 150 the loan officers knew about. All I know is that I bought 150 from the bank, and the same number from him. Those I bought from him were located in drops down labyrinthine roads I could not have retraced alone.

I took the bees to California, in many ways the promised land for beekeepers. The winters are warm, and there's nearly always something in bloom. In addition, the density of monocrops means extra money.

Modesto, California, is beautiful in February, with hills rolling for miles covered in white-blossomed almond trees. Hundreds of thousands of acres bloom in essential simultaneity, and if pollen isn't carried from flower to flower almonds won't form. Although monocropped miles of almond flowers may be beautiful, they're as unnatural as Frankenstein's monster; the staggering number of blossoms to be pollinated in these densely packed orchards grossly overmatches the capacity of such wild pollinators as bumblebees, moths, wasps, beetles, and so on to set fruit, prompting almond ranchers to pay beekeepers up to $40 per hive to bring in bees for the three week bloom.

Almonds aren't the only crop needing pollination. Apples, cherries, pears, raspberries, cranberries, blueberries, cucumbers, watermelons, muskmelons. Each of these densely packed crops requires similarly densely packed beehives to set fruit. The same is true for the seeds of other crops—onions, cauliflower, lettuce, carrots, cabbage, broccoli, radishes. Without bees, these crops disappear.

Beekeepers with the right contacts can turn a lot of cash. A few weeks after almonds comes prunes ($15), apples ($12), cherries ($12), and so on.

Moving bees is the hardest hard work I've ever done. You move them at night because they fly during the day; if you move hives then, you leave behind to die all those bees in the field, which would be a good portion of the hive. I shared work with another beekeeper and his wife, a wondrously generous couple who let me stay in their home for weeks at a time, and refused all offers of rent: they did let me take them out to dinner once in repayment, but insisted it be to Burger King so I wouldn't waste any money.

About three each afternoon, Glen and I began getting the forklift and flatbeds ready, so we could be out to a drop by dark. Then we'd load the truck—confused bees crawling everywhere— tie the hives down, untie the hives and unload the truck because the additional weight had sunk the truck to its axle in mud, pull the truck out with the forklift, reload the truck—confused bees *still* crawling everywhere—retie the hives, drive an hour or two to an orchard, get the truck stuck again, pull it free once more with the forklift, unload as many hives as the grower contracted for, drive to another orchard, and repeat the process till we'd unloaded the truck. Then we'd clean off the machinery, get it as ready as we could for the next night, sleep from maybe ten in the morning till two in the afternoon, get up, and start over. We'd do this for a week or ten days at a time.

It was exhausting. I remember one rainy night, toward the end of a series of moves, when I couldn't run the windshield wipers because they immediately hypnotized me, and another when for the final three hours of the drive the only words that passed through my mind, as taillights left red and blurry traces on the backs of my eyes, were "automobile mesmerization, automobile mesmerization." I remember a night, also, when Glen forgot his protective beesuit. Since it was a small load, and since our judgment was clouded, we decided to proceed anyway. Because they were his bees, we decided he'd wear my suit and do most of the work, while I would just drive. The load was the smoothest we could remember, as was the drive back to the drop, within the city of Modesto. The night was foggy, as February nights so often are there, and the only vehicles we saw were copcars and other beetrucks. It was four in the morning. We reached the drop, and Glen began to unload. I lost concentration, and drove too close underneath a tree. A branch swept the top row of hives off the back. I stopped the truck, and because this was an emergency, I ran out and, suit or no, began scooping frantic bees back into boxes. They crawled everywhere. Piles of them clumped together to comfort each other. Individuals crawled over my shoes and socks, and up my pant legs. I swatted at them, but there were hundreds. I began to curse, and curse louder. Telling Glen I'd be right back, I ran into the street—the only place light enough to see what I was doing—and whipped off my clothes. I put them back on, and, cursing the bees still in my pants and up my shirt, took them back off. I began to jump up and down on my shirt and pants, still cursing. Finally I stepped outside myself enough to realize I was standing in the middle of a four-lane road, wearing shoes, socks, underwear, and long leather beegloves, stomping my feet and shrieking. I began to laugh as I put my clothes back on, and laughed harder as I returned to help. Again the bees crawled up my pant legs, and all I could do, as I scooped handfuls back into their homes, was laugh at myself, and keep on laughing.

For the first time, my life was my own. Never again, at least that I could foresee, would I have to work for another. I didn't mind working through the night, nor through the next day, because the decision to work was my own. I didn't mind getting stung, because it happened with bees I cared about.

Each day became an adventure—*my* adventure—and time was never something to be wished away, but savored. I saw a dozen migrant workers playing baseball, and hopped the fence to join them. I know no Spanish, and the only English they knew was "Have a good one," so for the next three hours we said only that to each other, after each single, double, out, or error. And we smiled.

Soon after the almond bloom ended I moved the bees to Orosi, south of Fresno, in orange country. Small white blossoms filled the air with their scent. The bloom was so heavy I put all three hundred hives in one drop, and still the bees made honey: light, delicate, sweet.

Next to the field where I placed the hives lived another wondrously generous couple. They invited me for dinner, and gave me a place to shower. They ran the largest wasp ranch in the Western Hemisphere. Figs are pollinated by wasps. Not just any wasps, but a specific kind who lays her eggs only in a specific kind of nonedible fig. The eggs hatch and the grubs eat away at the fruit, then pupate there. The fruit falls to the ground. The tiny adults emerge, mate, and fly to find new fig blossoms. In laying her eggs, the wasp pollinates the fig. The next generation of both species is well served. This man collected nonedible figs from his ranch, put them in paper bags, and sold them to edible fig growers who placed them about their orchards. The new generation of wasps would emerge, enter the fig flowers, but then, sadly, find no suitable place to lay their eggs. Nonetheless, pollination occurred.

Because his great-great-grandparents had homesteaded the property, and because all succeeding generations had known better than to mortgage the land, he did not face the agricultural equivalent of the contradiction mentioned earlier as the one that dooms revolutions, a variant of which ultimately dooms efforts within our culture at sustainable agriculture. Economic production, once again, requires that resources be funneled toward producers, while ecosystemic production requires that resources be returned to all members of the natural community, including, especially, the ground. So he ran a loose ship. Like mine, his days seemed savored, and especially shared. He made regular trips to the pound to pick up animals about to be euthanized. I saw a blind horse, one three-legged dog and several who were partially blind, any number of scrawny yet happy (and spayed or neutered) cats, and a passel of peacocks ("Dad lives by himself in the old farmhouse, and if anything happens we can just listen for the peacocks to let us know."). Not even the horse was fenced, but all roamed free among the fig trees.

Every moment that spring was pregnant with meaning, as if I were seeing the world for the first time. I went to the Fresno zoo. I saw there a lone wolf—normally a social creature who lopes for days at fifteen miles per hour—pacing a small concrete pen. A woman stood next to me, and said to her child, "That's the big bad wolf"; I thought, "Another industrialist is born." I saw Colobus monkeys, who normally ascend to the tallest treetops at dawn and dusk, where they sit quietly facing the sun. These sat rocking in a small cage with no trees, and no view of the horizon.

I spent most of my time those days living in the front of my Toyota pickup, sharing space with my clothes, tools, notebook, baseball mitt, pillow, and two cocker spaniels. We slept together most nights in the front, or sometimes they slept in the front while I threw my sleeping bag on the ground. One of the dogs, a female, was going blind, and the other, a male, was nearly deaf. The male, especially, never seemed to slow down. He ran this way and that, ears flying and tongue flapping. He was an eternal child on an everlasting Christmas morning, wearing PJs and running from gift to gift saying, "Oh, Mom. A basketball! I've always wanted a basketb———Ah, man! You got me a book! I love books!" Had I told him to sit in a corner, and had he heard me, I'm sure he would have run to the spot, tail wagging as if to say, "Oh, man. I've always wanted to sit in this corner. Thank you. Thank you. Thank you." That's not to say he didn't have a mind of his own. Even when he heard me, he still disobeyed more often than not—one of his mottoes seemed to be "Rules are meant to be acknowledged and then ignored." Even, or especially, in ignoring my wishes he acted as he always did, exuberantly, joyously, with an abundance of life.

I can't imagine a better teacher.

Interconnection

"Our goal should be not the emulation of the ancients and their ways, but to experience for ourselves the aspects of human existence out of which arose those ancient forms which when we see them elicit such a feeling of . . . longing. Otherwise the modern will remain forever superficial while the real will remain ancient, far away, and therefore, outside of ourselves."

Mr. Aoki

A FEW YEARS AGO I had the opportunity to ask Grey Reynolds, second-in-command of the Forest Service, "If we discover that industrial forestry is incompatible with biodiversity, what then?" The question was of course absurd: I mentioned it that day to a high school jumper I was coaching, who said: "What a stupid question! Everyone knows they're incompatible." Reynolds' non-answer that evening unintentionally validated the teen's response: "What do you want us to do, live in mud huts?"

Pointing out that the needs of mass production are counter to the requirements of a good culture and incompatible with long-term survival doesn't mean I don't like hot showers, base-ball, good books, or Beethoven. I wish that the items we pro-duce—the good ones, at least—were separable from the larger processes: I wish we could have hot showers without building dams and nuclear power plants.

On some level of course that *is* possible. It wouldn't take long to rig up a system to heat water on my woodstove, then pour it into a reservoir that releases water over my head when I pull a cord. But where do I get the metal and glass for the woodstove? Where do I get the cord, or the reservoir? Where do I get the wood? We seem to have painted ourselves into a corner.

As Lewis Mumford observed, our choices have been grossly limited: "On the terms imposed by technocratic society, there is no hope for mankind except by 'going with' its plans for acceler-ated technological progress, even though man's vital organs will all be cannibalized in order to prolong the megamachine's mean-ingless existence." All is not lost, though, as he also remarked: "But for those of us who have thrown off the myth of the ma-chine, the next move is ours: for the gates of the technocratic prison will open automatically, despite their rusty hinges, as soon as we choose to walk out."

I think he's a bit optimistic. Although it's as possible as it is imperative to throw off the *myth* of the machine, it's not quite so simple to throw off the machine itself. The modern economy is a complicated web, sticky in every thread, and to disentangle oneself personally is difficult, requiring knowledge (much of it long lost), forethought, effort, vigilance, and access to land. For an entire community to disentangle itself from that web may be well-nigh impossible, given the modern economy's interconnected nature as well as the overpopulation, resource depletion, and environmental degradation that comes with civilization.

Food exemplifies the difficulty of withdrawing from the modern economy, because you can't live without it and because not many people produce all of their own. And if it's uncommon for a modern *person* to be food self-reliant, it is almost unheard of for a community to supply all of its own food. That is only recently the case; merely one hundred and fifty years ago here in Spokane, the natives lived self-reliantly and sustainably. One of their staples, for example, was salmon. During the massive runs, people placed boxes under falls over which salmon leapt on their way to spawn and die. Some of the salmon fell into the boxes; these the people who lived here ate, or dried, to eat later. Salmon and human communities coexisted, and could presumably have done so indefinitely. Now, even had the salmon not been killed by the dams that destroyed the Columbia as a free river, there are too many people here in Spokane—300,000 in the county—for the salmon to have supported all of us over the long-term. Nor can the community take other food from the river; signs near the Spokane River warn that its fish—native and introduced trout— are contaminated with PCBs.

I recently had dinner with George. We did not eat fish. Instead we ate at a wonderful Vietnamese restaurant. I had lemongrass chicken with chile, and George had stir-fried vegetables. Both meals were excellent, and both consisted of foods originating far from Spokane. Although we didn't ask the cook where the chicken and other foodstuffs came from, it isn't difficult to construct an entirely plausible scenario. Here it is: the chicken was raised on a factory farm in Arkansas. The factory is owned by Tyson Foods, which supplies one-quarter of this nation's chickens and sends them as far away as Japan. The chicken was fed corn from Nebraska and grain from Kansas. One of seventeen million chickens processed by Tyson that week, this bird was frozen and put onto a truck made by PACCAR. The truck was made from plastics manufactured in Texas, steel milled in Japan from ore mined in Australia and chromium from South Africa, and aluminum processed in the United States from bauxite mined in Jamaica. The parts were assembled in Mexico. As this truck, with its cargo of frozen chickens, made its way toward Spokane, it burned fuel refined in Texas, Oklahoma, California, and Washington from oil originating beneath Saudi Arabia, Venezuela, Mexico, Texas, and Alaska. All this, and I have chickens outside my door.

The making of the vegetarian dish was no less complex. The broccoli in George's stir-fried vegetables was grown in Mexico. The field was fertilized with, among other things, ammonium nitrate from the United States, phosphorous mined and processed by Freeport McMoRan from deposits in Florida, and potassium from potash deposits in Sasketchewan. This potash was processed by any one of the multinational mining, oil, and chemical companies: Texasgulf, Swift, PPG Industries, RTZ, or Noranda. The pesticides we ingested are equally cosmopolitan.

Another company associated with nearly every facet of our meal was AKZO, which has 350 facilities in 50 countries. The meal utilized many of their 10,000 chemical products: chicken vaccines that enable Tyson to keep their operations relatively disease-free; automobile coatings; chemicals used in many steps of the agricultural and manufacturing processes, and so on.

This was truly an international meal, and not merely because we ate at a Vietnamese restaurant. The simple pleasure of eating a fine meal is tied to processes involving literally thousands of people working for many companies in numerous countries, manifesting the intricate and interconnected nature of the global economy, which runs like a well-oiled machine.

The processes behind the meal manifest not only the complexity of the modern economy's web but also its destructiveness. Our meal was tied inescapably to pernicious activities across the globe: Tyson Food's monopoly and "virulently antiunion" attitudes, the unspeakable cruelty and debasement of factory farming, and water pollution in Arkansas; loss of topsoil and the depletion of the Oglala aquifer in Nebraska and Kansas; the indescribable immiseration and debasement of labor exploitation in Mexico; air pollution in Japan; toxic mining wastes in Australia, South Africa, and Jamaica; chemical pollution from refineries in four states, and degradation from oil exploration and extraction in four countries; soil toxification, the poisoning of groundwater, more labor exploitation, and the poisoning of agricultural workers in Mexico; air, water, and ground pollution in the United States and Canada, and so on. The food, the cruelty, the pollution, the exploitation, the debasement—all are tied together in this convoluted web that is the modern economy.

The point is not to confess George's and my own particular hypocrisy, nor to explicitly condemn Tyson, PACCAR, or Freeport McMoRan, although Freeport McMoRan *is* the single most polluting company in the United States, but instead to point out the interconnectedness of the modern economy and the ubiquity of the destruction it causes. The same exercise could be performed for the clothes we wear (sweat shops in Burma's military dictatorship, cotton pesticides, polypropylene petrochemicals), the houses we live in (formaldehyde in plywood, deforestation, extinction of fish and wildlife), other consumer products (40,000 American workers killed on the job each year), or any other activity that vibrates the strings of the web.

If our emphasis on production requires that resources be funneled toward producers, which seems self-evident; if the funneling of resources toward the already wealthy is a characteristic of a culture in which, as Ruth Benedict observed, "the advantage of one individual becomes a victory over another, and the majority who are not victorious must shift as they can"; if this funneling is also a cause of widespread inequality and insecurity, then it makes sense that our hyperemphasis on production leads to hypermilitarism. The rich have to protect what they've got, and take what they don't. This is precisely what I observed in myself when I wanted to destroy the chicken-killing coyotes. An emphasis on production requires an emphasis on private ownership requires a means to protect this ownership requires, in the end, murder.

You may say it's crazy to suggest that hot showers are predicated on dams, nuclear power plants, hydrogen bombs, and napalm. I'd say it's even crazier to think we've built these things if they aren't necessary for hot showers.

Although it seems clear to me that the two are linked—that is, hot showers, computers, vaccinations, major league baseball games, and compact disks of Mozart on one hand are tied inextricably to global warming, evolutionary meltdown, ubiquitous genocide, institutionalized cruelty to nonhumans, immiseration of the majority ("who must shift as they can"), high rates of incarceration, and NASA space probes on the other (not to mention the designated hitter rule)—it doesn't really matter whether they are or not. Pretend for a moment that they are. Are you going to argue that compact disks are worth genocide? Or to take a "more difficult" dilemma, are you going to suggest that the wonders of modern medicine (available to the few) are worth the immiseration of the majority? To state these trade-offs are fair, as Grey Reynolds seemed to be suggesting, would immediately show that one is not fit to be a member of a functioning community. It would suggest that one has become deafened to the sufferings of others, and to one's own conscience.

Now pretend that they are not linked. We can have hot showers and email and a computer that plays chess without having any of the negative characteristics of our culture. This leads immediately to an even more difficult question: in that case, why the hell the ubiquitous genocide, the mass rapes, the biological meltdown?

The primary link is not causal, in that my hot shower does not lead causally to the showers at Treblinka, but familial, in that my own shower and the other are distant cousins. Both ultimately spring from the same ancestor, which is the need for control, and a willingness to deafen oneself to all other considerations. I'm not talking about the simple act of heating water to pour over oneself: I'm talking about the systematic bending of others—human and nonhuman, animate and "inanimate"—to our will. There is obviously a difference between me taking a shower, and Jews being killed in gas chambers. And there is obviously a difference between hot showers and napalm. I've not said they're identical: they're kissing cousins. One seemingly benign—at least so long as we ignore the death of the salmon from dams, the irradiation of the region from nuclear power plants, the draw-down of the Spokane aquifer from wells, the toxication of the landscape caused by the production of metal and plastic used in plumbing, and so on—and the other obviously malevolent, but not without its uses, as those in power are only too aware.

Each bee is an individual. She has a personality and preferences. Although there is a general progression from job to job as bees get older—younger bees tend to do housework and nurse the babies, older bees fly out to collect nectar and pollen, and the oldest bees of all (bees live perhaps a month in the summer before they wear out their wings) perform the most dangerous task, which is to scout for new sources of nectar and pollen—it is also true that an individual bee may choose to spend her life cleaning the hive, or may skip the nursing phase and go directly to the field. For the most part they do whatever tasks they want, and that they perceive the hive as needing most at that moment. But they also spend a lot of time doing not much of anything (in the lingo of bee research, "loafing").

As observed earlier, hives, too, have personalities—some are gentle, some friendly, some short-tempered, some sickly—and it is not unfair to consider the hive as a whole a creature in its own right. Hives maintain a constant body temperature of about 95 degrees Fahrenheit, lowering it if necessary by bringing in water to evaporate in currents through their home, or raising it by metabolizing honey and clustering. They make community decisions, such as when to make a new queen (queens are made by feeding normal babies a special food: no one knows how they decide to make a new queen, or which grubs to so feed), when to kill an old queen, and so on. And they reproduce, throwing swarms in which some percentage of the bees move out, taking with them a new or old queen, to find a new home. Thus a new hive is born.

When bees swarm they almost never sting. This fact has been used by countless beekeepers to impress upon others their ostensible courage at virtually no risk. When I was staying with Glen and Susan, they received numerous calls from around town requesting they pick up swarms. If my friends were busy, I was always glad to go, in part because it meant a free bee colony, and in part because it meant the opportunity to show off. I went once on a call to a motel at a main intersection of Modesto. It was near noon, and hot. The street was crowded with cars, but no pedestrians went near the basketball-sized bundle of bees that hung from the branch of a waist-high bush. It should have taken me less than five minutes to pick up the swarm; I only needed to put a box beneath it, give the branch a hard shake to dislodge the cluster, cover the box, and go. But as I approached, wearing cut-offs, no shirt, and baseball cap, and as the loose bees at the edge of the swarm started to fly around my head, people began lining the plate glass at the front of the motel's office, and traffic started to back up as drivers rubbernecked to see this death-defying young man step into a cloud of crazed bees. I made it take a half an hour. When I got back to my friends' house, Glen asked what took so long. I said, "There were a lot of people there."

Smiling, he said, "Showtime."

Twice, though, I have been stung while collecting swarms. Once was nothing but an accident, the other was my fault. Bees often swarm high in trees. This makes sense, because when they leave their old home, they rarely have yet a new one in mind. So they hang, from a bush, rock, eave, tree limb, until scouts find a suitable new cavity they can call home. If they're going to cluster for a couple of days, and not sting much in the meantime, I can see why they would gravitate toward the tops of trees: less predation.

Often I've found myself shinnying up a pine, heavy canvas bag stuck into my waistband. The problem comes after I've got bees in the bag. For obvious reasons I no longer want to put the opening inside my pants. But only rarely have I been able to climb down one-handed, so I took to clamping the top of the bag between my teeth. This worked beautifully every time but once, when I accidentally bit down on a bee, who, understandably enough, stung me on the inside of my upper lip. It's hard to swear with a canvas bag of bees between your front teeth.

The other time was stupid on my part, and unforgivably rude. The bees taught me a painful lesson in return. The swarm was about sixty feet up a pine. The tree's lowest branch was twelve feet up, so I propped a ladder next to the tree. I started climbing, and when I reached the swarm, I saw the bees were six or seven feet out, at the end of a limb probably three inches in diameter: too small for me to crawl on. I climbed back down, and stapled two long, slender pieces of wood to the lip of the bag. I climbed back up, carrying this contraption, plus another long piece of wood: I would hold the two pieces in one hand, and position the open end of the bag beneath the swarm while I used the other to scrape bees off the bough and into the bag. Good idea, I thought, except how was I going to keep myself from falling? I left the equipment in the tree, climbed back down, got a rope, returned to my perch, wrapped the rope several times around the tree's trunk and my own, tied it off, and began to scrape. It didn't work. I tried for a couple of hours before I came up with an even worse idea: I would saw off the limb and allow it to crash to the ground. Sensing themselves falling, the bees would break their cluster and reform, I hoped at a place more conducive to their capture. Down again for the saw, and back up. The limb cracked, tore, and fell, right onto the next limb down, about five feet below. The bees remained clustered. I climbed down, tied myself in, and patiently began again to scrape away. I'd been working less than ten minutes when the bees finally lost patience. The whole time I'd been in the tree, bees had been flying about my head, seemingly more curious than anything, but suddenly they decided they'd had enough. Their mood turned angry, and in that one moment I had scores of bees burrowing into my hair, stinging my scalp, with more bees stinging my face and hands (because pine bark is rough I'd worn long pants and long sleeves). I started to climb down, only to realize I was tied to the tree. For one instant I pictured myself hanging there, dead of bee stings. I'd had catastrophes before, where bees suddenly turned angry and stung me forty, fifty, eighty times, but always before I could get away. I pushed hard against the rope, and because I'm terrible at tying knots the rope loosened enough for me to shimmy out. More bees in my hair, on my eyebrows, in my nose, on my eyelids. I pushed out from the tree and did a controlled fall, slapping my arms and legs against whatever limbs came my way to slow myself enough that when I hit the ground I wouldn't break a leg. I landed, rolled, and ran for the house. Inside, I turned on the water in the bathtub, cold and hard, and, moaning, put my head underneath.

After turning off the water, I began to pull soaked bees from my hair, and to scrape stingers from my scalp. Now that I was no longer in danger, I discovered I had a headache.

It didn't take long for me to realize what I'd done wrong. *Wu wei.* I had attempted to force it. I was no longer working with the bees, helping them into a new home, but instead, I was determined to capture these bees no matter their desires. And I was willing to saw a perfectly good limb from the tree for no unselfish reason. No wonder the bees got mad. The tree was probably cheering them on. The whole incident seemed to me a tangible manifestation of the consequences of an unwillingness to listen, of disobeying fundamental rules of neighborly compliance, and on the bees' part, of reasonable resistance to insanity. I apologized to the swarm, and to the tree, and let the swarm go wherever it wanted.

There is another kind of revolution, one that does not emerge from the culture, from philosophy, from theory, from thought abstracted from sense, but instead from our bodies, and from the land. It, too, is a part of this language older than words. It is the honeybee who stings in defense of the larger being that is her hive; it is the mother grizzly who charges again and again the train that took from her the two sons she carried inside, and that mangled their bodies beyond all but motherly recognition; it is the woman who submits to her rapist, knowing it's better to be violated than murdered, but who begins to fight when he reaches for the knife, or the hammer; it is Zapatista spokesperson Cecelia Rodriguez, who says, "I have a question of those men who raped me. Why did you not kill me? It was a mistake to spare my life. I will not shut up . . . this has not traumatized me to the point of paralysis." It is the indigenous Zapatistas, who declare, "There are those who resign themselves to being slaves. . . . But there are those who do not resign themselves, there are those who decide to be uncomfortable, there are those who do not sell themselves, there are those who do not surrender themselves. . . . There are those who decide to fight. In any place in the world, anytime, any man or woman rebels to the point of tearing off the clothes that resignation has woven for them and that cynicism has dyed grey. Any man, any woman, of whatever color in whatever tongue, says to himself, to herself, 'Enough already!'" It is Ogoni activist Ken Saro-Wiwa, murdered by the Nigerian government at the urging of Shell Oil, whose last words were, "Lord, take my soul but the struggle continues!" It is the U'wa people of South America, a part of whose community committed mass suicide 400 years ago by walking off a fourteen-hundred-foot cliff rather than submit to Spanish rule, and whose living members today vow to follow their ancestors if Occidental Petroleum and Shell move in to destroy their land. It is the U'wa woman who says, "I sing the traditional songs to my children. I teach them that everything is sacred and linked. How can I tell Shell and Oxy that to take the petrol is for us worse than killing your own mother? If you kill the Earth, then no one will live. I do not want to die. Nobody does." It is anyone who dares to think and speak for him- or herself. It is Nestor Makhno fighting for his Ukrainian homeland and for the autonomy of those who work the land, against the Germans, the Bolsheviks, the Whites, the Bolsheviks again, the Whites again, and again the Bolsheviks. It is the men and women who participated in the Warsaw Ghetto uprising, and it is those who rebelled at Treblinka. It is Jesus driving the moneylenders out of the temple. It is the women and men who lock themselves down in front of bulldozers. It is the Chipko movement in India, begun by women who clung tight to trees so the woodmen's axes would bite into their own, and not the trees', flesh. It is Crazy Horse, Sitting Bull, and Geronimo. It is the salmon battering themselves against the concrete, using the only thing they have, their flesh, to try to break down that which keeps them from their homes.

It is not the attempt to seize power or the industrial "means of production," but it is actions based upon the instinctual drive to survive, and to live with dignity.

This is not political theory. It is not philosophy. It is not religion. It is remembering what it is to be a human being—an animal. It is remembering what it means to love, and to be alive.

It is to learn the power of the word *no*. No more clearcuts. No more tumors on turtles. No more genocide. No more slavery, neither our own nor others.

So long as we, or I, continue to discuss this in the abstract, we, or I, still have too much to lose. Presumably the mother grizzly did not find herself paralyzed by theoretical discussions of what is right or wrong, and presumably the same is true for the woman who takes the weapons from her attacker's hands. If we only begin to feel in our bodies the immensity of what we are losing—intact ecosystems, hours sold for wages, childhoods lost to violence, women's capacity to walk unafraid—we will know precisely what we need to do.

Any revolution on the outside—any breaking down of current power structures—with no corresponding revolution in perceiving, being, and thinking, will merely further destruction, genocide, and ecocide. Any revolution on the inside—a revolution of the heart—which does not lead to a revolution on the outside plays just as false.

Anton Chekhov once said that he would like to read a story about a man who squeezes every drop of slave's blood from himself. That is first what we must do. For when a slave rebels without challenging the entire notion of slavery, we merely encounter a new boss. But if all the blood is painfully squeezed away, what emerges is a free man or woman, and not even death can stop those who are free.

I've been thinking about what I wrote before, about me being fucked up, manifesting in part by scenes of ecstasy and intimacy involving nonhuman others, and I've come to the conclusion I was wrong. Oh, I'm still fucked up in some ways: my sleep patterns are disturbed, confrontation is not always easy for me (not that you'd know it from this book), certain scenes remind me overmuch of my childhood (to this day I hate beans because I forced them down my too-tight throat, and only recently have I gained the ability to wash dishes when another is in the room). But I don't think that experiencing intimacy and ecstasy with nonhumans is a sign of mental illness. Rather it is the opposite. To experience these scenes *only* with nonhumans might be reason for concern, but one of the great losses we endure in this prison of our own making is the collapse of intimacy with others, the rending of community, like tearing and retearing a piece of paper until there only remains the tiniest scrap. To place our needs for intimacy and ecstasy—needs like food, water, acceptance—onto only one species, onto only one person, onto only the area of joined genitalia for only the time of intercourse, is to ask quite a lot of our sex.

I'm not suggesting we remedy this by having more sex with more partners, or with trees, high-jumping pits, or sheep. Sex is not the point at all. That's one of the problems of our mechanistic perspective. Because our science cannot measure and quantify existential loneliness, and because love, too, deigns not to be put on the rack and relieved of its secrets, we talk too much about that which we can comprehend, photograph, reproduce, commodify, which we can see: sex. But like an iceberg, or the entrance to a cave, or like the ocean itself, there is so much more beneath only hinted at by the surface.

I remember a midnight some ten years ago. I was walking through the late spring snow and looking at the sky. Suddenly, lightning began to dance from cloud to cloud. Billows and curves reflected purplish white behind the blinding glare of the bolts themselves. Opening my arms I fell into the clouds, then stood back in the snow, laughing, then finally moaning with delight as I saw for the first and only time in my life a lightning storm with snow on the ground.

I remember another night when northern lights coincided with the Perseid meteor shower. I carried a blanket into the dark, wearing only shoes. I spread the blanket, then took off those last bits of clothing. Lying in the cool August night, I watched the rhythmic pulsing of the Aurora, the sudden glint of meteor. I stayed there, naked, nearly till dawn. The feeling was not precisely sexual, but neither was it devoid of sexuality.

And I remember a third night, looking out the bedroom window of a house I rented in Nevada, and seeing the moon so bright it passed in front of any wispy clouds that happened by. I heard the quiet sounds of nightbirds, and beyond that the Humboldt River, soft and slow. I remember that I looked at the green blisters of paint on the windowsill, and I loved them just for what they were. I saw then the distant headlight of a train, carving out a bright helix as it swept toward me on its tracks. With it came its sounds, all the rush and roar and clatter that means a train, and the bumping of couplers straining as the train changes speed. It approached, and it held me tight, and then it passed on and left me alone again with the river, the night birds, and most of all, time.

There are some ways in which I'm fucked up, but that's not one of them.

The Plants Respond

"The body's carbon is simply carbon. Hence, 'at bottom' the psyche is simply 'world.' "
Carl Jung

SOMETIMES IT HAPPENS THAT a person can name the exact moment when his or her life changed irrevocably. For Cleve Backster, it was early morning on February 2, 1966, at thirteen minutes, fifty-five seconds of chart time for a polygraph he was administering. One of the world's experts on polygraphs, and the creator of the Backster Zone Comparison Test, the standard used by lie detection examiners worldwide, Backster had threatened the subject's well-being in hopes of triggering a response. The subject had responded electrochemically to this threat. The subject was a plant.

Some thirty-one years later, I had the opportunity to ask him about it.

He said, "I wasn't particularly into plants, but there was a going-out-of-business sale at a florist on the ground floor of the building, and the secretary bought a couple of plants for the office: a rubber plant, and this dracaena cane. I had done a saturation watering—putting them under the faucet until water ran out the bottom of the pots—and was curious to see how long it would take the moisture to get to the top. I was especially interested in the dracaena, because the water had to climb a long trunk, and then to the end of long leaves. I thought if I put the galvanic-skin-response detector of the polygraph at the end of a leaf, a drop in resistance would be recorded on the paper as the moisture arrived between the electrodes.

"That, at least, is the cover story. I'm not sure if there was another, more profound, reason. It could be that somebody at another level of consciousness was nudging me into doing this.

"I noticed something on the chart resembling a human response on a polygraph: not at all what I would have expected from water entering a leaf. Lie detectors work on the principle that when people perceive a threat to their well-being, they physiologically respond in predictable ways. If you were conducting a polygraph as part of a murder investigation, you might ask a suspect, 'Was it you who fired the shot fatal to so and so?' If the true answer were *yes*, the suspect will fear getting caught lying, and electrodes on his or her skin will pick up the physiological response to that fear. So I began to think of ways to threaten the well-being of the plant. First I tried dipping a neighboring leaf in a cup of warm coffee. The plant, if anything, showed what I now recognize as boredom—the line on the chart just kept trending downward.

"Then at thirteen minutes, fifty-five seconds chart time, the imagery entered my mind of burning the leaf. I didn't verbalize; I didn't touch the plant; I didn't touch the equipment. Yet the plant went wild. The pen jumped right off the top of the chart. The only new thing the plant could have reacted to was the mental image.

"I went into the next office to get matches from my secretary's desk, and lighting one, made a few feeble passes at a neighboring leaf. I realized, though, that I was already seeing such an extreme reaction that any increase wouldn't be noticeable. So I tried a different approach: I removed the threat by returning the matches to the secretary's desk. The plant calmed right back down.

"Immediately I understood something important was going on. I could think of no conventional scientific explanation. There was no one else in the lab suite, and I wasn't doing anything that might have provided a mechanistic trigger. From that split-second my consciousness hasn't been the same. My whole life has been devoted to looking into this."

I had flown to interview him for a magazine. I was glad I had come. I'd wanted to talk to him since I first read about his work when I was a kid. I don't think it's too much to say that his observations on February 2, 1966 changed not only his life but mine. Through my teens and early twenties, as my perception of an animate world wavered, a part of me kept returning to what I'd read of his work. He provided experimental verification of what I understood in my heart—that the world is alive and sentient. And it came when I still believed in science.

Backster continued, "After that first observation, I talked to scientists from different fields, to get their explanations for what was happening. But it was foreign to them. So I designed an experiment to explore in greater depth what I began to call primary perception."

I raised my eyebrows at the name. He said, "I couldn't call what I was witnessing extrasensory perception, because plants don't have most of the first five senses to start with. This perception on the part of the plant seemed to take place at a much more basic, or primary, level. Anyway, what emerged was an experiment in which I arranged for brine shrimp to be dropped automatically at random intervals into simmering water, while the plant's reaction was recorded at the other end of the lab."

He paused in his rapid-fire talk, then continued, "It's very very hard to eliminate the connection between the experimenter and the plants being tested. Even a brief association with the plants—just a few hours—is enough for them to become attuned to you. Then, even though you automate and randomize the experiment and leave the laboratory, guaranteeing you are entirely unaware of when the experiment starts, the plants will remain attuned to you, no matter where you go. At first, my partner and I would go to a bar a block away, but after a while we began to suspect the plants were not responding to the death of the brine shrimp at all, but instead to the rising and falling levels of excitement in our conversations.

"Finally, we had someone else buy the plants and store them in an unused part of the building. On the day of the experiment, we brought the plants in, hooked them up, and left. This meant the plants were in a strange environment, they had the pressure of the electrodes, they had a trickle of electricity going through their leaves, and they'd been deserted. Because they were not attuned to us or anyone else, they began 'looking around' for anything that would acquaint them with their environment. Then, and only then, did something so subtle as the deaths of the brine shrimp get picked up by the plants."

I asked, "Do they only become attuned to humans, or to others in their environment as well?"

"I'll answer that with an example," Cleve said. "Often I hook up a plant and just go about my business, then observe what makes it respond. One day, I was boiling water in a teakettle to make coffee. I realized I needed the teakettle for something else, and so poured the scalding water down the sink. The plant being monitored showed a huge reaction. It turns out that if you don't put chemicals or hot water down the sink for a long time, a little jungle begins to grow down there. The plant was responding to the death of the microbes.

"I've been amazed at the perception capability right down to the bacterial level. One sample of yogurt, for example, will pick up when another is being fed. Sort of like, 'That one's getting food. Where's mine?' That happens with a fair degree of repeatability. Or if you take two samples of yogurt, hook one up to electrodes, and drop antibiotics in the other, the electroded yogurt shows a huge response at the other's death. And they needn't even be the same kind of bacteria. The first Siamese cat I ever had would only eat chicken. I'd keep a cooked bird in the lab refrigerator and pull off a piece each day to feed the cat. By the time I'd get to the end, the carcass would be pretty old, and bacteria would have started to grow. One day I had some yogurt hooked up, and as I got the chicken out of the refrigerator to begin pulling off strips of meat, the yogurt responded. Next, I put the chicken under a heat lamp to bring it to room temperature, and heat hitting the bacteria created more huge reactions in the yogurt."

"How did you know you weren't influencing this?"

"I was unaware of the reaction at the time. I had pip switches all over the lab, and whenever I performed an action, I hit a switch, which placed a mark on a remote chart. Only later did I compare the reaction of the yogurt to what had been happening in the lab."

"Did the plant respond again when the cat started to eat?"

"Interestingly enough, bacteria appear to have a defense mechanism such that extreme danger causes them to go into a state similar to shock. In effect, they pass out. Many plants do this as well. If you hassle them enough they flatline. The bacteria apparently did this, because as soon as they hit the cat's digestive system, the signal went out. There was a flatline from then on."

I thought of the conversation of death, of the chickens who offered themselves to Amaru, of the duck who gave himself to me, and also of a story I read about the African explorer Dr. Livingstone being mauled by a lion. He later said that during the attack, he didn't feel pain, but rather a sense of bliss. He said it would have been no problem to give himself to the other.

I told Cleve this, and he nodded, laughing, then said, "I was on an airplane once, and had with me a little battery-powered galvanic response meter. Just as the attendants started serving lunch, I pulled out the meter and said to the guy next to me, 'You want to see something interesting?' I put a piece of lettuce between the electrodes, and when people started to eat their salads we got some reactivity, which stopped as the leaves went into shock. 'Wait until they pick up the trays,' I said, 'and see what happens.' When attendants removed our meals, the lettuce got back its reactivity. I had the aisle seat, and I can still remember him strapped in next to the window, no way to escape this mad scientist attaching an electronic gadget to lettuce leaves."

I could well imagine the passenger's shock. Cleve did seem the mad scientist, though with white hair cropped short instead of a tangle, and with a muscular build that betrays the body-building important to him when he was younger, after World War II, when he left the service. His manner was just what I would have expected. He spoke quickly, thoughts tripping too fast for the tongue, and he laughed readily, at his own jokes or those of others. The laboratory, too, was what I would have expected from a mad scientist-type: a jumble of galvanic-response meters, plants (including the original dracaena cane, now grown to cover the better part of a room), cats, lab benches, chemical hoods (leftovers from many years before, when this was a Drug Enforcement Agency lab, only now the hoods were home to plants, sealed off by plastic screens from the batting paws of playful cats), a huge aquarium, books, refrigerator, and bunches of closed-circuit television monitors (he receives reduced rent in exchange for providing electronic security to the jewelers in the office building). He works in the lab. He eats in the lab. He sleeps in the lab. It is his life. I admired the dedication.

As Cleve talked, I thought about a story he'd told me soon after I arrived, as he showed me around the lab and also the basement suite where he still teaches lie detection classes to law enforcement officials—"I've got to make a living, and I've never made a penny off the primary perception research." He'd said that when he was young, he'd been envious of high divers, but was himself afraid to dive even off lower boards. So he'd climbed a ten-meter diving tower and asked a friend to douse his sweat pants with gasoline and set him on fire. The bigger fear, consciously chosen, overrode the lesser fear. He ended up doing "fire dives" professionally for two summers as part of a show.

I came back to the present, and heard Cleve talking: "The point is that the lettuce was going into a protective state so it wouldn't suffer. When the danger left, the reactivity came back. This ceasing of electrical energy at the cellular level ties in, I believe, to the state of shock that people, too, enter in extreme trauma."

"Plants, bacteria, lettuce leaves. . . ."

"Eggs. I had a Doberman Pinscher back in New York whom I used to feed an egg a day. One day I had a plant hooked up to a large galvanic-response meter, and as I cracked the egg, the meter went crazy. That started hundreds of hours of monitoring eggs. Fertilized or unfertilized, it doesn't matter; it's still a living cell, and plants perceive when that continuity is broken. Eggs, too, have the same defense mechanism. If you threaten them, their tracing goes flat. If you wait about twenty minutes, they come back.

"After working with plants, bacteria, and eggs, I started to wonder how animals would react. But I couldn't get a cat or dog to sit still long enough to do meaningful monitoring. So I thought I'd try human sperm cells, which are capable of staying alive outside the body for long periods of time, and are certainly easy enough to obtain. I got a sample from a donor, and put it in a test tube with electrodes, then separated the donor from the sperm by several rooms. The donor inhaled amyl nitrate, which dilates blood vessels and is conventionally used to stop a stroke. Just crushing the amyl nitrate caused a big reaction in the sperm, and when the donor inhaled, the sperm went wild.

"So here I am, seeing single-cell organisms on a human level— sperm—that are responding to the donor's sensations, even when they are no longer in the same room as the donor. There was no way, though, that I could continue that research. It would have been scientifically proper, but politically stupid. The dedicated skeptics would undoubtedly have ridiculed me, asking where my masturbatorium was, and so on.

"Then I met a dental researcher who had perfected a method of gathering white cells from the mouth. This was politically feasible, easy to do, and required no medical supervision. I started doing split-screen videotaping of experiments, with the chart readout superimposed at the bottom of the screen showing the donor's activities. We took the white cell samples, then sent the people home to watch a preselected television program likely to elicit an emotional response—for example, showing a veteran of Pearl Harbor a documentary on Japanese air attacks. We found that cells outside the body still react to the emotions you feel, even though you may be miles away.

"The greatest distance we've tested has been about three hundred miles. Astronaut Brian O'Leary, who wrote *Exploring Inner and Outer Space,* left his white cells here in San Diego, then flew home to Phoenix. On the way, he kept track of events that aggravated him, carefully logging the time of each. The correlation remained, even over that distance."

"The implications of all this . . ."

He interrupted, laughing again. He said, "Yes, are staggering. I have file drawers full of high-quality anecdotal data showing time and again how bacteria, plants, and so on are all fantastically in tune with each other. And human cells, too, have this primary perception capability, but somehow it's gotten lost at the conscious level."

I smiled at the confirmation of my own deadening, and, more recently, reawakening. I asked, "How has the scientific community received your work?"

"With the exception of scientists at the margins, like Rupert Sheldrake, it was met first with derision, then hostility, and mostly now with silence.

"At first they called primary perception 'the Backster Effect,' perhaps hoping they could trivialize the observations by naming them after this wild man who claimed to see things missed by mainstream science. The name stuck, but because primary perception can't be readily dismissed, it is no longer a term of contempt."

"What's the primary criticism by mainstream scientists?"

"The big problem—and this is a problem as far as conscious-ness research in general is concerned—is repeatability. The events I've observed have all been spontaneous. They have to be. If you plan them out in advance, you've already changed them. It all boils down to a this: repeatability and spontaneity do not go together, and as long as members of the scientific community overemphasize repeatability in scientific methodology, they're not going to get very far in consciousness research.

"Not only is spontaneity important, but so is intent. You can't pretend. If you say you are going to burn a plant, but don't mean it, nothing will happen. I hear constantly from people in differ-ent parts of the country, wanting to know how to cause plant reactions. I tell them, 'Don't do anything special. Go about your work; keep notes so later you can tell what you were doing at specific times, and then compare them to your chart recording. But don't plan anything, or the experiment won't work.' People who do this often get equivalent responses to mine, and often win first prize in science fairs. But when they get to Biology 101, they're told that what they have experienced is not important.

"There have been a few attempts by scientists to replicate my experiments with brine shrimp, but these have all been method-ologically inadequate. When they learned they had to automate the experiment, they merely went to the other side of a wall and used closed-circuit television to watch what occurred. Clearly, they weren't removing their consciousness from the experiment."

Cleve paused, a rare event, then said, suddenly serious, "It is so very easy to fail at that experiment. And let's be honest: some of the scientists were relieved when they failed, because success would have gone against the body of scientific knowledge."

I said, "For scientists to give up predictability means they have to give up control, which means they have to give up West-ern culture, which means it's not going to happen until civiliza-tion collapses under the weight of its own ecological excesses."

He nodded, I'm not sure whether in agreement or thought, then said, "I have given up trying to fight other scientists on this, because I know that even if the experiment fails they still see things that change their consciousness. People who would not have said anything twenty years ago often say to me, I think I can safely tell you now how you really changed my life with what you were doing back in the early seventies.' These scientists didn't feel they had the luxury back then to rock the boat; their credibility, and thus their grant requests, would have been affected."

Faced with what Backster was saying, I had several options, presumably the same options with which readers are faced concerning my interactions with coyotes. I could believe he is lying, as is everyone else who has ever made similar observations. I could believe that what he was saying is true, which would validate everything I have experienced but would require that the whole notion of repeatability in the scientific method be reworked, along with preconceived notions of consciousness, communication, perception, and so on. Or I could believe that he's overlooked some strictly mechanistic explanation. I said all this, then mentioned that I'd seen an account of one scientist who insisted there had to be a loose wire in his lie detector.

He responded, "In thirty-one years of research I've found all my loose wires. No, I can't see any mechanistic solution. Some parapsychologists believe I've mastered the art of psychokinesis—that I move the pen with my mind—which would be a pretty good trick in itself. But they overlook the fact that I've automated and randomized many of the experiments to where I'm not even aware of what's going on until later, when I study the resulting charts and videotapes. The conventional explanations have worn pretty thin. One such explanation, proposed in *Harper's*, was static electricity: if you scuffle across the room and touch the plant, you get a response. But of course I seldom touch the plant during periods of observation, and in any case the response would be totally different."

"So, what *is* the signal picked up by the plant?"

"I don't know. I don't believe the signal, whatever it is, dissipates over distance, which is what we'd get if we were dealing with electromagnetic phenomenon. I used to hook up a plant, then take a walk with a randomized timer in my pocket. When the timer went off, I'd return home. The plant always responded the moment I turned around, no matter the distance. And the signal from Phoenix was just as strong as if Brian O'Leary were in the next room.

"Also, we've attempted to screen the signal using lead-lined containers, and other materials, but we can't screen it out. This makes me think the signal doesn't actually *go* from here to there, but instead manifests itself in different places. All this, of course, lands us firmly in the territory of the metaphysical, the spiritual. Think about prayer, for instance. If you were to pray to God, and God was hanging out on the far side of the galaxy, and your prayer traveled at the speed of light, your bones would long-since be dust before God could respond. But if God—however you define God—is everywhere, the prayer doesn't have to travel."

I thought not so much about God as I did of stars, and the courage they gave me when I was a child, and the thoughts and memories I gave to them. Cleve and I were both silent for a long moment. I looked at the tape recorder on the table between us, and saw the slow rotation of the spools. I thought again about the caring of the stars, and said, "Primary perception suggests a radical redefinition of consciousness."

"You mean it would do away with the notion of conscious-ness as something on which humans have a monopoly?" He hesi-tated a moment, then continued, "Western science exaggerates the role of the brain in consciousness. Whole books have been written on the consciousness of the atom. Consciousness might exist on an entirely different level. Some very good research has been done on remote viewing, that is, describing conditions at a distant location. More good research has been done on survival after bodily death. All of it points toward the notion that con-sciousness need not specifically be linked with gray matter. That is another straitjacket we need to rid ourselves of."

I thought of another story that Jeannette once told me. She had been interviewing a shaman from an indigenous group in the north of Russia. He told her that the year before the caribou had been very late. Hunting parties returned with no meat. The shaman had gone into a trance, and on coming out had told the hunters where to go. They went to the indicated valley, and found the caribou. Jeannette asked him, through a translator, "How did you know where they were?" He held his hands open in front of him, and said, "How do you know where your fingers are?"

Cleve continued, "The brain may have some things to do with memory, but a strong case can be made that much memory is not stored there."

I thought of my difficulty sleeping, then thought also of high jumping. I said, "The whole point of training in athletics seems to be to build memories in the muscles." He nodded, and I pushed the questioning about consciousness further, asking whether he has worked with materials that would normally be considered inanimate.

He answered, "I've shredded some things and suspended them in agar. I get electric signals, but not necessarily relating to anything going on in the environment. It's too crude an electroding pattern for me to decipher. But I do suspect that consciousness goes much much further.

"In 1987 I participated in a University of Missouri program that included a talk by Dr. Sidney Fox, then connected with the Institute for Molecular and Cellular Evolution at the University of Miami. Fox had recorded electric signals from proteinlike material that showed properties strikingly similar to those of living cells. The simplicity of the material he used and the self-organizing capability it displayed suggest to me that biocommunication was present at the earliest states in the evolution of life on this planet. Of course the Gaia hypothesis—the idea that the earth is a great big working organism, with a lot of corrections built in—fits in nicely with this. I don't think it would be a stretch to take the hypothesis further and presume that the planet itself is intelligent."

I asked how his work has been received in other parts of the world.

"The Russians and other eastern Europeans have always been very interested. And whenever I encounter Indian scientists—Buddhist or Hindu—and we talk about what I do, instead of giving me a bunch of grief they say, 'What took you so long?' My work dovetails very well with many of the concepts embraced by Hinduism and Buddhism."

"What *is* taking us so long?"

"The fear is that, if what I am observing is accurate, many of

the theories on which we've built our lives need complete re-
working. I've known biologists to say, 'If Backster is right, we're
in trouble.' It takes a certain kind of character and personality to
even attempt such a questioning of fundamental assumptions.
The Western scientific community, and actually all of us, are in
a difficult spot, because in order to maintain our current mode of
being, we must ignore a tremendous amount of information. And
more information is being gathered all the time. For instance,
have you heard of Rupert Sheldrake's work with dogs? He puts a
time-recording camera on both the dog at home and the human
companion at work. He has discovered that even if people come
home from work at a different time each day, at the moment the
person leaves work, the dog at home heads for the door.

"Even mainstream scientists are stumbling all over this
biocommunication phenomenon. It seems impossible, given the
sophistication of modern instrumentation, for us to keep missing this fundamental attunement of living things. Only for so
long are we going to be able to pretend it's the result of 'loose
wires.' We cannot forever deny that which is so clearly there."

It was good to receive this validation, but I didn't want to trust
Backster: he could be lying, or he could be crazy. Just because the
story hangs together doesn't mean it accurately represents reality.

We went to dinner, and then I took a long walk. I returned
late, and Cleve set me up on pads in the basement. I slept fit-
fully: the room was too large, too unfamiliar, and with too many
corners and too many doors. At last I dragged my sleeping bag
into a small room off to the side, barricaded one door with a chair
and the other with my feet, and began to doze.

He awakened me early, and we returned to the lab. I wanted
to see "the Backster Effect" for myself. He hooked up a plant,
and I watched the paper roll out of the recorder. I couldn't corre-
late the movement of the pen with anything I was feeling, or
with the conversation. One of his cats began to play with the
plant. The oscillations of the pen *seemed* to increase in magni-
tude, but I couldn't be sure. Halfheartedly, I suggested burning
the plant. No response from the plant. Cleve responded, "I don't
think you really want to, and besides, I wouldn't let you."

We moved to another part of the lab, and he put yogurt into a sterilized test tube, then inserted a pair of sterilized gold electrodes. We began again to talk. The pen wriggled up and down, and once again *seemed* to lurch just as I took in my breath to disagree with something he said. But I couldn't be sure. When we see something, how do we know if it is real, or do we see it only because we wish so much to believe?

Cleve left to take care of business elsewhere in the building. The line manifesting the electrical response of the yogurt immediately went flat. I tried to fabricate anger, thinking of clearcuts and the politicians who legislate them, thinking about abused children and their abusers. Still flat. Either fabricated emotions don't count (as Cleve had suggested), or it's a sham, or something else was terribly wrong. Perhaps the yogurt was not interested in me. Losing interest myself, I began to wander the lab. My eyes fell on a calendar, which on closer inspection I saw was actually an advertisement for a shipping company. I felt a surge of anger at the ubiquity of advertising. Then I realized—a spontaneous emotion! I dashed to the chart, and saw a sudden spike corresponding to the moment I'd felt the anger. Then more flatline. And more flatline. And more. Again I began to wander the lab, and again I saw something that triggered an emotion. This was a poster showing a map of the human genome. I thought of the Human Genome Diversity Project, a monumental study hated by many indigenous peoples and their allies for its genocidal implications (Backster is not affiliated with or particularly a fan of the program; I later found he simply likes the poster). Another surge of anger, another dash to the chart, and another spike in the graph, from instants before I started to move.

Finally Cleve came back. Even the scientist in me was happy. I had previously experienced this attunement in the field, felt it with coyotes, dogs, trees, stars. And now I had seen it in the laboratory.

Death and Awakening

"In the middle of the journey of our life, I came to myself in a dark wood, For the straight way was lost."
Dante Alighieri

MY BEES DIED FOR the first time in the spring of 1985.

Beekeeping in California promises not only cash, but danger. One of the reasons Glen and I pushed so hard when we moved bees is that growers generally want them in as soon as the bloom gets underway, but no sooner, because they want to apply insecticides until the last moment. They want the bees out when the petals drop, for the same reason. You never know precisely when blossoms are going to pop: rain may delay, or a nice day hasten, the flowers opening. Nor do you know when the petals will fall: a hot wind can rob the trees of flowers in just a couple of hours. Then you can bet growers will be spraying chemicals the next day. Even with this constant movement on the part of beekeepers, about 50,000 beehives—nearly ten percent of the total present—are killed each year in California by pesticides.

Oranges are one of the most dangerous crops. Even during the bloom, when growers are prohibited from applying insecticides except in the case of (routine) emergencies, every morning I found abnormally large piles of dead bees in front of each hive, and hundreds of walking wounded: disoriented bees dragging hind legs as if paralyzed, wings fluttering spasmodically.

Each day I called the county extension office to find when the ban on pesticides would be lifted, and one Thursday they announced it would end at dawn on Saturday morning. I immediately called a trucking broker to hire a flatbed semi to haul the bees to northeastern Nevada, where I had arranged sites on pastures of alfalfa and clover to keep the bees through the summer. The first broker I called didn't handle flatbeds, nor did the second. The third said he would check around for me and find something. I called him back late in the afternoon, and he said there were none to be found. He would, however, be able to rent me a refrigerated van.

I later learned that I was gullible, and intentionally deceived. Flatbeds were everywhere; I had merely called the wrong three brokers. The final one, not willing to send me on as had the others, merely lied. Though I didn't know all that at the time, I did know that on rare occasions beekeepers hire refrigerated vans to move their bees, refrigeration being crucial to keep the hives from overheating during the long drive in close confinement. Because my hives were on pallets for ease of loading, I insisted that the interior of the van be wide enough to accommodate two pallets side-by-side. The broker reassured me.

I woke up before dawn on Friday to perform a final check on the hives before strapping them four tight to a pallet. By now, because of swarms, I had about 320 colonies. I finished strapping about seven in the evening, and drove to meet the trucker at a restaurant. We returned to the drop. I had arranged for my friend the wasp farmer to help me with his forklift. He would place the pallets in the back of the trailer, and I would use a pallet jack to position them inside.

The truck was too small. I couldn't fit pallets two wide, which meant that in order to accommodate anywhere near all of my hives, I would have to remove many of them from the pallets to hand stack them in corners and spare spaces. Had I not been anticipating the massed arrival of cropdusters the next morning, I would have sent the trucker on his way and called another broker. But that was no longer an option.

I loaded what pallets I could, then began to hand stack. Plugged with honey, the hives weighed a hundred to a hundred and fifty pounds a piece. The bees, of course, were crawling everywhere. Sometime during the night the netting covering my face developed a rip, and I began to get stung. Since it was dark, I couldn't see the tear, and so didn't know where bees were getting into my suit. Holding a hundred-and-fifty-pound box full of tens of thousands of bees, you can't simply drop it to scrape away the stinger. And there was work to be done. For the first twenty or so times, I relied on my ability to wall off pain. For the next twenty, I cursed, not too loud because the wasp farmer was a devout Seventh-Day Adventist. For the third twenty, I begged the bees to stop. After that I lost count.

About seven-thirty in the morning we finished. We had been able to cram all but eight of the hives into the semi, and put the rest in the back of my pickup. I took off my suit, and at long last began to scrape stingers, their poison sacs by now long empty, off my face. I stopped to get some quick breakfast, and the waitress pointed out I had bees crawling in my hair.

I drove all day. The truck ended up miles behind me—some sort of problem getting gas money from the broker—but I had given the trucker careful directions to the drop site. It was a twelve-hour drive, and I looked forward to unloading the bees—another night's work—and finally going to my rented house in Carlin, Nevada (another hour-and-a-half drive), and sleeping for a couple of days. Then I would move the bees to their summer sites.

But that's not what happened. All day as I drove, I kept hearing the bees die. Of course they were hundreds of miles away. Perhaps it was Backster's "primary perception" brought to a conscious level. All I know is that I perceived first their distress and then their deaths all through the day and into the evening, and when the trucker finally arrived at the drop, I was not surprised when I opened the doors to see a two-foot-deep river of dead bees, honey, and melted wax pour out the rear of the trailer. The truck's refrigeration unit had broken down, and the inside had grown hot enough to melt beeswax, hot enough to kill bees. I was sad, I was tired—exhausted really—my head hurt, and my arms and legs ached. But I was not surprised.

I spent the night unloading the remains. The next morning, dawn creeping over the mountains to the east, I drove home, too tired to feel anything. I slept.

Not only bees died in 1985. I died also, from Crohn's disease, pain, internal bleeding, and self-control.

Looking back, it's clear I've had Crohn's since I was young, but it wasn't diagnosed until I was twenty-four. As a child I often had stomach cramps that doubled me over, or left me pressing my face to the surface of my desk at school, closing my eyes, and going away. Also, my growth spurt was late—I was five feet, two inches, in eighth grade, before shooting to six feet by the end of high school—something I've since learned is symptomatic of Crohn's. And then there's my metabolism: even among teenaged boys I had a reputation as a trencherman, easily putting away fifteen or twenty tacos at a meal and still, at six feet, weighing less than a hundred and forty pounds.

The real problems commenced in college. After I started jumping (my weight now up to one fifty-five), I began to suffer diarrhea the day of every meet. I thought it was nerves. Then I got diarrhea the day before, then the day before that, then the day before that, until more often than not, in season and out, I had the flux. At the time the cramps were not severe.

Crohn's is an incurable progressive disease which, during flareups, causes sores to appear along the gastrointestinal tract, anywhere from the lips to the anus, centering on the bowels, especially the colon. It has many side effects, some of which I have (arthritis, anemia, constant fatigue, clubbing of the fingers), and some of which I don't (fistulas, iridis, a horrifying skin condition called *pyoderma gangrenosum*). It is characterized, as I discovered in the summer of 1985, by abdominal cramping more painful than broken bones, more painful, I've since heard from women who have the disease, than childbirth.

No one knows what causes it. Studies have shown the bowels of those with Crohn's to be generally more permeable to large molecules than the norm, but no one knows what, if anything, that means. Studies have also shown that the disease is extremely rare in nonindustrialized nations, even after accounting for misdiagnoses at less sophisticated medical facilities; for example, believing that someone who actually died of Crohn's died of dysentery. Then as industries enter a region, so does the disease: Japan had few cases prior to World War II, and now has one of the highest rates in the world. This means that not only metaphorically but in all physical truth industrial civilization is eating away at my guts.

The disease came on hard in the weeks after the death of the bees, probably in great measure because of the physical strain of too little sleep for too many months in the front of the truck, and too many nights moving bees. But something else was happening as well. I was dying.

There are deaths such as the death of a chicken in the jaws of a coyote, an aphid in the jaws of a ladybug larva, a duck as I bring down the hatchet to split him head from body. And there are deaths such as that of the larva who falls asleep to awaken as a ladybug, the grub who spins a black cocoon before becoming a honeybee, and each of us each night dying to one world to find ourselves in another, and each morning dying in the other to walk again in the present.

My old way of living—or rather surviving—that had allowed me to persevere through the violence of my childhood was no longer sustainable. Perhaps it never had been, but was all along a stopgap response to a pathological environment. In any case, I could not continue controlling or ignoring my emotions, nor could I, and this amounts to the same thing, continue to ignore my body. A way of living based on ignoring the body can lead only to bodily collapse.

I didn't see it that way at the time. I just knew I hurt like hell, and that I was defecating thirty times per day (defecating what? I could keep nothing down, so in time I simply quit eating), and throwing up at least that many times, from the pain that rolled across my lower abdomen.

That summer, I could sleep in only one position: on my back, knees clutched to my chest. Any other position immediately precipitated cramps that caused me to dash doubled over to the toilet. This made nights especially difficult, because as a child I had trained myself to sleep only on my stomach, neck tucked under upraised shoulder to keep vampires or others from sucking me dry.

I didn't go to the hospital. I had no way to pay, nor did I have any sense. I kept thinking that if I ignored the symptoms with enough determination and for a long enough time, the sickness would go away on its own.

Then one morning I awoke to no pain at all, only a grainy pulling at my full bowels, not unlike the feel of rough-hewn lumber sliding under fingertips. I stood up straight and smiled briefly before tripping down the stairs to the toilet. What came out was liquid, but I couldn't expect all the symptoms to disappear in one night, could I? I cleaned myself, and looked in the bowl. Bright red. Blood. I was bleeding internally. I finally understood that it would not work to ignore the sickness. I checked into the hospital.

It didn't help. As I came to know later, the doctors misdiagnosed me and performed inappropriate and damaging procedures. They overprescribed some medications and underprescribed others.

One of the worst things they did—and there was obviously no reason for it—was to one night give me a laxative. The cramps worsened. I had not thought that possible. For the first time in my life—and I remember experiencing a sense of sickly wonder at this encounter with a new feeling—I could not cope. The pain was too much. At some point long after midnight I felt my will buckle and collapse, a feeling as physical as the implosion of an overburdened archway. Had someone entered the room, handed me a gun, and said, "I will let you sleep if you shoot the person in the other bed," I would have done it. Had this person suggested I shoot my nieces, who lived down the street from the hospital, I would have done that, too. I would have shot anyone or destroyed anything to sleep. Not so much because I was tired, though I was, but because I was empty. I had ceased entirely to care, nor even to exist. I was dead.

There is a language older by far and deeper than words. It is the language of the earth, and it is the language of our bodies. It is the language of dreams, and of action. It is the language of meaning, and of metaphor. This language is not safe, as Jim Nollman said of metaphor, and to believe in its safety is to diminish the importance of the embodied. Metaphors are dangerous because if true they open us to our bodies, and thus to action, and because they slip—sometimes wordlessly, sometimes articulated—between the seen and unseen. This language of symbol is the umbilical cord that binds us to the beginning, to whatever is the source of who we are, where we come from, and where we return. To follow this language of metaphor is to trace words back to our bodies, back to the earth.

We suffer from misperceiving the world. We believe ourselves separated from each other and from all others by words and by thoughts. We believe—rationally, we think—that we are separated by rationality, and that to perceive the world "rationally" is to perceive the world as it is. But perceiving the world "as it is" is also to misperceive it entirely, to blind ourselves to an even greater body of truth.

The world is a great dream. No, not fleeting, evanescent, unreal, immaterial, less than. These words do not describe even our dreams of night. But alive, vivid, every moment present to and pregnant with meaning, speaking symbolically. To perceive the world as we perceive our dreams would be to more closely perceive it as it is. The sky is crying, from joy or grief I do not know. Waves in a wild river form bowbacked lovers and speak to me of union. Industrial civilization tears apart my insides.

The world is speaking, every moment of every day, and because so often it does not choose to speak English—or in the case of caged apes, American Sign Language—we choose to believe it does not speak. How sad. Our bodies speak, too, and to them, too, so often we choose not to listen. A woman once said to me, "I love my children, and I'm glad they exist, but I now know I wanted so much to be born that three times I went through the process of giving birth. Finally I know what I wanted all along."

Our actions also speak to us of death. I've often wondered if the urge to destroy is really the desire to do away with a way of living that does not bring us joy. Perhaps what we want is not to destroy the world with plutonium, but to stop living the way we do. We know that to be reborn we must die, but we do not know what form this death must take. Having denied the existence of the spirit (it can't be measured in the laboratory), or at the very least having attempted to sever the ties between spirit and flesh (flesh bringing "the manly mind down from the heights"), we have forgotten their interconnectedness.

For my father to have stopped beating us, to have stopped raping us, he would have had to die to his own bitter childhood. Because he clearly did not beat my sister over the stated reason of finding drowned puppies, we can know that his anger had to be located elsewhere. It lurked among the internalized images of those who froze his psyche in a state of perpetual fear and anger. A bubbling pot frozen mid-boil. To let that go, he would have to fall into it, let the significance of his own actions—for actions, as they say, speak so much louder than words—surround him. He would have to let them speak to him. What does the rape of his daughter, his son, his wife, mean? What deep desires do they manifest? As he brings back his fist to strike his son, how does the fist signify?

It is not easy. Earlier I said that the way to step past atrocity is to step toward experience. But experience is tied intimately to perception, which is tied intimately to prior experience. How does one know that experiences are what they seem? My father's experience was undoubtedly of anger: *so listen to it, man, and pop that fucking smartass kid across the mouth.* It ends up that we must not stop at direct experience, but instead pause there to listen again to that voice of anger or sorrow or hatred or even perceived love, and then while stepping again forward even further into experience step also into meaning.

But even that is of no use. My earlier wish for my father— that he would understand the effects of his actions—is wishful thinking. It is likely that he, like so many of us, like the monkeys made psychotic by removing them from their community, like the race of the indecent mentioned by Viktor Frankl, is simply unreachable. If that is the case, trying to make someone like my father understand this is a waste of time. In order to understand, he would have to first die. As we all do.

Jesus in the grave, Jonah in the whale, Moses in the desert, Jesus once again and also in the desert, the Phoenix burning to rise from its own ashes, the snake shedding its old and dead skin, caterpillars forming cocoons, trees dropping leaves: *everyone* understands that for there to be growth, there must always be a dying away.

George Gurdjieff wrote, "A man may be born, but in order to be born he must first die, and in order to die he must first awake." Being born without dying is false, and leads only to a reaffirmation and strengthening of the same impulses that drive us terrified toward death while disallowing us from entering that cleansing abyss. Dying without awakening is just as false, playing out as we see in the unquenchable cannibalism of the somnambular undead, those who enact a death wish never realizing that what they want to kill—or rather to allow to die—is wholly inside. The trick is to walk that sharp line between death and life, and to allow yourself, with full cognizance of the risks involved, to collapse, to let a part of your life die so another may emerge, to dive as fully into death as you do life, to embrace it and let it embrace you, to eat the fish of collapse and death as well as the fish of life and experience, and to let its line also pull you to the bottom of the ocean.

Looking back, it is fitting that I last heard my father's voice as a part of the same larger experience that killed off the first part of my life, a part dominated by him and my reaction to him.

My first night in the hospital the telephone rang. I picked it up, heard my name. I asked, "Who is this?"

He said, "Your father."

I hung up.

The bleeding stopped soon after I entered the hospital. Not because of anything the doctors did, but simply because it stopped. I returned to my home in Carlin, Nevada, where the summer months passed in an unfocused tunnel of days and nights in which I crawled again and again from bedroom to bathroom and back. I lost weight, down to a hundred and fifteen pounds. I could no longer stand straight, or again I'd cramp, then stagger to the sink and toilet. I lost the capacity to think clearly, and to remember. My vocabulary disappeared, and I could say no words over four syllables, even directly after they were said by others.

The woman I dated through college and after, the one whose question sparked the dream of cranes, flew out to get me to eat. I could not, and after a few days she checked me back into the hospital. She called my mother in England, where she was thinking of staying, and said, "If you want to see your son alive, you need to come home." She then said to me, "I do not want to watch you die." She flew back to her home.

The doctors continued their maltreatment, and I continued to lose weight. They scheduled me for a colostomy. Had my mother not returned, and pulled me from the hospital, I would probably not have survived my death to be reborn: a decade later I speak easily of these deaths and rebirths, but in all truth they are dangerous, and messy. This spiritual death, this collapse, does not come without its price, exacted in pain and tears and oftentimes physical death as well.

After speaking with experts on Crohn's disease and ulcerative colitis (this latter the disease with which I'd been misdiagnosed), and after learning of the wrong tests done and right tests undone, my mother took me to another hospital, this in Salt Lake City. There, they diagnosed me immediately with Crohn's (a case so classic that later, when part of my colon was removed, they used it as a teaching tool). The doctors tried to strengthen me with intravenous feeding. They weaned me off the steroids I'd gotten from earlier doctors, and for several weeks tried many medications to control the disease.

The recurrence rate of Crohn's following surgery is high—according to one cheerful account, "greater than ninety-nine percent," and according to another about fifty percent per year—and for this reason the physicians were hesitant to operate. But I had another bleed, and then another, and despite transfusions began passing out from loss of blood.

I awoke the morning after surgery to a delicious absence of pain. Sure, my belly hurt where they'd opened me up, but it was nothing compared to the cramps. They were gone. I pulled myself up, and looked out the window to the dawn sunlight reflecting off scattered hills to the west. The surgeon came in, told me they'd removed about two-thirds of my colon ("We left as much as possible for next time"), and was followed shortly by a nurse who told me to pee. I told her I couldn't. She said I needed to so they could make sure my kidneys still worked. I told her I'd be happy to, but I couldn't just right then. She said they needed to know right away, so she'd go get a catheter. I told her I'd try real hard. When I handed back the bottle, it was closer to one-tenth full than nine-tenths empty.

I went home as soon as my guts awakened, and through that fall my mother cooked for me four or five meals per day to fatten me up. I remember that the first night back I was too weak to climb the stairs to my room, and so had to crawl. A week later, on my first walk outdoors, I made it only to the next city lot before returning home exhausted.

I spent that fall and winter taking long slow walks to the

river, or down to the town's park where I would stand alone and shoot baskets for hours on end. When other people showed up, I was not yet strong enough to play in games, but by spring I stood my own, and played pickup basketball and softball as often as I could.

Through that winter my mother often said to me, in response to my despair at the slow return of strength, "It took you a long time to get sick, and it will take you a long time to get well."

A Time of Sleeping

"The part of the mind that is dark to us
in this culture, that is sleeping in us, that
we name 'unconscious,' is the knowledge
that we are inseparable from all other
beings in the universe."
Susan Griffin

THIS PAST SUMMER I went to the beach with Julie. The sky was gray, the wind sharp. Tiny drops of rain hit our faces, or fell to the sand at our feet. We ate lunches of dry meat sandwiches—we'd forgotten mustard and mayonnaise. Seagulls circled above, or trotted toward us, only to scurry away.

One bird looked especially pathetic, a forlorn adolescent evidently unpracticed at scooping up starfish. He looked hungry. Julie tried to throw him the scrap-end of her meal. Another seagull swooped for the snatch of bread before it hit the sand. Julie reached into the bag for another piece. Another toss, and another seagull had a snack. The young bird still stood, still seeming pathetic and hungry. Again her hand went into the bag, and again another bird snatched the bread away.

I laughed, then said, "It's a bait-and-switch routine they've got set up. They take turns being the orphan."

Julie didn't think it was funny. She kept throwing food until the Pathetic One had tasted a bite.

A large part of me had not been laughing, but had instead been wanting to grab the bread and repeat to her the warning I'd heard repeatedly as a child: do not feed the animals. Do not cause them to become habituated to humans. It will only hurt them in the long run. Don't feed the seagulls, because they will just be a nuisance, and besides, they will not learn to fend for themselves. And if they can't learn to catch starfish they die. It's survival of the fittest. The same is true for all others. Don't feed the bears, or they'll lose their fear, and having lost their fear they may attack. Even if they do not attack they will knock over trash bins and iceboxes, and we will have to shoot them. Then I remembered the offerings I give the coyotes, and noted my own hypocrisy.

Julie said, "I've always loved feeding animals. Ever since I was a child. Do you think it's wrong?"

I wanted to say *yes* but heard myself say, "No."

"I don't think so, either," she said. "I think it's what we're supposed to do."

I didn't have to ask why. I just nodded, agreeing now, and thought of salmon swimming toward bears waiting for the food that would last them through their long winter's sleep. I thought of the duck, giving his life to me. Part of our task as members of a community is to feed each other. I thought again of our fundamental inversion of all relatedness, of how we nearly always ask precisely the wrong question—*What can I get from this?*—and so very rarely the right one—*What can I give back?* Even when we try to learn from others, it is from this same spirit of acquisition: *What can I learn from this forest ecosystem that will teach me how to manage it for maximum resource extraction?* Rarely: *What can I learn from this forest community that will teach me how to better serve it?*

We did not talk for a long time. Instead we sat watching seagulls lose interest and trot away to stand one-legged in the wind. My fingers picked at the huge log of driftwood on which we sat, and I felt the softly textured surface, worn smooth by sun, salt, water, and sand. For some reason I thought of bear baiting, a process in which for months prior to the season, a "hunter" places edibles at a spot in the forest. Come season, he sits in a tree, waits for a bear to show up for dinner, and shoots him or her at point-blank range. I've often wondered what that bear must think and feel while dying, lying next to an offering of food. I would imagine shock, sorrow, and a deep sense of betrayal. *How could you? I thought you were giving me this meal.*

Times like that—times I consider the duplicitous nature of so many of our relations—I think back to a time I've never known, when children painted the faces of wolf pups and placed them gently back in dens, and when wolves found lost families and led them home. A time when humans and nonhumans conversed, and when the world and all in it were not resources to be consumed but friends and neighbors to be loved and enjoyed, and even when killed and eaten to be perceived with a sense of gratitude and wonder. Times like that I think back to when men did not rape women, nor did they rape children, and when fathers did not strike their sons nor daughters. It really wasn't so very long ago, but it was a time I've never known.

I did not die for only one night, but for the several years it took for the lessons of that night to travel to every cell of my body, and for the layers of old skin—formed in an earlier time of trauma, when I had different requirements for survival—to scrape away or slough off and be replaced by new ones.

When we imprison another we must also place one of our own in prison as a guard. Likewise when we imprison a part of ourselves, other parts must move into that same dungeon. Prisons—whether made of steel, razor wire, floodlamps, and observation posts, or a steel will holding emotions and flesh in check—consume a tremendous amount of energy. When as a child I vowed to no longer feel anger, to no longer feel anything, not only did I lose access to banished feelings but I lost also the energy it took to keep them at bay. Where did those emotions go, what did they do? They did not vanish into the psychic equivalent of thin air. How did they twist and turn to find their way out, as ultimately they must? How do frustrated emotions make clear their need for expression, and how, in the end, are they expressed?

The collapse that night in the hospital taught me the inefficacy of attempted control: diarrhea was an embodied manifestation of a lesson I needed to learn, and Crohn's disease was a teacher. *Let go, Derrick. Let go.* If I could not control my bowels, how could I hope to control my emotions, and certainly how could I ever hope to control any other? If I could no longer cope with physical pain by simply walling it off, what made me think that process worked any better for psychological pain? That night made clear that my attempts to ignore pain were killing me, both physically and psychically. It also made clear that control was a dead-end street.

I still have a notebook from that time in which I wrote a tentative declaration of this new direction: "All my life I have trained myself to be guided intellectually by intuition [I always did well on tests, standardized and other, because I'm a good guesser], and emotionally and practically by will. Now I wish to begin training my intuition to govern those other aspects of my life, tempered by will." That was as far as I could say at the time. I hadn't yet realized I didn't need to "train" my intuition so much as I needed to quit trying to impose my will upon it, and to instead begin listening to it. I hadn't yet learned well enough the lesson the disease was bringing to me.

By speaking of Crohn's disease as a teacher—both literal and metaphorical—I'm not suggesting that everything in our lives is a result of our having called it forward to teach us what we need to learn. Napalmed children do not call fiery death into their lives, nor do salmon call into existence dams to teach them about extinction. The notion of all calamity being in some measure self-inflicted is just one more attempt to deny accountability to perpetrators, one more means to silence victims. It insults not only the victim but also objectifies the agent of calamity, diminishes it to just another resource to be consumed, this time for our education. But the agent may have a lesson to deliver, and it may not. That's up to the other, or sometimes to chance.

I got a lot of that "blame the victim" stuff soon after I came down with the disease. All through the summer of 1985, and over the next couple of years, perhaps a dozen people approached to tell me the disease was my responsibility, that somehow I had brought it on myself. This was annoying enough the first time; by the fourth or fifth I lost patience and began, exasperated, to ask, "Would you tell me to take responsibility for getting hurt in an earthquake?" I am not certain whether it was the question, or the vehemence with which I asked it, that usually shut them up.

One person didn't shut up. I was on a plane, stuck for hours on a runway at Chicago's O'Hare while the pilots waited for a break in a blizzard. My row-mate was a psychologist. We exchanged histories, and at some point I told her I had Crohn's. We talked of it for a while before she made what I had come to view as the inevitable reference to my responsibility. I responded by rote with my rhetorical question: Without hesitation she answered *yes*.

She didn't have to say anything else, for suddenly I understood. There is a difference between assigning causal responsibility to someone—I *caused* this Crohn's disease, the napalmed baby *caused* the atrocity—and someone becoming responsible (that is, capable of responding) to the events which engulf them. In other words, Crohn's disease had arrived, which meant it was now my responsibility to learn how to respond to it, enter into a dialogue with it. Obviously, in many cases—the napalmed baby; myself as a child; all of us, I fear, faced with the monumental momentum of our culture's death urge—the circumstances of any particular calamity can be so overwhelming as to disallow reasonable response. But so long as we are capable it is our duty and our joy to remain as present as we can to our circumstances.

At that moment something shifted inside. I was no longer simply a person afflicted with Crohn's disease, but instead a person with a new companion for life. This companion was not always going to be pleasant, and in fact could kill me if it so chose, but from now on our lives were inextricably bound. For better or for worse, I was accountable to this other, which (or who) was also accountable to me. Just as it would behoove me to learn to listen to the friends and family with whom I plan on maintaining any sort of relationship and to learn to speak honestly to them as well—hearing what they need and making clear what I need in order to continue—sitting on that plane I realized that if I were going to survive this disease, I had better learn to listen. I realized, too, that learning to listen to the disease might not only keep me alive, but might also help to release me from the prison of my own steel will, which I had built as a child to keep the world out, but which I now was finding kept me locked in even more firmly.

The psychologist Rollo May retells the story of Briar Rose, modifying the emphasis so that no longer is she a mere sleeping beauty waiting unchanging to be awakened by a kiss, but instead she— or rather her primarily unconscious processes of maturation— now runs the story. Far more important than the kiss is the time of sleeping—the hundred years of death—and it is now she and not the prince who determines the moment of reawakening. The lucky prince merely happens to be in the right place at the right time with the right attitude.

The story, if you recall, runs like this: A king and queen were unable to conceive, until one day when the queen was bathing a frog crawled onto land and said, "Before the year is out you shall have a daughter."

The daughter, named Briar Rose, was born, and the king gave a great feast. Because he hadn't enough golden plates, he was able to invite only twelve of the country's thirteen Wise Women. On the night of the feast, each of the first eleven Wise Women granted gifts to the princess: virtue, beauty, riches, and so on. Then the thirteenth, the uninvited one, showed up unannounced, and to avenge herself said that in the princess's fifteenth year she would prick herself with a spindle and fall down dead. The twelfth Wise Woman, who had not yet granted a boon, stated that while she could not undo the words of the other, she could soften them; instead of dying the princess would sleep for a hundred years.

Her father responded by removing every spindle from the kingdom, trying to protect his daughter from the death everyone knew must come. But it is no more possible to cheat fate than it is to resolve the nonrational through the purely rational. One day in her explorations the princess found an old woman spinning in a deserted room in the castle. Briar Rose "pricked" her finger on the spindle and began to bleed—the sexual imagery here is not tremendously subtle—and fell asleep.

The sleep extended to everyone in the castle, and round the castle grew a hedge of thorns so high as to hide even the flag on the roof (in the cocoon, the caterpillar must give up its former identity so that when the time is right it may assume another). For the next hundred years many princes tried to awaken this sleeping beauty with a kiss. But they never succeeded, because before they could get to her the hedge's thorns grabbed and killed them. Finally, at the end of the allotted time, another prince, really not so very different from the ones who came before, made the same attempt. But because the time had come for Briar Rose to rewaken, the thorns turned to flowers, which parted of their own accord—once again, the sexual symbolism is so obvious as to almost make me blush—and let him in. He kissed her, and you know the rest.

Rollo May calls this moment when Briar Rose grew ready

kairos, or *the time of destiny.* It is that moment when her pupating is done, and she is ready to emerge an adult. It is the moment when her purpose begins to be fulfilled (and let's hope her purpose in life is far more than to be a simple helpmate to her handsome prince). She is at last receptive to stimuli to which, in the time before, she was insensate. Because of internal changes she is ready for external change, ready to be reawakened with something so simple as a kiss.

The notion of *kairos* is important not only to sleeping princesses in fairy tales and to their suitors, successful or dead. It applies to anyone who undergoes any death and who must then await the necessary rebirth, and I believe it applies just as surely to cultures, which too must die to a way of living so that when the time is right they may reawaken mature, ripe, and ready to enter into fully mutual, adult relationships.

Every creature on the planet must be hoping, at the very least selfishly, that our culture's time of awakening comes soon. Perhaps someday the salmon and the rest of us will hurl ourselves against the dams expecting to feel the impermeability that has met us all along—the obstinate resistance that murdered Jesus, Spartacus, Tupac Amaru, and Thomas Münzer—and we will find at long last and instead the wild river that lay hidden there all the time.

I don't believe it would have been possible for me to undergo a meaningful death and rebirth had I been working a wage job. There would not have been time. No one expects a caterpillar to spin a cocoon, pop in for ten minutes, then emerge a butterfly, and at least my mother understood it would take me months or years to recover even physically from my episode of Crohn's disease, yet not many of us are willing or able to make the time necessary to begin asking the right questions about who we are, what we love, what we fear, and what we're doing to each other, much less answering these questions, and much much less living them.

I don't always know what the right questions are; I only know that they reside in my body, and that in order to discover them— or better, remember—I need to be still. In that sense the disease did me an immense favor; had I at any time been tempted by poverty, rampant deficit spending, and social pressure to get a job, my body would have killed me.

At the time, through my twenties, I did not know what was right, only what was wrong, and I didn't know what I wanted, only what I didn't want. I didn't know how to live, only how not to live. I knew a job wasn't what I wanted or needed.

We did not evolve working for others forty hours or more per week. We evolved, and one need only look at nonhumans or at remaining indigenous peoples to see this is so, spending a great deal of time doing not much of anything (or once again in the lingo of bee research, "loafing"). As the Dane Frederick Andersen Bolling said of the Khoikhoi of South Africa, "They find it strange that we, the Christians, work, and they say, that we are all mortal, that we gain nothing from our toil, but at the end are thrown underground, so that all we have done is in vain." Another colonist noted of these same people that "their contempt for riches is in reality nothing but their hatred of work," and a third remarked that "the principle work of the men is to laze about."

Had I encountered these comments in my twenties, they would have encouraged me by helping to blunt the voice inside: *What's the matter? Lazy?* Looking back, I can put a positive spin on my activities—or lack thereof—of those years by calling it a period of pupation, or saying I was undergoing a death and re-birth, or calling it my own forty days in the wilderness. But the truth is that for the next few years, living first in Nevada and later in Idaho, I didn't actually do much of anything. I felt guilty about this, but I couldn't find anything to do that interested me more than nothing. I certainly wasn't going to go back to phys-ics, or to any other means of selling my hours. I called myself a writer, but didn't write much: what was I going to write? I didn't have anything to say, because I didn't know who I was. To dis-cover that takes long, slow, uninterrupted time. Time enough to get bored, and then to move beyond boredom, which is really just another screen to deflect our attention away from the ardu-ous yet delightful, joyous though painful process of allowing ourselves the stillness to remember what we feel and to begin assuming responsibility for our lives.

Nearly every day I walked the railroad tracks to the Humboldt River, then climbed down to the concrete footing of a bridge.

There I sat in the sunlight and read, or more often just watched the river. I walked the banks, and in spring saw a mother bird feign a broken wing to distract me from her nest. I saw beetles crawling in and out of a beaver dead on the tracks, and I saw the beaver's teeth, orange as carrots. I saw plenty of trains.

Albert Einstein once observed that "the significant problems of the world cannot be solved at the same level of consciousness at which they were created." I think he's right. I believe Carl Jung was onto much the same thing when he wrote, "All the greatest and most important problems of life are fundamentally insoluble. . . . They can never be solved, but only outgrown. This 'outgrowing' proved on further investigation to require a new level of consciousness. Some higher or wider interest appeared on the patient's horizon, and through this broadening of his or her outlook the insoluble problem lost its urgency. It was not solved logically in its own terms but faded when confronted with a new and stronger life urge."

The first statement points out to me why there must always be a death for there to be a meaningful transition—one that sticks. We do not easily give up our acquired ways of being, even when they're killing us. Although when I sat on the couch as a child, or lay in bed feeling my father's flesh against mine, it had been unspeakably crucial for me to control my emotions and body, I could not later quit manifesting that same control until it had very nearly killed me. That level of consciousness had to play itself out to the end, or rather to *an* end. Only when that mindset had, like a plant in a too-small pot, exhausted its own possibilities did I begin casting about for another way to be; only when I no longer had any real choice, far past the time when what little choice there was—death or change—had become all-too-painfully obvious, did I begin to reject the earlier mindset. This is why I don't think our culture will stop before the world has been impoverished beyond our most horrifying imaginations.

The second statement reveals to me why the period of hibernation takes so long. We do not stand in front of a tree, shouting, "Grow, damn you, grow!" and we recognize the futility of wishing a broken foot to heal in a day. But in myself and in so many of my friends I've encountered an unwillingness to acknowledge that even having sloughed off an old level of consciousness, it takes a long time to grow a new one.

It could be argued that my own railing against the culture exhibits the same blindness to process as that of a person yelling at a broken foot: the culture is broken, and shouting ain't gonna fix it. But there are two differences.

The first is that if a person continues to pretend against all evidence that his foot is not broken, he may rebreak it, as I did high jumping. Had I allowed my foot to heal through the fall during my last year jumping, I could have jumped in the spring. I may even have fulfilled my potential as a jumper. I will never know. It might have been appropriate for my coach just that once to yell at me. Not at my foot, but at me for not listening to my foot.

The second difference is that there is a distinction to be made between shouting from frustration, and shouting because a house is being destroyed and no one is paying attention. Another way to say this is that given enough time—perhaps ten thousand years—even my father could probably heal, but what about the people whose souls he murders in the meantime? And what about the secondary damage caused by those whose own destructiveness had its genesis in the violence he did to them: my siblings, for example, when they pass on damage to their children. In contrast to the Buddhists on the panel who blew the question about compassion, my loyalty lies with the innocent, and I need to do whatever I can to stop the damage.

It's a fine line to walk, that of waiting for the arrival of understanding—for *kairos*—and the need for action. I am active now. In my twenties I was not. I believe my present level of energy is a result of having fallen deeply into my lethargy then. Had there been no time of sleep, there could not now be this time of awakening, but instead I would still be as I was before, turning most of my energy inward to maintain the imprisonment of my own emotions.

I need to now step away from much of what I've just been saying. To believe for a moment that what I was doing in Nevada and after constituted "lazing about," or "inaction," makes plain another form of silencing, once again of the unseen. Hidden here is the absurd presumption that to flip burgers or repair televisions is more important and difficult than to shake off the effects of a coercive upbringing and education, and insofar as possible to vomit out the internalized voices of a coercive and deeply violent culture. This is but one more way we value production over life.

We do what we reward, and we reward what we value. All fancy philosophy aside, we value asking someone if they would like fries with their burger more than we value a rich and healthy emotional and spiritual life and a vital community. Of course. The former does not threaten the foundations of our culture.

All choices involve the loss of unembraced opportunities. The time I spend trying to understand and stem the pervasive destructiveness of the culture cannot be spent shoveling fries, and were I to mix milkshakes I could not spend that time learning how to listen to coyotes, trees, aphids, dogs, the Dreamgiver, or my disease.

Just as Cleve Backster can name the moment when his consciousness forever changed, I can name the time when I began to be reborn. It was 1987. I had moved to north Idaho, because in driving around with my two dogs, it was the prettiest place I had seen. Presumably they agreed. I had by that time regained my weight and lost it again to Crohn's, then regained it and lost it again, and gained it once more: learning the lessons of the disease took time, and did not guarantee freedom from relapses. I had been in a dreadful car accident with my mother, hitting an overturned semi load of plywood at fifty-five. I walked away; she shattered her arm, broke her neck, and was made functionally blind by paralysis of the nerves controlling eye movement.

I was living in a small town called Spirit Lake. I was poor. I had not yet received a settlement from the trucker whose lack of refrigeration had killed the bees, and so was unable to buy new bees to start over. I was not very happy.

I did not have a telephone, and used to walk to the grocery store to use the pay phone outside. I remember an evening in early September, dark gray sky growing darker by the moment, bats swooping circles around the lights overhanging the parking lot, finding their meals of daily bugs. I was on the phone to an old friend. He lived in California, and we'd not talked for a couple of years. Craig said, "I'm worried about you, buddy. I always thought you'd do something, go somewhere."

"I'm here."

"Where the hell's that? The back side of Idaho, living in a dinky apartment doing nothing? You have gifts, man, and with any gift comes responsibility. You can't just walk away. If you don't give back to the universe what the universe gives you, then you really aren't worth shit. I hate to say it, but I hate even more to see you like you are."

I didn't say anything. What could I say?

"I'm not saying you have to get some fucking job at PayLess, not at all. What I'm saying is that if you are ever going to succeed at anything, it has to become the most important thing in your life. What do you value, Derrick? Where do you live? Can you answer that?"

Had he said these things a year, or maybe even a day, before, they would have hurt and upset me. But because the time was right, they helped. Later that night, hours after we'd hung up, and hours after I'd taken a walk to Spirit Lake and sat quietly by the shore, I began to realize that I'd long since answered Craig's questions. I'd begun answering them by refusing to follow the path blazed for me by my father, and by his father before him, and his before him, and later by refusing to remain in the wage economy, and later by doing nothing at all, and by taking the time to begin my own life. Now it was time to get on with it.

That American settler was right when he wrote, "As long as we keep ourselves busy tilling the earth, there is no fear of any of us becoming wild." So long as we keep ourselves busy removing spindles from our kingdom and building dams to block rivers, taking notes in boring classes and counting hours in tedious workdays, there is no fear of any of us becoming wild. Nor, and this is much the same thing, is there any fear of us becoming who we are.

I began again with bees. I spread the hives around the Hoodoo Valley in north Idaho, and driving to drop sites I often saw the abandoned ruin of a partially constructed church. The builders were wise, I thought, in discontinuing their project: what could be more ludicrous than building a house for God amongst all these trees and hills and meadows full of grasses? The wood frame would serve only to separate those inside from those out. But I guess that's been the point all along.

My last summer in Idaho I lost a stand of hives to bears. I arrived at the site to see boxes scattered and honeycombs torn and tossed, as though the bears had sampled their way through colony after colony, selecting only the most delectable foods from this buffet. Frightened bees clustered in clumps down among the deep clover.

Contrary to what we were taught by A.A. Milne in *Winnie The Pooh,* when bears rip apart a beehive, they aren't so much interested in honey as they are baby bees. I'd heard old-timers (beekeepers, not bears) say the grubs are sweet, which only made sense, considering their food. After I cleaned up what hives I could and put what bees I could find back into their homes, I had several honeycombs full of brood left over. I knew the babies chill quickly, and that the bears had been to this site at least a day before, so the babies were either dead or dying. What's good enough for bears, I thought, is good enough for me, so I started munching on bee grubs. I'm not sure why the bears bothered; while succulent, the grubs were disappointingly pasty and not so very sweet at all.

I moved to Spokane, to go back to graduate school, this time to study writing, and I brought the bees with me. I placed the hives in fields of alfalfa around eastern Washington, and kept some at the house just to watch. I remember once I saw a hive throw a swarm: tens of thousands of bees swirling in a cloud three times the size of a house. I couldn't follow the flight of any individual bee—they were too many, flying too chaotically—but after a time I noticed the cloud's center of mass begin to shift, at first subtly and then substantially, toward a tall pine. The tree shimmered with bees. It was alive with humming. Slowly the seething mass coalesced on a limb—high up, of course, later necessitating a hard climb—shrinking, shrinking until they formed a tight bundle the size of a basketball.

One summer I noticed that each night a long line of ants ran single file back and forth thirty yards from the barn to the nearest of the beehives. I'd seen ants kill hives before, overwhelming the guards by numbers, standing six to a bee and clasping fur or legs in mandibles while she furiously maneuvered her stinger to jab at them again and again, then more ants, and more, until the bee is covered. Having overrun the colony, the ants carry honey and grubs back to their nest. So I presumed these ants were up to no good.

Having grown up in a coercive culture I find it sometimes hard to rid myself of all vestiges of the desire to control (Vestiges? Who am I kidding? It's hard to rid myself of vast unbroken stretches of *that* territory). I tried to sweep the ants away with a broom. After that I stepped on some. I placed blocks of wood in their way as barriers. Finally it occurred to me to simply watch them. They weren't hurting the hives at all. The ants, like the grasshoppers so many years before, were simply carrying away the bees' trash. I looked more closely, and more closely still, and saw that though the hive was full and healthy, the guards merely checked the ants as they walked in and out, then waved them through to continue about their business.

When I returned to school in 1989 I began to teach. Or rather not to teach but to participate in classes. I knew from my own experiences in school that I wanted the classes to be different than what I had been put through. I knew that the most important words any instructor had ever said to me were, "Never believe anything you read, and rarely believe anything you think." I knew that the best teacher I ever had was that excitable cocker spaniel. I knew I was somehow supposed to be helping students become better writers, but I knew also that the best writing springs from passion, love, hate, fear, hope. So by definition the class had to be as much a class in life—in passion, love, fear, experience, relation—as in writing. I knew also that we teach best what we most need to learn, so thinking of the lessons of Crohn's disease I knew I'd have to strive my hardest to get members of the class, including myself, to begin to feel, and to express that feeling through writing, and perhaps even our lives. And finally, the night before I was first to enter a class, I encountered words by

Carl Rogers, in his book *On Becoming a Person,* that seemed to speak to my experience as a learning human being: "It seems to me that anything that can be taught to another is relatively inconsequential, and has little or no significant influence on behavior. . . . I have come to feel that the only learning which significantly influences behavior is self-discovered, self-appropriated learning. Such self-discovered learning, truth that has been personally appropriated and assimilated in experience, cannot be directly communicated to another. As soon as the individual tries to communicate such experience directly, often with a quite natural enthusiasm, it becomes teaching, and its results are inconsequential. . . . When I try to teach, as I do sometimes, I am appalled by the results, which seem a little more than consequential, because sometimes the teaching seems to succeed. When this happens I find that the results are damaging. It seems to cause the individual to distrust his [or her] own experience, and to stifle significant learning. Hence I have come to feel that the outcomes of teaching are either unimportant or hurtful. When I look back at the results of my past teaching, the real results seem the same—either damage was done, or nothing significant occurred. . . . As a consequence, I realize that I am only interested in being a learner, preferably learning things that matter, that have some significant influence on my own behavior. . . . I find that one of the best, but most difficult ways for me to learn is to drop my own defensiveness, at least temporarily, and to try to understand the way in which [another's] experience seems and feels to the other person. I find that another way of learning is for me to state my own uncertainties, to try to clarify my puzzlements, and thus get closer to the meaning that my experience actually seems to have. . . . It seems to mean letting my experience carry me on, in a direction which appears to be forward, toward goals that I can but dimly define, as I try to understand at least the current meaning of that experience." Of course I did not accept Rogers's words merely because he said them, but I fit them to my own experience of learning, and soon, of "teaching."

I walked in that first day of that first class, and the first thing I did was to change the name from "Principles of Thinking and Writing," to "Intellectual, Philosophical, and Spiritual Liberation and Exploration for the Fine, Very Fine, and Extremely Fine Human Being." Many of the students reached for their class lists to make sure they were in the right room. As I took role, I asked each person what he or she loved. At first suspicious, they began to open up within minutes.

I soon realized I could not give grades: it would be immoral to ask someone to write from the heart, then give the writing a C. This created a problem, since the department required I assign grades. I suggested assigning grades randomly, but neither the students nor the department liked that idea. So I suggested giving everyone a 4.0. This was fine with the students, but not the administration. My next plan was to give everyone a grade of 3.14159, or π. Math majors in the class thought this was a hoot, but the administrators didn't get the joke.

Eventually here's what we (the students and I) devised. Because the way to learn to think is by thinking, we would spend most class time on open discussions of important issues: What is love? What is the difference (if any) between emotional, intellectual, spiritual, and physical intimacy? Is there such a thing as a universal good? What do you want out of life? If you had only a limited time to live (which is of course the case), how would you spend your time? Is the universe a friendly place or not? (This last question, by the way, Einstein thought to be the most important a person can ask.) Irish students took it upon themselves to teach us about the Irish Republican Army, and African-American students taught us about their own experience of racism. A Samoan man told us of his earlier life in a gang. The sons and daughters of farmers told us what it was like to grow up on a farm. Volleyball players told us of volleyball, and football players of football.

Similarly, the way to learn how to write is by doing plenty of it, so my main job in the classroom would be to cheerlead them into writing more. The students could, of course, write anything they wanted about anything they wanted. I would not judge any papers, but merely give the writers positive feedback, and I would try to guide them wherever they wished to go in their explorations. I asked (not told, but asked) students to write about the thing they'd done in their lives they were most proud of, and asked them to write about that which caused them the most shame. We took the latter papers (mostly unread) into the hall and burned them, causing police to show up one quarter to question us about vandalism. One student, getting married the next summer, wrote her wedding vows as well as a letter to her fiancé, to be delivered moments before he walked down the aisle. Another, a wine salesman by trade, spent the quarter writing sales pitches. Many people explored their own abuse, some wrote fiction. For each piece of writing a person did, he or she received a check mark (longer pieces received more). The final grade corresponded to the number of check marks. If a person had thirty-four check marks by the end of the quarter, for example, the grade was 3.4. Simple enough. The people in the class wrote about five times as much as people in other sections, but loved the work because it pertained to their own lives. When people wrote pieces they particularly loved, we scheduled private conferences to go over these pieces again and again until every word was magic. In the context of sharing an important piece of themselves, suddenly even grammar became crucial: the bride, for example, didn't want the pastor stumbling over her sentences or her groom wondering what the hell she was trying to say. Given the opportunity to express themselves, these people wanted to learn how to do that.

I asked each student to hand in a couple of pieces composed in different forms of expression besides writing. Many brought in food, some paintings, a few tape-recordings of their own music. A chef from Kuwait cooked us a seven-course meal and showed us pictures of his country. Another student brought a videotape of himself doing technical rock climbing.

It took us a couple of quarters to realize something was still missing. Experience. It's madness to think all learning comes from putting pen to paper. What about life itself? We decided that people would get check marks every time they did something they'd never done before. People went to symphonies, rock concerts, Vietnamese restaurants. They watched foreign films ("That Akira Kurosawa guy can be pretty funny"). They got in car wrecks (not for the check mark, but it having happened, they may as well get credit). They got counseling (I hope not as a result of the class). One fellow told his father for the first time that he loved him (a big baseball fan, he watched the movie *Field of Dreams* over and over that day to psyche himself up).

Something else was missing. I still had too much control of the class. How to let go more? I didn't know. Finally it occurred to me to break them into groups, and ask each group to run the class for one two-hour period (we generally met two evenings per week). They could do whatever they wanted. One group wanted to play Capture the Flag. I thought, "What does *this* have to do with writing?" But we did it, then wrote about it, and I felt closer to that class after our group's physical activity than I had even after intense emotional discussions (besides, my team won).

Next class period we talked about the relationship between shared physical activities and feelings of intimacy. Another group had us eat popsicles and watch cartoons, then draw pictures from our childhood with our opposite hands (it broke my heart when one fellow shared his picture with the class: "This is my father taking me out in the woods to smoke my first vial of crack"). In the same group we played Duck Duck Goose and Hide and Go Seek in the basement of the near-empty building. Many of the people were continuing students, and thus were older. Looking back, I don't know how anyone could possibly say that he or she has successfully run a writing class without having played Hide and Go Seek with overweight old men, twenty year olds, middle-aged mothers of five, and a half-dozen men and women whose native language is not English, all of them dead serious about finding or not being found. One group taught us how to do the Country and Western dance, the Tush Push. This was especially difficult for me, a confirmed nondancer. Because the room was too small, we did this in the building's central courtyard. Midway through one of our times pushing our respective tushes, a couple of the department's most humorless administrators walked by, evidently having worked into the evening. I smiled and waved. Even this class taught me much. I had been working on letting go in my writing for years by this point, and I sometimes became frustrated at the baby steps many students were taking toward manifesting their passion in words. But when it came to me attempting to let go in dancing, I suddenly comprehended their inhibitions: I would push my tush only three or four inches, while many who were too shy to open up in words were wildly swinging their hips (including a fifty-year-old sheriff's deputy I never would have pegged for a tush-pusher). In another class we made marshmallow figures representing our hopes and dreams. One fellow, a bow hunter, made a big marshmallow buck with toothpick antlers, and a huge toothpick arrow jutting from its chest; mine was a broken marshmallow dam with marshmallow salmon swimming in a river of marshmallow (surprise, surprise). We played blindfolded soccer in the classroom, with four people at a time blindfolded, being told where to move by sighted partners ("Left, left," my partner shouted as I ran into the wall. "Oh, sorry, wrong way"). We broke into groups, each group picking out of a hat the rough plot for a screenplay (our group was to come down from a mountain to find that everyone else in the world had disappeared), and then each person in the group picked from a different hat a character to be played in the drama (I was to play the actress Sharon Stone), after which we had an hour to write our scripts, to be performed and videotaped in what we later dubbed "An Exercise in Embarrassment." For Halloween, we plopped sleeping bags on the floor, sat around a flashlight surrounded by small pieces of wood (simulating a campfire), ate s'mores, and told ghost stories. For Valentine's Day, we wrote stories about first loves, and memories of hearts broken or overflowing. Mainly we had fun.

I did assign one topic each quarter that the people in the class had to write on. It was the final paper. The assignment was for each of them to walk on water, and then write about it. They had to decide to do something impossible, do it, and then describe what it was like. A few people filled their bathtubs with a quarter-inch of water, walked across that, and considered themselves done. Others walked across frozen lakes. But one quit smoking, another ended an abusive relationship, a very shy woman asked a man out (he said *yes*), another woman for the first time admitted her bulimia and sought help, one man told his parents he did not want to be an accountant but instead an artist.

The people in my classes, including me, did not need to be controlled, managed, nor even taught. What we needed was to be encouraged, accepted, and loved just for who we were. We needed not to be governed by a set of rules that would tell us what we needed to learn and what we needed to express, but to be given time in a supportive space to explore who we were and what we wanted, with the assistance of others who had our best interests at heart. I believe that is true not only for my students, but for all of us, human and nonhuman alike. All we want, whether we are honeybees, salmon, trash-collecting ants, ponderosa pines, coyotes, human beings, or stars, is to love and be loved, to be accepted, cherished, and celebrated simply for being who we are. Is that so very difficult?

Out of Mourning, Play

"The Great Way has no gate;
There are a thousand paths to it.
If you pass through the barrier,
you walk the universe alone."
Wu-Men

THE PAST FEW YEARS I've begun to burn my beekeeping equipment. Frames and boxes, varnished with beeswax from years of use, keep the house warm. Other equipment I've stored in the barn. Chickens roost on the lip of the extractor, and last year a hen started setting in a settling tank.

I'd love to start with bees again. I look at empty hives still standing in my yard and feel the urge to hear again the hum of thousands of bees flying in all directions, but I'm scared.

The fear began for me in 1992. The year started wonderfully, a hot, wet spring that produced a waist-deep carpet of blue and purple wildflowers. Hives bubbled with bees, and each colony filled boxes with seventy pounds of honey as fast as I put them on. The bees were happy, and so was I.

Then bees started dying. At first I blamed the weather—it was dry from mid-June to early September. Then I blamed pesticides. Then urban sprawl. But most of all I blamed myself. I didn't know what I was doing wrong, but it had to be something.

It was strange solace to learn that bees were dying everywhere: solace because this meant I hadn't caused the deaths; strange because I had to ask what sort of solace it was to be discovered in such loss. A 1996 American Beekeeping Federation survey of the previous winter's kill reads like the casualty count of a horrific battle: "Maine, 80 percent loss . . . Massachusetts, 55–75 percent . . . Michigan, 60 percent. . . ."

Why? Varroa mites. They cause deformities and paralysis, introduce viruses, and ultimately kill entire colonies. The best guess on how these mites got here is that in the 1980s a beekeeper smuggled honeybee queens from South America or Europe, hoping their offspring would pollinate more effectively and give more honey than American honeybees. But along with queens the beekeeper accidentally brought varroa mites. Because bees groom each other constantly, mites spread throughout hives into which the queens were introduced, then clung to bees as they entered other colonies, quickly invading hive after hive. Since commercial beekeepers often follow blooms across the country, mites soon overspread the continent.

It would be pointless to blame the die-off on the smuggling beekeeper. The collapse was inevitable anyway.

The strengths that have made modern beekeeping the foundation upon which the agricultural infrastructure rests are precisely the weaknesses that have made beekeeping, and modern agribusiness, vulnerable to something tiny as the mite. These are the intertwined attributes of standardization (the use of one pollinator across many crops), density (the annual gathering of a half-million hives to pollinate almonds, for example), and mobility (the transport of bees, and consequently mites, to and from all parts of the country).

Years ago, working with bees provided me a somatic understanding of cooperation. More recently they taught me about loss. Now, as I watch modern beekeeping collapse under the weight of its own strengths, they're teaching me once again that the modern industrial economy—based as it is upon these same traits of standardization (the conversion of forests to tree farms, grasslands to cornfields, diverse cultures to capitalism), the short-term maximization of resource usage, and the absolute mobility of resources—faces the same vulnerabilities as beekeeping.

Despite the high losses, it's not the end of beekeeping. Each year, new people discover the richness of this craft, and for them high losses and an ever-widening spiral of chemicals may simply be part of the bargain.

As for me, this year I watched a pair of nuthatches try to squeeze into an empty beehive. No matter how they tried, they couldn't make it. With saw and file, I made them a home. They raised babies there, and seemed to like it. So did I.

Even though I often have nightmares, I have never felt unsafe with the Dreamgiver. The horrifying dreams, I feel, have never been without purpose (Yeah, I know my father never beat anyone without good reason, but this *feels* different). They remind me often of things my conscious mind wants to ignore. It is such with the symbolic underpinnings of our actions of the day—as when my father beat his children attempting to retell the buried story of beatings he'd received, and when we collectively destroy the planet because we so wish to end our way of being—and it is such with the symbolic underpinnings of our actions of the night.

I once asked the Dreamgiver what sort of relationship it wanted with me, and what sort of relationship we had. I fell asleep and soon dreamed I was bobbing up and down far from shore in a deep and warm ocean. I was happy. A huge creature swam up from below to rest just behind me. I did not turn around, nor was I scared. The creature began to play with me, and reached to touch my genitals. Suddenly I was standing on the shore, using a shovel to pick up dog manure and put it in trash cans. I awoke laughing. The Dreamgiver would like nothing more than to come up from the depths to play intimately with me, but, unfortunately, both of us have to spend most of our time cleaning up other people's shit.

It occurred to me not moments later that this is the relationship with the world at large into which most of us have been forced. It would be nice to simply be able to play intimately with and in an old growth forest, as humans have been doing for hundreds of thousands of years, without having to worry that next year or the year after you will learn that the trees have been murdered, the forest has been cut.

As usual, I walked outside to feed the chickens this afternoon. Because it is now winter, and snow covers the ground, songbirds gather to eat the bread and vegetables I set out for the chickens. After feedtime I walked to the coyote tree, carrying my daily offering of bread. I know now that it is coyotes who eat it, and not deer or magpies, because I can see the small prints of a dog in the fresh snow. My own dogs scamper ahead of me. I shield my eyes from the sun's reflection: it's the first time the sun has broken through the clouds in a week.

I placed the bread at the base of the tree, touched its trunk in welcoming, and began to walk home, passing the still-standing stakes the surveyors left behind: tomorrow I will pick them up. Then I passed a rock outcropping onto which also I daily place a piece of bread. A few times I've seen a chipmunk standing atop the rock, and I've got enough bread to share. After the outcropping I followed the trail down a gentle slope that winds among trees to eventually open out at my home. Today, as I stepped beneath the first tree, it chose that moment to unload its burden of the last few days' snow directly atop my head.

It is not true that for the last few hundred thousand years it is only humans who have played with forests. Forests, too, have been playing with us.

Trauma and Recovery

"The struggle of man against power is the
struggle of memory against forgetting."
Milan Kundera

EARLY ON I ASKED what level of violence it will take to make the destructiveness of our way of living obvious. That's not a fair question, because the relationship between the perpetration or even receipt of violence and the awareness of that violence is not linear. As violence becomes more ubiquitous it also becomes more transparent. If one woman out of four is raped within her lifetime, and two out of five are either raped or fend off rape attempts, is the condition of having been sexually assaulted now normal? Is the condition of being capable of, or even having committed, sexual assault also now normal? Add to this the isolating effects of trauma—the erection of internal walls to keep a dangerous world at bay—and the way these walls later facilitate—at least make possible and in some cases make inevitable—the committing of further violence (emotional, spiritual, and physical), and the result can be no other than a constantly expanding sphere of traumatized, isolated individuals. Those on the inside—the already traumatized—will consume those at the frontier (the new children, the newly contacted indigenous peoples, the newly discovered reserves of exploitable human and nonhuman resources), never once seeing the damage they cause nor the isolation they engender. To see the damage would be to revisit their original insult. If they did that, where would they be, and what would they do?

Recall the monkeys made permanently insane by their artificial removal from the social embeddedness in which they evolved. These creatures were too fearful to interact normally with other beings, and became the best "monster mothers" the scientists could devise. Isolation leads to psychopathology. Isolated from the rest of nature, isolated from each other by walls of fear, isolated from our own bodies, and isolated most of all from our own horrifying experience, is it any wonder that we are all crazy?

If we have become so inured to the coercion that engulfs, forms, and deforms us that we no longer perceive it for the aberration it is, how much more is this true for our ignorance of the trauma that characterizes our way of life? Salmon are going extinct? *Pass the toast, man, I'm hungry.* A quarter of a million dead in Iraq? *Damnit, I'm gonna be late for work.* If coercion is our habitat, then trauma is the food we daily take into our bodies.

I spoke with Dr. Judith Herman, one of the world's experts on the effects of psychological trauma. I asked her about the relationship between atrocity and silence.

She said, "Atrocities are actions so horrifying they go beyond words. For people who witness or experience atrocities, there is a kind of silencing that comes from not knowing how to put these experiences into speech. At the same time, atrocities are the crimes perpetrators most want to hide. This creates a powerful convergence of interest: no one wants to speak about them. No one wants to remember them. Everyone wants to pretend they didn't happen."

I asked her about a line she once wrote: "In order to escape accountability the perpetrator does everything in his power to promote forgetting."

"This is something with which we are all familiar. It seems that the more extreme the crimes, the more determined the efforts to deny the crimes happened. So we have, for example, almost a hundred years after the fact, an active and apparently state-sponsored effort on the part of the Turkish government to deny there was ever an Armenian genocide. We still have a whole industry of Holocaust denial. I just came back from Bosnia where, because there hasn't been an effective medium for truth-telling and for establishing a record of what happened, you have the nationalist governmental entities continuing to insist that ethnic cleansing didn't happen, that the various war crimes and atrocities committed in that war simply didn't occur."

"How does this happen?"

"On the most blatant level, it's a matter of denying the crimes took place. Whether it's genocide, military aggression, rape, wife beating, or child abuse, the same dynamic plays itself out, beginning with an indignant, almost rageful denial, and the suggestion that the person bringing forward the information—whether it's the victim or another informant—is lying, crazy, malicious, or has been put up to it by someone else. Then of course there are a number of fallback positions to which perpetrators can retreat if the evidence is so overwhelming and irrefutable it cannot be ignored, or rather, suppressed. This, too, is something we're familiar with: the whole raft of predictable rationalizations used to excuse everything from rape to genocide: the victim exaggerates; the victim enjoyed it; the victim provoked or otherwise brought it on herself; the victim wasn't really harmed; and even if some slight damage has been done, it's now time to forget the past and get on with our lives: in the interests of preserving peace—or in the case of domestic violence, preserving family harmony—we need to draw a veil over these matters. The incidents should never be discussed, and preferably should be forgotten altogether."

I asked her a question that has bothered, entranced, and terrified me since childhood: "To what degree do perpetrators and their apologists believe their own claims? Did my father really believe he wasn't beating us?"

Her response made clear what I understood as a child: that I'll never know. She responded, "Do perpetrators believe their own lies? I have no idea, and I don't have much trust in those who claim they do. Certainly we in the mental health profession don't have a clue when it comes to what goes on in the hearts and minds of perpetrators of either political atrocities or sexual and domestic crimes.

"For one thing, we don't get to know them very well. They aren't interested in being studied—by and large they don't volunteer—so we study them when they're caught. But when they're caught, they tell us whatever they think we want to hear.

"This leads to a couple of problems. The first is that we have to wend our way through lies and obfuscation to attempt to discover what's really going on. The second problem is even larger and more difficult. Most of the psychological literature on perpetrators is based on studies of convicted or reported offenders, which represents a very small and skewed, unrepresentative group. If you're talking about rape, for example, since the reporting rates are, by even the most generous estimates, under twenty percent, you lose eighty percent of the perpetrators off the top. Your sample is reduced further by the rates at which arrests are made, charges are filed, convictions are obtained, and so forth, which means convicted offenders represent about one percent of all perpetrators. Now, if your odds of being caught and convicted of rape are basically one in one hundred, you have to be extremely inept to become a convicted rapist. Thus the folks we are normally able to study look fairly pathetic, and often have a fair amount of psychopathology and violence in their own histories. But they're not representative of your ordinary, garden-variety rapist or torturer, or the person who gets recruited to go on an ethnic cleansing spree. We don't know much about these people. The one thing victims say most often is that these people look normal, and that nobody would have believed it about them. That was true even of Nazi war criminals. From a psychiatric point of view, these people didn't look particularly disturbed. In some ways that's the scariest thing of all."

"Given the misogyny, genocide, and ecocide endemic in our culture," I said, "I wonder how much of that normality is only *seeming*."

"If you're part of a predatory and militaristic culture, then to behave in a predatory and exploitative way is not deviant, *per se*. Of course there are rules as to who, if you want to use these terms, might be a legitimate victim, a person who may be attacked with impunity. And most perpetrators are exquisitely sensitive to these rules."

I wondered out loud, "Why is our behavior so predatory? What are the common factors among predatory cultures?"

"It's interesting," she responded. "The anthropologist Peggy Reeves Sanday looked at data from over a hundred cultures as to the prevalence of rape, and divided them into high- or low-rape cultures. She found that high-rape cultures are highly militarized and sex-segregated. There is a lot of difference in status between men and women. The care of children is devalued and delegated to subordinate females. She also found that the creation myths of high-rape cultures recognize only a male deity rather than a female deity or a couple. When you think about it, that is rather bizarre. It would be an understandable mistake to think women make babies all by themselves, but it's preposterous to think men do that alone. So you've got to have a fairly elaborate and counterintuitive mythmaking machine in order to fabricate a creation myth that recognizes only a male deity. There was another interesting finding, which is that high-rape cultures had recent experiences—meaning in the last few hundred years—of famine or migration. That is to say, they had not reached a stable adaptation to their ecological niche. Sadly enough, when you tally these risk factors, you realize you've pretty much described our culture."

If words alone could bring down our culture, I would write them. If actions by themselves would stop the atrocities, I would commit them. If a change of heart would bring back the salmon, I would change my heart again and again and again.

It is not enough at this point (necessary, as they say, but not sufficient) to merely right ourselves from trauma, to dismantle the walls we've so laboriously and necessarily constructed to constrict our broken hearts, and then to try to pick up the shredded and scattered fragments of our experience to reassemble like a precious vase that won't quite go back together no matter how we try, or better, like the lifeless body of a loved one who is never coming back.

The dog going blind, with whom I traveled in my truck so many years ago, eventually was hit by a train. Focused only on me, her friend, farther along the way, she never knew what hit her but merely tumbled off the tracks into the tall weeds by the side. I ran to her, found her, picked her up and could not believe she was dead until I saw the gash that split her, back to belly, white flesh that never had time to bleed. There was nothing I could do except hurl sobs at my stupidity for taking a blind dog for a walk on railroad tracks, and to wish that just this once I could go back to before and this time do it right.

In our case, too, seeing the mistake after it is done is not enough. Nor is wishing it away. Nor, especially in this case, is grieving.

When I took her for that walk, I found myself wandering far ahead of this ancient, arthritic, overweight pup. I worried about a train, but not overmuch, because we were in the midst of a long straightaway, at the far end of which, beyond the dog, was a tight curve. When I saw a train round this corner, I began to run toward the dog. Not because I needed to run, but for the joy of running. Then I saw the train had more speed than I had anticipated, and I ran faster than I ever had. And then I saw her tumble into space.

What do you do—what do you feel—when you see destruction rushing down steel rails toward someone you love, and you see that nothing you can do will stop it? You may be a fast runner, but you cannot outrun a train.

I have read that while every culture has invented comedy, tragedies are the unique invention of civilizations. A hero, doomed, stupid, blind to his own faults, falls quickly—or more accurately inexorably—toward a fate he can neither comprehend nor avoid.

I can try to make right those parts inside of me which should never have been made wrong, and I can grieve losses both inside and out, and I can try for all my life to improve my relationships with those around me, human and nonhuman alike. I can even accept that the oncoming train will most likely crush us— or rather continue to crush us—and will stop only under the weight of our bodies and the gumming of its gears by our flesh.

But I will not give up. I know in my bones what it is like to sit stone-faced and frozen in the face of inevitable evil, and I know in my flesh what it is to lie down and take it. I know also what it is like to resist. I know that I am no longer a child, faced with only the options of a child. I know that I am now an adult, and I know that it is at long last time I began to act like one. It is time for me to fight back.

One of the difficulties of our predicament is that once having suffered atrocity, the walls you've constructed become a part of your body, and do not come down of their own when the immediate danger has passed.

Judith Herman said, "In the aftermath of trauma people see danger everywhere. They're jumpy, they startle easily, and they have a hard time sleeping. They're irritable, and more prone to anger. This seems to be a biological phenomenon, not just a psychological one. People also relive the experience in nightmares and flashbacks. Any little reminder can set them off. For example, a Vietnam veteran involved in helicopter combat might react years later when a news or weather helicopter flies overhead."

I remembered that all through my teens and twenties when someone asked me to go waterskiing, my response externally was, "No, thanks," but my internal response was, "Fuck you." I never could figure out why until a few years ago I asked my mother, who said there had been beatings associated with waterskiing trips when I was a small child. I never knew that. I just always knew that waterskiing pissed me off. I told this to Judith.

She said, "Sometimes people understand the trigger, but sometimes they won't have complete memory of the event. They may respond to the reminder as you did, by becoming terrified or agitated or angry. Sometimes it's very subtle. Someone who was raped in the backseat of a car may have a lot of feelings every time she gets into a car, particularly one that resembles the one in which she was raped.

"This reliving, these intrusions, are not a normal kind of re-membering, where the smell of cinnamon rolls, for example, may remind you of your grandmother. Instead, it's like playing the same videotape over and over, a repetitive sequence of terrifying images and sensations."

She continued, "The third group of symptoms people have— and these are almost the opposite of the intrusive nightmares and flashbacks, the dramatic symptoms—is a shutting-down of feelings, a constriction of emotions, intellect, and behavior. It's characteristic of traumatized people to oscillate between feeling overwhelmed, enraged, terrified, desperate, or in extreme grief and pain, and feeling nothing at all. People describe themselves as numb. They don't feel anything, they aren't interested in things that used to interest them, they avoid situations that might re-mind them of the trauma. You, for example, probably avoided waterskiing in order to avoid the traumatic memories. Waterskiing may not be much to give up, but people sometimes avoid rela-tionships, they avoid sexuality, they make their lives smaller, in an attempt to stay away from the overwhelming feelings."

"What happens," I asked, thinking not just of myself, "if a

person is traumatized repeatedly or systematically?"

"People begin to lose their identity, their self-respect. They begin to lose their autonomy and independence.

"Because people in captivity are most often isolated from other relationships—that this is so in normal captivity is obvious and intentional, but it is overwhelmingly the case in domestic violence as well, as perpetrators often demand their victims increasingly cut all other social ties—they are forced to depend for basic survival on the very person who is abusing them. This creates a complicated bond between the two, and skews the victim's perception of the nature of human relationships. The situation is even worse for children raised in these circumstances, because their personality is formed in the context of an exploitative relationship, in which the overarching principles are those of coercion and control, of dominance and subordination.

"Whether we are talking about adults or children, it often happens that a kind of sadistic corruption enters into the captive's emotional relational life. People lose their sense of faith in themselves, in other people. They come to believe or view all relationships as coercive, and come to feel that the strong rule, the strong do as they please, that the world is divided into victims, perpetrators, bystanders, and rescuers. They believe that all relations are contaminated and corrupted, that sadism is the principle that rules all relationships."

"Might makes right," I said. "Social Darwinism. The selfish-gene theory. Original Sin. You've just described the principles that undergird our political, economic, scientific, and religious systems."

"And there are other losses involved. A loss of basic trust. A loss of feeling of mutuality of relatedness. In its stead is emplaced a contempt for self and others. If you've been punished for showing autonomy, initiative, or independence, after a while you're not going to show them. In the aftermath of this kind of brutalization, victims have a great deal of difficulty taking responsibility for their lives. Often, people who try to help get frustrated because we don't understand why the victims seem so passive, seem so unable to extricate themselves or to advocate on their own behalf. They seem to behave as though they're still under the perpetrator's control, even though we think they're now free. But in some ways the perpetrator has been internalized."

All of the traditional Indians I have spoken with have mentioned the importance to each of us to decolonize our minds, removing the internalized messages of the dominant culture.

Judith said, "Captivity also creates disturbances in intimacy, because if you view the world as a place where everyone is either a victim, a perpetrator, an indifferent or helpless bystander, or a rescuer, there's no room for relationships of mutuality, for cooperation, for responsible choices. There's no room to follow agreements through to everyone's mutual satisfaction. The whole range of cooperative relational skills, and all the emotional fulfillment that goes with them, is lost. And that's a great deal to lose."

"It seems to me that part of the reason for this loss is not simply the physical trauma itself, but also the fact that the traumatizing actions can't be acknowledged."

She agreed, then added, "And much more broadly, because they take place within a relationship motivated by a need to dominate, and in which coercive control is the central feature."

I thought again of our culture.

She said, "When I teach this, I describe the methods of coercive control perpetrators use. It turns out that violence is only one of the methods, and it's not even one of the most frequent. It doesn't have to be used all that often; it just has to be convincing. In the battered-women's movement, there's a saying: 'One good beating lasts a year.'"

"What constitutes a good beating?"

"If it's extreme enough, when the victim looks into the eyes of the perpetrator she realizes, 'Oh, my God, he really could kill me.'

"Going along with this violence are other methods of coercive control that have as their aim the victim's isolation, and the breakdown of the victim's resistance and spirit. You have capricious enforcement of lots of petty rules, and you have concomitant rewards. Prisoners and hostages talk about this all the time: if you're good, maybe they'll let you take a shower, or give you something extra to eat. You have the monopolization of perception that follows from the closing off of any outside relationships or sources of information. Finally, and I think this is the thing that really breaks people's spirits, perpetrators often force victims to engage in activities the victims find morally reprehensible or disgusting. Once you've forced a person to violate his or her moral codes, to break faith with him- or herself—the fact that it's done under duress does not remove the shame or guilt of the experience—you may never again even need to use threats. At that point the victim's self-hatred, self-loathing, and shame will be so great that you don't have to beat her up, because she's going to do it herself."

I thought immediately of the secret collaboration into which my father initiated me by my mere acquiescence. I thought, too, of the other members of my family, and of the deal we each one of us had to daily make to get through the day—*I will not break the silence, if only you do not kill me. If you are going to kill me, do not let me know about it beforehand.* I mentioned to Judith a description I'd read of Jews who collaborated with Nazis: "A man who had knowingly compromised himself did not revolt against his masters, no matter what idea had driven him to collaboration: too many mutual skeletons in the closet. . . . There were so many proofs of the absolute obedience that could be expected of men of honor who had drifted into collaboration."

She responded, "Perpetrators know this. These methods are known, they're taught. Pimps teach them to one another. Torturers in the various clandestine police forces involved in state-sponsored torture teach them to each other. They're taught at taxpayer expense at our School of the Americas. The Nazi war criminals who went to Latin America passed on this knowledge. It is apparently a point of pride among many Latin American torturers that they have come up with techniques the Nazis didn't know about."

Practice doesn't make perfect. If our hearts and minds are wrong, it doesn't matter what we do, nor what justifications we emplace to buttress our decisions, our actions will further destruction. Consider the consecutive claims to virtue for deforestation. Consider the fact that my father never beat anyone without good reason. If we learn nothing else from the insistent cooptation of the words of Jesus by those who would destroy, we should learn this: if your heart is wrong—if you are a member of the race of the indecent, as Viktor Frankl put it; if you are a cannibal, as Jack Forbes said—you can and will twist any words to serve vile ends. It doesn't much matter whether you are raping a woman because Eve sinned, because you need to determine if she is a witch, or because she provoked you by the clothes she was wearing, the fact is that you are raping her. Whether the tinder is lit because a woman "does marvellous things with regard to male organs," or "in honor of Christ Our Saviour and the Apostles," or because you've got to clear slash piles from clearcuts, the result is that the world and those in it burn. In the beginning is the urge. . . .

Jesus knew this. And I believe he knew he never had a prayer. Like the salmon who hurl themselves against concrete, he knew there could only be one ending. He could not have been so stupid as to think otherwise.

The opposite is true as well. If your heart and mind are right, it doesn't matter what you do; it will be the right thing. A father who loves his children would not and could not rape them, nor beat them. He may make mistakes, but he will not traumatize them. A person who loves the world and those in it will not destroy it. A person who loves will not rob others of their voices.

Jesus would have known this also. We all know it. Anyone who has ever been in a bad or a good relationship knows it. If the magic isn't there, it doesn't matter how many roses you send nor chocolates you receive, the most you can hope to achieve is that the both of you agree to carry on a fiction (As Kahlil Gibran wrote: "It is wrong to think that love comes from long companionship and persevering courtship. Love is the offspring of spiritual affinity, and unless that affinity is created in a moment, it will not be created in years or even generations." This is true whether the lover is a human, a piece of art, the coyote tree, or the world). The same is true for writing: no amount of rewrites will awaken words that lie dead on the page. The same is true for music: if you have to ask, it ain't jazz.

While it is true that we all know this, it is also true that on another level those who would destroy are consistently able to convince themselves that they too love the world and that they too would act only in the best interests of those around them. Recall the Nazi doctors who convinced themselves they were acting in the best interests of the Jews. Recall the Boise Cascade advertisement likening clearcuts to smallpox vaccinations. Recall that in order to maintain our way of living, we must tell lies to each other, and especially to ourselves.

Recall finally our collective response to self-evident, if inconvenient, truths. A grenade rolls across the floor. This time, with all the world at stake, do not look away.

"What is the relationship," I asked, "between breaking the silence and healing? You've written that, 'When the truth is finally recognized, survivors can begin their recovery.' How does that work? What happens inside survivors when the truth *is* recognized?"

She laughed. "I wish I knew. It's miraculous. I don't understand it. I just observe it, and try to facilitate it. I think it's a natural healing process that has to do with the restoration of human connection and agency. If you think of trauma as the moment when those two things are destroyed, then there is something about telling the trauma story in a place where it can be heard and acknowledged that seems to restore both agency and connection. The possibility of mutuality returns. People feel better.

"The most important principles for recovery are restoring power and choice or control to the person who has been victimized, and the facilitation of the person's reconnection with her or his natural social supports, the people who are important in that person's life. In the immediate aftermath, of course, the first step is always to reestablish some sense of safety. That means getting out of physical danger, and means also creating some sort of minimally safe social environment in which the person has people to count on, to rely on, to connect to. Nobody can recover in isolation.

"It's only after safety is established that it becomes appropriate for this person to have a chance to tell the trauma story in more depth. There we run into two kinds of mistakes. One is the idea that it's not necessary to tell the story, and that the person would be much better off not talking about it."

"It's over. Just get on with your life."

"That may work for a while, and it might be the right choice in any given circumstance, but there comes a time eventually where if the story isn't told it festers. So one mistake is suppressing it, which comes back to the silencing we spoke of earlier. These are horrible things and nobody really wants to hear or think about them. The victim doesn't, the bystander doesn't, the perpetrator certainly doesn't. So there's a very natural tendency on everyone's part to say, 'Let's forget the whole thing.'

"The other mistake is to try to push people into talking about it prematurely, or when the circumstances aren't right, or when it isn't the person's choice. If the timing, pacing, and setting isn't right, all you're going to have is another reenactment. You're not going to have the integrative experience of putting the story into a context that makes meaning out of it and gives a sense of resolution, which is what you're really aiming for. You don't want just a simple recitation of facts, you want the person to be able to talk about how it felt, how she feels about it now, what it meant to her then, what it means to her now, how she made sense of it then, how she's trying to make sense of it now. It's in that kind of processing that people reestablish their sense of continuity with their own lives and connection with others."

"This seems to be tied to mourning what was lost."

"Part of the motivation for the idea of 'Let's not talk about it' is the belief that you can go back to the way you were before the trauma, and what people find is that's just not possible. Once you've seen up close the evil human beings are capable of, you're not going to see the world the same way, you're not going to see other people the same way, and you're not going to see yourself the same way. We can all fantasize about how brave or cowardly we would be in extreme situations, but people who've been exposed know what they did, and what they didn't do. And almost inevitably they failed to live up to some kind of expectation of themselves. There has to be a sense of grieving what was lost. It's only after that mourning process that people can come through it and say, 'That was a hard lesson, and I wouldn't wish it on my worst enemy, but I am stronger or wiser.' There is a way that people learn from adversity. People will say, 'I had a crisis of faith and I found out what's important, what I really believe in.'"

"How especially does an abused child mourn what he's never known?" (I was, of course, asking about myself.)

"It's what you've never had that is the hardest to grieve. It's unfair. You only get one childhood, and you were cheated out of the one that every child is entitled to."

There was a long silence between us. I thought now not just of myself, but of all of us who have never seen the sky darkened by passenger pigeons or a vast plain covered with bison, who have never experienced a healthy and "good" community, who have never experienced the world as whole, who have never known the joy of walking alone through a night with no fear of attackers. And who never will. Finally, I asked, "What comes next?"

She said, "The recovery doesn't end with the telling and hearing of the story. There is another step after that, which has to do with people reforming their connections, moving from a preoccupation with the past to feeling more hopeful for the future, feeling that they *have* a future, that it's not just a matter of enduring and going through life as a member of the walking dead. Instead there is an ability to knowingly affirm life even after surviving the worst other people have to dish out. And I do think that what renews people is the hope and belief that their own capacity to love has not been destroyed. When people feel damned and doomed, and feel they can't go on living, the fear often has to do with the feeling that they have been so contaminated with the perpetrator's hate, and taken so much of it into themselves, that there is nothing left but rage, and hate, and distrust, and fear and contempt.

"When people go through mourning, and through their crisis of faith, what they come back to as bedrock is their own capacity to love. Sometimes that connection is frail and tenuous, but whether it is with animals, nature, music, or other humans, that's the bedrock to which they must return, to that one caring relationship the perpetrator was never able to destroy. And then they build from there.

"I think as people move into their lives again, the ones who do best are the ones who've developed what Robert Jay Lifton calls a survivor mission. I've seen it happen so many times, that people turn this experience around, and make it a gift to others. That really is the only way you can transcend an atrocity. You can't bury it. You can't make it go away. You can't dissociate it. It comes back. But you can transcend it, first by telling the truth about it, and then by using it in the service of humanity, saying, 'This isn't the way we want to live. We want to live differently.'

"In the aftermath of terror many survivors find themselves much clearer and more daring about going after what they want in life, and in relationships. They straighten things out with their families and lovers and friends, and they often say, 'This is the kind of closeness I want, and this is the kind of stuff I don't want.' When people are sensitized to the dynamics of exploitation, they are able to say, 'I don't want this in my life.' And they often become very courageous about speaking truth to power.

"I have heard so many survivors say, 'I know what terror is. I will live in fear every day for the rest of my life. But I also know that I will be all right, and that I feel all right.' And I have heard them join others in saying, 'This is the thing we want to protect, and this is the thing we want to stop. We don't know how we're going to do it, but we do know that this is what we want. And we're not indifferent.' Sometimes through atrocity people discover in themselves courage that they didn't know they had."

It's not possible to recover from atrocity in isolation, and it is hard to discover a new way to be—or remember an old way— when all signals from the culture pull you in the direction of coercion, control, and ultimately annihilation. I did not walk directly out of my childhood and out of the Colorado School of Mines into a conversation with coyotes, and into the understanding that ours is a culture of atrocity. There were many rebirths along the way, many times of dying—to the control of my emotions, to the silencing of my body, to a belief in Judeo-Christianity, to a belief in the goodness of the United States government, to a belief in the capacity of those in power to act in the best interests of living beings, to a belief in the capacity of a bad culture to reform, to a belief in the superiority or even fundamental specialness of human beings—many times of silent waiting, and many times of *kairos,* large and small.

I could not have learned to listen to coyotes without having first learned to listen to my unwillingness to sell my hours, then to listen to the signals of my body, then to listen to the disease that has made my insides its home, and thus has become a part of me. And I could not have learned to listen to coyotes without having talked to other people courageous enough to validate my perception of an animate world. I talked to the writer Christopher Manes, who said, "For most cultures throughout history—including our own in preliterate times—the entire world used to speak. Anthropologists call this animism, the most pervasive worldview in human history. Animistic cultures listen to the natural world. For them, birds have something to say. So do worms, wolves, and waterfalls." Later the philosopher Thomas Berry told me, "The universe is composed of subjects to be communed with, not objects to be exploited. Everything has its own voice. Thunder and lightning and stars and planets, flowers, birds, animals, trees—all these have voices, and they constitute a community of existence that is profoundly related."

Without the courage of other people who were willing to speak their own truths, I would not have had the courage to be able to listen again, as I did as a child.

We are what we eat. If daily we take into our bodies the knowledge that Coke is the real thing, and that one can buy happy meals at McDonald's, then we will soon enough believe that Coke *is* the real thing, and that happiness is only a hamburger away. This means also that if we begin to listen to those other voices that have been speaking to us all along, of women, children, other races, other cultures, our own experiences, the songbirds that sing outside our doors and the ladybugs that land on our windows, we will soon enough reenter their world, the world into which we were born, the world in which we evolved, the world we have inhabited all along, though sometimes without knowing.

Connection
and Cooperation

"The future of man-
kind lies waiting for
those who will come to
understand their lives
and take up their re-
sponsibility to all liv-
ing things."
Vine Deloria, Jr.

THE COOPERATION I'VE BEEN invoking as a central tenet of existence is not a sentimentalized version in which death is vanquished, all beings live happily ever after, and the only suffering is incurred by villains, who even themselves suffer only inconvenience: a pie in the face, a fiery auto accident in which they walk away clothes blackened and mustache singed. Instead, this is a ruthless cooperation in which those who do not cooperate are extinguished—sooner or later, depending on their degree of insulation from the effects of their actions—but more importantly and to the point are by their refusal to cooperate banished from meaningful participation in the larger community.

A man owns a falcon. He moves from the west side of Washington to a small town near Spokane. His new home is by a lake. Every day he sees an eagle floating far above, circling by the hour and never seeming to move its wings. After the man has lived there a few days, he takes the falcon out back to let it fly. The falcon has barely left his hand when the eagle hurtles down to kill it. The domesticated falcon presumably had not known the rules of the lake, or knowing them had faced no choice when released from its master's hand, and the domesticated owner had not bothered to learn: *I am here, so you should not be. Your presence is not helpful to this community, so I will kill you now.* The community already had enough birds of prey: more would harm its prey base.

We say that Native Americans had, and some still have, good relationships with the natural world, and it is undoubtedly true, as Jeannette told me, that a primary difference between Western and indigenous philosophies is that indigenous philosophies do not view listening to the land as a metaphor, but it is also true that these nations devised complex rules to guarantee their cooperation with nonhuman members of their larger communities. An intricate network of treaties governed the take of salmon from the Columbia River system: each Indian nation could kill only so many, making certain to leave enough for other nations, for bears, eagles, ravens, for future generations of salmon. The relationship between the Indians of this region and the salmon was and is deeply spiritual and reciprocal, but the treaties were hardheaded policy agreements that worked for thousands of years. Similarly, the relationship between the Indians of the plains and the buffalo was deep and respectful. This did not stop Indians from enacting and enforcing sharp strictures against overkill. Tom McHugh describes what happened to a hunter who violated these rules: "After flogging him, marshalls confiscated or killed his dogs and horses, cut his lodge into pieces, burned his tipi poles, broke his bow or gun, took his meat supplies, and ripped his hides, reducing him to total beggary." As Richard Manning comments on these rules: "The buffalo culture depended upon cooperation and the rules were meant to ensure it." Note that McHugh described enforcement as it occurred long after this buffalo culture had been contacted by civilization. It is possible that prior to contact, neither laws nor violence were necessary: the economic and familial incentives of living in a functioning community would of themselves discourage overkill. Another way to say this is that other cultures with more fully intact systems to siphon wealth from rich to poor have not needed to use violence to enforce cooperation: the desire to cooperate inheres in the values of those present. Besides, when your life depends on the buffalo, who could be stupid enough to kill too many?

It is spring. Deep within a pocket of remaining old growth the seed of a douglas fir germinates. A tiny root reaches its tip toward the fresh fecal pellet of a deer mouse. The night before, the mouse ate truffles, and so the pellet contains a half-million truffle spores that passed intact through the mouse's digestive system. Because the pellet is fresh, the root tip penetrates easily, and comes in contact with the spores and also a yeast extract that is food for nitrogen-fixing bacteria. The yeast stimulates the spores to germinate, and they grow into and around the tip of the root, and grow also to envelope the nitrogen-fixing bacteria and yeast. The bacteria feeds off both fungus and yeast, and in turn fixes nitrogen crucial to both fungus and tree. The truffle continues to expand, and forms a mantle around the tree's feeder root: the association is called mycorrhiza, which literally means "fungus-root." The tree provides simple sugars and metabolites without which the fungus cannot live. The fungus provides minerals, nutrients, nitrogen, and water without which the tree would die. The fungus also grows new truffles to feed new deer mice, and the whole symphony begins again.

A termite uses its powerful jaws to chew wood. But it cannot digest this food. That task is accomplished by a protozoan that lives in its gut. There is, however, another problem: the protozoan requires more nitrogen than decaying wood provides. The solution? Bring another creature into the dance: nitrogen-fixing bacteria. Termites feed wood to the protozoa and bacteria, both of whom reside in its gut. The bacteria feed nitrogen to the protozoa, and the protozoa digest wood and nitrogen to feed acetic acid to the termite. Everyone's satisfied.

An ancient tree is ready to die. It is a lodgepole pine. After its death its body will be used by birds, squirrels, mice, termites, ants, bees, fungi as their home. It may take centuries to decay and become the soil it used to be. But it is not yet dead. For that it needs help. So it speaks. It emits an audible signal heard by a species of beetle that has been listening for just this sound. Hearing, the beetle comes. It kills the tree.

This is how the world works.

Last month, a handful of environmental activists walked into the office of Frank Riggs, a congressman from Eureka, California, who is deeply beholden to big timber corporations. The activists—young women, including two teenaged girls—dumped sawdust on the floor as a protest against Riggs' efforts to deforest the last of this continent's old growth redwoods, then handcuffed themselves in a circle around a stump they had also brought. Riggs' secretary called the police. When the police arrived, they sprayed pepper into the eyes of the handcuffed and helpless women from a range of less than three inches. Over the women's screams they then forced open their eyes and daubed a concentrated liquid form of this substance directly onto their eyeballs.

Remember that the women were already handcuffed. It would be comforting, as always, to believe these policemen were acting alone, or were somehow rogues. We would, as always, be wrong. The policemen videotaped themselves applying the pepper to show that they were correctly following official policy. A poll taken in Eureka two weeks later revealed that 86 percent of the residents believed it is appropriate for police to use pepper spray on nonviolent, nonresisting political and environmental protestors. Two weeks after that a judge refused to grant an injunction against further use of pepper spray or its concentrate by police, saying, "the hardship to law enforcement in being deprived of the ability to use pepper spray on recalcitrant demonstrators was greater than the discomfort suffered and the risk incurred by those on whom it is used." The police defended their use of pepper spray as not only "cost-effective" but in the best interests of the protestors themselves. The activists sued the county, and their case was thrown out of court by a judge who said that this use of pepper spray was appropriate because these activists were, among other things, interfering with the normal course of business. Thus again—as inevitably happens in our culture—is production valued over life.

The use of pepper spray against nonviolent political and environmental protestors is routine. More than sixty people have been killed by police through the use of pepper spray. A mere two weeks before the incident in Eureka, the same police force did the same thing to other environmentalists, but failed to videotape it. Shortly before that, police in Eugene, Oregon, dumped six jars of pepper spray onto one environmentalist's face before spraying pepper into the eyes of citizens who had stopped to see what all the fuss was about. These police also used a cherry-picker to approach two young women locked-down demonstrating in trees, then raised the women's skirts to spray pepper onto their genitals.

This is how our system works.

If we are to survive, we need to discern the difference between real and false hopes. We must eliminate false hopes, which blind us to real possibilities, and bind us to unlivable situations. Does anyone really believe that Weyerhaeuser or other timber transnationals will stop destroying forests? Does anyone really believe that the same corporate administrators who say they "wish salmon would go extinct so we could just get on with living" will act other than to fulfill their stated desires? Does anyone really believe that a pattern of exploitation old as our civilization can be halted legislatively, judicially, or through any means other than an absolute rejection of the mindset that engineers the exploitation in the first place, followed by actions based on that rejection? This means if we want to stop the destruction, we have to root out the mindset.

To expect police to do other than use pepper spray or worse on those who prefer life over production is to delude ourselves. To expect the institutions created by our culture to do any other than to poison waters, denude hillsides, eliminate alternative ways of living, commit genocide, and so on, is to engage in magical thinking. After bearing witness to the horrors of Hanford, Rocky Flats, the Salvage Rider, dams, governmental inaction in the face of Bhopal, the ozone hole, global warming, the greatest mass extinction in the history of the planet, surely by now there are few who still believe the purpose of government is to protect citizens from the activities of those who would destroy. At last most of us must understand that the opposite is true: that Adam Smith was correct in noting that the primary purpose of government is to protect those who run the economy from the outrage of injured citizens.

Ours is a politics, economics, and religion of occupation, not of inhabitation, and as such the methods by which we are formed and governed ultimately have no legitimacy save that sprouting from the end of a gun, from a can of pepper spray, from the tip of a rapist's penis, from the travesty of modern education, from the instilled dread of a distant hell and the false promise of a future technotopia, from the chains that bind children to beds and looms and from the everyday fear of starvation—as well as an internalized notion of what constitutes social success or failure—that binds so many to wage slavery. Any political, economic, theological, or philosophical system that in practice rewards production over life is illegitimate because, tautologically enough, it does not value the lives of its citizens over the needs of production. Such is sufficient to define illegitimacy. No other measure is needed. The same is true—for the same reasons, because the results play out the same—for any system that is unsustainable.

The responsibility for holding destructive institutions—more broadly systems, and more broadly yet cultures—accountable falls on each of us. We are the governors as well as the governed; it is only when we daily allow our servants—our so-called "elected representatives"—to act outside our behalf that they can actually do so. This means that all of us who care about life need to force accountability onto those who do not; we must learn to be accountable to ourselves, our consciences, our neighbors, and the nonhuman members of our community—to salmon, for example, and grizzly bears—rather than be loyal to political, economic, religious, penal, educational, and other institutions that do not serve us well. If salmon, to return to a creature who once spawned not two miles from where I live, are to be saved, we must give the corporations and bureaucracies that are driving them extinct, such as Kaiser Aluminum, the Bonneville Power Administration, and the United States government, a reason to save them. We must tell these institutions that if they cause salmon to go extinct, we will cause these institutions to go extinct. And we must mean it. We must then say the same to every other destructive institution, and we must act on our words; we must do whatever is necessary to protect our homes and our land bases from those who are destroying them. Only then will salmon be saved. Only when we as citizens and communities begin to act as though we value life over production will we begin to act as though we value life over production. It really is that simple.

In a speech a few years ago, former House Speaker Newt Gingrich threatened drug smugglers: "When you make the decision that you'll get rich at the expense of our children, you are signing your own death warrant." In a larger context this is not a threat at all, but a simple statement of fact. All of us who participate in a system that "makes" money at the expense of our ecological base—upon which not only our economics but our lives depend—are signing our own death warrants. Allowing our crazy system to destroy our land base is not merely unethical and unwise but suicidal.

The Declaration of Independence states, "That whenever any Form of Government becomes destructive of these ends [Life, Liberty, and the Pursuit of Happiness], it is the Right of the People to alter or abolish it. . . ." It would be more precise to say that it is not the *Right* of the People, nor even their responsibility, but instead something more like breathing—something that if we fail to do we die. If we as a people fail to rid our community of destructive institutions, those institutions will destroy our community. And if we as a community cannot provide meaningful and nondestructive ways for people to gain food, clothing, and shelter then we must recognize it's not just destructive institutions but our entire economics—our entire civilization—that's pushing biological systems past breaking points. Once we've recognized the destructiveness of our civilization we've no choice, unless we wish to sign our own and our children's death warrants, but to fight for all we're worth and in every way we can to change it. There is nothing else to do.

It is customary when winding down a book about the destruction of the planet to offer tangible solutions for readers to pursue. After learning about the apocalypse, we are told to write our senators, send faxes to CEOs, and especially to send money to those who delivered the message. There are several reasons I can't and won't be more specific than to tell people to fight like hell. The first is that to propose discrete solutions trivializes the efforts of those who have come before. If the solution were that simple—merely a matter of capturing a sudden flash of cognitive insight—don't you think somebody would have delivered the golden key? We whisper, *Hey, my friend, whatever you do, don't walk into the showers,* and suddenly the skeletal figure of the concentration camp inmate slaps his open palm against his forehead. *It's so simple,* the woman says as she deftly avoids the rapist, *Why didn't I think of that before?*

The next reason I can't offer solutions is that the "problem"—whatever that means—is unconsciously though intentionally structured to make solutions impossible. A double bind is defined as a situation where if you choose the first option you lose, if you choose the second option you lose, and you cannot withdraw. Would you like to vote for the Republican or the Democrat? Should you step into the line on the left or the right? Should you fish the puppies out of the pool or get your brother? Should you work for IBM or Microsoft? Try leaving the wage economy. The only way to defeat a double bind is to obliterate it.

In the seventeenth century the Zen poet Bunan wrote, "Die while you're alive and be absolutely dead. Then do whatever you want: it's all good." We are, of course, already dead. There is no hope. The machine is too powerful, the damage too severe. There are too many child abusers, too many rapists, too many corporations, too many tanks and guns and airplanes. And I'm just one person; I can't do anything. You're dead right, so what the hell are you waiting for? An Irish friend of mine once told me his favorite saying: "Is this a private fight, or can anyone enter?" Give up. Capitulate. Realize there's no hope, then have at it. If you're dead, you have nothing to lose and a world to gain.

The third reason I can't propose solutions is that to attempt to do so presupposes that solutions exist. But to believe that we can rationally "solve the problems" is to pretend the "problems" are rational, and is to manifest the same megalomania that got us here in the first place. We can no more manage the problems than we can manage a forest.

The best I can offer is the suggestion that if we are to survive, we must not only begin to learn the difference between real and false hopes, but we must also remember how to surrender. No, not to the destructive forces guiding our culture toward its own collapse, nor even to the despair caused by seeing the murder of so many peoples and so many species and biomes, so much beauty, but instead we must remember how to surrender to the land itself, to immerse ourselves in the implications of the natural and social circumstances in which we find ourselves engulfed. If we do not allow ourselves to attend to our surroundings and what is happening to them, to feel the implications deep in our bones, how can we respond appropriately and deeply to the situation?

What are the dying salmon telling you, and the dying forests? What lessons are whispered to you by the ghosts of the passenger pigeons, or the ghostly roll of thunder of a mammoth herd of bison? Allow these voices to inform your actions.

There are some lines from the Tao Te Ching that I dearly love. They are: "Do you have the patience to wait until your mud settles and the water is clear? Can you remain unmoving until the right action arises by itself?"

None of this is to say that we shouldn't work to revoke corporate charters, revest corporate-claimed lands, file timber sale appeals, vote, write, work at battered-women's shelters, throw pies, blow up dams, or even write letters to Slade Gorton and Larry Craig. All of those actions are necessary to the degree that they arise organically from the situation. If we listen carefully enough I believe our bodies, the land, and circumstance will tell us what to do. If someone were to ask me what to do about the problems we face in the world today, I would say, "Listen. If you listen carefully enough you will in time know exactly what to do."

Change is coming. We are in the midst of it. Ecological system after system is collapsing around us, and we wander dazed through our days as though we have become in reality the automatons we so often strive to be.

Often when I awaken I hear the voices of those who will come after, and sometimes I see their faces. They speak to me of hunger, and ask, always, where are the salmon? They speak to me, too, of beauty, and ask again that same question. I have no answer for them. Sometimes I hand them a book or an article I've written. They read it, nod, smile sadly, and ask again about the fish. They do not care so much how deftly we rationalize our actions—and inactions—nor even how deeply we discuss the destruction. What they want, reasonably enough, is an intact and livable world. They ask what we have done to their home.

They ask not only about salmon, but also about forests, bears, fisher, marten, lynx, cutthroat trout, bull trout, sturgeons. They ask about them all. And there is nothing I can do except hand them my book, and say I'm sorry.

I sometimes wonder if the other creatures on the planet are doing what they can to shut down the machine. Perhaps salmon are leaving not just because of dams, and not just because they do not like our unwillingness to participate in reciprocal relationships, and not just because we make life intolerable for all others, but also to deprive us of calories; perhaps they are willing to give away their existence in order to stop civilization. Perhaps trees sometimes refuse to grow on clearcuts because they do not want to give their bodies to be used to enrich those in power. Perhaps Eskimo curlews—whose appetite for grasshoppers was legendary—left the planet so we would poison ourselves with pesticides. Perhaps the planet as a whole is now pushing us along in our own headlong rush to self-extinguishment, so that whatever creatures remain behind can at last and again breathe easily.

Or perhaps the salmon and the trees are not acting merely physically but also symbolically, and perhaps then it becomes our task to ask them clearly and carefully what it is they are saying through their own deaths, what it is that they are dying to tell us. It becomes our task after that to listen to their stories, and to act upon what they have to say.

Here is another thought: perhaps the others—the extirpated salmon, the disappearing frogs—have not gone away forever. Perhaps they have only gone into hiding, and will return after civilization collapses, once we learn, or remember, how to behave. When we are ready to receive them, and to give ourselves up to them in relationship as all along they have given themselves up to us and to each other, they will return. Only then.

At that point we will again see herds of bison stretching from horizon to horizon, the huge creatures eating grasses taller than a human. We'll see flocks of passenger pigeons that stretch also to every horizon, and that take days to pass overhead. Then, too, we'll see so many Eskimo curlews that we could not count them if we lived a thousand years. Salmon will keep us awake at night with the slapping of their tails against the water, and we will have plenty to eat. We need only dip a basket weighted with a stone in order to catch a fish for dinner, in fact enough fish to feed the whole village.

And at night, we will talk to each other, and talk to the moon, who looks down not quite so sadly, and we will talk to wolves, and to bears and to porcupines and weasels. And they will talk to us. Children will paint the faces of wolf pups. Perhaps women and children will not need to dread the night. Women may walk alone with no fear of rape—*rape? I do not know that word*—and children will sleep soundly with no worry of nightly visits from their fathers. Fathers and mothers will look at their children and say, "It was not always this way," and the children will listen, puzzled.

Stars, too, will speak, and will no longer find themselves the holders of memories too painful to be held by children, but will hold other memories, and other conversations, of celebration, of the changing of the seasons, of growing old or perhaps dying young but in any case living within the larger community of existence.

Or perhaps not. Perhaps the salmon really are gone. Perhaps extinction really is forever, and when at long last we do awaken from our nightmare of plutonium, rape, genocide, and coercion, we will find ourselves finally facing the world we have created. Perhaps we will awaken in an exterior landscape that is barren and lonely enough to match the landscape of our hearts and minds. Perhaps we'll awaken to find that at least one tenet of Christianity is literally true—that hell does in fact exist, and that we are in it. Hell, after all, is the too-late realization of interdependence.

Several years ago, a few days after speaking with Thomas Berry and a few days before my first encounter with the coyotes, I walked into a cold January afternoon to take care of the chickens. My breath hung white in the air. Dogs danced at my feet.

I heard in the distance the clamor of geese, then stood speechless to watch a huge v fly low overhead. I opened my mouth to say something—I didn't know what it would be—and heard my voice say three times, "Godspeed." Suddenly, and for no reason I could understand, I burst into tears. Then I ran into the house. Walking back outside later, and staring into the now empty sky, I realized that in speaking not only had I been wishing them well for their journey south but that they, too, had been using my voice and my breath to wish me just-as-well on my own just-as-difficult journey. The tears, it became clear to me, had been neither from sorrow nor joy, but from homecoming, like a sailor who has been too long at sea, and who spontaneously bursts into sobs on smelling land, and feeling those tentative first steps on solid ground, at home.

It is not possible to recover from atrocity in isolation. It is, in fact, precisely this isolation that induces the atrocities. If we wish to stop the atrocities, we need merely step away from the isolation. There is a whole world waiting for us, ready to welcome us home. It has missed us as sorely as we have missed it. And it is time to return.

Godspeed.

Acknowledgments

MEISTER ECKHART SAID THAT if the only prayer you say in your life is Thank you, that would suffice. This book is, among many other things, a prayer of thanksgiving.

Long before the first word found the page, many people helped me disentangle my thinking from civilization's sticky web. Without their support and assistance, I do not know whether I would have had the courage to start making sense of what I was experiencing, and later, to follow my experience wherever it led. This book would not have existed without countless long and loving conversations with these friends. Many of them read significant portions of the book, often through multiple drafts. Their suggestions shaped the form and content, and their enthusiasm revitalized me when my energy flagged. These people include Melanie Adcock, Jeannette Armstrong, Paul Bond, Brian Brothers, George Draffan, Molly Eichar, Bruce Hutton, Mary Jensen, Claire and John Keeble, Vicki Lopez, Laiman Mai, Julie Mayeda, Melissa McCann, John Osborn, Laurel Pederson, Carolyn Raffensperger, Royann Richardson, Lee Running, and Bethanie Walder.

My friend Julie Mayeda line-edited most of the book for me. Her ear never failed, even when mine did.

George Draffan helped me write a couple sections of the book, as part of our *End Game* project.

I am blessed to have found Beau Friedlander as a friend and as a publisher. His courage is matched only by his integrity.

I am grateful to Sy Safransky and others at *The Sun* for giving me the opportunity to interview Jim Nollman, Cleve Backster, and Judith Herman.

Julie Burke did a better job of designing the book than I could ever have hoped.

I need to thank the members of my family who did their best to protect me from my father's violence: my mother, my brothers, and my sisters. I could not have survived without you.

The support of my mother has been instrumental in my recovery from the trauma of my childhood. Crucial also have been the many conversations with many of my friends listed above.

Nor could I have survived without the nonhuman others who have nurtured me all along, even when I did not know it. Stars, bees, the ponderosa pine outside my window, the coyote tree, coyotes, dogs, cats, poultry, the duck who gave me his life, the Dreamgiver, the muse, even Crohn's disease pathogens, and all of the others too numerous even to remember.

I would not be who I am without your guidance and love.

Notes on Sources

None of the information in this book is in any way arcane, or even difficult to find. Many fine researchers have compiled thorough and often devastating histories and analyses of our culture's horrible trajectory, and have articulated viable alternatives. I am thankful that these other authors were able to point me toward original sources. I include here the primary sources where I can, otherwise, the secondary sources.

SILENCING

The epigraph (and all other R.D. Laing quotes) is from R.D. Laing's extraordinary book *The Politics of Experience*. This book, along with Neil Evernden's *The Natural Alien*, helped me perhaps more than any others to understand the alienation that characterizes our culture, and to understand also that it is possible to *experience* the world—to not be alienated.

For the description of a factory slaughterhouse I unfortunately had to rely on a composite of friends' descriptions and published accounts. My attempts to enter slaughterhouses were met with polite yet insistent refusals. The public relations hacks with whom I spoke *did* provide me lots of nifty literature, none of which mentions death or killing.

My figure for rates of rape within our culture come from Judith Herman's classic *Trauma and Recovery*, and Diane E. H. Russel's *Sexual Exploitation, Rape, Child Sexual Abuse, and Sexual Harassment*.

"I suppose, then . . ." is from Descartes' *Meditations on First Philosophy*.

"Let the woman . . ." is from *First Timothy*.

My source for many of the quotes concerning the European hatred of indigenous Africans is Noël Mostert's comprehensive *Frontiers: The Epic of South Africa's Creation and the Tragedy of the Xhosa People*. He pointed me toward many informative primary documents.

"extremely ugly . . ." is from Raven-Hart's *Cape of Good Hope*, citing Leguat's 1708 *New Voyage to the East*

"when they speak . . ." is also from *Cape of Good Hope*, this time citing Baptiste Tavernier.

"it is a great pittie . . ." is from Raven-Hart's *Before Van Riebeeck*.

I have two sources for many of my quotes concerning the European hatred of indigenous North Americans. The first is David Stannard's

American Holocaust. The second is Frederick Turner's *Beyond Geography.* Both are invaluable references to the primary documents, both provide wonderful analyses, and both are extremely difficult to read because of the atrocities they detail.

"animals who do . . ." and "were born for . . ." is from Stannard.

The quote about scientists administering beatings is from *When Elephants Weep,* by Jeffrey Moussaieff Masson and Susan McCarthy.

I became aware of the study by Allport, Bruner, and Jandorf through an article someone handed to me at a reading, entitled "The Psychology of Smog," by Ira J. Winn, from *The Nation,* March 5, 1973.

The figure of one hundred and fifty million enslaved children comes from cross-referencing two sources, and then being extremely conservative in my extrapolation. The Anti-Slavery Society finds more than one hundred million enslaved children just in Asia, and the International Programme on the Elimination of Child Labour, which puts the estimate of enslaved children worldwide in "only" the tens of millions, finds that Africa has an incidence of child labor nearly twice that of Asia. The mere fact that I can even consider estimates differing by one hundred million (I think an estimate of two hundred and fifty million enslaved children worldwide would be defensible) disturbs me greatly. Lost in the numbers—in fact worse than lost, but masked—is the misery inherent in each one of these cases. This little girl enslaved to prostitution in Thailand, this little boy enslaved to rugmaking in Pakistan. My source for the Anti-Slavery Society figure was the *Spokesman-Review,* September 19, 1995.

Evernden's story about cutting the vocal cords is from *The Natural Alien.*

The Okanagan definition of "violation of a woman" is from Jeannette Armstrong.

Coyotes, Kittens, and Conversations

"We are the . . ." is in Dolores LaChapelle's extraordinary *Sacred Land Sacred Sex,* citing Paula Gunn Allen's "The Psychological Landscape of Ceremony."

"Since nature . . ." is from Aristotle's *Poetics.*

"I perceived it to be . . ." is from Descartes' *Discourse on Method.*

"My only earthly wish . . ." is from Bacon's *New Organon.*

"I am come . . ." is from Bacon's *Temporis Partus Masculus.*

The account of the robo-roaches is from the *Spokesman-Review,* January 10, 1997.

The vivisection accounts come from Singer's *Animal Liberation,* Ruesch's *Slaughter of the Innocent,* and Levin's and Danielson's *Cardiac Arrest.* None of these books are for the faint of heart.

For information on the Sand Creek Massacre I am indebted to Stannard, who provided an excellent analysis, and pointed me toward three earlier sources, Svaldi's *Sand Creek,* Hoig's *The Sand Creek Massacre,* and the U.S. Congressional inquiry volumes.

Taking a Life

"Today we took . . ." is from Jack Forbes' *Columbus and Other Cannibals,* a short but crucial book.

The "conversation of death" materials are from Barry Lopez's *Of Wolves and Men.*

Cultural Eyeglasses

"All through school . . ." is from E.F. Schumacher's *A Guide For the Perplexed.*

The incidence study for child abuse is put out by the Centers For Disease Control.

The headlines "Defiant activist defends guerrillas" and "Mother bear charges trains" are from the *Spokesman-Review,* Jan 9, 1996, and April 29, 1996, respectively.

I learned about the levels of alcoholism among *einsatzgruppen* from Robert Jay Lifton's important *The Nazi Doctors.*

I don't remember where I first heard about the "black line" in Tasmania—it must have been when I was a child—but the image had long haunted me. When my dart hit the map there (no, that wasn't a literary device), I headed to the library and Internet. A very good source is *Fate of a Free People: A Radical Re-examination of the Tasmanian Wars,* by Henry Reynolds. The quote "It was a favourite . . ." is from Lehman's *The Battle for Tasmanian Aboriginal Heritage,* citing Hull's 1850 *Experience of Forty Years in Tasmania.*

"the races who rest . . ." was cited in Stannard. The citation for the awful incident where settlers kicked the heads of infants is the book *Massacres to Mining: The Colonisation of Aboriginal Australia,* by Janine P. Roberts.

The quotes regarding Africans are cited in Mostert.

The quote concerning Hawai'ians is cited in Stannard.

The political cartoon by my neighbor was in the now-defunct *New Press* of Spokane.

"Some Christians encounter . . ." is from Todorov's *The Conquest of America.* "At about 1:00 p.m. . . ." is from Jonas' *Battle for Guatemala.* Stannard pointed me toward both of these books.

CRANES

"God does not send us . . ." is from Hesse's *Reflections*.

THE SAFETY OF METAPHOR

"The most striking . . ." is cited in Susan Griffin's *Pornography and Silence: Culture's Revenge Against Nature*.

"no human bodies . . ." is from the *Spokesman-Review,* June 3, 1996.

CLAIMS TO VIRTUE

"Exploitation must not . . ." is from Laing's *Politics*.

"And seest among . . ." is from *Deuteronomy*.

"shall welcome [her] husband's . . ." is from *Genesis*.

"I thank thee . . ." is cited in Mary Daly's *Beyond God the Father*.

John Perlin succinctly tells the story of the planet's deforestation in *A Forest Journey*.

Many books describe the beauty and natural opulence of North America prior to the arrival of civilization. One of the best, and most heartbreaking, is Farley Mowat's *Sea of Slaughter*.

The exchange described by Captain John Chester is from Quinn's *The Voyages and Colonizing Enterprises of Sir Humphrey Gilbert*.

"a rich heiress . . ." is from Sobel's *Wall Street*.

The Tertullian quote is from "On the Apparel of Women." The whole quotation is: "You are the devil's gateway. . . . You are the first deserter of the divine law; you are she who persuaded him whom the devil was not valiant enough to attack. You destroyed so easily God's image, man. On account of your desert—that is, death—even the Son of God had to die." I guess what he's saying is that things would be okay for men—who are of course the images of God—if it weren't for those damned women.

The story of Origen is not unique. Many early Christians castrated themselves, following *Matthew* 19.

For explorations of the Christian hatred of the body, see Stannard, Daly, Turner, French (*Beyond Power*), Griffin (*Woman and Nature*), or many others. Specifically "What is seen . . ." is from Origen, Selecta in Exodus xviii.17, Migne, Patrologia Graeca, volume 12, column 296. "I know nothing . . ." is from St. Augustine *Basic Writings of St. Augustine.*

"They built a . . ." is from de Las Casas's *Brief Account*.

"did no other . . ." is cited in Stannard.

The story of the woman who was a role model for Spokane was in the

Spokesman-Review on April 27, 1997.

"Act provocatively and . . ." is from the *Spokesman-Review,* November 7, 1997.

SEEKING A THIRD WAY

"For those in . . ." is from Campbell's *Masks of God,* volume IV.

For accounts of prisoner exchanges between the Indians and whites, see especially Stannard and Turner.

Demonic Males was written by Richard Wrangham and Dale Peterson.

Information on the Semai is from Dentan's *The Semai.*

One of many books to read as antidotes to *Demonic Males* might be Eleanor Burke Leacock's *Myths of Male Dominance.*

BREAKING OUT

"The world of . . . " is cited in Daly, *Beyond God the Father.*

Richard Dawkins' quotes are from *The Selfish Gene.*

The account of the trial for animal abuse was in the *Spokesman-Review,* June 27, 1997. The verdict, and the account of the judge's tongue-lashing, was in the paper on June 28.

"I never knew . . ." is from Hearne's *Journals.*

There are many extraordinary books giving examples of interspecies communication. The stories I told here are a representative collage from many sources. But if you want to learn about interspecies communication, put the books away (including this one) and go ask a nonhuman.

The best general exploration of the history of civilization's assault on wolves is Rick McIntyre's *War Against the Wolf.*

The economics textbook I reference is Froyen's *Macroeconomics.* The "≡" symbol means "equals by definition."

"There is not . . ." is from an interview of Noam Chomsky by David Barsamian.

ECONOMICS

"scarcely admit either . . ." is in Raven-Hart, *Cape of Good Hope,* citing Ovington.

"A woman must . . ." is cited in Daly's *Beyond God the Father.*

The story of the extermination of the great auk is given in Mowat's *Sea of Slaughter.* Here is the destruction of the last egg: "As they clambered up they saw two Geirfugel [great auks] sitting among numberless other sea-birds, and at once gave chase. The Geirfugel showed not the slightest disposition to repel the invaders, but immediately ran along the high cliff, their heads erect, their little wings extended. They uttered no cry of alarm and moved, with their short steps, about as quickly as a man could walk. Jon, with outstretched arms, drove one onto a corner, where he soon had it fast. Sigurder and Ketil pursued the second and seized it close to the edge of the rock. Ketil then returned to the sloping shelf whence the birds had started and saw an egg lying on the lava slab, which he knew to be a Geirfugel's. He took it up, and finding it was broken, dropped it again. All this took place in much less time than it took to tell." I really do hate this culture.

The accounts of fecundity prior to the arrival of civilization are from Mowat's *Sea of Slaughter*.

THE GOAL IS THE PROCESS
"It's life that . . ." is from Dostoyevski's *The Idiot*.

HEROES
"If I were . . ." is from a 1704 letter from Fletcher to the Marquise of Montrose.

U.S. Crimes Against Humanity are described in Ramsey Clark's *The Fire This Time*.

METAMORPHOSIS
"Between living and . . ." is from Stephen Mitchell's *The Enlightened Heart*.

INSATIABILITY
"We need to . . ." is from the *Anderson Valley Advertiser*, December, 10, 1997.

If you want information about the fight to save Mount Graham, go to the people and organizations leading the fight. I would probably start with the Apache Survival Coalition. If you've got Internet access, you might look there.

VIOLENCE
"We kill when . . ." is from Hesse's *Reflections*.

"There are only . . ." is from an AP story in the *Spokesman-Review* on September 4, 1997.

If you crave information about the MRTA—and about various other liberation struggles worldwide—you could do far worse than to check out the Arm The Spirit website. Other than that just pore over various news sources, recognizing of course the unreliability of the corporate press.

The Parable of the Box

Ruth Benedict wrote up her study for a series of lectures she gave at Bryn Mawr College in 1941. Her notes were lost. But her assistant, Abraham Maslow, was able to assemble fragments. These are presented in his *The Farther Reaches of Human Nature*. Erich Fromm expanded on these for his necessary book *The Anatomy of Human Destructiveness*. LaChapelle also does a wonderful job of drawing crucial conclusions from Benedict's study in her *Sacred Land, Sacred Sex*.

I discovered Janus's and Bess's book, *A Sexual Profile of Men in Power*, in J.C. Smith's *Psychoanalytic Roots of Patriarchy*.

"While Mexico does . . ." is from Riordan Rhett's January 13, 1995, Mexico-Political Update.

Violence Revisited

"What I fear . . ." is from *Newsweek*, December 19, 1988.

"New York Stock . . ." and "It is probable . . ." are cited in Olday's *March to Death*.

"done in such . . ." was, ironically, in *Life*. It was in the November 18, 1957, issue.

"For what the . . ." is from Dunnigan and Nofi's fascinating book, *Dirty Little Secrets: Military Information You're Not Supposed to Know*. They've spent much of their lives working intimately with and for the military, yet they seem to understand how horrid it all is.

Lethality of plutonium assembled from Gordon Edwards article "Plutonium Anyone?" and a number of other easily accessible sources.

The biblical quotes in the paragraph beginning "There can be . . ." are of course from *Revelation*.

The story of the largest white pine in Idaho is from the *Spokesman-Review*, September 7, 1997.

The story of injecting heart rot fungus is from the *Eugene Register-Guard*, September 10, 1997.

The information about Cassini was assembled from many web sites, and with conversations with activists opposed to it. Activists all over the world worked against Cassini. The "Stop Cassini Website" is probably as good a place as any to start looking. For the relative lethality of plutonium-238 compared to plutonium-239, I spoke with Dr. Horst Poehler.

"I feel no . . ." is from Wenkam's *The Great Pacific Ripoff: Corporate Rape in the Far East*.

Coercion

"I have never . . ." is from a letter from Jefferson to A. L. C. Destutt de

Tracy in 1811.

"Shell operations still . . ." from a May 12, 1994, memo obtained by the Movement for the Survival of Ogoni People. It goes on to recommend that soldiers begin "wasting" Ogoni leaders who are "especially vocal individuals," and concludes by recommending pressure on oil companies for "prompt, regular" payments to support the cost of the military operation.

"to protect the . . ." is from Noam Chomsky's, "Market Democracy in a Neoliberal Order: Doctrines and Reality," *Z Magazine*.

"Civil government . . ." is from Adam Smith's *Wealth of Nations*, Book Five.

"Government has no . . ." is from John Locke's *Second Treatise of Government*.

"The American national . . ." is from the *Anderson Valley Advertiser*, January 20, 1999.

HONEYBEES

"Happiness is love . . ." is from Hesse's *Reflections*.

A TURNING OVER

"This country, with . . ." is from Abraham Lincoln's first Inaugural Address, March 4, 1861.

"The tumors themselves . . ." is from an Associated Press report in the *Spokesman-Review*, October 24, 1997.

"melted ice caps . . ." is from the *Spokesman-Review*, October 24, 1997. The editorial's title is "Chicken Littles running scared."

"The first questions . . ." is from Marilyn Robinson's *Mother Country*. The story about the missing "suitcase bombs" is from a *60 Minutes* broadcast on September 7, 1997.

Breast cancer statistics are from Samuel Epstein's monumental *The Politics of Cancer Revisited*.

A LIFE OF MY OWN

Nothing to cite.

INTERCONNECTION

"Our goal should . . ." is cited in LaChapelle's *Sacred Land, Sacred Sex*.

"On the terms . . ." is from Lewis Mumford's *The Pentagon of Power*. This is the second and final volume of his *Myth of the Machine*, an exploration that cannot be too-highly recommended.

Where our dinner came from was derived mostly from George Draffan's phenomenal *Directory of Transnational Corporations*. Find it on the

Internet. Or better, give George a call. He's got lots more information in his head than in the directory.

"I have a . . ." is from the "Zapatista Posters Series" put out by *Resistant Strains*. The poster's creator is Nick Jehlen.

"There are those . . ." is from the "Second Declaration of La Realidad: Words of the Zapatista Army of National Liberation in the closing act of the First Intercontinental Encounter for Humanity and Against Neoliberalism (read by Subcomandante Insurgente Marcos)," August 3, 1996.

If you want to help get Shell out of Ogoniland, probably the best place to start would be with the Movement for the Survival of Ogoni People.

A good place to get started on issues surrounding the U'wa is with the U'wa Defense Working Group. The following October 27, 1997, open letter to the presidents of Occidental and Shell from U'wa traditional authority Roberto Cobaría is worth quoting in full for the straightforward wisdom it reveals, and for the sad story so often heard that it represents: "I write to you asking that you hear my people's request and stop your oil project on U'wa ancestral lands. We hope that you will comply with the request that the U'wa send in this letter. At this point, there is nothing else for you to do.

"The U'wa have always had a law that existed before the sun and the moon. We have always taken good care of our land, because we have always followed this law. Our law is our culture, our song, and our dance. In this world there are many laws, but Mother Earth also has her laws. Before, these laws were respected. Are Occidental and Shell going to respect these laws or not? Occidental and Shell must hear these laws and leave U'wa territory please.

"Today I speak for the first time in public of the threat and beating I have received by hooded men in the night, demanding I sign an authorization agreement or die. Can you see how the U'wa are already suffering from oil exploitation? The war that spreads throughout Colombia will spread to U'wa land if your oil project starts. Can you see how it is already arriving? Oil may be good to sell, but it causes war.

"You speak of negotiation and consultation with the U'wa. My people say that they cannot negotiate. Our Father has not authorized it. We cannot sell oil, the blood of our Mother Earth. Mother Earth is sacred. It is not for negotiation, so please do not try to confuse us with offers. Please hear our request, a request that comes from our ancestral right by virtue of being born on our territory: Halt your oil project on U'wa ancestral land.

"The U'wa people need your sign of respect."

As this book goes to press, 5,000 U.S.-backed Columbian troops have invaded U'Wa territory to facilitate further drilling.

The Plants Respond

"The body's carbon . . ." is from Jung's *The Archetypes and the Collective Unconscious.* The full quote is: "The deeper 'layers' of the psyche lose their individual uniqueness as they retreat farther and farther into darkness. 'Lower down'—that is to say, as they approach the autonomous functional systems—they become increasingly collective until they are universalized and extinguished in the body's materiality, i.e., in the chemical bodies. The body's carbon is simply carbon. Hence 'at bottom' the psyche is simply 'world.'"

Death and Awakening

"In the middle . . ." is from Dante's *Divine Comedy.*
"A man may . . ." is cited in James Moore's *Gurdjieff: A Biography.*

A Time of Sleeping

"The part of . . ." is from Griffin's *Pornography and Silence.*
Rollo May retells the story in *The Cry For Myth.*
"They find it . . ." and "their contempt for . . ." and "the principle work . . ." are all from Raven-Hart, *Cape of Good Hope.* The first is citing Bolling, the second de la Loubère, and the third Shreyer.
I couldn't track down the original source for "the significant problems. . . ." Either ol' Al Einstein, the aphorism king, said this one about thirty different ways, or the saying is twisted even more than most to fit locutional needs (neither of which is necessarily bad). Here are a few versions I've seen: "No problem can be solved from the same level of consciousness that created it." "The problems of the world will not be solved with the level of thinking that created them." "The problems of the world cannot be solved with mechanisms, but only by changing the hearts and minds of man and speaking courageously." And, "We can't solve the problems of the world from the level of thinking we were at when we created them." Not being wildly anal-retentive, and because these all mean basically the same thing, the differences don't bother me. But I'll tell you what does: a good portion of the Internet sites where I found these were promoting seminars where corporate managers will learn how to better solve problems in their businesses. I doubt that these seminars will ask the managers to question corporate dominance of the world, the profit motive, private property, or human (read Euroamerican male) supremacy. *That's* a problem.
"It seems to . . ." is from Carl Rogers' *On Becoming a Person.*

Out of Mourning, Play

"The Great Way . . ." is from Mitchell's *Enlightened Heart.*

TRAUMA AND RECOVERY

"The struggle of . . ." is spoken by one of the characters in Milan Kundera's novel, *The Book of Laughter and Forgetting.*

"It is wrong . . ." is from Kahlil Gibran's *The Prophet.*

"For most cultures . . ." and "The universe is . . ." are from my book *Listening to the Land.*

CONNECTION AND COOPERATION

"The future of . . ." is from Vine Deloria's *God is Red.*

"After flogging him . . ." is from Tom McHugh's *The Time of the Buffalo.*

"The buffalo culture . . ." is from Richard Manning's *Grassland.*

The story about the ancient tree calling the beetles is from Richard Manning's *The Last Stand.*

"When you make . . ." is from a speech given on August 26, 1995.

"Die while you're . . ." is from Mitchell's *Enlightened Heart.*

"Do you have . . ." is from Stephen Mitchell's translation.

Bibliography

Barsamian, David, "Expanding the Floor of the Cage, Part II," *Z Magazine,* April 1997.

Casas, Bartholomé de Las, *Brief Account of the Destruction of the Indies.*

Campbell, Joseph, *Masks of God, Volume IV: Creative Mythology,* Penguin, NY, 1968.

Chomsky, Noam, "Market Democracy in a Neoliberal Order: Doctrines and Reality," *Z Magazine.*

Clark, Ramsey, *The Fire This Time: U.S. War Crimes in the Gulf,* Thunder's Mouth Press, Emeryville, 1994.

Daly, Mary, *Beyond God the Father: Toward a Philosophy of Women's Liberation,* Beacon, Boston, 1985.

Dante, *Divine Comedy*

Dawkins, Richard, *The Selfish Gene,* Oxford University Press, NY, 1990.

Deloria, Vine, Jr., *God is Red: A Native View of Religion,* Fulcrum, Golden, 1994.

Dentan, Robert Knox, *The Semai: A Nonviolent People of Malaya,* Holt, Rinehart, and Winston, NY, 1979.

Dostoyevski, Fyodor, *The Idiot,* Dell, NY, 1959.

Dunnigan, James F., and Nofi, Albert A., *Dirty Little Secrets: Military Information You're Not Supposed to Know,* Morrow, NY, 1990.

Draffan, George, *Directory of Transnational Corporations.*

Edwards, Gordon, "Plutonium Anyone?" From the Internet, reprinted from the spring 1995 issue of *Ploughshares Monitor.*

Epstein, Samuel S, *The Politics of Cancer Revisited,* East Ridge Press, Fremont Center, 1998.

Evernden, Neil, *The Natural Alien: Humankind and Environment,* University of Toronto, Toronto, 1985

Forbes, Jack D., *Columbus and Other Cannibals,* Autonomedia, Brooklyn, 1992.

French, Marilyn, *Beyond Power: On Women, Men, and Morals,* Ballentine, NY, 1985.

Fromm, Erich, *The Anatomy of Human Destructiveness,* Holt, Rinehart, and Winston, NY, 1973.

Froyen, Richard T., *Macroeconomics: Theories and Policies,* MacMillan, NY, 1983.

Gibran, Kahlil, *The Prophet,* Citadel, NY, 1957.

Griffin, Susan, *Pornography and Silence: Culture's Revenge Against Nature,* Harper & Row, NY, 1981.

Griffin, Susan, *Woman and Nature: The Roaring Inside Her,* Harper & Row, NY, 1978.

Hearne, Samuel, *Journals of Samuel Hearne and Philip Turnor,* Greenwood, 1969.

Herman, Judith, *Trauma and Recovery: The aftermath of violence—from domestic abuse to political terror,* Basic Books, NY 1997.

Hesse, Hermann, *Reflections,* translated by Ralph Manheim, Farrar, Straus and Giroux, NY, 1974.

Hoig, Stan, *The Sand Creek Massacre,* University of Oklahoma Press, Norman, 1961.

Janus, Sam, Barbara Bess, and Carol Saltus, *A Sexual Profile of Men in Power,* Prentice-Hall, Englewood-Cliffs, 1977.

Jensen, Derrick, *Listening to the Land: Conversations About Nature, Cul-*

ture, and Eros, Sierra Club, San Francisco, 1995.

Jonas, Susanne, *The Battle for Guatemala: Rebels, Death Squads, and U.S. Power,* Westview Press, Boulder, 1991.

Jung, C.G., *The Archetypes and the Collective Unconscious,* Princeton University Press, Princeton, 1968.

Kautsky, Karl, *Communism in Central Europe in the Time of the Reformation,* Russell & Russell, NY, 1959.

Kundera, Milan, *The Book of Laughter and Forgetting,* Harper Perennial, NY, 1999.

LaChapelle, Dolores, *Sacred Land, Sacred Sex: Rapture of the Deep: Concerning Deep Ecology—And Celebrating Life,* Kivaki Press, Durango, 1988.

Laing, R.D., *The Politics of Experience,* Ballentine, NY, 1967.

Leacock, Eleanor Burke, *Myths of Male Dominance,* Monthly Review Press, 1981.

Lehman, Greg, "The battle for Tasmanian Aboriginal heritage," *Green Left,* April 9, 1991.

Levin, Emil, and Diane Danielson, *Cardiac Arrest,* Civitas, Swain, 1991

Lifton, Robert Jay, *The Nazi Doctors: Medical Killing and the Psychology of Genocide,* Basic, NY, 1986.

Locke, John, *Second Treatise of Government.*

Lopez, Barry, *Of Wolves and Men,* Scribner's, NY, 1978.

Manning, Richard, *Grassland: The History, Biology, Politics, and Promise of the American Prairie,* Viking, New York, 1995.

Manning, Richard, *The Last Stand: A Riveting Expose of Environmental Pillage and a Lone Journalist's Struggle to Keep Faith,* Penguin, 1992.

Maslow, Abraham H., *The Farther Reaches of Human Nature,* Viking, NY, 1971.

Masson, Jeffrey Moussaieff, and Susan McCarthy, *When Elephants Weep: The Emotional Lives of Animals,* Delecorte Press, NY, 1995.

May, Rollo, *The Cry For Myth,* Delta, NY, 1992.

McHugh, Tom, *The Time of the Buffalo,* Alfred A. Knopf, New York, 1972.

McIntyre, Rick, *War Against the Wolf: America's Campaign to Exterminate the Wolf,* Voyageur, Stillwater, 1995.

Mitchell, Stephen, *The Enlightened Heart: An Anthology of Sacred Poetry,* Harper & Row, NY, 1989.

Mitchell, Stephen, *Tao Te Ching,* Harper Perennial, NY, 1991.

Moore, James, *Gurdjieff: A Biography,* Element, 1999.

Mostert, Noël, *Frontiers: The Epic of South Africa's Creation and the Tragedy of the Xhosa People,* Alfred A. Knopf, New York, 1992.

Mowat, Farley, *Sea of Slaughter,* Seal, Toronto, 1989.

Mumford, Lewis, *The Pentagon of Power,* Harcourt Brace Jovanovich, NY, 1970.

Olday, John, *The March to Death,* Freedom Press, London, 1943.

Perlin, John, *A Forest Journey: The Role of Wood in the Development of Civilization,* Harvard University Press, Cambridge, 1991.

Quinn, David Beers, *The Voyages and Colonizing Enterprises of Sir Humphrey Gilbert,* London, 1940.

Raven-Hart, Major R., *Cape of Good Hope, 1652–1702: The First Fifty Years,* 2 vols., (A.A. Balkema, Cape Town, 1971).

Raven-Hart, Major R., *Before Van Riebeeck: Callers at South Africa from 1488 to 1652,* C. Struik, Cape Town, 1967.

Reynolds, Henry, *Fate of a Free People: A Radical Re-examination of the Tasmanian Wars,* Penguin, NY, 1995.

Roberts, Janine P, *Massacres to Mining: the Colonisation of Aboriginal Aus-*

tralia, Dove, 1981.

Robinson, Marilyn, *Mother Country: The Truth About the Secret Toxic Dumping That is Destroying the Environment,* Ballantine, NY, 1979.

Rogers, Carl, *On Becoming a Person,* Houghton Mifflin, Boston, 1961.

Rousselle, Aline, *Porneia: On Desire and the Body in Antiquity,* Basil Blackwell, Oxford, 1988.

Ruesch, Hans, *Slaughter of the Innocent,* Civitas, Swain, 1983.

Russell, D.E.H., *Sexual Exploitation: Rape, Child Sexual Abuse, and Sexual Harassment,* Sage, Beverly Hills, 1984

Schumacher, E.F., *A Guide for the Perplexed,* Harper Colophon, NY, 1977.

"Second Declaration of La Realidad: Words of the Zapatista Army of National Liberation in the closing act of the First Intercontinental Encounter for Humanity and Against Neoliberalism (read by Subcomandante Insurgente Marcos)," August 3, 1996.

Smith, J.C., *Psychoanalytic Roots of Patriarchy: The Neurotic Foundations of Social Order,* New York University Press, NY, 1990.

Singer, Peter, *Animal Liberation: A New Ethics For Our Treatment of Animals,* Avon, New York, 1975.

Smith, Adam, *The Wealth of Nations,* book Five.

Sobel, Robert, *Panic on Wall Street,* E.P. Dutton, NY, 1988.

Stannard, David E., *American Holocaust: Columbus and the Conquest of the New World,* Oxford University Press, NY, 1992.

Svaldi, David, *Sand Creek and the Rhetoric of Extermination: A Case Study in Indian-White Relations,* University Press of America, New York, 1989.

Todorov, Tzvetan, *The Conquest of America: The Question of the Other,* Harper & Row, NY, 1984.

Turner, Frederick, *Beyond Geography: The Western Spirit Against The Wildnerness,* Rutgers University Press, New Brunswick, 1992.

Weast, Robert C., editor, *CRC Handbook of Chemistry and Physics*, CRC, West Palm Beach, 1978.

Wenkam, Robert, *The Great Pacific Ripoff: Corporate Rape in the Far East*, Follett, Chicago, 1974.

Winn, Ira J., "The Psychology of Smog," *The Nation*, March 5, 1973

Wrangham, Richard, and Peterson, Dale, *Demonic Males: Apes and the Origins of Human Violence*, Houghton Mifflin, Boston, 1997.

DERRICK JENSEN is the author of *Listening to the Land: Conversations about Nature, Culture, and Eros,* a *USA Today* Critics Choice for one of the best nature books of 1995, and *Railroads and Clearcuts*. He writes for *The New York Times Magazine, Audubon,* and *The Sun Magazine,* among many others. He now lives among the redwoods in Crescent City, California, near the ocean where he works to improve habitat for the coho salmon who swim upstream near his home, and for the California red-legged frogs who sing nightly outside his windows. He teaches writing at Pelican Bay State Prison.